PRIVACY,
LAW ENFORCEMENT,
AND NATIONAL SECURITY

Aspen Custom Publishing Series

PRIVACY,
LAW ENFORCEMENT,
AND NATIONAL SECURITY

First Edition

Daniel J. Solove
John Marshall Harlan Research Professor of Law
George Washington University Law School

Paul M. Schwartz
Jefferson E. Peyser Professor of Law
U.C. Berkeley School of Law
Faculty Director, Berkeley Center for Law & Technology

Published by Wolters Kluwer in New York.

Wolters Kluwer serves customers worldwide with CCH, Aspen Publishers, and Kluwer Law International products. (www.wolterskluwerlb.com)

To contact Customer Care, e-mail customer.service@wolterskluwer.com, call 1-800-234-1660, fax 1-800-901-9075, or mail correspondence to:

Wolters Kluwer
Attn: Order Department
PO Box 990
Frederick, MD 21705

Printed in the United States of America.

1 2 3 4 5 6 7 8 9 0

ISBN 978-1-4548-6153-9

About Wolters Kluwer Law & Business

Wolters Kluwer Law & Business is a leading global provider of intelligent information and digital solutions for legal and business professionals in key specialty areas, and respected educational resources for professors and law students. Wolters Kluwer Law & Business connects legal and business professionals as well as those in the education market with timely, specialized authoritative content and information-enabled solutions to support success through productivity, accuracy and mobility.

Serving customers worldwide, Wolters Kluwer Law & Business products include those under the Aspen Publishers, CCH, Kluwer Law International, Loislaw, ftwilliam.com and MediRegs family of products.

CCH products have been a trusted resource since 1913, and are highly regarded resources for legal, securities, antitrust and trade regulation, government contracting, banking, pension, payroll, employment and labor, and healthcare reimbursement and compliance professionals.

Aspen Publishers products provide essential information to attorneys, business professionals and law students. Written by preeminent authorities, the product line offers analytical and practical information in a range of specialty practice areas from securities law and intellectual property to mergers and acquisitions and pension/benefits. Aspen's trusted legal education resources provide professors and students with high-quality, up-to-date and effective resources for successful instruction and study in all areas of the law.

Kluwer Law International products provide the global business community with reliable international legal information in English. Legal practitioners, corporate counsel and business executives around the world rely on Kluwer Law journals, looseleafs, books, and electronic products for comprehensive information in many areas of international legal practice.

Loislaw is a comprehensive online legal research product providing legal content to law firm practitioners of various specializations. Loislaw provides attorneys with the ability to quickly and efficiently find the necessary legal information they need, when and where they need it, by facilitating access to primary law as well as state-specific law, records, forms and treatises.

ftwilliam.com offers employee benefits professionals the highest quality plan documents (retirement, welfare and non-qualified) and government forms (5500/PBGC, 1099 and IRS) software at highly competitive prices.

MediRegs products provide integrated health care compliance content and software solutions for professionals in healthcare, higher education and life sciences, including professionals in accounting, law and consulting.

Wolters Kluwer Law & Business, a division of Wolters Kluwer, is headquartered in New York. Wolters Kluwer is a market-leading global information services company focused on professionals.

To my parents and grandparents—DJS

To Steffie, Clara, and Leo—PMS

SUMMARY OF CONTENTS

Contents		*xi*
Preface		*xv*
Acknowledgments		*xvii*
1	**PRIVACY AND LAW ENFORCEMENT**	**1**
	A. The Fourth Amendment and Emerging Technology	6
	B. Information Gathering about First Amendment Activities	82
	C. Federal Electronic Surveillance Law	95
	D. Digital Searches and Seizures	111
2	**NATIONAL SECURITY AND FOREIGN INTELLIGENCE**	**155**
	A. The Intelligence Community	157
	B. The Fourth Amendment Framework	157
	C. Foreign Intelligence Gathering	166
	D. NSA Surveillance	194
Index		*225*

CONTENTS

Preface   *xv*

Acknowledgments   *xvii*

1 PRIVACY AND LAW ENFORCEMENT   1

A. THE FOURTH AMENDMENT AND EMERGING TECHNOLOGY   6

1. How the Fourth Amendment Works   6
   (a) Applicability: Searches and Seizures   6
   (b) Reasonable Searches and Seizures   7
   (c) Enforcement: The Exclusionary Rule and Civil Remedies   9
   (d) Subpoenas and Court Orders   10
2. Wiretapping, Bugging, and Beyond   13
   • Olmstead v. United States   14
   • Lopez v. United States   21
   • Katz v. United States   24
   • United States v. White   30
3. The Reasonable Expectation of Privacy Test and Emerging Technology   34
   (a) The Third Party Doctrine   34
      • Smith v. Maryland   34
   (b) Items Abandoned or Exposed to the Public   45
      • California v. Greenwood   45
   (c) Surveillance and the Use of Sense-Enhancing Technologies   52
      • Florida v. Riley   53
      • Dow Chemical Co. v. United States   60
      • Kyllo v. United States   64
      • United States v. Jones   72

B. INFORMATION GATHERING ABOUT FIRST AMENDMENT ACTIVITIES — 82

- Stanford v. Texas — 84
- Gonzales v. Google — 91

C. FEDERAL ELECTRONIC SURVEILLANCE LAW — 95

1. Section 605 of the Federal Communications Act — 95
2. Title III — 97
3. The Electronic Communications Privacy Act — 97
   (a) The Wiretap Act — 99
   (b) The Stored Communications Act — 102
   (c) The Pen Register Act — 103
4. The Communications Assistance for Law Enforcement Act — 104
5. The USA PATRIOT Act — 106
6. State Electronic Surveillance Law — 108

D. DIGITAL SEARCHES AND SEIZURES — 111

1. Searching Computers and Electronic Devices — 111
   - United States v. Andrus — 113
   - Riley v. California — 119
2. Encryption — 125
3. Video Surveillance — 129
4. E-mail and Online Communications — 129
   - Steve Jackson Games, Inc. v. United States Secret Service — 129
   - United States v. Warshak — 135
5. ISP Account Information — 142
   - United States v. Hambrick — 142
6. IP Addresses, URLs, and Internet Searches — 150
   - United States v. Forrester — 150

2 NATIONAL SECURITY AND FOREIGN INTELLIGENCE — 155

A. THE INTELLIGENCE COMMUNITY — 157

B. THE FOURTH AMENDMENT FRAMEWORK — 157

- United States v. United States District Court (The *Keith* Case) — 159

C. FOREIGN INTELLIGENCE GATHERING — 166

1. The Foreign Intelligence Surveillance Act — 166
   - Global Relief Foundation, Inc. v. O'Neil — 169
   - United States v. Isa — 171

2. The USA-PATRIOT Act   173
- The 9/11 Commission Report   178
- In re Sealed Case   178

3. National Security Letters   186

4. Internal Oversight   190
   (a) The Attorney General's FBI Guidelines   190
   (b) The Homeland Security Act   192
   (c) The Intelligence Reform and Terrorism Prevention Act   192

D. NSA SURVEILLANCE   **194**

1. Standing   196
- Clapper v. Amnesty International USA   196

2. The Snowden Revelations   205
- Klayman v. Obama   207
- In re FBI   216

Index   *225*

PREFACE

New technology presents profound challenges for how to balance privacy and security. The leaks by Edward Snowden about the National Security Agency have raised extensive discussion about the role that various types of law should play regarding government surveillance and data gathering.

In today's digital world, the Fourth and Fifth Amendments are not the only way that government surveillance and data gathering are regulated. Federal statutes such as the Electronic Communications Privacy Act (ECPA) also play a major role. There are state constitutions and electronic surveillance laws as well. In addition, the line between ordinary law enforcement and national security is quite fuzzy and contested. The Constitution regulates national security somewhat differently, and there are laws specific to national security and foreign intelligence surveillance such as the Foreign Intelligence Surveillance Act (FISA).

This text aims to pull all of these various laws together to provide a coherent introduction to how government surveillance and data gathering are regulated. Our goal is to provide a comprehensive and accessible introduction. We have provided the relevant background so that no prior knowledge of Constitutional law or criminal procedure is required. The text includes extensive notes and commentary, and it integrates cases and statutes with policy and jurisprudential perspectives. To facilitate discussion and debate, we have included excerpts from commentators with a wide range of viewpoints. Technical terms are clearly explained.

A Note on the Casebook Website. We strive to keep the book up to date between editions, and we maintain a web page for the book with downloadable updates and other useful information. We invite you to visit the website:

http://informationprivacylaw.com

The website contains links to useful news sites, blogs, and online resources pertaining to information privacy law issues. We also provide a list of recommended books that can be read in conjunction with this book.

A Note on Privacy Law Fundamentals. Students may find our short volume, *Privacy Law Fundamentals,* to be a useful companion to the casebook. *Privacy Law Fundamentals* is designed to be a distilled overview of information privacy law for both practitioners and students. More information about this book can be found at http://informationprivacylaw.com.

A Note on the Editing. We have deleted many citations and footnotes from the cases to facilitate readability. The footnotes that have been retained in the cases have been renumbered. When discussing books, articles, and other materials in the notes and commentary, we have included full citations in footnotes in order to make the text easier to read. We have also included many citations to additional works in the footnotes that may be of interest to the reader.

Daniel J. Solove
Paul M. Schwartz

November 2014

ACKNOWLEDGMENTS

Daniel J. Solove: I would like to thank Carl Coleman, Scott Forbes, Susan Freiwald, Tomás Gómez-Arostegui, Stephen Gottlieb, Marcia Hofmann, Chris Hoofnagle, John Jacobi, Orin Kerr, Raymond Ku, Peter Raven-Hansen, Joel Reidenberg, Neil Richards, Michael Risinger, Lior Strahilevitz, Peter Swire, William Thompson, and Peter Winn for helpful comments and suggestions. Charlie Sullivan and Jake Barnes provided indispensable advice about how to bring this project to fruition. Special thanks to Richard Mixter at Aspen Publishers for his encouragement and faith in this project. Thanks as well to the other folks at Aspen who have contributed greatly to the editing and development of this book: John Devins, Christine Hannan, Carmen Reid, Jessica Barmack, John Burdeaux, and Sandra Doherty. I would like to thank my research assistants Peter Choy, Monica Contreras, Carly Grey, Maeve Miller, James Murphy, Poornima Ravishankar, Sheerin Shahinpoor, Vladimir Semendyai, John Spaccarotella, Tiffany Stedman, Lourdes Turrecha, Eli Weiss, and Kate Yannitte. I would also like to thank Dean Blake Morant for providing the resources I needed. And thanks to my wife Pamela Solove and son Griffin Solove, who kept me in good cheer throughout this project.

Paul M. Schwartz: For their suggestions, encouragement, and insights into information privacy law, I would like to thank Ken Bamberger, Fred Cate, Malcolm Crompton, Christopher Gulotta, Andrew Guzman, Chris Hoofnagle, Ted Janger, Ronald D. Lee, Lance Liebman, Steven McDonald, Viktor Mayer-Schönberger, Deirdre Mulligan, Karl-Nikolaus Peifer, Joel Reidenberg, Ira Rubinstein, Pam Samuelson, Lior Strahilevitz, Peter Swire, William M. Treanor, and Peter Winn. I benefited as well from the help of my talented research assistants: Cesar Alvarez, Benedikt Burger, Kai-Dieter Classen, Leah Duranti, Alpa Patel, Karl Saddlemire, Brian St. John, Laura Sullivan, and Sebastian Zimmeck. Many thanks to my co-author, Daniel Solove. Many thanks as well to my mother, Nancy Schwartz, and to Laura Schwartz and Ed Holden; David Schwartz and Kathy Smith; and Daniel Schwartz.

A profound debt is owed Spiros Simitis. My interest in the subject of information privacy began in 1985 with his suggestion that I visit his office of the Hessian Data Protection Commissioner in Wiesbaden and sit in on meetings there. Through his scholarship, example, and friendship, Professor Simitis has provided essential guidance during the decades since that initial trip to Wiesbaden. My portion of the book is dedicated to Steffie, Clara, and Leo, with my gratitude and love.

Finally, both of us would like to thank Marc Rotenberg, who helped us shape the book in its first two editions and provided invaluable input.

We are grateful to the following sources for their permission to reprint excerpts of their scholarship:

Anita L. Allen, *Coercing Privacy*, 40 William & Mary L. Rev. 723 (1999). Used by permission. © 1999 by William & Mary Law Review and Anita L. Allen.

William C. Banks & M.E. Bowman, *Executive Authority For National Security Surveillance*, 50 Am. U. L. Rev. 1 (2000). Reprinted with permission.

Fred H. Cate, *The Privacy Problem: A Broader View of Information Privacy and the Costs and Consequences of Protecting It*, 4 First Reports 1 (March 2003). Reprinted with permission.

Julie E. Cohen, *Examined Lives: Informational Privacy*, 52 Stan. L. Rev. 1371 (2000). © 2000. Reprinted by permission of the Stanford Law Review in the format textbook via Copyright Clearance Center and Julie Cohen.

Mary DeRosa, *Data Mining and Data Analysis for Counterterrorism*, Center for Strategic and International Studies 6-8 (CSIS) (2004). Reprinted with permission.

Richard Epstein, *The Legal Regulation of Genetic Discrimination: Old Responses to New Technology*, 74 B.U. L. Rev. 1, 2-4, 8-13, 18-19 (1994). Reprinted with permission of Richard Epstein.

Eric Goldman, *The Privacy Hoax*, Forbes (Oct. 14, 2002) available at http://www.ericgoldman.org/Articles/privacyhoax.htm. Reprinted with permission.

Lawrence O. Gostin, Health Information Privacy, 80 Cornell L. Rev. 451 (1995). Reprinted with permission.

Steven Hetcher, *The FTC as Internet Privacy Norm Entrepreneur*, 53 Vand. L. Rev. 2041 (2000). Reprinted with the permission of Steven Hetcher.

Orin S. Kerr, *A User's Guide to the Stored Communications Act — and a Legislator's Guide to Amending It*, 72 Geo. Wash. L. Rev. 1208 (2004). Reprinted with permission.

Orin S. Kerr, *The Fourth Amendment and New Technologies: Constitutional Myths and the Case for Caution*, 102 Mich. L. Rev. 801 (2004). © 2004 by the Michigan Law Review Association. Reprinted with permission.

Pauline T. Kim, *Privacy Rights, Public Policy, and the Employment Relationship*, 57 Ohio St. L.J. 671 (1996). Reprinted with permission.

Catharine A. MacKinnon, Toward a Feminist Theory of the State 190-193 (1989). © 1989 by Harvard University Press. Reprinted with permission.

Richard A. Posner, *The Right of Privacy*, 12 Ga. L. Rev. 393 (1978). Reprinted with permission.

Radhika Rao, *Property, Privacy and the Human Body*, 80 B.U. L Rev. 359 (2000). Reprinted with permission of the Boston University Law Review and Radhika Rao.

Joel Reidenberg, *E-Commerce and Trans-Atlantic Privacy*, 38 Hous. L. Rev. 717 (2001). Reprinted with permission.

Marc Rotenberg, *Fair Information Practices and the Architecture of Privacy (What Larry Doesn't Get)*, 2001 Stan. Tech. L. Rev. 1, 43 (2001). Reprinted with permission.

Paul M. Schwartz, *Privacy and Democracy in Cyberspace*, 52 Vand. L. Rev. 1609 (1999). Reprinted with the permission of Paul Schwartz.

Paul M. Schwartz, *Privacy and the Economics of Health Care Information*, 76 Tex. L. Rev. 1 (1997). © 1997 the Texas Law Review. Reprinted with permission.

Reva B. Seigel, *The Rule of Love: Wife Beating as Prerogative of Privacy*, 105 Yale L.J. 2117 (1996). Reprinted by permission of the *Yale Law Journal* Company and the William S. Hein Company, from the *Yale Law Journal,* vol. 105, pages 2117-2207.

Spiros Simitis, *Reviewing Privacy in an Informational Society*, 135 U. Pa. L. Rev. 707, 709-710, 724-726, 732-738, 746 (1987). © 1987 by the University of Pennsylvania Law Review. Reprinted by permission of the University of Pennsylvania Law Review and Spiros Simitis.

Richard Sobel, *The Degradation of the Moral Economy of Political Identity Under a Computerized National Identification System*, 8 B.U. J. Sci. & Tech. L. 37 (2002). Reprinted with permission.

Daniel J. Solove, *Conceptualizing Privacy,* 90 California Law Review 1087 (2002). © 2002 by the California Law Review.

Daniel J. Solove, *Reconstructing Electronic Surveillance Law*, 72 George Washington Law Review 1264 (2004). © 2004 by Daniel J. Solove.

Jeff Sovern, *Opting In, Opting Out, or No Options at All: The Fight for Control of Personal Information,* 74 Wash. L. Rev. 1033 (1999). Reprinted with permission.

Michael E. Staten & Fred H. Cate, *The Impact of Opt-In Privacy Rules on Retail Markets: A Case Study of MBNA*, 52 Duke L.J. 745 (2003). Reprinted with permission.

Alan Westin, Privacy and Freedom 7, 31-38 (1967). A study sponsored by the Association of the Bar of the City of New York. Reprinted with permission.

James Q. Whitman, *The Two Western Cultures of Privacy: Dignity Versus Liberty,* 113 Yale L.J. 1151 (2004). Reprinted with permission.

Peter A. Winn, *Online Court Records: Balancing Judicial Accountability and Privacy in an Age of Electronic Information*, 79 Wash. L. Rev. 307 (2004). Reprinted with permission.

PRIVACY, LAW ENFORCEMENT, AND NATIONAL SECURITY

CHAPTER 1

PRIVACY AND LAW ENFORCEMENT

CHAPTER OUTLINE

A. THE FOURTH AMENDMENT AND EMERGING TECHNOLOGY

   1. How the Fourth Amendment Works

     (a) Applicability: Searches and Seizures

     (b) Reasonable Searches and Seizures

     (c) Enforcement: The Exclusionary Rule and Civil Remedies

     (d) Subpoenas and Court Orders

   2. Wiretapping, Bugging, and Beyond

   3. The Reasonable Expectation of Privacy Test

     (a) The Third Party Doctrine

     (b) Items Abandoned or Exposed to the Public

     (c) Surveillance and the Use of Sense Enhancement Technologies

B. INFORMATION GATHERING ABOUT FIRST AMENDMENT ACTIVITIES

C. FEDERAL ELECTRONIC SURVEILLANCE LAW

   1. Section 605 of the Federal Communications Act

   2. Title III

   3. The Electronic Communications Privacy Act

     (a) The Wiretap Act

     (b) The Stored Communications Act

     (c) The Pen Register Act

   4. The Communications Assistance for Law Enforcement Act

   5. The USA Patriot Act

   6. State Electronic Surveillance Law

D. DIGITAL SEARCHES AND SEIZURES

1. Searching Computers and Electronic Devices

2. Encryption

3. Video Surveillance

4. E-mail and Online Communications

5. ISP Account Information

6. IP Addresses, URLs, and Internet Searches

One of the central tensions in information privacy law is between privacy and security. Security involves society's interest in protecting its citizens from crimes, including physical and monetary threats. One way that government promotes security is by investigating and punishing crimes. To do this, law enforcement officials must gather information about suspected individuals. Monitoring and information gathering pose substantial threats to privacy. At the same time, however, monitoring and information gathering offer the potential of increasing security. Throughout the twentieth century, technology provided the government significantly greater ability to probe into the private lives of individuals.

The prevailing metaphor for the threat to privacy caused by law enforcement surveillance techniques is George Orwell's novel *Nineteen Eighty-Four*. Written in 1949, the novel depicted an all-powerful and omniscient government called "Big Brother" that monitored and controlled every facet of individuals' lives:

> Outside, even through the shut window-pane, the world looked cold. Down in the street little eddies of wind were whirling dust and torn paper into spirals, and though the sun was shining and the sky a harsh blue, there seemed to be no colour in anything, except the posters that were plastered everywhere. The black moustachio'd face gazed down from every commanding corner. There was one on the house-front immediately opposite. BIG BROTHER IS WATCHING YOU, the caption said, while the dark eyes looked deep into Winston's own. Down at streetlevel another poster, torn at one corner, flapped fitfully in the wind, alternately covering and uncovering the single word INGSOC. In the far distance a helicopter skimmed down between the roofs, hovered for an instant like a bluebottle, and darted away again with a curving flight. It was the police patrol, snooping into people's windows. The patrols did not matter, however. Only the Thought Police mattered.
>
> Behind Winston's back the voice from the telescreen was still babbling away about pig-iron and the overfulfilment of the Ninth Three-Year Plan. The telescreen received and transmitted simultaneously. Any sound that Winston made, above the level of a very low whisper, would be picked up by it, moreover, so long as he remained within the field of vision which the metal plaque commanded, he could be seen as well as heard. There was of course no way of knowing whether you were being watched at any given moment. How often, or on what system, the Thought Police plugged in on any individual wire was guesswork. It was even conceivable that they watched everybody all the time. But at any rate they could plug in your wire whenever they wanted to. You had to live — did live, from habit that became instinct — in the assumption that

every sound you made was overheard, and, except in darkness, every movement scrutinized.[1]

Orwell's harrowing portrait of a police state illustrates the importance of limiting the power of the government to monitor its citizens. But consider the reverse as well: Will overly restrictive limitations on the power of the police restrict their ability to protect the public?

Although privacy and security may at times be viewed in conflict, consider the opening words of the Fourth Amendment: "The right of the people to be *secure* in their persons, houses, papers, and effects . . ." (emphasis added). Are the interests in public security and privacy fated to be always at odds? Are there times when the opposition between security and privacy proves a false dichotomy?

In the United States, policing is predominantly carried out by local governments. The Constitution, however, provides a national regulatory regime for police conduct. The Fourth and Fifth Amendments significantly limit the government's power to gather information. The Fourth Amendment regulates the government's activities in searching for information or items as well as the government's seizure of things or people.[2] The Fifth Amendment guarantees that "[n]o person . . . shall be compelled in any criminal case to be a witness against himself. . . ." The Fifth Amendment establishes a "privilege against self-incrimination," and it prohibits the government from compelling individuals to disclose inculpatory information about themselves.

In addition to the U.S. Constitution, federal statutes can regulate law enforcement activity. One of the predominant areas of law enforcement that has been regulated by federal law is electronic surveillance. This chapter will focus extensively on these statutes, as they play an increasingly important role in criminal procedure as more searches involve electronic devices, computers, and the Internet.

At the state level, most state constitutions have provisions similar to the Fourth and Fifth Amendments — sometimes the language is even identical. State courts, however, have sometimes interpreted their state constitutional provisions as being more strict than the way the U.S. Supreme Court has interpreted the Fourth and Fifth Amendments. States have also passed their own statutory regulation of law enforcement, often also in the realm of electronic surveillance. State law enforcement officials will be bound by their state constitutions and laws, as well as by the U.S. Constitution and federal laws. Federal officials are not subject to these state constitutional and statutory restrictions.

---

[1] George Orwell, *Nineteen Eighty-Four* 3-4 (1949).

[2] For a comprehensive historical account of the origins of the Fourth Amendment, see William J. Cuddihy, *The Fourth Amendment: Origins and Original Meaning* 602-1791 (2009).

A. THE FOURTH AMENDMENT AND EMERGING TECHNOLOGY

1. HOW THE FOURTH AMENDMENT WORKS

The Fourth Amendment governs the investigatory power of government officials. The language of the Fourth Amendment reads:

> The right of the people to be secure in their persons, houses, papers, and effects, against unreasonable searches and seizures, shall not be violated, and no warrants shall issue, but upon probable cause, supported by oath or affirmation, and particularly describing the place to be searched, and the persons or things to be seized.

This section explains briefly how the Fourth Amendment works. The first issue is the *applicability of the Fourth Amendment*. Is a particular instance of government information gathering regulated by the Fourth Amendment? There are many instances when the government gathers information about people in a fashion that is not considered to be a search or seizure in the sense of the Fourth Amendment. In those cases, the behavior is considered free from the constraints of the Fourth Amendment. In these instances, however, a federal statute or state constitutional or statutory provision might still limit or otherwise regulate the governmental behavior. If not, then the government information gathering might not be regulated at all.

The second issue is *whether the search or seizure is reasonable*. Generally, a search is reasonable if government officials have obtained a search warrant supported by probable cause. The warrant must be properly circumscribed, and the search must not exceed the scope of the warrant. Only in very rare circumstances will a search within the scope of a valid warrant be deemed unreasonable. There are many instances, however, where a search without a warrant or probable cause will be deemed to be reasonable.

The third issue is *how the Fourth Amendment is enforced*. The primary method of enforcing the Fourth Amendment is by excluding from trial the use of evidence obtained in violation of the Fourth Amendment. People can also bring civil lawsuits for Fourth Amendment violations.

(a) Applicability: Searches and Seizures

The Fourth Amendment applies every time government officials (not just police) conduct a "search" or the "seizure" of an object, document, or person.

Searches. What is a "search" under the Fourth Amendment? This question has proven to be immensely challenging to answer. The cases in this chapter predominantly focus on this question, and the Supreme Court has used different approaches to answering this question. Its current approach is the "reasonable expectation of privacy test," which will be discussed later in this chapter.

Some paradigmatic examples of "searches" include peeking into one's pockets or searching one's person; entering into and looking around one's house, apartment, office, hotel room, or private property; and opening up and examining

defines whether it's a "search"

the contents of one's luggage or parcels. However, when government officials happen to observe something in plain view, then it is not a search.

Seizures. A "seizure" is a taking away of items by the police. A seizure can be of physical things or of persons (arrests).

(b) Reasonable Searches and Seizures

If there is a search or seizure, then the Fourth Amendment applies. It does not bar the search or seizure—it just requires that the search or seizure be "reasonable." What is reasonable and unreasonable under the Fourth Amendment?

Warrants and Probable Cause. Generally, a search or seizure is reasonable if the police have obtained a valid search warrant. To obtain a warrant, the police must go before a judge or magistrate and demonstrate that they have "probable cause" to conduct a search or seizure.

For a search warrant, probable cause requires that government officials have "reasonably trustworthy information" that is sufficient to "warrant a man of reasonable caution in the belief that an offense has been or is being committed" or that evidence will be found in the place to be searched. *Brinegar v. United States*, 338 U.S. 160 (1949). Probable cause is more than "bare suspicion." Probable cause must be measured on a case-by-case basis, via the facts of particular cases. *See Wong Sun v. United States*, 371 U.S. 471 (1963). The purpose of a warrant is to have an independent party (judges) ensure that police really do have probable cause to conduct a search.

A search warrant may be issued if there is probable cause to believe that there is incriminating evidence in the place to be searched. This is not limited to places owned or occupied by the criminal suspect. In certain instances, incriminating documents or things may be possessed by an innocent party.

A search is valid if the warrant is supported by probable cause and the search is within the scope of the warrant.

Unreasonable Searches with Warrants. Even with a warrant, certain searches are unreasonable. For example, in *Winston v. Lee*, 470 U.S. 753 (1985), the removal of a bullet lodged deep in the accused's chest was deemed unreasonable. However, this is one of the very rare circumstances where a search pursuant to a valid warrant will be deemed unreasonable. For example, the taking of blood from a suspect is a reasonable search. *See Schmerber v. California*, 384 U.S. 757 (1966). Barring truly exceptional circumstances, most searches undertaken with a valid warrant will be reasonable.

The Scope of Search Warrants. Search warrants do not authorize an unfettered search. The search must be circumscribed to the evidence being searched for and any other limits the court establishes in the warrant. In *Horton v. California*, 496 U.S. 128 (1990), the Supreme Court held that "[i]f the scope of the search exceeds that permitted by the terms of a validly issued warrant or the character of the relevant exception from the warrant requirement, the subsequent seizure is unconstitutional without more."

Warrants not only limit the search but also who is permitted to enter a person's home if it is being searched. In *Wilson v. Layne*, 526 U.S. 603 (1999), the police obtained a warrant to search the home of Charles and Geraldine Wilson because they were seeking to find their son who had violated his probation. The police entered the Wilsons's home in the early morning hours, accompanied by a reporter and a photographer from the *Washington Post*. After the search came up empty, the officers left. The Supreme Court held that the officers were not entitled to bring along reporters because they "were not present for any reason related to the justification for the police entry into the home."

Exceptions to the Warrant and Probable Cause Requirements. Under a number of circumstances, a search can be reasonable even when government officials do not have a warrant or probable cause to conduct a search or seizure. Some of these exceptions require government officials to have probable cause, but there are other exceptions where neither a warrant nor probable cause is required. For example, one exception is when exigent circumstances make obtaining a warrant impractical. Another exceptions is when a person consents to a search.

The Fourth Amendment applies not just to law enforcement officials but to all government officials. In some instances, however, searches by officials in certain places may fall under the "special needs" exception. Under this doctrine, searches and seizures are reasonable without a warrant or probable cause if "special needs, beyond the normal need for law enforcement, make the warrant and probable-cause requirement impracticable." *Griffin v. Wisconsin*, 483 U.S. 868 (1987). "The validity of a search is judged by the standard of 'reasonableness . . . under all the circumstances.' " *O'Connor v. Ortega*, 480 U.S. 709 (1987).

Searches that may fall under the "special needs" exception include searches by government employers, public school officials, and public hospital officials. As an example, the Supreme Court has upheld random drug tests for high school students participating in any competitive extracurricular activities, including academic extracurricular activities. *Board of Education v. Earls*, 536 U.S. 822 (2002). The special needs doctrine applies only when a search is not for a law enforcement purpose. Thus, in *New Jersey v. T.L.O.*, the Court upheld a search of a student's purse by school officials and noted that the search was "carried out by school authorities acting alone and on their own authority" as opposed to searches that might be conducted "in conjunction with or at the behest of law enforcement officials." *New Jersey v. T.L.O*, 469 U.S. 337 (1985).

Another exception to the warrant and probable cause requirement is a *Terry stop*. In *Terry v. Ohio*, 392 U.S. 1 (1968), the Court held that a police officer can "stop" an individual if the officer has "reasonable suspicion" that criminal activity is afoot. "Reasonable suspicion" is a standard that is lower than probable cause. A stop must be brief or temporary. If it lasts too long, it becomes a seizure, which requires probable cause. During the stop, the officer may "frisk" an individual for weapons if the officer has reasonable suspicion that the person is armed and dangerous. A frisk is not a full search. The officer cannot search the person for other items — only weapons. If, in the course of searching a person for weapons, the officer finds evidence of a crime, it will still be admissible if it was found within the scope of a valid frisk. For example, in *Minnesota v. Dickerson*, 508 U.S. 366 (1993), a police officer was searching a suspect for weapons and felt an object in the suspect's pocket. The officer did not believe it to be a weapon, but continued to inspect it. The Court concluded that this behavior was an invalid search that extended beyond the limited confines of a frisk.

In addition to *Terry* stops, government officials can engage in certain checkpoint stops and information-seeking stops. For example, fixed sobriety checkpoints are constitutional. *See Michigan Dep't of State Police v. Sitz*, 496 U.S. 444 (1990). Such a checkpoint search does not require "particularized suspicion." On the other hand, in *Delaware v. Prouse*, 440 U.S. 648 (1979), the Court held that the police cannot randomly stop cars to check license and registration. In *Indianapolis v. Edmond*, 531 U.S. 32 (2000), the Court held that checkpoints established to investigate possible drug violations were indistinguishable from a general purpose crime control search and were therefore unconstitutional:

> We have never approved a checkpoint program whose primary purpose was to detect evidence of ordinary criminal wrongdoing. Rather, our checkpoint cases have recognized only limited exceptions to the general rule that a seizure must be accompanied by some measure of individualized suspicion. We suggested in *Prouse* that we would not credit the "general interest in crime control" as justification for a regime of suspicionless stops. Consistent with this suggestion, each of the checkpoint programs that we have approved was designed primarily to serve purposes closely related to the problems of policing the border or the necessity of ensuring roadway safety. Because the primary purpose of the Indianapolis narcotics checkpoint program is to uncover evidence of ordinary criminal wrongdoing, the program contravenes the Fourth Amendment.

The Supreme Court in *Illinois v. Lidster*, 540 U.S. 419 (2004), upheld the constitutionality of so-called "information-seeking highway stops." Following a hit-and-run accident that killed a 70-year-old bicyclist, the police in Lombard, Illinois set up a checkpoint at the approximate scene of the accident. The police stopped vehicles, asked the occupants of the car whether they had seen anything the previous weekend, and gave each driver a flyer that described the fatal accident and asked for assistance in identifying the vehicle and driver in the accident. The Court held that the stop was reasonable. The "relevant public concern was grave," the stops were appropriately tailored to the investigatory need, and the stops were minimal because "each stop required only a brief wait," "[c]ontact with the police lasted only a few seconds," and the "contact provided little reason for anxiety or alarm."

(c) Enforcement: The Exclusionary Rule and Civil Remedies

When law enforcement officials violate an individual's Fourth Amendment rights, the individual can seek at least two forms of redress. First, if the individual is a defendant in a criminal trial, she can move to have the evidence obtained in violation of the Fourth Amendment suppressed. This is known as the "exclusionary rule." In *Weeks v. United States*, 232 U.S. 383 (1914), the Court established the exclusionary rule as the way to enforce the Fourth Amendment on federal officials. Later, in *Mapp v. Ohio*, 367 U.S. 643 (1961), the Court held that the exclusionary rule applies to all government searches, whether state or federal. The purpose of the exclusionary rule is to deter law enforcement officials from violating the Constitution.

If the police illegally search or seize evidence in violation of the Constitution, not only is that evidence suppressed but all other evidence derived from the illegally obtained evidence is also suppressed. This is known as the "fruit of the poisonous tree" doctrine. For example, suppose the police illegally search a person's luggage and find evidence that the person is a drug trafficker. Armed with that evidence, the police obtain a warrant to search the person's home, where they uncover new evidence of drug trafficking along with a weapon used in a murder. The person is charged with drug trafficking and murder. Under the Fourth Amendment, the evidence found in the person's luggage will be suppressed. Additionally, since the search warrant could not have been obtained but for the evidence turned up in the illegal search, the evidence found at the house, including the additional drug trafficking evidence as well as the murder evidence, will be suppressed. However, if the police obtained a warrant or located evidence by an "independent source," then the fruit of the poisonous tree doctrine does not apply. *See Silverthorne Lumber Co. v. United States*, 251 U.S. 385 (1920). Returning to the example above, if the police had evidence supplied from the person's cohort that the person was engaged in drug trafficking out of his home and had murdered somebody, this evidence may suffice to give the police probable cause to have a warrant issued to search the person's house. This evidence is independent from the illegal search, and it is admissible.[3]

The second form of redress for a violation of the Fourth Amendment is a civil remedy. A person, whether a criminal defendant or anybody else, can obtain civil damages for a Fourth Amendment violation by way of 42 U.S.C. § 1983.

(d) Subpoenas and Court Orders

A common means for the government to gather information is through a court order or subpoena. Court orders are specified by statutes or regulations as a protection against unfettered government information gathering. Court orders often have different standards than warrants, which require probable cause. When Fourth Amendment applies to the information gathering, it provides the baseline of protection. If the Fourth Amendment requires a warrant before the government can engage in the specific behavior, the government cannot conduct a search or gather the information under a lesser standard. In instances where the Fourth Amendment does not apply, the standards set forth in a court order (if required by a law) will govern. These standards vary considerably depending upon the

---

[3] The exclusionary rule has received significant scholarly attention. A number of scholars question its efficacy and advocate that the Fourth Amendment be enforced through other mechanisms such as civil sanctions. *See* Akhil Reed Amar, *The Constitution and Criminal Procedure* 28 (1997); Christopher Slobogin, *Why Liberals Should Chuck the Exclusionary Rule*, 1999 U. Ill. L. Rev. 363, 400-01 (1999). Other commentators contend that civil sanctions will be ineffective. *See* Arnold H. Loewy, *The Fourth Amendment as a Device for Protecting the Innocent*, 81 Mich. L. Rev. 1229, 1266 (1983); Tracey Maclin, *When the Cure for the Fourth Amendment Is Worse Than the Disease*, 68 S. Cal. L. Rev. 1, 62 (1994).

particular law that defines them. In many cases, the standards are less stringent than probable cause.

A subpoena is an order to obtain testimony or documents. Numerous statutes authorize federal agencies to issue subpoenas. In *Doe v. Ashcroft,* 334 F. Supp. 2d 471 (S.D.N.Y. 2004), the court explained:

> For example, the Internal Revenue Service (IRS) may issue subpoenas to investigate possible violations of the tax code, and the Securities Exchange Commission (SEC) may issue subpoenas to investigate possible violations of the securities laws. More obscure examples include the Secretary of Agriculture's power to issue subpoenas in investigating and enforcing laws related to honey research, and the Secretary of Commerce's power to issue subpoenas in investigating and enforcing halibut fishing laws. . . .
>
> Where an agency seeks a court order to enforce a subpoena against a resisting subpoena recipient, courts will enforce the subpoena as long as: (1) the agency's investigation is being conducted pursuant to a legitimate purpose, (2) the inquiry is relevant to that purpose, (3) the information is not already within the agency's possession, and (4) the proper procedures have been followed. The Second Circuit has described these standards as "minimal." Even if an administrative subpoena meets these initial criteria to be enforceable, its recipient may nevertheless affirmatively challenge the subpoena on other grounds, such as an allegation that it was issued with an improper purpose or that the information sought is privileged.

In contrast to an administrative subpoena, an ordinary subpoena may be issued in civil or criminal cases. For criminal cases, the government may obtain a subpoena from the clerk of court. Subpoenas are not issued directly by judges. Instead, "[t]he clerk must issue a blank subpoena — signed and sealed — to the party requesting it, and that party must fill in the blanks before the subpoena is served." Fed. R. Crim. P. 17(a). Failure to comply with a subpoena can lead to contempt of court sanctions. A subpoena can broadly compel the production of various documents and items:

> A subpoena may order the witness to produce any books, papers, documents, data, or other objects the subpoena designates. The court may direct the witness to produce the designated items in court before trial or before they are to be offered in evidence. When the items arrive, the court may permit the parties and their attorneys to inspect all or part of them. Fed. R. Crim. P. 17(c)(1).

If the party served with the subpoena has an objection, she may bring a motion to quash or modify the subpoena. "[T]he court may quash or modify the subpoena if compliance would be unreasonable or oppressive." Fed. R. Crim. P. 17(c)(2). As *Doe v. Ashcroft,* 334 F. Supp. 2d 471 (S.D.N.Y. 2004) explains:

> The reasonableness of a subpoena depends on the context. For example, to survive a motion to quash, a subpoena issued in connection with a criminal trial "must make a reasonably specific request for information that would be both relevant and admissible at trial." By contrast, a grand jury subpoena is generally enforced as long as there is a "reasonable possibility that the category of materials the Government seeks will produce information relevant to the general subject of the grand jury's investigation." Considering the grand jury's broad investigatory power and minimal court supervision, it is accurate to observe, as

the Second Circuit did long ago, that "[b]asically the grand jury is a law enforcement agency."

When do subpoenas violate the Fourth or Fifth Amendments? Subpoenas can compel people to produce documents with incriminating information. One of the early cases addressing this issue was *Boyd v. United States*, 116 U.S. 616 (1886). The government issued a subpoena to compel Boyd, a merchant, to produce invoices on cases of imported glass for use in a civil forfeiture proceeding. The Court held that the subpoena violated the Fourth and Fifth Amendments:

> . . . [B]y the proceeding now under consideration, the court attempts to extort from the party his private books and papers to make him liable for a penalty or to forfeit his property. . . .
> . . . It is not the breaking of his doors, and the rummaging of his drawers, that constitutes the essence of the offence; but it is the invasion of his indefeasible right to personal security, personal liberty and private property, where the right has never been forfeited by his conviction of some public offence. . . . Breaking into a house and opening boxes and drawers are circumstances of aggravation; but any forcible and compulsory extortion of a man's own testimony or of his private papers to be used as evidence to convict him of crime or to forfeit his goods, is within the condemnation of that judgment. In this regard the Fourth and Fifth Amendments run almost into each other.

In *Gouled v. United States*, 255 U.S. 298 (1921), the Court held that law enforcement officials could not use search warrants to search a person's "house or office or papers" to obtain evidence to use against her in a criminal proceeding. The holdings of *Boyd* and *Gouled* became known as the "mere evidence" rule — the government could only seize papers if they were instrumentalities of a crime, fruits of a crime, or illegal contraband. This idea was based on a property-based approach to the Fourth Amendment.

The holding in *Boyd* has been significantly cut back. In *Warden v. Hayden*, 387 U.S. 294 (1967), the Court abolished the mere evidence rule. As the Court currently interprets the Fifth Amendment, the government can require a person to produce papers and records. *See Shapiro v. United States*, 335 U.S. 1 (1948). The Fifth Amendment also does not protect against subpoenas for a person's records and papers held by third parties. In *Couch v. United States*, 409 U.S. 322 (1973), the Court upheld a subpoena to a person's accountant for documents because "the Fifth Amendment privilege is a personal privilege: it adheres basically to the person, not to information that may incriminate him." The Fifth Amendment, the Court reasoned, only prevents "[i]nquisitorial pressure or coercion against a potentially accused person, compelling her, against her will, to utter self-condemning words or produce incriminating documents." Similarly, in *Fisher v. United States*, 425 U.S. 391 (1976), the Court upheld a subpoena to a person's attorney for documents pertaining to that person. The Fifth Amendment is not a "general protector of privacy" but protects against the "compelled self-incrimination."

Cases expanding the government's ability to use subpoenas to gather information used to maintain a distinction between corporate records (which could be obtained via subpoena) and personal papers (which could not).

Christopher Slobogin observes that the Court gradually abandoned this distinction.[4]

In *United States v. Dionisio*, 410 U.S. 1 (1973), the Court held that the Fourth Amendment does not restrict a grand jury subpoena to produce documents (subpoena duces tecum) or to testify:

> It is clear that a subpoena to appear before a grand jury is not a 'seizure' in the Fourth Amendment sense, even though that summons may be inconvenient or burdensome. . . .
>
> The compulsion exerted by a grand jury subpoena differs from the seizure effected by an arrest or even an investigative 'stop' in more than civic obligation. For, as Judge Friendly wrote for the Court of Appeals for the Second Circuit: "The latter is abrupt, is effected with force or the threat of it and often in demeaning circumstances, and, in the case of arrest, results in a record involving social stigma. A subpoena is served in the same manner as other legal process; it involves no stigma whatever; if the time for appearance is inconvenient, this can generally be altered; and it remains at all times under the control and supervision of a court."
>
> Thus the Court of Appeals for the Seventh Circuit correctly recognized in a case subsequent to the one now before us, that a 'grand jury subpoena to testify is not that kind of governmental intrusion on privacy against which the Fourth Amendment affords protection once the Fifth Amendment is satisfied.'

The Court was not quite ready to conclude that subpoenas fall entirely outside the Fourth Amendment, stating that "[t]he Fourth Amendment provides protection against a grand jury subpoena duces tecum too sweeping in its terms 'to be regarded as reasonable.'"

2. WIRETAPPING, BUGGING, AND BEYOND

At common law, eavesdropping was considered a nuisance. "Eavesdropping," as William Blackstone defined it, meant to "listen under walls or window, or the eaves of a house, to hearken after discourse, and thereupon to frame slanderous and mischievous tales."[5] Before the advent of electronic communication, people could easily avoid eavesdroppers by ensuring that nobody else was around during their conversations.

The invention of the telegraph in 1844 followed by the telephone in 1876 substantially altered the way people communicated with each other. Today, the telephone has become an essential part of everyday communications. The advent of electronic communications was soon followed by the invention of recording and transmitting devices that enabled new and more sophisticated forms of eavesdropping than overhearing a conversation with the naked ear. One feature of electronic surveillance is that unlike the unsealing of letters, the interception of communications is undetectable. Some of the current forms of electronic surveillance technology include wiretaps, bugs, and parabolic microphones. New

---

[4] For an excellent history of the Supreme Court's jurisprudence regarding subpoenas, see Christopher Slobogin, *Subpoenas and Privacy,* 53 DePaul L. Rev. 805 (2005).

[5] 4 Blackstone, *Commentaries* 168 (1769).

legal questions are raised by modern technology such as a cell phone, which can provide information about the physical location of the person using it.

A "wiretap" is a device used to intercept telephone (or telegraph) communications. Wiretapping began before the invention of the telephone. Wiretapping was used to intercept telegraph communications during the Civil War and became very prevalent after the invention of the telephone. The first police wiretap occurred in the early 1890s. In the first half of the twentieth century, wiretaps proliferated due to law enforcement attempts to monitor protests over bad industrial working conditions, social unrest caused by World War I, and the smuggling of alcohol during the Prohibition Years.[6]

A "bug" is a device, often quite miniature in size, that can be hidden on a person or in a place that can transmit conversations in a room to a remote receiving device, where the conversation can be listened to.

A "parabolic microphone" can pick up a conversation from a distance. Typically, a small dish behind the microphone enables the amplification of sound far away from the microphone itself.

Electronic surveillance devices were not in existence at the time that the Fourth Amendment was drafted. How, then, should the Fourth Amendment regulate these devices? In 1928, the Supreme Court attempted to answer this question in *Olmstead v. United States*, the first electronic surveillance case to come before the Court.

OLMSTEAD V. UNITED STATES

277 U.S. 438 (1928)

TAFT, C.J. The petitioners were convicted in the District Court for the Western District of Washington of a conspiracy to violate the National Prohibition Act by unlawfully possessing, transporting and importing intoxicating liquors and maintaining nuisances, and by selling intoxicating liquors. Seventy-two others, in addition to the petitioners, were indicted. Some were not apprehended, some were acquitted, and others pleaded guilty. . . .

The information which led to the discovery of the conspiracy and its nature and extent was largely obtained by intercepting messages on the telephones of the conspirators by four federal prohibition officers. Small wires were inserted along the ordinary telephone wires from the residences of four of the petitioners and those leading from the chief office. The insertions were made without trespass upon any property of the defendants. They were made in the basement of the large office building. The taps from house lines were made in the streets near the houses. . . .

The well-known historical purpose of the Fourth Amendment, directed against general warrants and writs of assistance, was to prevent the use of governmental force to search a man's house, his person, his papers, and his

---

[6] For more background on the history of wiretapping, see generally Robert Ellis Smith, *Ben Franklin's Web Site: Privacy and Curiosity from Plymouth Rock to the Internet* (2000); Priscilla M. Regan, *Legislating Privacy: Technology, Social Values, and Public Policy* (1995); James G. Carr, *The Law of Electronic Surveillance* (1994); Whitfield Diffie & Susan Landau, *Privacy on the Line: The Politics of Wiretapping and Encryption* (1998).

effects, and to prevent their seizure against his will. This phase of the misuse of governmental power of compulsion is the emphasis of the opinion of the court in the *Boyd* Case. . . .

. . . The Fourth Amendment may have proper application to a sealed letter in the mail, because of the constitutional provision for the Post Office Department and the relations between the government and those who pay to secure protection of their sealed letters. . . . It is plainly within the words of the amendment to say that the unlawful rifling by a government agent of a sealed letter is a search and seizure of the sender's papers or effects. The letter is a paper, an effect, and in the custody of a government that forbids carriage, except under its protection.

The United States takes no such care of telegraph or telephone messages as of mailed sealed letters. The amendment does not forbid what was done here. There was no searching. There was no seizure. The evidence was secured by the use of the sense of hearing and that only. There was no entry of the houses or offices of the defendants. . . .

The language of the amendment cannot be extended and expanded to include telephone wires, reaching to the whole world from the defendant's house or office. The intervening wires are not part of his house or office, any more than are the highways along which they are stretched. . . .

Congress may, of course, protect the secrecy of telephone messages by making them, when intercepted, inadmissible in evidence in federal criminal trials, by direct legislation, and thus depart from the common law of evidence. But the courts may not adopt such a policy by attributing an enlarged and unusual meaning to the Fourth Amendment. The reasonable view is that one who installs in his house a telephone instrument with connecting wires intends to project his voice to those quite outside, and that the wires beyond his house, and messages while passing over them, are not within the protection of the Fourth Amendment. Here those who intercepted the projected voices were not in the house of either party to the conversation. . . .

BRANDEIS, J. dissenting. The government makes no attempt to defend the methods employed by its officers. Indeed, it concedes that, if wire tapping can be deemed a search and seizure within the Fourth Amendment, such wire tapping as was practiced in the case at bar was an unreasonable search and seizure, and that the evidence thus obtained was inadmissible. But it relies on the language of the amendment, and it claims that the protection given thereby cannot properly be held to include a telephone conversation.

"We must never forget," said Mr. Chief Justice Marshall in *McCulloch v. Maryland*, "that it is a Constitution we are expounding." Since then this court has repeatedly sustained the exercise of power by Congress, under various clauses of that instrument, over objects of which the fathers could not have dreamed. We have likewise held that general limitations on the powers of government, like those embodied in the due process clauses of the Fifth and Fourteenth Amendments, do not forbid the United States or the states from meeting modern conditions by regulations which "a century ago, or even half a century ago, probably would have been rejected as arbitrary and oppressive." Clauses guaranteeing to the individual protection against specific abuses of power, must have a similar capacity of adaptation to a changing world. It was with reference to such a clause that this court said in *Weems v. United States*, 217 U.S. 349, 373:

> Legislation, both statutory and constitutional, is enacted, it is true, from an experience of evils, but its general language should not, therefore, be necessarily confined to the form that evil had theretofore taken. Time works changes, brings into existence new conditions and purposes. Therefore a principle to be vital must be capable of wider application than the mischief which gave it birth. This is peculiarly true of Constitutions. They are not ephemeral enactments, designed to meet passing occasions. They are, to use the words of Chief Justice Marshall, "designed to approach immortality as nearly as human institutions can approach it." The future is their care and provision for events of good and bad tendencies of which no prophecy can be made. In the application of a Constitution, therefore, our contemplation cannot be only of what has been but of what may be. Under any other rule a Constitution would indeed be as easy of application as it would be deficient in efficacy and power. Its general principles would have little value and be converted by precedent into impotent and lifeless formulas. Rights declared in words might be lost in reality.

When the Fourth and Fifth Amendments were adopted, "the form that evil had theretofore taken" had been necessarily simple. Force and violence were then the only means known to man by which a government could directly effect self-incrimination. It could compel the individual to testify — a compulsion effected, if need be, by torture. It could secure possession of his papers and other articles incident to his private life — a seizure effected, if need be, by breaking and entry. Protection against such invasion of "the sanctities of a man's home and the privacies of life" was provided in the Fourth and Fifth Amendments by specific language. *Boyd v. United States*, 116 U.S. 616 (1886). But "time works changes, brings into existence new conditions and purposes." Subtler and more far-reaching means of invading privacy have become available to the government. Discovery and invention have made it possible for the government, by means far more effective than stretching upon the rack, to obtain disclosure in court of what is whispered in the closet.

Moreover, "in the application of a Constitution, our contemplation cannot be only of what has been, but of what may be." The progress of science in furnishing the government with means of espionage is not likely to stop with wire tapping. Ways may some day be developed by which the government, without removing papers from secret drawers, can reproduce them in court, and by which it will be enabled to expose to a jury the most intimate occurrences of the home. Advances in the psychic and related sciences may bring means of exploring unexpressed beliefs, thoughts and emotions. "That places the liberty of every man in the hands of every petty officer" was said by James Otis of much lesser intrusions than these. To Lord Camden a far slighter intrusion seemed "subversive of all the comforts of society." Can it be that the Constitution affords no protection against such invasions of individual security?

A sufficient answer is found in *Boyd v. United States*, 116 U.S. 616 (1886), a case that will be remembered as long as civil liberty lives in the United States. This court there reviewed the history that lay behind the Fourth and Fifth Amendments. We said with reference to Lord Camden's judgment in *Entick v. Carrington*, 19 Howell's State Trials, 1030:

The principles laid down in this opinion affect the very essence of constitutional liberty and security. They reach farther than the concrete form of the case there before the court, with its adventitious circumstances; they apply to all invasions on the part of the government and its employees of the sanctities of a man's home and the privacies of life. It is not the breaking of his doors, and the rummaging of his drawers, that constitutes the essence of the offense; but it is the invasion of his indefeasible right of personal security, personal liberty and private property, where that right has never been forfeited by his conviction of some public offense — it is the invasion of this sacred right which underlies and constitutes the essence of Lord Camden's judgment. Breaking into a house and opening boxes and drawers are circumstances of aggravation; but any forcible and compulsory extortion of a man's own testimony or of his private papers to be used as evidence of a crime or to forfeit his goods, is within the condemnation of that judgment. In this regard the Fourth and Fifth Amendments run almost into each other.

In *Ex parte Jackson*, 96 U.S. 727 (1877), it was held that a sealed letter entrusted to the mail is protected by the amendments. The mail is a public service furnished by the government. The telephone is a public service furnished by its authority. There is, in essence, no difference between the sealed letter and the private telephone message. . . .

The evil incident to invasion of the privacy of the telephone is far greater than that involved in tampering with the mails. Whenever a telephone line is tapped, the privacy of the persons at both ends of the line is invaded, and all conversations between them upon any subject, and although proper, confidential, and privileged, may be overheard. Moreover, the tapping of one man's telephone line involves the tapping of the telephone of every other person whom he may call, or who may call him. As a means of espionage, writs of assistance and general warrants are but puny instruments of tyranny and oppression when compared with wire tapping.

Time and again this court, in giving effect to the principle underlying the Fourth Amendment, has refused to place an unduly literal construction upon it. . .

The protection guaranteed by the amendments is much broader in scope. The makers of our Constitution undertook to secure conditions favorable to the pursuit of happiness. They recognized the significance of man's spiritual nature, of his feelings and of his intellect. They knew that only a part of the pain, pleasure and satisfactions of life are to be found in material things. They sought to protect Americans in their beliefs, their thoughts, their emotions and their sensations. They conferred, as against the government, the right to be let alone — the most comprehensive of rights and the right most valued by civilized men. To protect that right, every unjustifiable intrusion by the government upon the privacy of the individual, whatever the means employed, must be deemed a violation of the Fourth Amendment. And the use, as evidence in a criminal proceeding, of facts ascertained by such intrusion must be deemed a violation of the Fifth.

Applying to the Fourth and Fifth Amendments the established rule of construction, the defendants' objections to the evidence obtained by wire tapping must, in my opinion, be sustained. It is, of course, immaterial where the physical connection with the telephone wires leading into the defendants' premises was made. And it is also immaterial that the intrusion was in aid of law enforcement. Experience should teach us to be most on our guard to protect liberty when the government's purposes are beneficent. Men born to freedom are naturally alert to repel invasion of their liberty by evil-minded rulers. The greatest dangers to liberty lurk in insidious encroachment by men of zeal, well-meaning but without understanding. . . .

NOTES & QUESTIONS

1. *Background and Epilogue.* Roy Olmstead, known as the "King of Bootleggers," ran a gigantic illegal alcohol distribution operation on the Pacific Coast during Prohibition. Formerly a police officer, Olmstead had long avoided trouble with state police by bribing them, but federal officials soon caught up with him. The federal investigators, led by Roy Lyle, Director of Prohibition, were wiretapping all of the telephones in Olmstead's home for around five months. The case was widely followed in the press, and it was dubbed "the case of the whispering wires." Olmstead was careful not to leave evidence in his very large home; when the agents searched it, they turned up no evidence. Most of the evidence in the case came from the wiretaps. Olmstead knew he was being wiretapped; he had been tipped off by a freelance wiretapper the government had hired. But Olmstead believed that because wiretapping was illegal in the state of Washington, the wiretap evidence could not be used against him at trial. He was wrong. At trial, Olmstead was convicted and sentenced to four years in prison. He was later pardoned by President Roosevelt in 1935. In an ironic twist, while Olmstead was in prison, Roy Lyle was arrested for conspiring with rumrunners. Olmstead testified against Lyle at Lyle's trial. While in prison, Olmstead became a Christian Scientist, and after his release, he repudiated alcohol as one of the ills of society.[7]

2. *The Physical Trespass Doctrine, Detectaphones, and "Spike Mikes."* In *Olmstead*, the Supreme Court concluded that Fourth Amendment protections are triggered only when there is a physical trespass. The Court followed this approach for nearly 40 years. In *Goldman v. United States*, 316 U.S. 129 (1942), the police placed a device called a "detectaphone" next to a wall adjacent to a person's office. The device enabled the police to listen in on conversations inside the office. The Court concluded that since there was no trespass, there was no Fourth Amendment violation.

   In *Silverman v. United States*, 365 U.S. 505 (1961), the police used a device called a "spike mike" to listen in from a vacant row house to conversations in an adjoining row house. The device consisted of a microphone with a spike of about a foot in length attached to it. The spike was

---

[7] Samuel Dash, *The Intruders: Unreasonable Searches and Seizures from King John to John Ashcroft* 74-78 (2004); Robert C. Post, *Federalism, Positive Law, and the Emergence of the American Administrative State: Prohibition in the Taft Court Era*, 48 Wm. & Mary L. Rev. 1, 139-50 (2006).

inserted into a baseboard of the vacant row house on the wall adjoining the row house next door. The spike hit the heating duct serving the next-door row house, which transformed the heating system into a sound conductor. The Court held that the use of the "spike mike" violated the Fourth Amendment because it constituted an "unauthorized physical encroachment" into the adjoining row house. The Court distinguished *Olmstead* and *Goldman* because those cases did not involve any "physical invasion" or "trespass" onto the defendant's property, whereas the "spike mike" "usurp[ed] part of the [defendant's] house or office." Do you agree with the Court's distinction between *Goldman/Olmstead* and *Silverman* — between surveillance involving physical intrusion (however slight) and surveillance not involving any trespassing on the premises?

3. ***Brandeis's Dissent and the Warren and Brandeis Article.*** Justice Brandeis's dissent is one of the most famous dissents in Supreme Court history. Note the similarities between Brandeis's 1890 article, *The Right to Privacy*, and his dissent nearly 40 years later in *Olmstead*. What themes are repeated? Recall that *The Right to Privacy* concerned locating common law roots for privacy protection. What is Brandeis saying about the roots of constitutional protection of privacy?

4. ***Changing Technology and the Constitution.*** Brandeis contends that the Constitution should keep pace with changing technology. But given the rapid pace of technological change and the fact that the Constitution must serve as the stable foundation for our society, can the Constitution keep pace? How adaptable should the Constitution be?

5. ***Wiretapping vs. Mail Tampering.*** Brandeis contends that wiretapping is more insidious than tampering with the mail. Why? How would you compare wiretapping with intercepting e-mail or instant messages?

6. ***State Wiretapping Law.*** In the state of Washington, where the wiretapping in *Olmstead* took place, wiretapping was a criminal act, and the officers had thus violated the law. In a separate dissenting opinion, Justice Holmes noted that:

> . . . [A]part from the Constitution the government ought not to use evidence obtained and only obtainable by a criminal act. . . . It is desirable that criminals should be detected, and to that end that all available evidence should be used. It also is desirable that the government should not itself foster and pay for other crimes, when they are the means by which the evidence is to be obtained. If it pays its officers for having got evidence by crime I do not see why it may not as well pay them for getting it in the same way, and I can attach no importance to protestations of disapproval if it knowingly accepts and pays and announces that in future it will pay for the fruits. We have to choose, and for my part I think it a less evil that some criminals should escape than that the government should play an ignoble part.

Should it matter in Fourth Amendment analysis whether particular federal law enforcement surveillance tactics are illegal under state law?

7. ***The Birth of Federal Electronic Surveillance Law.*** The *Olmstead* decision was not well received by the public. In 1934, Congress responded to *Olmstead* by enacting § 605 of the Federal Communications Act, making

wiretapping a federal crime. This statute will be discussed later in the part on electronic surveillance law.

8. ***Secret Agents and Misplaced Trust.*** In *Hoffa v. United States*, 385 U.S. 293 (1966), an undercover informant, Edward Partin, befriended James Hoffa and elicited statements from him about his plans to bribe jurors in a criminal trial in which Hoffa was a defendant. According to the Court:

> In the present case . . . it is evident that no interest legitimately protected by the Fourth Amendment is involved. It is obvious that the petitioner was not relying on the security of his hotel suite when he made the incriminating statements to Partin or in Partin's presence. Partin did not enter the suite by force or by stealth. He was not a surreptitious eavesdropper. Partin was in the suite by invitation, and every conversation which he heard was either directed to him or knowingly carried on in his presence. The petitioner, in a word, was not relying on the security of the hotel room; he was relying upon his misplaced confidence that Partin would not reveal his wrongdoing.

Likewise, in *Lewis v. United States*, 385 U.S. 206 (1966), the defendant sold drugs to an undercover agent in his house. The Court held:

> In the instant case . . . the petitioner invited the undercover agent to his home for the specific purpose of executing a felonious sale of narcotics. Petitioner's only concern was whether the agent was a willing purchaser who could pay the agreed price. . . . During neither of his visits to petitioner's home did the agent see, hear, or take anything that was not contemplated, and in fact intended, by petitioner as a necessary part of his illegal business. Were we to hold the deceptions of the agent in this case constitutionally prohibited, we would come near to a rule that the use of undercover agents in any manner is virtually unconstitutional per se. Such a rule would, for example, severely hamper the Government in ferreting out those organized criminal activities that are characterized by covert dealings with victims who either cannot or do not protest. A prime example is provided by the narcotics traffic. . . .

Hoffa and *Lewis* establish that a person does not have a privacy interest in the loyalty of her friends. The government may deceive a person by sending in secret agents to befriend her. Is it problematic that government is permitted to use spies and deception as a law enforcement technique? Consider the following observation by Anthony Amsterdam:

> I can see no significant difference between police spies . . . and electronic surveillance, either in their uses or abuses. Both have long been asserted by law enforcement officers to be indispensable tools in investigating crime, particularly victimless and political crime, precisely because they both search out privacies that government could not otherwise invade. Both tend to repress crime in the same way, by making people distrustful and unwilling to talk to one another. The only difference is that under electronic surveillance you are afraid to talk to anybody in your office or over the phone, while under a spy system you are afraid to talk to anybody at all.[8]

---

[8] Anthony G. Amsterdam, *Perspectives on the Fourth Amendment*, 58 Minn. L. Rev. 349, 407 (1974). For a detailed analysis of undercover agents, see Gary T. Marx, *Under Cover: Police Surveillance in America* (1988).

9. ***Bugs, Transmitters, and Recording Devices.*** In *On Lee v. United States*, 343 U.S. 747 (1952), Chin Poy, a government informant with a concealed transmitter, engaged On Lee in conversation for the purpose of eliciting that On Lee was a drug dealer. The conversation was transmitted to a law enforcement agent, who later testified at trial about the content of the conversation. The Court held that the Fourth Amendment did not apply:

> Petitioner was talking confidentially and indiscreetly with one he trusted, and he was overheard. This was due to aid from a transmitter and receiver, to be sure, but with the same effect on his privacy as if agent Lee had been eavesdropping outside an open window. The use of bifocals, field glasses or the telescope to magnify the object of a witness' vision is not a forbidden search or seizure, even if they focus without his knowledge or consent upon what one supposes to be private indiscretions. It would be a dubious service to the genuine liberties protected by the Fourth Amendment to make them bedfellows with spurious liberties improvised by farfetched analogies which would liken eavesdropping on a conversation, with the connivance of one of the parties, to an unreasonable search or seizure. We find no violation of the Fourth Amendment here.

Does the use of electronic devices distinguish *On Lee* from *Hoffa* and *Lewis* in a material way?

LOPEZ V. UNITED STATES
373 U.S. 427 (1963)

[The petitioner, German S. Lopez, was tried in a federal court on a four-count indictment charging him with attempted bribery of an Internal Revenue agent, Roger S. Davis. The evidence against him had been obtained by a series of meetings between him and Davis. The last meeting was recorded by Davis with a pocket wire recorder. Prior to trial, Lopez moved to suppress the recorded conversation.]

HARLAN, J. . . . [Petitioner's] argument is primarily addressed to the recording of the conversation, which he claims was obtained in violation of his rights under the Fourth Amendment. Recognizing the weakness of this position if Davis was properly permitted to testify about the same conversation, petitioner now challenges that testimony as well, although he failed to do so at the trial. . . .

Once it is plain that Davis could properly testify about his conversation with Lopez, the constitutional claim relating to the recording of that conversation emerges in proper perspective. The Court has in the past sustained instances of "electronic eavesdropping" against constitutional challenge, when devices have been used to enable government agents to overhear conversations which would have been beyond the reach of the human ear. *See, e.g., Olmstead v. United States.* It has been insisted only that the electronic device not be planted by an unlawful physical invasion of a constitutionally protected area. . . . Indeed this case involves no "eavesdropping" whatever in any proper sense of that term. The Government did not use an electronic device to listen in on conversations it could not otherwise have heard. Instead, the device was used only to obtain the most reliable evidence possible of a conversation in which the Government's own agent was a participant and which that agent was fully entitled to disclose. And the device was not planted by means of an unlawful physical invasion of petitioner's premises under circumstances which would violate the Fourth Amendment. It was carried in and out by an agent who was there with petitioner's assent, and it neither saw nor heard more than the agent himself. . . .

Stripped to its essentials, petitioner's argument amounts to saying that he has a constitutional right to rely on possible flaws in the agent's memory, or to challenge the agent's credibility without being beset by corroborating evidence that is not susceptible of impeachment. For no other argument can justify excluding an accurate version of a conversation that the agent could testify to from memory. We think the risk that petitioner took in offering a bribe to Davis fairly included the risk that the offer would be accurately reproduced in court, whether by faultless memory or mechanical recording. . . .

WARREN, C.J. concurring. I also share the opinion of Mr. Justice Brennan that the fantastic advances in the field of electronic communication constitute a great danger to the privacy of the individual; that indiscriminate use of such devices in law enforcement raises grave constitutional questions under the Fourth and Fifth Amendments; and that these considerations impose a heavier responsibility on this Court in its supervision of the fairness of procedures in the federal court system. However, I do not believe that, as a result, all uses of such devices should be proscribed either as unconstitutional or as unfair law enforcement methods. One of the lines I would draw would be between this case and *On Lee*. . . .

The use and purpose of the transmitter in *On Lee* was substantially different from the use of the recorder here. Its advantage was not to corroborate the testimony of Chin Poy, but rather, to obviate the need to put him on the stand. The Court in *On Lee* itself stated:

> We can only speculate on the reasons why Chin Poy was not called. It seems a not unlikely assumption that the very defects of character and blemishes of record which made On Lee trust him with confidences would make a jury distrust his testimony. Chin Poy was close enough to the underworld to serve as bait, near enough the criminal design so that petitioner would embrace him as a confidante, but too close to it for the Government to vouch for him as a witness. Instead, the Government called agent Lee.

However, there were further advantages in not using Chin Poy. Had Chin Poy been available for cross-examination, counsel for On Lee could have explored the nature of Chin Poy's friendship with On Lee, the possibility of other unmonitored conversations and appeals to friendship, the possibility of entrapments, police pressure brought to bear to persuade Chin Poy to turn informer, and Chin Poy's own recollection of the contents of the conversation. . . .

Thus while I join the Court in permitting the use of electronic devices to corroborate an agent under the particular facts of this case, I cannot sanction by implication the use of these same devices to radically shift the pattern of presentation of evidence in the criminal trial, a shift that may be used to conceal substantial factual and legal issues concerning the rights of the accused and the administration of criminal justice.

BRENNAN, J. joined by DOUGLAS and GOLDBERG, JJ. dissenting. . . . [T]he Government's argument is that Lopez surrendered his right of privacy when he communicated his "secret thoughts" to Agent Davis. The assumption, manifestly untenable, is that the Fourth Amendment is only designed to protect secrecy. If a person commits his secret thoughts to paper, that is no license for the police to seize the paper; if a person communicates his secret thoughts verbally to another, that is no license for the police to record the words. *On Lee* certainly rested on no such theory of waiver. The right of privacy would mean little if it were limited to a person's solitary thoughts, and so fostered secretiveness. It must embrace a concept of the liberty of one's communications, and historically it has. "The common law secures to each individual the right of determining, ordinarily, to what extent his thoughts, sentiments, and emotions shall be communicated to others . . . and even if he has chosen to give them expression, he generally retains the power to fix the limits of the publicity which shall be given them." Warren and Brandeis, *The Right to Privacy*, 4 Harv. L. Rev. 193, 198 (1890).

That is not to say that all communications are privileged. On Lee assumed the risk that his acquaintance would divulge their conversation; Lopez assumed the same risk vis-à-vis Davis. The risk inheres in all communications which are not in the sight of the law privileged. It is not an undue risk to ask persons to assume, for it does no more than compel them to use discretion in choosing their auditors, to make damaging disclosures only to persons whose character and motives may be trusted. But the risk which both *On Lee* and today's decision impose is of a different order. It is the risk that third parties, whether mechanical auditors like the Minifon or human transcribers of mechanical transmissions as in *On Lee* — third parties who cannot be shut out of a conversation as conventional eavesdroppers can be, merely by a lowering of voices, or withdrawing to a private place — may give independent evidence of any conversation. There is only one way to guard against such a risk, and that is to keep one's mouth shut on all occasions. . . .

The risk of being overheard by an eavesdropper or betrayed by an informer or deceived as to the identity of one with whom one deals is probably inherent in the conditions of human society. It is the kind of risk we necessarily assume whenever we speak. But as soon as electronic surveillance comes into play, the risk changes crucially. There is no security from that kind of eavesdropping, no way of mitigating the risk, and so not even a residuum of true privacy. . . .

NOTES & QUESTIONS

1. *Is Electronic Surveillance Different?* Should electronic surveillance be treated similarly or differently than regular eavesdropping? Is it consistent to agree that Davis could testify as to what Lopez said via his memory but cannot introduce a recording of what Lopez said?

KATZ V. UNITED STATES

389 U.S. 347 (1967)

STEWART, J. The petitioner was convicted in the District Court for the Southern District of California under an eight-count indictment charging him with transmitting wagering information by telephone from Los Angeles to Miami and Boston in violation of a federal statute. At trial the Government was permitted, over the petitioner's objection, to introduce evidence of the petitioner's end of telephone conversations, overheard by FBI agents who had attached an electronic listening and recording device to the outside of the public telephone booth from which he had placed his calls. In affirming his conviction, the Court of Appeals rejected the contention that the recordings had been obtained in violation of the Fourth Amendment, because "[t]here was no physical entrance into the area occupied by, (the petitioner)." We granted certiorari in order to consider the constitutional questions thus presented.

The petitioner had phrased those questions as follows:

A. Whether a public telephone booth is a constitutionally protected area so that evidence obtained by attaching an electronic listening recording device to the top of such a booth is obtained in violation of the right to privacy of the user of the booth.

B. Whether physical penetration of a constitutionally protected area is necessary before a search and seizure can be said to be violative of the Fourth Amendment to the United States Constitution.

We decline to adopt this formulation of the issues. In the first place the correct solution of Fourth Amendment problems is not necessarily promoted by incantation of the phrase "constitutionally protected area." Secondly, the Fourth Amendment cannot be translated into a general constitutional "right to privacy." That Amendment protects individual privacy against certain kinds of governmental intrusion, but its protections go further, and often have nothing to do with privacy at all. Other provisions of the Constitution protect personal privacy from other forms of governmental invasion. But the protection of a person's general right to privacy — his right to be let alone by other people — is, like the protection of his property and of his very life, left largely to the law of the individual States.

Because of the misleading way the issues have been formulated, the parties have attached great significance to the characterization of the telephone booth from which the petitioner placed his calls. The petitioner has strenuously argued that the booth was a "constitutionally protected area." The Government has maintained with equal vigor that it was not. But this effort to decide whether or not a given "area," viewed in the abstract, is "constitutionally protected" deflects attention from the problem presented by this case. For the Fourth Amendment protects people, not places. What a person knowingly exposes to the public, even in his own home or office, is not a subject of Fourth Amendment protection. But what he seeks to preserve as private, even in an area accessible to the public, may be constitutionally protected.

The Government stresses the fact that the telephone booth from which the petitioner made his calls was constructed partly of glass, so that he was as visible after he entered it as he would have been if he had remained outside. But what he sought to exclude when he entered the booth was not the intruding eye — it was the uninvited ear. He did not shed his right to do so simply because he made his calls from a place where he might be seen. No less than an individual in a business office, in a friend's apartment, or in a taxicab, a person in a telephone booth may rely upon the protection of the Fourth Amendment. One who occupies it, shuts the door behind him, and pays the toll that permits him to place a call is surely entitled to assume that the words he utters into the mouthpiece will not be broadcast to the world. To read the Constitution more narrowly is to ignore the vital role that the public telephone has come to play in private communication.

The Government contends, however, that the activities of its agents in this case should not be tested by Fourth Amendment requirements, for the surveillance technique they employed involved no physical penetration of the telephone booth from which the petitioner placed his calls. It is true that the absence of such penetration was at one time thought to foreclose further Fourth Amendment inquiry, *Olmstead v. United States*, *Goldman v. United States*, for that Amendment was thought to limit only searches and seizures of tangible property. But "[t]he premise that property interests control the right of the Government to search and seize has been discredited." . . . [O]nce this much is acknowledged, and once it is recognized that the Fourth Amendment protects people — and not simply "areas" — against unreasonable searches and seizures it becomes clear that the reach of that Amendment cannot turn upon the presence or absence of a physical intrusion into any given enclosure.

We conclude that the underpinnings of *Olmstead* and *Goldman* have been so eroded by our subsequent decisions that the "trespass" doctrine there enunciated can no longer be regarded as controlling. . . .

The question remaining for decision, then, is whether the search and seizure conducted in this case complied with constitutional standards. In that regard, the Government's position is that its agents acted in an entirely defensible manner: They did not begin their electronic surveillance until investigation of the petitioner's activities had established a strong probability that he was using the telephone in question to transmit gambling information to persons in other States, in violation of federal law. Moreover, the surveillance was limited, both in scope and in duration, to the specific purpose of establishing the contents of the petitioner's unlawful telephonic communications. The agents confined their surveillance to the brief periods during which he used the telephone booth, and they took great care to overhear only the conversations of the petitioner himself. . . .

. . . It is apparent that the agents in this case acted with restraint. Yet the inescapable fact is that this restraint was imposed by the agents themselves, not by a judicial officer. They were not required, before commencing the search, to present their estimate of probable cause for detached scrutiny by a neutral magistrate. They were not compelled, during the conduct of the search itself, to observe precise limits established in advance by a specific court order. Nor were they directed, after the search had been completed, to notify the authorizing magistrate in detail of all that had been seized. In the absence of such safeguards, this Court has never sustained a search upon the sole ground that officers reasonably expected to find evidence of a particular crime and voluntarily confined their activities to the least intrusive means consistent with that end. Searches conducted without warrants have been held unlawful "notwithstanding facts unquestionably showing probable cause." . . . "Over and again this Court has emphasized that the mandate of the [Fourth] Amendment requires adherence to judicial processes," and that searches conducted outside the judicial process, without prior approval by judge or magistrate, are per se unreasonable under the Fourth Amendment — subject only to a few specifically established and well-delineated exceptions. . . .

HARLAN, J. concurring. . . . As the Court's opinion states, "the Fourth Amendment protects people, not places." The question, however, is what protection it affords to those people. Generally, as here, the answer to that question requires reference to a "place." My understanding of the rule that has emerged from prior decisions is that there is a twofold requirement, first that a person have exhibited an actual (subjective) expectation of privacy and, second, that the expectation be one that society is prepared to recognize as "reasonable." Thus a man's home is, for most purposes, a place where he expects privacy, but objects, activities, or statements that he exposes to the "plain view" of outsiders are not "protected" because no intention to keep them to himself has been exhibited. On the other hand, conversations in the open would not be protected against being overheard, for the expectation of privacy under the circumstances would be unreasonable.

The critical fact in this case is that "(o)ne who occupies it, (a telephone booth) shuts the door behind him, and pays the toll that permits him to place a call is surely entitled to assume" that his conversation is not being intercepted. The point is not that the booth is "accessible to the public" at other times, but that it is a temporarily private place whose momentary occupants' expectations of freedom from intrusion are recognized as reasonable.

BLACK, J. dissenting. . . . My basic objection is twofold: (1) I do not believe that the words of the Amendment will bear the meaning given them by today's decision, and (2) I do not believe that it is the proper role of this Court to rewrite the Amendment in order "to bring it into harmony with the times" and thus reach a result that many people believe to be desirable.

While I realize that an argument based on the meaning of words lacks the scope, and no doubt the appeal, of broad policy discussions and philosophical discourses on such nebulous subjects as privacy, for me the language of the Amendment is the crucial place to look in construing a written document such as our Constitution. The Fourth Amendment says that

> The right of the people to be secure in their persons, houses, papers, and effects, against unreasonable searches and seizures, shall not be violated, and no Warrants shall issue, but upon probable cause, supported by Oath or affirmation, and particularly describing the place to be searched, and the persons or things to be seized.

The first clause protects "persons, houses, papers, and effects, against unreasonable searches and seizures. . . ." These words connote the idea of tangible things with size, form, and weight, things capable of being searched, seized, or both. The second clause of the Amendment still further establishes its Framers' purpose to limit its protection to tangible things by providing that no warrants shall issue but those "particularly describing the place to be searched, and the persons or things to be seized." A conversation overheard by eavesdropping, whether by plain snooping or wiretapping, is not tangible and, under the normally accepted meanings of the words, can neither be searched nor seized. . . .

NOTES & QUESTIONS

1. *Who Was Charlie Katz?* David Sklansky describes the background to *Katz*:

> Charlie Katz was a Damon Runyon character plopped into 1960s Los Angeles. Katz was a professional bettor . . . Katz wagered on sports events, sometimes for himself and sometimes on commission for others. He specialized in basketball games, and he had his own, elaborate system for ranking teams and predicting outcomes. In February 1965, he was living in a poolside hotel room on the Sunset Strip.[9]

Sklanksy describes how the FBI would observe Katz leaving his hotel to place his bets from the telephone booth. An agent stationed outside would radio the news to another agent near the booth. This second agent would turn on a tape recorder placed on top of the telephone booth, observe Katz making his calls, and once Katz was finished and left the telephone booth, turn the recorder off and take it down from the top of the booth.

2. *The Reasonable Expectation of Privacy Test.* The *Katz* decision established a widely cited test for whether the Fourth Amendment is applicable in a given situation. That test was articulated not in the majority opinion but in the concurring opinion by Justice Harlan. The rule as articulated in Justice Harlan's concurrence has become known as the "reasonable expectation of privacy test." Under the test, (1) a person must exhibit an "actual (subjective) expectation of privacy" and (2) "the expectation [must] be one that society is prepared to recognize as 'reasonable.' "

According to Christopher Slobogin and Joseph Schumacher:

> For the most part, the Court has been content with fleshing out the meaning of the phrase[] "reasonable expectations of privacy" . . . through [its] application to specific cases. But the Court has also provided two significant guidelines as to how [this phrase] should be interpreted. The first guideline came in *Rakas v. Illinois*, where the majority opinion, by then-Associate Justice Rehnquist, stated that "legitimation of expectations of privacy by law must have a source outside of the Fourth Amendment, either by reference to concepts of real or personal property law or to understandings that are recognized and permitted by society." Most important for present purposes is the last clause of this excerpt, which indicates the Court's willingness to rely on societal understandings in defining "reasonable expectations of privacy."

---

[9] David A. Sklansky, *Katz v. United States*, in *Criminal Procedure Stories* (Carol S. Steiker ed., 2006).

Although this language appeared in a footnote, and was directed solely toward defining the standing concept, it has since been relied upon in the text of several other cases involving the "search" issue, often rephrased in terms of expectations of privacy "society is prepared to recognize as 'reasonable.'"

The second guideline came from the same footnote in *Rakas*. According to the Court, the use of the word "legitimate" or "reasonable" before "expectations of privacy" is meant to convey "more than a subjective expectation of not being discovered." As the Court explained,

> [a] burglar plying his trade in a summer cabin during the off season may have a thoroughly justified subjective expectation of privacy, but it is not one which the law recognizes as "legitimate." His presence . . . is "wrongful"; his expectation is not "one that society is prepared to recognize as 'reasonable.'"

In short, the Fourth Amendment does not protect expectations of privacy that only a criminal would have.[10]

3. *Variations on* **Katz.** What if the door to the telephone booth in *Katz* had been open? Would the Court still have concluded that the Fourth Amendment applied? What if the cop stood outside the booth, and Katz spoke loud enough for the cop to hear? Suppose the police placed a sound recording device outside the phone booth, and the device could pick up Katz's voice, which would be inaudible to the naked ear outside the phone booth. Would this be a violation of the Fourth Amendment?

4. *"Conditioned" Expectations of Privacy.* Before *Katz*, police sometimes tapped phones. How would this behavior affect a person's expectations of privacy when speaking on the phone? Consider the following observation by the Court in *Smith v. Maryland*, 442 U.S. 735, 741 n.5 (1979):

> Situations can be imagined, of course, in which Katz' two-pronged inquiry would provide an inadequate index of Fourth Amendment protection. For example, if the Government were suddenly to announce on nationwide television that all homes henceforth would be subject to warrantless entry, individuals thereafter might not in fact entertain any actual expectation or privacy regarding their homes, papers, and effects. Similarly, if a refugee from a totalitarian country, unaware of this Nation's traditions, erroneously assumed that police were continuously monitoring his telephone conversations, a subjective expectation of privacy regarding the contents of his calls might be lacking as well. In such circumstances, where an individual's subjective expectations had been "conditioned" by influences alien to well-recognized Fourth Amendment freedoms, those subjective expectations obviously could play no meaningful role in ascertaining what the scope of Fourth Amendment protection was. In determining whether a "legitimate expectation of privacy" existed in such cases, a normative inquiry would be proper.

5. **Berger v. New York.** *Berger v. New York*, 388 U.S. 41 (1967), is an important Fourth Amendment case decided after the Supreme Court agreed to

---

[10] Christopher Slobogin & Joseph E. Schumacher, *Reasonable Expectations of Privacy and Autonomy in Fourth Amendment Cases: An Empirical Look at "Understandings Recognized and Permitted by Society,"* 42 Duke L.J. 727, 731-32 (1993).

hear *Katz* but before it heard oral arguments in that case. In *Berger*, the Court struck down portions of New York's eavesdropping statute as violating the Fourth Amendment. The New York law authorized the installation of electronic surveillance devices for 60 days, and it allowed the surveillance to be extended beyond the 60 days without a showing of present probable cause to continue the eavesdrop. The Court held:

. . . The Fourth Amendment commands that a warrant issue not only upon probable cause supported by oath or affirmation, but also "particularly describing the place to be searched, and the persons or things to be seized." New York's statute lacks this particularization. It merely says that a warrant may issue on reasonable ground to believe that evidence of crime may be obtained by the eavesdrop. It lays down no requirement for particularity in the warrant as to what specific crime has been or is being committed, nor "the place to be searched," or "the persons or things to be seized" as specifically required by the Fourth Amendment. The need for particularity and evidence of reliability in the showing required when judicial authorization of a search is sought is especially great in the case of eavesdropping. By its very nature eavesdropping involves an intrusion on privacy that is broad in scope. . . .

. . . New York's statute . . . lays down no . . . "precise and discriminate" requirements. . . . New York's broadside authorization rather than being "carefully circumscribed" so as to prevent unauthorized invasions of privacy actually permits general searches by electronic devices, the truly offensive character of which was first condemned in *Entick v. Carrington*, 19 How. St. Tr. 1029, and which were then known as "general warrants." The use of the latter was a motivating factor behind the Declaration of Independence. In view of the many cases commenting on the practice it is sufficient here to point out that under these "general warrants" customs officials were given blanket authority to conduct general searches for goods imported to the Colonies in violation of the tax laws of the Crown. The Fourth Amendment's requirement that a warrant "particularly describ(e) the place to be searched, and the persons or things to be seized," repudiated these general warrants and "makes general searches . . . impossible and prevents the seizure of one thing under a warrant describing another. As to what is to be taken, nothing is left to the discretion of the officer executing the warrant."

We believe the statute here is equally offensive. First, as we have mentioned, eavesdropping is authorized without requiring belief that any particular offense has been or is being committed; nor that the "property" sought, the conversations, be particularly described. The purpose of the probable cause requirement of the Fourth Amendment, to keep the state out of constitutionally protected areas until it has reason to believe that a specific crime has been or is being committed, is thereby wholly aborted. Likewise the statute's failure to describe with particularity the conversations sought gives the officer a roving commission to "seize" any and all conversations. . . . As with general warrants this leaves too much to the discretion of the officer executing the order. Secondly, authorization of eavesdropping for a two-month period is the equivalent of a series of intrusions, searches, and seizures pursuant to a single showing of probable cause. Prompt execution is also avoided. During such a long and continuous (24 hours a day) period the conversations of any and all persons coming into the area covered by the device will be seized indiscriminately and without regard to their connection with the crime under investigation. Moreover, the statute permits, and there were authorized here, extensions of the original two-month period — presumably for two months each — on a mere showing that such extension is "in the public interest." Apparently the original grounds on which the eavesdrop order was initially issued also form the basis of the renewal. This we believe insufficient without a showing of present probable cause for the continuance of the eavesdrop. Third, the statute places no termination date on the eavesdrop once the conversation sought is seized. This is left entirely in the discretion of the officer. Finally, the statute's procedure, necessarily because its success depends on secrecy, has no requirement for notice as do conventional warrants, nor does it overcome this defect by requiring some showing of special facts. On the contrary, it permits uncontested entry without any showing of exigent circumstances. . . . In short, the statute's blanket grant of permission to eavesdrop is without adequate judicial supervision or protective procedures. . . .

As Sklansky points out, the effect of *Berger* combined with two other cases decided immediately before *Katz* — *Warden v. Hayden*, 387 U.S. 294 (1967) and *Camara v. Municipal Court*, 387 U.S. 523 (1967) — was to underscore the "centrality of the warrant requirement to the Fourth Amendment."[11]

UNITED STATES V. WHITE

401 U.S. 745 (1971)

WHITE, J. In 1966, respondent James A. White was tried and convicted under two consolidated indictments charging various illegal transactions in narcotics. . . . He was fined and sentenced as a second offender to 25-year concurrent sentences. The issue before us is whether the Fourth Amendment bars from evidence the testimony of governmental agents who related certain conversations which had occurred between defendant White and a government informant, Harvey Jackson, and which the agents overheard by monitoring the frequency of a radio transmitter carried by Jackson and concealed on his person. On four occasions the conversations took place in Jackson's home; each of these conversations was overheard by an agent concealed in a kitchen closet with Jackson's consent and by a second agent outside the house using a radio receiver. Four other conversations — one in respondent's home, one in a restaurant, and two in Jackson's car — were overheard by the use of radio equipment. The prosecution was unable to locate and produce Jackson at the trial and the trial court overruled objections to the testimony of the agents who conducted the electronic surveillance. The jury returned a guilty verdict and defendant appealed. . . .

Concededly a police agent who conceals his police connections may write down for official use his conversations with a defendant and testify concerning them, without a warrant authorizing his encounters with the defendant and without otherwise violating the latter's Fourth Amendment rights. For constitutional purposes, no different result is required if the agent instead of

---

[11] Sklansky, *supra*.

immediately reporting and transcribing his conversations with defendant, either (1) simultaneously records them with electronic equipment which he is carrying on his person, *Lopez v. United States*; (2) or carries radio equipment which simultaneously transmits the conversations either to recording equipment located elsewhere or to other agents monitoring the transmitting frequency. *On Lee v. United States*. If the conduct and revelations of an agent operating without electronic equipment do not invade the defendant's constitutionally justifiable expectations of privacy, neither does a simultaneous recording of the same conversations made by the agent or by others from transmissions received from the agent to whom the defendant is talking and whose trustworthiness the defendant necessarily risks.

Our problem is not what the privacy expectations of particular defendants in particular situations may be or the extent to which they may in fact have relied on the discretion of their companions. Very probably, individual defendants neither know nor suspect that their colleagues have gone or will go to the police or are carrying recorders or transmitters. Otherwise, conversation would cease and our problem with these encounters would be nonexistent or far different from those now before us. Our problem, in terms of the principles announced in *Katz*, is what expectations of privacy are constitutionally "justifiable" — what expectations the Fourth Amendment will protect in the absence of a warrant. So far, the law permits the frustration of actual expectations of privacy by permitting authorities to use the testimony of those associates who for one reason or another have determined to turn to the police, as well as by authorizing the use of informants in the manner exemplified by *Hoffa* and *Lewis*. If the law gives no protection to the wrongdoer whose trusted accomplice is or becomes a police agent, neither should it protect him when that same agent has recorded or transmitted the conversations which are later offered in evidence to prove the State's case.

Inescapably, one contemplating illegal activities must realize and risk that his companions may be reporting to the police. If he sufficiently doubts their trustworthiness, the association will very probably end or never materialize. But if he has no doubts, or allays them, or risks what doubt he has, the risk is his. In terms of what his course will be, what he will or will not do or say, we are unpersuaded that he would distinguish between probably informers on the one hand and probable informers with transmitters on the other. . . .

Nor should we be too ready to erect constitutional barriers to relevant and probative evidence which is also accurate and reliable. An electronic recording will many times produce a more reliable rendition of what a defendant has said than will the unaided memory of a police agent. It may also be that with the recording in existence it is less likely that the informant will change his mind, less chance that threat or injury will suppress unfavorable evidence and less chance that cross-examination will confound the testimony. Considerations like these obviously do not favor the defendant, but we are not prepared to hold that a defendant who has no constitutional right to exclude the informer's unaided testimony nevertheless has a Fourth Amendment privilege against a more accurate version of the events in question. . . .

HARLAN, J. dissenting. . . . Since it is the task of the law to form and project, as well as mirror and reflect, we should not, as judges, merely recite the expectations and risks without examining the desirability of saddling them upon society. The critical question, therefore, is whether under our system of government, as reflected in the Constitution, we should impose on our citizens the risks of the electronic listener or observer without at least the protection of a warrant requirement.

This question must, in my view, be answered by assessing the nature of a particular practice and the likely extent of its impact on the individual's sense of security balanced against the utility of the conduct as a technique of law enforcement. For those more extensive intrusions that significantly jeopardize the sense of security which is the paramount concern of Fourth Amendment liberties, I am of the view that more than self-restraint by law enforcement officials is required and at the least warrants should be necessary. The impact of the practice of third-party bugging, must, I think, be considered such as to undermine that confidence and sense of security in dealing with one another that is characteristic of individual relationships between citizens in a free society. It goes beyond the impact on privacy occasioned by the ordinary type of "informer" investigation upheld in *Lewis* and *Hoffa*. The argument of the plurality opinion, to the effect that it is irrelevant whether secrets are revealed by the mere tattletale or the transistor, ignores the differences occasioned by third-party monitoring and recording which insures full and accurate disclosure of all that is said, free of the possibility of error and oversight that inheres in human reporting.

Authority is hardly required to support the proposition that words would be measured a good deal more carefully and communication inhibited if one suspected his conversations were being transmitted and transcribed. Were third-party bugging a prevalent practice, it might well smother that spontaneity — reflected in frivolous, impetuous, sacrilegious, and defiant discourse — that liberates daily life. Much offhand exchange is easily forgotten and one may count on the obscurity of his remarks, protected by the very fact of a limited audience, and the likelihood that the listener will either overlook or forget what is said, as well as the listener's inability to reformulate a conversation without having to contend with a documented record. All these values are sacrificed by a rule of law that permits official monitoring of private discourse limited only by the need to locate a willing assistant. . . .

Interposition of a warrant requirement is designed not to shield "wrong-doers," but to secure a measure of privacy and a sense of personal security throughout our society. The Fourth Amendment does, of course, leave room for the employment of modern technology in criminal law enforcement, but in the stream of current developments in Fourth Amendment law I think it must be held that third-party electronic monitoring, subject only to the self-restraint of law enforcement officials, has no place in our society.

DOUGLAS, J. dissenting. . . . *On Lee* and *Lopez* are of a vintage opposed to *Berger* and *Katz*. However they may be explained, they are products of the old common-law notions of trespass. *Katz*, on the other hand, emphasized that with few exceptions "searches conducted outside the judicial process, without prior approval by judge or magistrate, are per se unreasonable under the Fourth Amendment.". . .

Monitoring, if prevalent, certainly kills free discourse and spontaneous utterances. Free discourse — a First Amendment value — may be frivolous or serious, humble or defiant, reactionary or revolutionary, profane or in good taste; but it is not free if there is surveillance. . . .

Now that the discredited decisions in *On Lee* and *Lopez* are resuscitated and revived, must everyone live in fear that every word he speaks may be transmitted or recorded and later repeated to the entire world? I can imagine nothing that has a more chilling effect on people speaking their minds and expressing their views on important matters. The advocates of that regime should spend some time in totalitarian countries and learn firsthand the kind of regime they are creating here. . . .

NOTES & QUESTIONS

1. **White *vs.* Katz.** Is this case more akin to the bugging in *On Lee* and *Lopez* rather than the wiretapping of *Katz*? Does it matter whether the police heard the conversation simultaneously? Suppose the conversation had been recorded by a hidden recorder and then handed over later to the police.

2. ***Covert Agents and the Misplaced Trust Doctrine.*** *White* suggests that the misplaced trust doctrine in *Hoffa, Lewis, Lopez,* and *On Lee* survives after *Katz*. Under the misplaced trust doctrine, people place their trust in others at their own peril and must assume the risk of betrayal. But should the misplaced trust doctrine survive after *Katz*? Do we have a reasonable expectation that our friends aren't government agents in disguise?

In a comparative study of how the United States and Germany regulate undercover policing, Jacqueline Ross identifies numerous differences in the two legal systems.[12] She argues:

> Germany's concern with individual dignity is part of the German Constitution's concern with safeguarding the "free development of personality," in direct reaction to the totalitarian oppression and violations of personal dignity under the Nazi regime. Invasions of privacy also have special salience for residents of the five new eastern states who remember the encompassing surveillance practiced more recently in the GDR [German Democratic Republic, also known as East Germany]. Given these concerns, police infiltration is deeply problematic. It interferes with the rights of all persons to control the face they present to the world; it reveals too much about the intimate details of a person's life; and it disrupts personal relationships. Giving constitutional status to these harms means that the government must satisfy certain requirements before inflicting them. Constitutional protection entails a warrant procedure, a showing of need, and statutory limits on the crimes that the government may target in this way.
>
> By contrast, the United States legal system does not treat undercover policing as an intrinsic invasion of privacy rights. Undercover policing is not recognized as a search or seizure under the Fourth Amendment. Because they have no Fourth Amendment significance, undercover investigations require no

---

[12] Jacqueline E. Ross, *The Place of Covert Surveillance in Democratic Societies: A Comparative Study of the United States and Germany*, 55 Am. J. Comp. L. 493 (2007).

warrant and no showing of probable cause or even reasonable suspicion as a matter of constitutional law.

What would be the impact on law enforcement if *White* came out the other way after *Katz*? In other words, suppose that *Katz* eliminated the misplaced trust doctrine. How would the Fourth Amendment apply to covert agents or informers? Would this unduly hamper police investigations of drug rings, mafia activity, and terrorist cells?

3. *Electronic Surveillance and the First Amendment.* Justice Douglas contends that electronic surveillance impinges upon and chills freedom of expression for all individuals in society. Is electronic surveillance without a warrant consistent with the First Amendment? What kind of process should be required to make use of the warrant consistent with the First Amendment?

3. THE REASONABLE EXPECTATION OF PRIVACY TEST

(a) The Third Party Doctrine

SMITH V. MARYLAND

442 U.S. 735 (1979)

BLACKMUN, J. This case presents the question whether the installation and use of a pen register[13] constitutes a "search" within the meaning of the Fourth Amendment, made applicable to the States through the Fourteenth Amendment.

On March 5, 1976, in Baltimore, Md., Patricia McDonough was robbed. She gave the police a description of the robber and of a 1975 Monte Carlo automobile she had observed near the scene of the crime. After the robbery, McDonough began receiving threatening and obscene phone calls from a man identifying himself as the robber. On one occasion, the caller asked that she step out on her front porch; she did so, and saw the 1975 Monte Carlo she had earlier described to police moving slowly past her home. On March 16, police spotted a man who met McDonough's description driving a 1975 Monte Carlo in her neighborhood. By tracing the license plate number, police learned that the car was registered in the name of petitioner, Michael Lee Smith.

The next day, the telephone company, at police request, installed a pen register at its central offices to record the numbers dialed from the telephone at petitioner's home. The police did not get a warrant or court order before having the pen register installed. The register revealed that on March 17 a call was placed from petitioner's home to McDonough's phone. On the basis of this and other evidence, the police obtained a warrant to search petitioner's residence. [A search of Smith's home revealed more evidence that Smith was the robber. Smith moved to suppress all evidence obtained from (and derived from) the pen

---

[13] "A pen register is a mechanical device that records the numbers dialed on a telephone by monitoring the electrical impulses caused when the dial on the telephone is released. It does not overhear oral communications and does not indicate whether calls are actually completed." A pen register is "usually installed at a central telephone facility [and] records on a paper tape all numbers dialed from [the] line" to which it is attached.

register. The trial court denied his motion, and Smith was convicted and sentenced to six years' imprisonment.] . . .

The Fourth Amendment guarantees "[t]he right of the people to be secure in their persons, houses, papers, and effects, against unreasonable searches and seizures." In determining whether a particular form of government-initiated electronic surveillance is a "search" within the meaning of the Fourth Amendment,[14] our lodestar is *Katz v. United States*, 389 U.S. 347 (1967). . . .

Consistently with *Katz*, this Court uniformly has held that the application of the Fourth Amendment depends on whether the person invoking its protection can claim a "justifiable," a "reasonable," or a "legitimate expectation of privacy" that has been invaded by government action. This inquiry, as Mr. Justice Harlan aptly noted in his *Katz* concurrence, normally embraces two discrete questions. The first is whether the individual, by his conduct, has "exhibited an actual (subjective) expectation of privacy," — whether, in the words of the *Katz* majority, the individual has shown that "he seeks to preserve [something] as private." The second question is whether the individual's subjective expectation of privacy is "one that society is prepared to recognize as 'reasonable,' — whether, in the words of the *Katz* majority, the individual's expectation, viewed objectively, is "justifiable" under the circumstances.[15]

In applying the *Katz* analysis to this case, it is important to begin by specifying precisely the nature of the state activity that is challenged. The activity here took the form of installing and using a pen register. Since the pen register was installed on telephone company property at the telephone company's central offices, petitioner obviously cannot claim that his "property" was invaded or that police intruded into a "constitutionally protected area." Petitioner's claim, rather, is that, notwithstanding the absence of a trespass, the State, as did the Government in *Katz*, infringed a "legitimate expectation of privacy" that petitioner held. Yet a pen register differs significantly from the listening device employed in *Katz*, for pen registers do not acquire the contents of communications. This Court recently noted:

> Indeed, a law enforcement official could not even determine from the use of a pen register whether a communication existed. These devices do not hear sound. They disclose only the telephone numbers that have been dialed — a means of

---

[14] In this case, the pen register was installed, and the numbers dialed were recorded, by the telephone company. The telephone company, however, acted at police request. In view of this, respondent appears to concede that the company is to be deemed an "agent" of the police for purposes of this case, so as to render the installation and use of the pen register "state action" under the Fourth and Fourteenth Amendments. We may assume that "state action" was present here.

[15] Situations can be imagined, of course, in which *Katz*'s two-pronged inquiry would provide an inadequate index of Fourth Amendment protection. For example, if the Government were suddenly to announce on nationwide television that all homes henceforth would be subject to warrantless entry, individuals thereafter might not in fact entertain any actual expectation or privacy regarding their homes, papers, and effects. Similarly, if a refugee from a totalitarian country, unaware of this Nation's traditions, erroneously assumed that police were continuously monitoring his telephone conversations, a subjective expectation of privacy regarding the contents of his calls might be lacking as well. In such circumstances, where an individual's subjective expectations had been "conditioned" by influences alien to well-recognized Fourth Amendment freedoms, those subjective expectations obviously could play no meaningful role in ascertaining what the scope of Fourth Amendment protection was. In determining whether a "legitimate expectation of privacy" existed in such cases, a normative inquiry would be proper.

establishing communication. Neither the purport of any communication between the caller and the recipient of the call, their identities, nor whether the call was even completed is disclosed by pen registers. *United States v. New York Tel. Co.*, 434 U.S. 159, 167 (1977).

Given a pen register's limited capabilities, therefore, petitioner's argument that its installation and use constituted a "search" necessarily rests upon a claim that he had a "legitimate expectation of privacy" regarding the numbers he dialed on his phone.

This claim must be rejected. First, we doubt that people in general entertain any actual expectation of privacy in the numbers they dial. All telephone users realize that they must "convey" phone numbers to the telephone company, since it is through telephone company switching equipment that their calls are completed. All subscribers realize, moreover, that the phone company has facilities for making permanent records of the numbers they dial, for they see a list of their long-distance (toll) calls on their monthly bills. In fact, pen registers and similar devices are routinely used by telephone companies "for the purposes of checking billing operations, detecting fraud and preventing violations of law." Electronic equipment is used not only to keep billing records of toll calls, but also "to keep a record of all calls dialed from a telephone which is subject to a special rate structure." Pen registers are regularly employed "to determine whether a home phone is being used to conduct a business, to check for a defective dial, or to check for overbilling." Although most people may be oblivious to a pen register's esoteric functions, they presumably have some awareness of one common use: to aid in the identification of persons making annoying or obscene calls. Most phone books tell subscribers, on a page entitled "Consumer Information," that the company "can frequently help in identifying to the authorities the origin of unwelcome and troublesome calls." Telephone users, in sum, typically know that they must convey numerical information to the phone company; that the phone company has facilities for recording this information; and that the phone company does in fact record this information for a variety of legitimate business purposes. Although subjective expectations cannot be scientifically gauged, it is too much to believe that telephone subscribers, under these circumstances, harbor any general expectation that the numbers they dial will remain secret.

Petitioner argues, however, that, whatever the expectations of telephone users in general, he demonstrated an expectation of privacy by his own conduct here, since he "us[ed] the telephone *in his house* to the exclusion of all others." But the site of the call is immaterial for purposes of analysis in this case. Although petitioner's conduct may have been calculated to keep the *contents* of his conversation private, his conduct was not and could not have been calculated to preserve the privacy of the number he dialed. Regardless of his location, petitioner had to convey that number to the telephone company in precisely the same way if he wished to complete his call. The fact that he dialed the number on his home phone rather than on some other phone could make no conceivable difference, nor could any subscriber rationally think that it would. Second, even if petitioner did harbor some subjective expectation that the phone numbers he dialed would remain private, this expectation is not "one that society is prepared to recognize as 'reasonable.' " This Court consistently has held that a person has no legitimate expectation of privacy in information he voluntarily turns over to third parties. In [*United States v.*] *Miller*, for example, the Court held that a bank depositor has no "legitimate 'expectation of privacy' " in financial information "voluntarily conveyed to . . . banks and exposed to their employees in the ordinary course of business." The Court explained:

> The depositor takes the risk, in revealing his affairs to another, that the information will be conveyed by that person to the Government. . . . This Court has held repeatedly that the Fourth Amendment does not prohibit the obtaining of information revealed to a third party and conveyed by him to Government authorities, even if the information is revealed on the assumption that it will be used only for a limited purpose and the confidence placed in the third party will not be betrayed.

Because the depositor "assumed the risk" of disclosure, the Court held that it would be unreasonable for him to expect his financial records to remain private.

This analysis dictates that petitioner can claim no legitimate expectation of privacy here. When he used his phone, petitioner voluntarily conveyed numerical information to the telephone company and "exposed" that information to its equipment in the ordinary course of business. In so doing, petitioner assumed the risk that the company would reveal to police the numbers he dialed. The switching equipment that processed those numbers is merely the modern counterpart of the operator who, in an earlier day, personally completed calls for the subscriber. Petitioner concedes that if he had placed his calls through an operator, he could claim no legitimate expectation of privacy. We are not inclined to hold that a different constitutional result is required because the telephone company has decided to automate.

Petitioner argues, however, that automatic switching equipment differs from a live operator in one pertinent respect. An operator, in theory at least, is capable of remembering every number that is conveyed to him by callers. Electronic equipment, by contrast can "remember" only those numbers it is programmed to record, and telephone companies, in view of their present billing practices, usually do not record local calls. Since petitioner, in calling McDonough, was making a local call, his expectation of privacy as to her number, on this theory, would be "legitimate."

This argument does not withstand scrutiny. The fortuity of whether or not the phone company in fact elects to make a quasi-permanent record of a particular number dialed does not in our view, make any constitutional difference. Regardless of the phone company's election, petitioner voluntarily conveyed to it information that it had facilities for recording and that it was free to record. In these circumstances, petitioner assumed the risk that the information would be divulged to police. . . .

STEWART, J. joined by BRENNAN, J. dissenting. . . . The numbers dialed from a private telephone — although certainly more prosaic than the conversation itself — are not without "content." Most private telephone subscribers may have their own numbers listed in a publicly distributed directory, but I doubt there are any who would be happy to have broadcast to the world a list of the local or long distance numbers they have called. This is not because such a list might in some sense be incriminating, but because it easily could reveal the identities of the persons and the places called, and thus reveal the most intimate details of a person's life.

MARSHALL, J. joined by BRENNAN, J. dissenting. . . . Privacy is not a discrete commodity, possessed absolutely or not at all. Those who disclose certain facts to a bank or phone company for a limited business purpose need not assume that this information will be released to other persons for other purposes.

The crux of the Court's holding, however, is that whatever expectation of privacy petitioner may in fact have entertained regarding his calls, it is not one "society is prepared to recognize as 'reasonable.'" In so ruling, the Court determines that individuals who convey information to third parties have "assumed the risk" of disclosure to the government. This analysis is misconceived in two critical respects.

Implicit in the concept of assumption of risk is some notion of choice. At least in the third-party consensual surveillance cases, which first incorporated risk analysis into Fourth Amendment doctrine, the defendant presumably had exercised some discretion in deciding who should enjoy his confidential communications. By contrast here, unless a person is prepared to forgo use of what for many has become a personal or professional necessity, he cannot help but accept the risk of surveillance. It is idle to speak of "assuming" risks in contexts where, as a practical matter, individuals have no realistic alternative.

More fundamentally, to make risk analysis dispositive in assessing the reasonableness of privacy expectations would allow the government to define the scope of Fourth Amendment protections. For example, law enforcement officials, simply by announcing their intent to monitor the content of random samples of first-class mail or private phone conversations, could put the public on notice of the risks they would thereafter assume in such communications. . . .

In my view, whether privacy expectations are legitimate within the meaning of *Katz* depends not on the risks an individual can be presumed to accept when imparting information to third parties, but on the risks he should be forced to assume in a free and open society. . . .

The use of pen registers, I believe, constitutes such an extensive intrusion. To hold otherwise ignores the vital role telephonic communication plays in our personal and professional relationships, as well as the First and Fourth Amendment interests implicated by unfettered official surveillance. Privacy in placing calls is of value not only to those engaged in criminal activity. The prospect of unregulated governmental monitoring will undoubtedly prove disturbing even to those with nothing illicit to hide. Many individuals, including members of unpopular political organizations or journalists with confidential sources, may legitimately wish to avoid disclosure of their personal contacts. Permitting governmental access to telephone records on less than probable cause may thus impede certain forms of political affiliation and journalistic endeavor that are the hallmark of a truly free society. Particularly given the Government's previous reliance on warrantless telephonic surveillance to trace reporters' sources and monitor protected political activity, I am unwilling to insulate use of pen registers from independent judicial review. . . .

NOTES & QUESTIONS

1. ***Pen Registers and Trap and Trace Devices.*** A pen register records outgoing telephone calls. Another device, known as a trap and trace device, records all incoming calls. In *Smith v. Maryland*, the Supreme Court ruled that a use of pen registers or trap and trace devices was not a form of wiretap (akin to that in *Katz*). What are the critical differences between the pen register and trap and device, on the one hand, and the wiretap, on the other?

2. ***Critiques of the* Smith *Decision.*** Consider the following observation by Laurence Tribe about *Smith*:

> The "assumption of risk" — more aptly, "assumption of broadcast" — notion underling the holding in *Smith* . . . reveals alarming tendencies in the Supreme Court's understanding of what privacy means and ought to mean. The Court treats privacy almost as if it were "a discrete commodity, possessed absolutely or not at all" [quoting Justice Marshall's dissent]. Yet what could be more commonplace than the idea that it is up to the *individual* to *measure out information* about herself *selectively* — to whomever she chooses?[16]

> Patricia Bellia contends that *Smith* conflicts with *Katz:* "In *Katz,* the phone company necessarily carried the defendant's telephone call, and the phone company no doubt had the technical ability to hear the contents of that call. That technical ability, however, was no impediment to the Court's conclusion that Katz had an expectation of privacy in the conversation."[17] Likewise, Susan Freiwald contends: "The *Smith* court ignored the lesson of *Katz:* We do not lose privacy in communications merely because they may be intercepted." She goes on to argue that the Court in *Smith* "avoided normative analysis and failed to consider how much privacy the law should actually grant to information. If the law treats information as private, then it will not be acceptable to acquire it, even when it possible to do so."[18]

> Deirdre Mulligan explains that the Court addressed the discrepancies between *Katz* and *Smith* by discussing in *Smith* "at some length the limited information that can be gleaned from a phone number, contrasting it with what may be revealed from a telephone conversation."[19] Does the holding of *Smith* rest on the fact that the numbers were exposed to a third party or on the fact that the numbers revealed limited information about a person or on both of these factors?

3. ***The Third Party Doctrine and Bank Records*: United States v. Miller.** The Supreme Court has also applied the third party doctrine to bank records. The Bank Secrecy Act of 1970, 31 U.S.C. § 1081, requires the retention of bank

---

[16] Laurence Tribe, *American Constitutional Law* 1391 (2d ed. 1988). For another critique of *Smith v. Maryland*, see Daniel J. Solove, *Digital Dossiers and the Dissipation*, 75 S. Cal. L. Rev. 1083 (2002).

[17] Patricia Bellia, *Surveillance Law Through Cyberlaw's Lens*, 72 Geo. Wash. L. Rev. 1375, 1405 (2004).

[18] Susan Freiwald, *Online Surveillance: Remembering the Lessons of the Wiretap Act*, 56 Ala. L. Rev. 9, 40, 66 (2004).

[19] Deirdre K. Mulligan, *Reasonable Expectations in Electronic Communications: A Critical Perspective on the Electronic Communications Privacy Act*, 72 Geo. Wash. L. Rev. 1557, 1581 (2004).

records and creation of reports that would be useful in criminal, tax, or regulatory investigations or proceedings. The Act requires that federally insured banks record the identities of account holders as well as copies of each check, draft, or other financial instrument. The Act authorizes the Secretary of the Treasury to promulgate regulations for the reporting of domestic financial transactions, which require that a report be made for every deposit, withdrawal, or other transfer of currency exceeding $10,000. *See* 31 C.F.R. § 103.22. For transactions exceeding $5,000 into or out of the United States, the amount, the date of receipt, the form of financial instrument, and the person who received it must be reported. *See* 31 C.F.R. §§ 103.23, 103.25.

In *California Bankers Association v. Shultz*, 416 U.S. 21 (1974), a group of bankers as well as depositors challenged the Bank Secrecy Act as a violation of the First, Fourth, and Fifth Amendments. The Court held that the Act did not violate the Fourth Amendment. First, the Court held that the bankers did not possess Fourth Amendment rights in the information because "corporations can claim no equality with individuals in the enjoyment of a right to privacy." Second, as to the constitutional rights of the individual depositors, the Court concluded that they lacked standing to pursue their claims because none alleged that they "were engaged in the type of $10,000 domestic currency transaction which would necessitate that their bank report it to the Government."

In a dissent, Justice Douglas wrote:

> The records of checks — now available to the investigators — are highly useful. In a sense a person is defined by the checks he writes. By examining them the agents get to know his doctors, lawyers, creditors, political allies, social connections, religious affiliation, educational interests, the papers and magazines he reads, and so on ad infinitum. These are all tied to one's social security number; and now that we have the data banks, these other items will enrich that storehouse and make it possible for a bureaucrat — by pushing one button — to get in an instant the names of the 190 million Americans who are subversives or potential and likely candidates.

The privacy of bank records was again before the Court two years later. In *United States v. Miller*, 425 U.S. 435 (1976), agents from the Alcohol, Tobacco, and Firearms Bureau obtained the defendant's records at two banks where he maintained accounts. The banks provided the records to the government without notifying him. The defendant argued that the records were protected by the Fourth Amendment and that the government needed a warrant to obtain them. The Supreme Court concluded that there is no reasonable expectation of privacy in bank records.

> The checks are not confidential communications but negotiable instruments to be used in commercial transactions. All of the documents obtained, including financial statements and deposit slips, contain only information voluntarily conveyed to the banks and exposed to their employees in the ordinary course of business. . . . .
>
> The depositor takes the risk, in revealing his affairs to another, that the information will be conveyed by that person to the Government. This Court has held repeatedly that the Fourth Amendment does not prohibit the

obtaining of information revealed to a third party and conveyed by him to Government authorities, even if the information is revealed on the assumption that it will be used only for a limited purpose and the confidence placed in the third party will not be betrayed. . . .

4. ***The Scope of the Third Party Doctrine.*** How broadly does the third party doctrine extend? To any information exposed to a third party? In *Smith v. Maryland,* the phone numbers were deemed not to be as sensitive as the contents of what was communicated during a phone call. But in *Miller,* the Court held there was no reasonable expectation of privacy in bank records without regard for the sensitivity of the information contained in them. What about medical records maintained by a physician? Is there no reasonable expectation of privacy in a person's health information if maintained by a doctor, hospital, or insurance company? If the Court were to draw a line to cabin the scope of the third party doctrine, is there a principled manner in which such a line could be drawn?

5. ***Federal and State Law.*** Sometimes when the Court fails to identify a privacy interest involving some aspect of the collection of personal information, Congress responds by enacting legislation that provides protection by statutory means. That happened after *Smith* with the Pen Register Act, 18 U.S.C. §§ 3121–3127. This statute requires that the government obtain a court order by certifying that the use of a pen register is "relevant to an ongoing investigation." This standard, however, is significantly less stringent than the probable cause required to obtain a Fourth Amendment warrant.

   Two years after *Miller,* in 1978, Congress passed the Right to Financial Privacy Act (RFPA), Pub. L. No. 95-630, which partially filled the void left by *Miller.* The RFPA prevents banks and other financial institutions from disclosing a person's financial information to the government unless the records are disclosed pursuant to subpoena or search warrant. *See* 29 U.S.C. §§ 3401–3422.

   Some states have rejected the *Smith* holding under their constitutions. For example, in *State v. Hunt,* 450 A.2d 952 (N.J. 1982), the New Jersey Supreme Court rejected *Smith* and held that under the New Jersey Constitution, there is a reasonable expectation of privacy in telephone records:

   > The telephone has become an essential instrument in carrying on our personal affairs. It has become part and parcel of the home. When a telephone call is made, it is as if two people are having a private conversation in the sanctity of their living room. . . .
   >
   > The telephone caller is . . . entitled to assume that the numbers he dials in the privacy of his home will be recorded solely for the telephone company's business purposes. From the viewpoint of the customer, all the information which he furnishes with respect to a particular call is private. The numbers dialed are private. . . .
   >
   > It is unrealistic to say that the cloak of privacy has been shed because the telephone company and some of its employees are aware of this information. Telephone calls cannot be made except through the telephone company's property and without payment to it for the service. This disclosure has been necessitated because of the nature of the instrumentality, but more

significantly the disclosure has been made for a limited business purpose and not for release to other persons for other reasons. . . .

In an analysis of state constitutional law, Stephen Henderson concludes that 11 states have rejected the third party doctrine. Ten more states have not explicitly rejected the third party doctrine, but have case law suggesting that they might do so in the future.[20]

6. *Privacy of the Mail.* People provide letters and parcels to the government to deliver in the mail. Does this implicate the third party doctrine?

In *Ex Parte Jackson,* 96 U.S. 727 (1877), one of its earliest Fourth Amendment cases, decided long before the third party doctrine, the Supreme Court held that the Fourth Amendment required a warrant to search sealed letters sent via the U.S. Postal Service:

> The constitutional guaranty of the right of the people to be secure in their persons against unreasonable searches and seizures extends to their papers, thus closed against inspection, wherever they may be. Whilst in the mail, they can only be opened and examined under like warrant, issued upon similar oath or affirmation, particularly describing the thing to be seized, as is required when papers are subjected to search in one's own household.

Although the Fourth Amendment protects the contents of a sealed letter, it does not protect the outside of letters, where addressing of information is typically located. As the Court noted in *Ex Parte Jackson,* "the outward form and weight" of letters and sealed packages are unprotected by the Fourth Amendment. Modern caselaw follows this distinction.

Today, federal law also restricts the government's ability to search people's mail. Pursuant to 39 U.S.C. §3623(d):

> No letter of such a class of domestic origin shall be opened except under authority of a search warrant authorized by law, or by an officer or employee of the Postal Service for the sole purpose of determining an address at which the letter can be delivered, or pursuant to the authorization of the addressee.

However, the government can search letters sent from abroad. *See United States v. Various Articles of Obscene Merchandise, Schedule No. 1213,* 395 F. Supp. 791 (S.D.N.Y. 1975), *aff'd,* 538 F.2d 317.

7. *Third Party Doctrine in the Information Age.* Daniel Solove contends that *Miller* and *Smith* pose a substantial threat to privacy in the modern world given the dramatic extent to which third parties hold personal information:

> In the Information Age, an increasing amount of personal information is contained in records maintained by private sector entities, Internet Service Providers, phone companies, cable companies, merchants, bookstores, websites, hotels, landlords and employers. Many private sector entities are beginning to aggregate the information in these records to create extensive digital dossiers.

---

[20] Stephen E. Henderson, *Learning from All Fifty States: How to Apply the Fourth Amendment and Its State Analogues to Protect Third Party Information from Unreasonable Seizure,* 55 Cath. U. L. Rev. 373, 395 (2006).

The data in these digital dossiers increasingly flows from the private sector to the government, particularly for law enforcement use. . . . Detailed records of an individual's reading materials, purchases, magazines, diseases and ailments, and website activity, enable the government to assemble a profile of an individual's finances, health, psychology, beliefs, politics, interests, and lifestyle. This data can unveil a person's anonymous speech, groups and personal associations.

The increasing amount of personal information flowing to the government poses significant problems with far-reaching social effects. Inadequately constrained government information gathering can lead to at least three types of harms. First, it can result in the slow creep toward a totalitarian state. Second, it can chill democratic activities and interfere with individual self-determination. Third, it can lead to the danger of harms arising in bureaucratic settings. Individuals, especially in times of crisis, are vulnerable to abuse from government misuse of personal information. Once government entities have collected personal information, there are few regulations in how it can be used and how long it can be kept. The bureaucratic nature of modern law enforcement institutions can enable sweeping searches, the misuse of personal data, improper exercises of discretion, unjustified interrogation, arrests, roundups of disfavored individuals, and discriminatory profiling.[21]

Because of the third party doctrine in *Miller* and *Smith*, the Fourth Amendment fails to limit the government from gathering personal information maintained by businesses. *Miller* and *Smith* were decided in the 1970s. Should they be reconsidered in light of the extensive computerized records maintained today? What would be the consequences of overruling *Miller* and *Smith*?

8. ***Can a Contract or Promise Create a Reasonable Expectation of Privacy?*** In many instances, companies promise people that they will keep their data confidential — either through express or implied contractual terms or through promises that customers might rely upon. Should contracts or promises be sufficient to create a reasonable expectation of privacy? Consider the following argument of Daniel Solove:

> According to the third party doctrine . . . even a written contract isn't enough to give people an expectation of privacy. But promises and contracts are the foundation of modern civil society. If people couldn't reply on them, business and commerce would grind to a halt. Yet when it comes to privacy, the U.S. Supreme Court thinks that promises and contracts don't matter.[22]

9. ***Critiques and Defenses of the Third Party Doctrine.*** Susan Brenner and Leo Clark argue that the third party doctrine is flawed because it assumes that a "disclosure to a trusted, reputable [third party] is the same as indiscriminate disclosure to the public." If we disclose information on a public website, "we have clearly demonstrated our lack of interest in controlling access to the information in question." In contrast, when we share information with third

---

[21] Daniel J. Solove, *Digital Dossiers and the Dissipation of Fourth Amendment Privacy*, 75 S. Cal. L. Rev. 1083, 1084-86 (2002).

[22] Daniel J. Solove, *Nothing to Hide: The False Tradeoff Between Privacy and Security* 13, 108-09 (2011).

parties, these are "controlled disclosures, in that they represent the limited, focused sharing of information with a [third party] as an integral part of a legitimate transaction."[23]

Taking a different approach, Thomas Crocker contrasts the third party doctrine with the Supreme Court's protection of interpersonal relations in *Lawrence v. Texas,* 539 U.S. 558 (2003), where it invalidated a Texas state statute criminalizing homosexual sodomy. While the *Lawrence* Court protected "conduct important to interpersonal relations," the third party doctrine leads to a view that "privacy protects only what we keep to ourselves."[24]

Orin Kerr defends the third party doctrine. In his view, it "ensures technological neutrality in Fourth Amendment rules." He argues that

> criminals could use third-party agents to fully enshroud their criminal enterprises in Fourth Amendment protection. A criminal could plot and execute his entire crime from home knowing that the police could not send in undercover agents, record the fact of his phone calls, or watch any aspect of his Internet usage without first obtaining a warrant. He could use third parties to create a bubble of Fourth Amendment protection around the entirety of his criminal activity.

Kerr concludes that the "third-party doctrine blocks such efforts, resulting in a rough equivalence in the overall amount of privacy for criminals acting alone and the amount of privacy for those using third parties."[25] Does modern technology make detecting crime more difficult as Kerr contends? It can also make investigating crime easier. How should the Fourth Amendment respond when new technology affects the way crimes are committed and investigated?

10. *The First Amendment and the Third Party Doctrine.* Daniel Solove argues that the First Amendment should be understood as a source of criminal procedure and should protect pen register information:

> Although the Supreme Court has focused on the Fourth Amendment, obtaining pen register data without a warrant potentially violates the First Amendment. A log of incoming and outgoing calls can be used to trace channels of communication. It is relatively easy to link a phone number to a person or organization. Pen registers can reveal associational ties, since association in contemporary times often occurs by way of telephone or e-mail. As David Cole argues, modern communications technology has made association possible without physical assembly. For example, if the

---

[23] Susan W. Brenner & Leo L. Clarke, *Fourth Amendment Protection for Shared Privacy Rights in Stored Transactional Data,* 14 J.L. & Pol'y 211, 258 (2006). For another critique of the third party doctrine, see Stephen E. Henderson, Beyond the (Current) Fourth Amendment: Protecting Third-Party Information, Third Parties, and the Rest of Us Too, 34 Pepp. L. Rev. 975 (2007).

[24] Thomas P. Crocker, *From Privacy to Liberty: The Fourth Amendment After* Lawrence, 57 UCLA L. Rev. 1 (2009).

[25] Orin S. Kerr, *The Case for the Third-Party Doctrine,* 107 Mich. L. Rev. 561, 575-76 (2009). For a critique of Kerr's article, see Richard A. Epstein, *Privacy and the Third Hand: Lessons from the Common Law of Reasonable Expectations,* 24 Berkeley Tech. L.J. 1199 (2009); Erin Murphy, *The Case Against the Case for the Third Party Doctrine: A Response to Epstein and Kerr,* 24 Berkeley Tech. L.J. 1239 (2009).

government scrutinized the phone logs of the main office of the Communist Party, it might discover many of the Party's members. The information would not be equivalent to a membership list, but it would probably include identifying data about countless individuals who would not want the government to discover their connection to the Communist Party. If the government were to examine the phone logs or e-mail headers of a particular individual, it might discover that the individual contacted particular organizations that the individual wants to keep private. The pen register information, therefore, implicates First Amendment values.[26]

Solove contends that government access to pen register information can violate the First Amendment, and he goes on to argue that the First Amendment should require a warrant before the government can obtain such information. Does pen register information implicate the First Amendment? If so, what kind of protections should the First Amendment require?

Neil Richards also contends that the First Amendment protects what he calls "intellectual privacy," which he defines as the ability "to develop ideas and beliefs away from the unwanted gaze or interference of others." According to Richards, the "ability to freely make up our minds and to develop new ideas thus depends upon a substantial measure of intellectual privacy. In this way, intellectual privacy is a cornerstone of meaningful First Amendment liberties." Richards argues that the government can implicate intellectual privacy when it seeks to "obtain from third parties intellectual records such as book purchases, library records, Web-use histories, and search-engine queries." Doing so "threaten[s] both the freedom of thought and the freedom of intellectual exploration."[27] When intellectual privacy is involved, heightened constitutional protections should be required. How would Richards's notion of intellectual privacy apply to pen registers?

(b) Items Abandoned or Exposed to the Public

CALIFORNIA V. GREENWOOD

486 U.S. 35 (1988)

[Police investigators searched the plastic garbage bags that Greenwood left on the curb in front of his house to be picked up by the trash collector. The officers found indications of drug use from the search of Greenwood's trash and obtained a warrant to search the house, where they uncovered more evidence of drug trafficking. Greenwood was arrested.]

WHITE, J. . . . The warrantless search and seizure of the garbage bags left at the curb outside the Greenwood house would violate the Fourth Amendment only if respondents manifested a subjective expectation of privacy in their garbage that society accepts as objectively reasonable.

---

[26] Daniel J. Solove, *The First Amendment as Criminal Procedure,* 82 N.Y.U. L. Rev. 112, 169 (2007).

[27] Neil M. Richards, *Intellectual Privacy,* 87 Tex. L. Rev. 387, 389, 439 (2008).

. . . [The Greenwoods] assert . . . that they had, and exhibited, an expectation of privacy with respect to the trash that was searched by the police: The trash, which was placed on the street for collection at a fixed time, was contained in opaque plastic bags, which the garbage collector was expected to pick up, mingle with the trash of others, and deposit at the garbage dump. The trash was only temporarily on the street, and there was little likelihood that it would be inspected by anyone.

It may well be that respondents did not expect that the contents of their garbage bags would become known to the police or other members of the public. An expectation of privacy does not give rise to Fourth Amendment protection, however, unless society is prepared to accept that expectation as objectively reasonable.

Here, we conclude that respondents exposed their garbage to the public sufficiently to defeat their claim to Fourth Amendment protection. It is common knowledge that plastic garbage bags left on or at the side of a public street are readily accessible to animals, children, scavengers, snoops, and other members of the public. Moreover, respondents placed their refuse at the curb for the express purpose of conveying it to a third party, the trash collector, who might himself have sorted through respondents' trash or permitted others, such as the police, to do so. Accordingly, having deposited their garbage "in an area particularly suited for public inspection and, in a manner of speaking, public consumption, for the express purpose of having strangers take it," respondents could have had no reasonable expectation of privacy in the inculpatory items that they discarded. . .

BRENNAN, J. joined by MARSHALL, J. dissenting. . . . Scrutiny of another's trash is contrary to commonly accepted notions of civilized behavior. I suspect, therefore, that members of our society will be shocked to learn that the Court, the ultimate guarantor of liberty, deems unreasonable our expectation that the aspects of our private lives that are concealed safely in a trash bag will not become public.

"A container which can support a reasonable expectation of privacy may not be searched, even on probable cause, without a warrant." *United States v. Jacobsen*, 466 U.S. 109, 120, n.17 (1984) (citations omitted). Thus, as the Court observes, if Greenwood had a reasonable expectation that the contents of the bags that he placed on the curb would remain private, the warrantless search of those bags violated the Fourth Amendment. . . .

Our precedent, therefore, leaves no room to doubt that had respondents been carrying their personal effects in opaque, sealed plastic bags — identical to the ones they placed on the curb — their privacy would have been protected from warrantless police intrusion. . . .

Respondents deserve no less protection just because Greenwood used the bags to discard rather than to transport his personal effects. Their contents are not inherently any less private, and Greenwood's decision to discard them, at least in the manner in which he did, does not diminish his expectation of privacy.

A trash bag, like any of the above-mentioned containers, "is a common repository for one's personal effects" and, even more than many of them, is "therefore . . . inevitably associated with the expectation of privacy." "[A]lmost every human activity ultimately manifests itself in waste products. . . ." *Smith v.*

State, 510 P.2d 793, 798 (Alaska 1973). A single bag of trash testifies eloquently to the eating, reading, and recreational habits of the person who produced it. A search of trash, like a search of the bedroom, can relate intimate details about sexual practices, health, and personal hygiene. Like rifling through desk drawers or intercepting phone calls, rummaging through trash can divulge the target's financial and professional status, political affiliations and inclinations, private thoughts, personal relationships, and romantic interests. It cannot be doubted that a sealed trash bag harbors telling evidence of the "intimate activity associated with the 'sanctity of a man's home and the privacies of life,'" which the Fourth Amendment is designed to protect. . . .

. . . Most of us, I believe, would be incensed to discover a meddler — whether a neighbor, a reporter, or a detective — scrutinizing our sealed trash containers to discover some detail of our personal lives. . . .

The mere possibility that unwelcome meddlers might open and rummage through the containers does not negate the expectation of privacy in their contents any more than the possibility of a burglary negates an expectation of privacy in the home; or the possibility of a private intrusion negates an expectation of privacy in an unopened package; or the possibility that an operator will listen in on a telephone conversation negates an expectation of privacy in the words spoken on the telephone. "What a person . . . seeks to preserve as private, even in an area accessible to the public, may be constitutionally protected." *Katz*, 389 U.S. at 351-52. . . .

NOTES & QUESTIONS

1. ***Recycling and Surveillance of Garbage.*** In dissent in *Greenwood*, Justice Brennan states, "Scrutiny of another's trash is contrary to commonly accepted notions of civilized behavior." The Supreme Court decided *Greenwood* in 1988. In the twenty-first century, however, an increasing number of communities have imposed recycling obligations on their citizens. Sanitation departments sometimes oversee the recycling by routinely checking people's trash, and, in the case of noncompliance, imposing fines. Does this development alter the extent of any reasonable expectation of privacy in one's trash vis-à-vis the police?

2. ***Surveillance 24/7.*** In addition to searching through Greenwood's trash, the police were staking out his home, watching who came and went from his house. Does the Fourth Amendment protect against such surveillance? Imagine that for one year, the police were to stake out a person's home and follow the person wherever he or she went throughout the day. The person would be under 24-hour surveillance, seven days a week. Assume that the police would simply observe the person anytime he or she was in public. Is this more invasive to privacy than a one-time search of particular items, such as one's luggage? Does the Fourth Amendment provide any limitation on the police activities described above?

3. ***State Courts and State Constitutions.*** In examining the same issue as *Greenwood*, some state supreme courts have come to a different conclusion in

interpreting their state constitutions. For example, the Supreme Court of Vermont declared that "the Vermont Constitution protects persons from warrantless police searches into the contents of secured opaque trash bags left at curbside for garbage collection and disposal." *State of Vermont v. Morris*, 680 A.2d 90 (Vt. 1996). It observed that the California, Hawaii, New Jersey, and Washington state supreme courts had already declined to follow the *Greenwood* analysis. The court argued that "the mere possibility that unwelcome animals or persons might rummage through one's garbage bags does not negate the expectation of privacy in the contents of those bags any more than the possibility of a burglary or break-in negates an expectation of privacy in one's home or car, or the possibility that a cleaning person or house guest will exceed the scope of a visit negates an expectation of privacy in a hotel room or home." Is one or more of these comparisons more convincing than the other?

4. **"Abandoned" DNA?** Frequently, the law views the police's collection of discarded DNA as similar to its examination of trash. In *California v. Greenwood*, 486 U.S. 35 (1988), the Supreme Court held that there was no reasonable expectation of privacy in trash set out at the curb for collection. Law enforcement officials have collected discarded DNA from a smoked cigarette, a recently used coffee cup, and a licked envelope sent through the mail. In a *New York Times* article, Amy Harmon warns: "The police could collect DNA deemed 'abandoned' from targeted individuals and monitor their movements even if they are not suspected of committing a serious crime. Innocent people whose DNA turns up unexpectedly may find themselves identified by a database." Several hundred suspects over the last few years have been implicated by traces of DNA collected from them secretly. In addition, "[m]any more were eliminated from suspicion without ever knowing that their coffee cups, tissue, straws, utensils and cigarette butts were subject to DNA analysis by the police." Harmon also notes that most people fail to realize that there may be no way to avoid shedding DNA in public "short of living in a bubble."[28] Does *Greenwood* foreclose finding a reasonable expectation of privacy in DNA from discarded items? Should DNA in discarded items be treated differently from regular trash?

For Elizabeth Joh, however, instead of thinking of the collection and analysis of such samples as involving "abandoned" DNA, we should view it as "covert involuntary DNA sampling." Joh argues that the law should end its grant of virtually limitless discretion to the police in collecting such DNA. More limits on police procedures are needed in this context because of the vast potential uses of this information, and the rapidity of scientific research in genetics, which makes it difficult to predict the amount of information about an individual that a single genetic sample might reveal. In Joh's view, the police should be required to obtain a warrant whenever they seek covert, involuntary DNA from a target. She also calls for the more modest step of

---

[28] Amy Harmon, *Lawyers Fight Gene Material Gained on Sly*, N.Y. Times, Apr. 3, 2008, at A1.

having legislatures clarify "the applicability of DNA database laws, both federal and state, to the collection of abandoned DNA."[29] What standard, if any, should be required in order for law enforcement officials to collect "abandoned" DNA?

5. ***DNA by Deceit.*** In *State v. Athan*, 158 P.3d 27 (Wash. 2007), police wanted to pursue a cold case involving the rape and murder of a young girl. They had suspected John Athan of the crime but lacked evidence. Twenty years later, they wanted to find out whether the crime scene DNA matched Athan's DNA profile. To obtain Athan's DNA, the police sent Athan a letter pretending to be from a law firm. The letter stated that Athan was part of a class action and that he had to send back a form to receive compensation from the litigation proceeds. Athan sent in the form, and the police used his saliva in sealing the letter to obtain his DNA. The police matched Athan's DNA to the crime scene. Athan challenged the police practice under the Fourth Amendment. The Washington Supreme Court held:

> Police may surreptitiously follow a suspect to collect DNA, fingerprints, footprints, or other possibly incriminating evidence, without violating that suspect's privacy. No case has been cited challenging or declaring this type of police practice unreasonable or unconstitutional. People constantly leave genetic material, fingerprints, footprints, or other evidence of their identity in public places. There is no subjective expectation of privacy in discarded genetic material just as there is no subjective expectation of privacy in fingerprints or footprints left in a public place. Physical characteristics which are exposed to the public are not subject to Fourth Amendment protection. The analysis of DNA obtained without forcible compulsion and analyzed by the government for comparison to evidence found at a crime scene is not a search under the Fourth Amendment.

Regarding the deceitful tactic used by the police, the court concluded:

> Public policy allows for a limited amount of deceitful police conduct in order to detect and eliminate criminal activity. . . . The police's use of a ruse to obtain evidence against a suspect is not determinative. We have upheld police ruses designed to gain warrantless entry into a suspect's house for the purpose of buying illegal drugs. . . . Although the police violated a state statute by posing as lawyers, the trial court noted the effect of the conduct on the integrity of the legal system is not as severe as where the ruse was directed at obtaining confidential information. Public policy allows for some deceitful conduct and violation of criminal laws by police officers in order to detect and eliminate criminal activity. The claimed misconduct in this case does not involve actions similar to those cases which found misconduct warranting dismissal. The police did not induce Athan to commit any crime here nor did they attempt to gain any confidential information from the ruse. The conduct here is not so outrageous as to offend a sense of justice or require dismissal of this case.

Should law enforcement officials be allowed to use deceitful tactics such as the one used in *Athan* in order to obtain people's DNA?

---

[29] Elizabeth E. Joh, *Reclaiming "Abandoned" DNA*, 100 Nw. U. L. Rev. 857, 860, 881 (2006).

6. *Who Decides What Constitutes a Reasonable Expectation of Privacy?* Currently, judges decide whether a defendant has a reasonable expectation of privacy in a particular activity. Is this question appropriate for judges to decide? Or should juries decide it? In all of the cases so far, observe the sources that the Court cites to for support that there is no reasonable expectation of privacy. How is a reasonable expectation of privacy to be measured? Is it an empirical question about what most people in society would generally consider to be private? If so, why aren't polls taken? If you're an attorney arguing that there is a reasonable expectation of privacy in something, what do you cite to? How should courts measure what society as a whole thinks is private?

Christopher Slobogin and Joseph Schumacher conducted a survey of individuals, asking them to rate on a scale of 0 to 100 the intrusiveness of certain types of searches or seizures, with 0 being nonintrusive and 100 being extremely intrusive. Several searches that the Court has concluded do not trigger a reasonable expectation of privacy rated in the middle of the scale. The flyover in *Florida v. Riley* rated at 40.32 on this scale; the dog sniff in *United States v. Place* rated at 58.33; the search of garbage in *California v. Greenwood* rated at 44.95; and the use of a beeper to track a car in *United States v. Knotts* rated at 54.46. Certain searches that the Court held do not involve a reasonable expectation of privacy rated highly on the scale, such as examining bank records in *United States v. Miller,* rated at 71.60. In other highly ranked searches, the Court has concluded that the Fourth Amendment applies, such as monitoring a phone for 30 days, rating at 87.67 and a body cavity search at the border, rating at 90.14. The body cavity search was the highest rated search, and a search of foliage in a public park was the lowest rated at 6.48. Slobogin and Schumacher conclude that "the Supreme Court's conclusions about the scope of the Fourth Amendment are often not in tune with commonly held attitudes about police investigative techniques."[30]

To what extent should empirical evidence such as this study be used by courts in determining whether or not there is a reasonable expectation of privacy? If such evidence should be used, at what point in the scale should the line be drawn to establish the existence of a reasonable expectation of privacy?

7. *Should the Reasonable Expectation of Privacy Test Be Empirical or Normative?* There is an interesting paradox at the heart of the reasonable expectation of privacy test: Legal protection is triggered by people's expectations of privacy, but those expectations are, to a notable extent, shaped by the extent of the legal protection of privacy. Consider the following argument by Daniel Solove regarding the privacy of the postal letters:

> [I]n America, the privacy of letters was formed in significant part by a legal architecture that protected the confidentiality of letters from other people and government officials. In colonial America, mail was often insecure; it was

---

[30] Christopher Slobogin & Joseph E. Schumacher, *Reasonable Expectations of Privacy and Autonomy in Fourth Amendment Cases: An Empirical Look at "Understandings Recognized and Permitted by Society,"* 42 Duke L.J. 727 (1993).

difficult to seal letters; and the wax often used to keep letters sealed was not very effective. There was widespread suspicion of postal clerks reading letters; and a number of prominent individuals, such as Thomas Jefferson, Alexander Hamilton, and George Washington, decried the lack of privacy in their letters and would sometimes even write in code. . . . Despite these realities, and people's expectation that letters would not be confidential, the law evolved to provide strong protection of the privacy of letters. Benjamin Franklin, who was in charge of the colonial mails, required his employees to swear an oath not to open mail. In the late eighteenth and early nineteenth centuries, Congress passed several laws prohibiting the improper opening of mail. And the Supreme Court held in 1877 that despite the fact that people turned letters over to the government for delivery in the postal system, sealed parcels were protected from inspection by the Fourth Amendment. This example illustrates that privacy is not just found but constructed. By erecting a legal structure to protect the privacy of letters, our society shaped the practices of letter writing and using the postal system. It occurred because of the desire to make privacy an integral part of these practices rather than to preserve the status quo.[31]

Solove argues that societies seek to protect privacy with the law when they do not expect privacy but desire to have it. If Solove is right, then what should courts look to when applying the reasonable expectation of privacy test?

8. ***Critiques of the Reasonable Expectation of Privacy Test.*** Thomas Crocker argues that the Fourth Amendment protects more than privacy — it protects "political liberty." According to Crocker, "the Fourth Amendment fits into a broader political liberty framework, as it has increasingly focused on protecting a narrow conception of privacy and regulating everyday police practice." Instead, it should broadly "enable freedom of movement and social interaction in private and in public, secure from arbitrary search and seizure."[32] Crocker's argument suggests that the Fourth Amendment should protect assembly in public and other activities out in the open. Some might contend that his view of the Fourth Amendment is too broad and vague. Is it? What are the benefits and problems with Crocker's approach?

Daniel Solove argues that the reasonable expectation of privacy test should be abandoned because "current Fourth Amendment coverage often bears little relation to the problems caused by government investigative activities. It also bears little relation to whether it is best to have judicial oversight of law enforcement activity, what that oversight should consist of, how much limitation we want to impose on various government information gathering activities, and how we should guard against abuses of power." He recommends that "the Fourth Amendment should provide protection whenever a problem of reasonable significance can be identified with a

---

[31] Daniel J. Solove, *Conceptualizing Privacy*, 90 Cal. L. Rev. 1087, 1142-43 (2002); *see also* Shaun Spencer, *Reasonable Expectations and the Erosion of Privacy*, 39 San Diego L. Rev. 843 (2002).

[32] Thomas P. Crocker, *The Political Fourth Amendment*, 88 Wash. U. L. Rev. 303, 310-11 (2010).

particular form of government information gathering."[33] Is this approach workable? What are the benefits and problems with such an approach?

Susan Freiwald makes a similar argument in the context of communications:

> Courts should focus on the normative inquiry into whether users should be entitled to view their communications as private, but in doing so they should shift the inquiry away from users' apparent knowledge about whether their communications were vulnerable to interception. Instead, courts should discharge their responsibility to mediate the tension between law enforcement's interest in obtaining as much information as possible and users' interest in avoiding excessive government intrusion into their lives.[34]

Is looking at people's expectations the wrong inquiry? Freiwald suggests that courts look to four factors to determine whether Fourth Amendment regulation is appropriate — whether the surveillance is hidden, intrusive, indiscriminate, and continuous. Are these factors, as opposed to people's expectations of privacy, a more coherent and workable approach to determining whether the Fourth Amendment should regulate government surveillance activities?

(c) Surveillance and the Use of Sense Enhancement Technologies

The Plain View Doctrine. "[I]t has long been settled that objects falling in the plain view of an officer who has a right to be in the position to have that view are subject to seizure and may be introduced in evidence." *Harris v. United States,* 390 U.S. 234, 236 (1968). This has become known as the "plain view" doctrine. If it is possible for something to be seen or heard from a public vantage point, there can be no reasonable expectation of privacy.

The Open Fields Doctrine. An extension of the plain view rule is the "open fields" doctrine. An individual does not have a reasonable expectation of privacy in the open fields that she owns. In *Oliver v. United States,* 466 U.S. 170 (1984), the defendant placed "No Trespassing" signs throughout his farm and maintained a locked gate around the farm's entrance. The fields could not be seen from any public vantage point. The police trespassed onto the fields and found marijuana. The Court held, however, that there is no reasonable expectation of privacy in open fields, and the defendant's attempt to keep them secluded and shielded from public view was irrelevant.

An exception to the open fields doctrine is the legal treatment of a house's so-called "curtilage." Under the curtilage doctrine, parts of one's property immediately outside one's home do not fall within the open fields rule. This exception does not mean that the curtilage is automatically afforded Fourth Amendment protection; a reasonable expectation of privacy analysis still must be performed. The question of whether an area constitutes a curtilage depends upon

---

[33] Daniel J. Solove, *Fourth Amendment Pragmatism,* 51 B.C. L. Rev. 1511, 1513-14 (2010). For more about these issues, see Daniel J. Solove, *Nothing to Hide: The False Tradeoff Between Privacy and Security* (2011).

[34] Susan Freiwald, *First Principles of Communications Privacy,* 2007 Stan. Tech. L. Rev. 3, 9.

"whether the area in question is so intimately tied to the home itself that it should be placed within the home's 'umbrella' of Fourth Amendment protection." *United States v. Dunn*, 480 U.S. 294, 301 (1987).

FLORIDA V. RILEY

488 U.S. 445 (1989)

WHITE, J. . . . Respondent Riley lived in a mobile home located on five acres of rural property. A greenhouse was located 10 to 20 feet behind the mobile home. Two sides of the greenhouse were enclosed. The other two sides were not enclosed but the contents of the greenhouse were obscured from view from surrounding property by trees, shrubs, and the mobile home. The greenhouse was covered by corrugated roofing panels, some translucent and some opaque. At the time relevant to this case, two of the panels, amounting to approximately 10% of the roof area, were missing. A wire fence surrounded the mobile home and the greenhouse, and the property was posted with a "DO NOT ENTER" sign.

This case originated with an anonymous tip to the Pasco County Sheriff's office that marijuana was being grown on respondent's property. When an investigating officer discovered that he could not see the contents of the greenhouse from the road, he circled twice over respondent's property in a helicopter at the height of 400 feet. With his naked eye, he was able to see through the openings in the roof and one or more of the open sides of the greenhouse and to identify what he thought was marijuana growing in the structure. A warrant was obtained based on these observations, and the ensuing search revealed marijuana growing in the greenhouse. Respondent was charged with possession of marijuana under Florida law. . . .

We agree with the State's submission that our decision in *California v. Ciraolo*, 476 U.S. 207 (1986), controls this case. There, acting on a tip, the police inspected the back-yard of a particular house while flying in a fixed-wing aircraft at 1,000 feet. With the naked eye the officers saw what they concluded was marijuana growing in the yard. A search warrant was obtained on the strength of this airborne inspection, and marijuana plants were found. The trial court refused to suppress this evidence, but a state appellate court held that the inspection violated the Fourth and Fourteenth Amendments to the United States Constitution, and that the warrant was therefore invalid. We in turn reversed, holding that the inspection was not a search subject to the Fourth Amendment. We recognized that the yard was within the curtilage of the house, that a fence shielded the yard from observation from the street, and that the occupant had a subjective expectation of privacy. We held, however, that such an expectation was not reasonable and not one "that society is prepared to honor." Our reasoning was that the home and its curtilage are not necessarily protected from inspection that involves no physical invasion. "'What a person knowingly exposes to the public, even in his own home or office, is not a subject of Fourth Amendment protection.'" As a general proposition, the police may see what may be seen "from a public vantage point where [they have] a right to be." Thus the police, like the public, would have been free to inspect the backyard garden from the street if their view had been unobstructed. They were likewise free to inspect the yard from the vantage point of an aircraft flying in the navigable airspace as this plane was. "In an age where private and commercial flight in the public airways is routine, it is unreasonable for respondent to expect that his marijuana plants were constitutionally protected from being observed with the naked eye from an altitude of 1,000 feet. The Fourth Amendment simply does not require the police traveling in the public airways at this altitude to obtain a warrant in order to observe what is visible to the naked eye."

We arrive at the same conclusion in the present case. In this case, as in *Ciraolo*, the property surveyed was within the curtilage of respondent's home. Riley no doubt intended and expected that his greenhouse would not be open to public inspection, and the precautions he took protected against ground-level observation. Because the sides and roof of his greenhouse were left partially open, however, what was growing in the greenhouse was subject to viewing from the air. Under the holding in *Ciraolo*, Riley could not reasonably have expected the contents of his greenhouse to be immune from examination by an officer seated in a fixed-wing aircraft flying in navigable airspace at an altitude of 1,000 feet or, as the Florida Supreme Court seemed to recognize, at an altitude of 500 feet, the lower limit of the navigable airspace for such an aircraft. Here, the inspection was made from a helicopter, but as is the case with fixed-wing planes, "private and commercial flight [by helicopter] in the public airways is routine" in this country, and there is no indication that such flights are unheard of in Pasco County, Florida. Riley could not reasonably have expected that his greenhouse was protected from public or official observation from a helicopter had it been flying within the navigable airspace for fixed-wing aircraft.

Nor on the facts before us, does it make a difference for Fourth Amendment purposes that the helicopter was flying at 400 feet when the officer saw what was growing in the greenhouse through the partially open roof and sides of the structure. We would have a different case if flying at that altitude had been contrary to law or regulation. But helicopters are not bound by the lower limits of the navigable airspace allowed to other aircraft.[35] Any member of the public could legally have been flying over Riley's property in a helicopter at the altitude of 400 feet and could have observed Riley's greenhouse. The police officer did no more. . . . As far as this record reveals, no intimate details connected with the use of the home or curtilage were observed, and there was no undue noise, and no wind, dust, or threat of injury. In these circumstances, there was no violation of the Fourth Amendment.

O'CONNOR, J. concurring in the judgment. Ciraolo's expectation of privacy was unreasonable not because the airplane was operating where it had a "right to be," but because public air travel at 1,000 feet is a sufficiently routine part of modern life that it is unreasonable for persons on the ground to expect that their curtilage will not be observed from the air at that altitude. Although "helicopters

---

[35] While Federal Aviation Administration regulations permit fixed-wing-aircraft to be operated at an altitude of 1,000 feet while flying over congested areas and at an altitude of 500 feet above the surface in other than congested areas, helicopters may be operated at less than the minimums for fixed-wing-aircraft "if the operation is conducted without hazard to persons or property on the surface. In addition, each person operating a helicopter shall comply with routes or altitudes specifically prescribed for helicopters by the [FAA] Administrator." 14 CFR § 91.79 (1988).

are not bound by the lower limits of the navigable airspace allowed to other aircraft," there is no reason to assume that compliance with FAA regulations alone determines "'whether the government's intrusion infringes upon the personal and societal values protected by the Fourth Amendment.'" Because the FAA has decided that helicopters can lawfully operate at virtually any altitude so long as they pose no safety hazard, it does not follow that the expectations of privacy "society is prepared to recognize as 'reasonable'" simply mirror the FAA's safety concerns. . . .

. . . However, if the public can generally be expected to travel over residential backyards at an altitude of 400 feet, Riley cannot reasonably expect his curtilage from such aerial observation. In my view, the defendant must bear the burden of proving that his expectation of privacy was a reasonable one, and thus that a "search" within the meaning of the Fourth Amendment even took place.

Because there is reason to believe that there is considerable public use of airspace at altitudes of 400 feet and above, and because Riley introduced no evidence to the contrary before the Florida courts, I conclude that Riley's expectation that his curtilage was protected from naked-eye aerial observation from that altitude was not a reasonable one. However, public use of altitudes lower than that — particularly public observations from helicopters circling over the curtilage of a home — may be sufficiently rare that public surveillance from such altitudes would violate reasonable expectations of privacy, despite compliance with FAA air safety regulations.

BRENNAN, J. joined by MARSHALL and STEVENS, JJ. dissenting. Under the plurality's exceedingly grudging Fourth Amendment theory, the expectation of privacy is defeated if a single member of the public could conceivably position herself to see into the area in question without doing anything illegal. It is defeated whatever the difficulty a person would have in so positioning herself, and however infrequently anyone would in fact do so. In taking this view the plurality ignores the very essence of *Katz*. The reason why there is no reasonable expectation of privacy in an area that is exposed to the public is that little diminution in "the amount of privacy and freedom remaining to citizens" will result from police surveillance of something that any passerby readily sees. To pretend, as the plurality opinion does, that the same is true when the police use a helicopter to peer over high fences is, at best, disingenuous. . . .

It is a curious notion that the reach of the Fourth Amendment can be so largely defined by administrative regulations issued for purposes of flight safety.[36] It is more curious still that the plurality relies to such an extent on the legality of the officer's act, when we have consistently refused to equate police violation of the law with infringement of the Fourth Amendment.

---

[36] The plurality's use of the FAA regulations as a means for determining whether Riley enjoyed a reasonable expectation of privacy produces an incredible result. Fixed-wing aircraft may not be operated below 500 feet (1,000 feet over congested areas), while helicopters may be operated below those levels. Therefore, whether Riley's expectation of privacy is reasonable turns on whether the police officer at 400 feet above his curtilage is seated in an airplane or a helicopter. This cannot be the law.

The police officer positioned 400 feet above Riley's backyard was not, however, standing on a public road. The vantage point he enjoyed was not one any citizen could readily share. His ability to see over Riley's fence depended on his use of a very expensive and sophisticated piece of machinery to which few ordinary citizens have access. In such circumstances it makes no more sense to rely on the legality of the officer's position in the skies than it would to judge the constitutionality of the wiretap in *Katz* by the legality of the officer's position outside the telephone booth. The simple inquiry whether the police officer had the legal right to be in the position from which he made his observations cannot suffice, for we cannot assume that Riley's curtilage was so open to the observations of passersby in the skies that he retained little privacy or personal security to be lost to police surveillance. The question before us must be not whether the police were where they had a right to be, but whether public observation of Riley's curtilage was so commonplace that Riley's expectation of privacy in his backyard could not be considered reasonable. . . .

. . . The Fourth Amendment demands that we temper our efforts to apprehend criminals with a concern for the impact on our fundamental liberties of the methods we use. I hope it will be a matter of concern to my colleagues that the police surveillance methods they would sanction were among those described 40 years ago in George Orwell's dread vision of life in the 1980's:

> The black-mustachio'd face gazed down from every commanding corner. There was one on the house front immediately opposite. BIG BROTHER IS WATCHING YOU, the caption said. . . . In the far distance a helicopter skimmed down between the roofs, hovered for an instant like a bluebottle, and darted away again with a curving flight. It was the Police Patrol, snooping into people's windows.

Who can read this passage without a shudder, and without the instinctive reaction that it depicts life in some country other than ours? I respectfully dissent.

NOTES & QUESTIONS

1. ***Privacy in Public.*** The court quotes from *Katz v. United States* that "[w]hat a person knowingly exposes to the public . . . is not a subject of Fourth Amendment protection." How far does this principle extend? Can there be situations where a person might have a reasonable expectation of privacy even when exposed in public?

2. ***Drones.*** The future of law enforcement surveillance likely rests not with helicopters, as in *Florida v. Riley*, but with drones, also known as unmanned aircraft vehicles or unmanned (UAV's). In the words of the N.Y. Times, "Drones are becoming a darling of law enforcement authorities across the country."[37] Law enforcement authorities seek use of drones to locate bombs, find lost children, and assist rescue workers. As part of the 2012 federal budget, Congress ordered it to establish rules for integrating UAV's into the national airspace. The FAA has already designated drone test sites in six

---

[37] Somini Sengupta, *Rise of Drones in U.S. Drives Efforts to Limit Police Use*, N.Y. Times (Feb. 15, 2013).

states, Alaska, Nevada, New York, North Dakota, Texas, and Virginia. In 2014, it plans to launch its rulemaking process for UAV's. The FAA has also noted that its mission "does not include developing or enforcing policies to pertaining privacy or civil liberties" although its experience with the drone test sites can help inform the regulatory dialogue concerning these issues.[38] Does *Florida v. Riley* provide useful Fourth Amendment doctrine for the coming age of law enforcement drones?

3. *Surveillance Cameras.* The use of surveillance cameras is increasing. Since 1994, in response to terrorist bombings, Britain has been watching city streets through a system of surveillance cameras monitored by closed circuit television (CCTV).[39] In 2002, the National Park Service announced plans to set up a surveillance system at all major monuments on the National Mall in Washington, D.C. Given the frequent use of surveillance cameras, do we still have an expectation of privacy not to be filmed in our day-to-day activities? Consider Marc Blitz:

> People also need privacy and anonymity in many aspects of public life — for example, when they explore controversial films, books, or ideas, have conversations in public places, or seek aid or counsel of a sort they can only find by venturing into the public sphere. Although walls and windows do not shield these public activities from everyone's view, other features of physical and social architecture, distinctive to public space, do shield them. Crowds and the diversity and separateness of the social circles that people move in allow people to find anonymity; the existence of isolated and unmonitored islands of public space allow them to find seclusion. . . . These privacy-enhancing features of public space cannot easily survive in a world of ubiquitous cameras, and the task of preserving them requires courts to do in a sense the opposite of what *Katz* recommends: They must abandon the task of identifying difficult-to-identify expectations of privacy . . . and instead return to the task of preserving the environment that makes privacy possible.[40]

What precisely are the harms of surveillance cameras? Consider Christopher Slobogin:

> Virtually all of us, no matter how innocent, feel somewhat unnerved when a police car pulls up behind us. Imagine now being watched by an officer, at a discreet distance and without any other intrusion, every time you walk through certain streets. Say you want to run (to catch a bus, for a brief bit of exercise or just for the hell of it). Will you? Or assume you want to obscure your face (because of the wind or a desire to avoid being seen by an officious acquaintance)? How about hanging out on the street corner (waiting for friends or because you have nothing else to do)?

---

[38] FAA, *Integration of Civil Unmanned Aircraft Systems in the National Airspace System* 11 (1st ed. 2013).

[39] For more background about CCTV, see Clive Norris & Gary Armstrong, *The Maximum Surveillance Society: The Rise of CCTV* (1999); Jeffrey Rosen, *A Cautionary Tale for a New Age of Surveillance*, N.Y. Times Mag. (Oct. 7, 2001).

[40] Marc Jonathan Blitz, *Video Surveillance and the Constitution of Public Space: Fitting the Fourth Amendment to a World that Tracks Image and Identity*, 82 Tex. L. Rev. 1349, 1481 (2004).

In all of these scenarios, you will probably feel and perhaps act differently than when the officer is not there. Perhaps your hesitancy comes from uncertainty as to the officer's likely reaction or simply from a desire to appear completely law-abiding; the important point is that it exists. Government-run cameras are a less tangible presence than the ubiquitous cop, but better at recording your actions. A police officer in Liverpool, England may have said it best: A camera is like having a cop "on duty 24 hours a day, constantly taking notes."[41]

Are there any other harms you can think of? What are the benefits of surveillance cameras? Should they not be permissible as a low-cost way to extend the reach of police? Do the benefits outweigh the harms? Regarding the benefits of surveillance cameras, consider Jeff Rosen:

> In 2000, Britain's violent-crime rates actually increased by 4.3 percent, even though the cameras continued to proliferate. But CCTV cameras have a mysterious knack for justifying themselves regardless of what happens to crime. When crime goes up, the cameras get the credit for detecting it, and when crime goes down, they get the credit for preventing it.[42]

Would it be possible to design an empirical study that would test the effectiveness of surveillance cameras in preventing crime?

4. *Face Recognition Systems.* In Tampa, a computer software program called "FaceIt" linked to 36 cameras attempts to scan the faces of individuals on public streets to match them against mug shots of wanted fugitives. A similar system was used to scan faces at Super Bowl XXXV in January 2001. The Tampa Police Department argues that "FaceIt" is analogous to a police officer standing on a street holding a mug shot. Philip Agre contends that face recognition systems are different:

> A human being who spots me in the park has the accountability that someone can spot them as well. Cameras are much more anonymous and easy to hide. More important is the question of scale. Most people understand the moral difference between a single chance observation in a park and an investigator who follows you everywhere you go.[43]

Further, contends Agre, the information used and collected by face recognition systems could fall into the wrong hands and be potentially abused by the government to exercise social control. Additionally, such systems can have errors, resulting in the tracking and potential arrest of innocent persons. As a policy matter, do the costs of facial recognition systems outweigh the benefits? Given the information privacy law you have learned so far, assess the legality and constitutionality of facial recognition systems.

The Tampa face recognition system was ultimately scrapped because of high errors and general ineffectiveness.

---

[41] Christopher Slobogin, *Public Privacy: Camera Surveillance of Public Places and the Right to Anonymity*, 72 Miss. L.J. 213, 247 (2002).

[42] Jeffrey Rosen, *The Naked Crowd: Reclaiming Security and Freedom in an Anxious Age* 49 (2004).

[43] Philip E. Agre, *Your Face Is Not a Bar Code: Arguments Against Automatic Face Recognition in Public Places* (Sept. 9, 2001), http://dlis.gseis.ucla.edu/people/pagre/bar-code.html.

5. *The First Amendment and Government Surveillance:* **Laird v. Tatum.** In *Florida v. Riley,* the Fourth Amendment failed to limit government surveillance in public places. Does government surveillance implicate First Amendment rights? Christopher Slobogin contends that expressive public conduct and public associations implicate the First Amendment because "such surveillance can chill conduct, even though it takes place in public and is meant to be seen by others."[44]

In *Laird v. Tatum*, 408 U.S. 1 (1972), a group of individuals brought a First Amendment challenge to the Department of the Army's surveillance of civil rights activities in the aftermath of Dr. Martin Luther King, Jr.'s assassination. The Army harvested the information from news reports and from intelligence agents attending public meetings.[45] Although the Supreme Court noted that chilling the exercise of First Amendment rights could constitute a First Amendment violation, the Court concluded that the plaintiffs failed to establish a cognizable First Amendment injury and that their mere allegations of a "subjective 'chill' are not an adequate substitute for a claim of specific present objective harm or a threat of specific future harm." According to the Court, the plantiffs merely articulated "speculative apprehensiveness that the Army may at some future date misuse the information in some way that would cause direct harm to respondents."

Why doesn't surveillance create a cognizable injury under the First Amendment? Being watched inhibits one's ability to be free and candid in one's expression.

How broad is the Supreme Court's holding? Would the plaintiffs have established standing if they produced evidence that the surveillance was deterring their First Amendment activities? Would the case have come out differently had the surveillance involved gatherings in private as opposed to in public?

If *Laird* had been decided in the plaintiffs' favor, could individuals challenge wiretapping and other forms of police surveillance as a violation of the First Amendment? Such a holding could have far-reaching implications because many forms of police monitoring and investigation would be subject not only to Fourth Amendment limitations but to First Amendment ones as well. Where should the line be drawn?

In *Philadelphia Yearly Meeting of the Religious Society of Friends v. Tate*, 519 F.3d 1335 (3d Cir. 1975), the police engaged in surveillance of the plaintiffs' public demonstrations and assemblies. The police shared the information with other government agencies as well as leaked it to the media. Distinguishing *Laird v. Tatum,* the court held that the plaintiffs sufficiently established evidence of a chilling effect. The court reasoned that making the information about the plaintiffs available to non-police entities "could interfere with the job opportunities, careers or travel rights of the individual plaintiffs." Additionally, "disclosure on nationwide television that certain named persons or organizations are subjects of police intelligence files has a

---

[44] Christopher Slobogin, *Public Privacy: Camera Surveillance of Public Places and the Right to Anonymity,* 72 Miss. L.J. 213, 253-55 (2002).

[45] *Id.* at 6.

potential for a substantial adverse impact on such persons and organizations even though tangible evidence of the impact may be difficult, if not impossible, to obtain." Does *Tate* adequately distinguish *Laird*? Is public disclosure always a more injurious privacy violation than government surveillance and information collection?

DOW CHEMICAL CO. V. UNITED STATES

476 U.S. 227 (1986)

BURGER, C.J. . . . Petitioner Dow Chemical Co. operates a 2,000-acre facility manufacturing chemicals at Midland, Michigan. The facility consists of numerous covered buildings, with manufacturing equipment and piping conduits located between the various buildings exposed to visual observation from the air. At all times, Dow has maintained elaborate security around the perimeter of the complex barring ground-level public views of these areas. It also investigates any low-level flights by aircraft over the facility. Dow has not undertaken, however, to conceal all manufacturing equipment within the complex from aerial views. Dow maintains that the cost of covering its exposed equipment would be prohibitive.

In early 1978, enforcement officials of EPA, with Dow's consent, made an on-site inspection of two power plants in this complex. A subsequent EPA request for a second inspection, however, was denied, and EPA did not thereafter seek an administrative search warrant. Instead, EPA employed a commercial aerial photographer, using a standard floor-mounted, precision aerial mapping camera, to take photographs of the facility from altitudes of 12,000, 3,000, and 1,200 feet. At all times the aircraft was lawfully within navigable airspace.

EPA did not inform Dow of this aerial photography, but when Dow became aware of it, Dow brought suit in the District Court alleging that EPA's action violated the Fourth Amendment and was beyond EPA's statutory investigative authority. The District Court granted Dow's motion for summary judgment on the ground that EPA had no authority to take aerial photographs and that doing so was a search violating the Fourth Amendment. EPA was permanently enjoined from taking aerial photographs of Dow's premises and from disseminating, releasing, or copying the photographs already taken. . . .

The photographs at issue in this case are essentially like those commonly used in mapmaking. Any person with an airplane and an aerial camera could readily duplicate them. In common with much else, the technology of photography has changed in this century. These developments have enhanced industrial processes, and indeed all areas of life; they have also enhanced law enforcement techniques. . . .

. . . Dow claims EPA's use of aerial photography was a "search" of an area that, notwithstanding the large size of the plant, was within an "industrial curtilage" rather than an "open field," and that it had a reasonable expectation of privacy from such photography protected by the Fourth Amendment. . . .

. . . Dow concedes that a simple flyover with naked-eye observation, or the taking of a photograph from a nearby hillside overlooking such a facility, would give rise to no Fourth Amendment problem.

In *California v. Ciraolo*, 476 U.S. 207 (1986), decided today, we hold that naked-eye aerial observation from an altitude of 1,000 feet of a backyard within the curtilage of a home does not constitute a search under the Fourth Amendment.

In the instant case, two additional Fourth Amendment claims are presented: whether the common-law "curtilage" doctrine encompasses a large industrial complex such as Dow's, and whether photography employing an aerial mapping camera is permissible in this context. Dow argues that an industrial plant, even one occupying 2,000 acres, does not fall within the "open fields" doctrine of *Oliver v. United States* but rather is an "industrial curtilage" having constitutional protection equivalent to that of the curtilage of a private home. Dow further contends that any aerial photography of this "industrial curtilage" intrudes upon its reasonable expectations of privacy. Plainly a business establishment or an industrial or commercial facility enjoys certain protections under the Fourth Amendment. . . .

. . . The curtilage area immediately surrounding a private house has long been given protection as a place where the occupants have a reasonable and legitimate expectation of privacy that society is prepared to accept. . . .

Dow plainly has a reasonable, legitimate, and objective expectation of privacy within the interior of its covered buildings, and it is equally clear that expectation is one society is prepared to observe. Moreover, it could hardly be expected that Dow would erect a huge cover over a 2,000-acre tract. In contending that its entire enclosed plant complex is an "industrial curtilage," Dow argues that its exposed manufacturing facilities are analogous to the curtilage surrounding a home because it has taken every possible step to bar access from ground level. . . .

. . . The intimate activities associated with family privacy and the home and its curtilage simply do not reach the outdoor areas or spaces between structures and buildings of a manufacturing plant. . . .

It may well be, as the Government concedes, that surveillance of private property by using highly sophisticated surveillance equipment not generally available to the public, such as satellite technology, might be constitutionally proscribed absent a warrant. But the photographs here are not so revealing of intimate details as to raise constitutional concerns. Although they undoubtedly give EPA more detailed information than naked-eye views, they remain limited to an outline of the facility's buildings and equipment. The mere fact that human vision is enhanced somewhat, at least to the degree here, does not give rise to constitutional problems. An electronic device to penetrate walls or windows so as to hear and record confidential discussions of chemical formulae or other trade secrets would raise very different and far more serious questions; other protections such as trade secret laws are available to protect commercial activities from private surveillance by competitors. . . .

We hold that the taking of aerial photographs of an industrial plant complex from navigable airspace is not a search prohibited by the Fourth Amendment. . . .

POWELL, J. joined by BRENNAN, MARSHALL, and BLACKMUN, JJ. concurring in part and dissenting in part. The Fourth Amendment protects private citizens from arbitrary surveillance by their Government. For nearly 20 years, this Court has adhered to a standard that ensured that Fourth Amendment rights would retain their vitality as technology expanded the Government's capacity to commit unsuspected intrusions into private areas and activities. Today, in the context of administrative aerial photography of commercial premises, the Court retreats from that standard. It holds that the photography was not a Fourth Amendment "search" because it was not accompanied by a physical trespass and because the equipment used was not the most highly sophisticated form of technology available to the Government. Under this holding, the existence of an asserted privacy interest apparently will be decided solely by reference to the manner of surveillance used to intrude on that interest. Such an inquiry will not protect Fourth Amendment rights, but rather will permit their gradual decay as technology advances. . . .

NOTES & QUESTIONS

1. *New Surveillance Technologies.* One of the rationales of *Dow Chemical* is that the device could have been acquired by a member of the general public. Does the case turn on this point? Suppose the police used a special camera that was developed exclusively for law enforcement purposes.

   The *Dow Chemical* Court stated: "It may well be, as the Government concedes, that surveillance of private property by using highly sophisticated surveillance equipment not generally available to the public, such as satellite technology, might be constitutionally proscribed absent a warrant." But does this sentence reflect contemporary technological reality? Mark Monmonier describes the rapid increase in the availability of commercial satellite capacities once the Cold War ended and the U.S. government lifted its restrictions in this area. The public now has cheaper and more detailed satellite images available to it than ever before.[46] As an example, look at maps.google.com, where free high-quality satellite imagery is available for most street maps.

   Recall that in *The Right to Privacy*, Warren and Brandeis complained in 1890 of the then new ability to take candid photographs of individuals. Before the invention of the snap camera, people did not expect to be photographed without their consent. Clearly today the ability to take pictures in public is greatly enhanced. There are video cameras, night-vision cameras, powerful zoom lenses, and satellite images available for sale. Google Street View has mapped most of the United States at street level. Are these new technologies eroding our reasonable expectation of privacy?[47] How should the law respond?

2. *Flashlights.* The use of a flashlight "to illuminate a darkened area simply does not constitute a search, and thus triggers no Fourth Amendment protection." *Texas v. Brown*, 460 U.S. 730 (1983). If this conclusion seems evident, how is a flashlight different from other devices that enhance human

---

[46] Mark Monmonier, *Spying with Maps* (2002).

[47] For an argument that people do have reasonable expectations of privacy in public, see Helen Nissenbaum, *Protecting Privacy in an Information Age: The Problem of Privacy in Public*, 17 Law & Phil. 559 (1998).

senses? Is any device that enhances the human senses merely an extension of ordinary senses? What factors should be considered in determining which sense enhancement devices trigger a search under the Fourth Amendment and which do not?

3. ***Canine Sniffs.*** In *United States v. Place*, 462 U.S. 696 (1983), the Court held that a canine sniff by a narcotics detection dog does not infringe upon a reasonable expectation of privacy. It declared:

> A "canine sniff" by a well-trained narcotics detection dog, however, does not require opening the luggage. It does not expose noncontraband items that otherwise would remain hidden from public view, as does, for example, an officer's rummaging through the contents of the luggage. Thus, the manner in which information is obtained through this investigative technique is much less intrusive than a typical search. Moreover, the sniff discloses only the presence or absence of narcotics, a contraband item. Thus, despite the fact that the sniff tells the authorities something about the contents of the luggage, the information obtained is limited. This limited disclosure also ensures that the owner of the property is not subjected to the embarrassment and inconvenience entailed in less discriminate and more intrusive investigative methods.
>
> In these respects, the canine sniff is *sui generis*. We are aware of no other investigative procedure that is so limited both in the manner in which the information is obtained and in the content of the information revealed by the procedure.

The Court revisited the issue of canine sniffs in *Illinois v. Caballes*, 543 U.S. 405 (2005) where it found that the conducting a dog sniff did not change the constitutional character of a "traffic stop that is lawful at its interception and otherwise executed in a reasonable manner." A dog sniff performed on the exterior of a car whose driver was "lawfully seized for a traffic violation" did not rise to the level of a constitutionally cognizable infringement."

Finally, in *Florida v. Harris*, 568 U.S. ___ (2013), the Supreme Court considered when a canine sniff would constitute probable cause for a further search, in this case of the interior of a truck. Aldo, the dog in the *Harris*, alerted on two separate occasions involving the same individual. The search on the first occasion turned up only chemicals that Aldo was not trained to detect; the search on the second revealed nothing of interest to law enforcement.

A unanimous Supreme Court found that a probable cause assessment based on a trained narcotics dog's alert turned on "whether all the facts surrounding a dog's alert, viewed through the lens of common sense, would make a reasonably prudent person think a search would reveal contraband or evidence of a crime." Writing for the *Harris* Court, Justice Kagan added: "A sniff is up to snuff when it meets that test." One key factor is making this determination is whether "the State has produced proof from controlled settings that a dog performs reliably in detecting drugs." A defendant is able to contest the State's case "by disputing the reliability of the drug overall or of a particular alert."

In an empirical study of the reliability of dog sniffs, dogs trained to detect narcotics or explosives responded to subconscious cuing by their handlers.[48] In dissenting in *Illinois v. Caballes*, Justice Souter took a similar view: "The infallible dog . . . is a creature of legal fiction."

In *Florida v. Jardines* (2013), the Court considered the issue of sniffs by narcotic canines of the front porch of a house. That case is discussed in a note following *Kyllo v. United States*.

KYLLO V. UNITED STATES

533 U.S. 27 (2001)

SCALIA, J. In 1991 Agent William Elliott of the United States Department of the Interior came to suspect that marijuana was being grown in the home belonging to petitioner Danny Kyllo, part of a triplex on Rhododendron Drive in Florence, Oregon. Indoor marijuana growth typically requires high-intensity lamps. In order to determine whether an amount of heat was emanating from petitioner's home consistent with the use of such lamps, at 3:20 A.M. on January 16, 1992, Agent Elliott and Dan Haas used an Agema Thermovision 210 thermal imager to scan the triplex. Thermal imagers detect infrared radiation, which virtually all objects emit but which is not visible to the naked eye. The imager converts radiation into images based on relative warmth — black is cool, white is hot, shades of gray connote relative differences; in that respect, it operates somewhat like a video camera showing heat images. The scan of Kyllo's home took only a few minutes and was performed from the passenger seat of Agent Elliott's vehicle across the street from the front of the house and also from the street in back of the house. The scan showed that the roof over the garage and a side wall of petitioner's home were relatively hot compared to the rest of the home and substantially warmer than neighboring homes in the triplex. Agent Elliott concluded that petitioner was using halide lights to grow marijuana in his house, which indeed he was. Based on tips from informants, utility bills, and the thermal imaging, a Federal Magistrate Judge issued a warrant authorizing a search of petitioner's home, and the agents found an indoor growing operation involving more than 100 plants. Petitioner was indicted on one count of manufacturing marijuana, in violation of 21 U.S.C. § 841(a)(1). He unsuccessfully moved to suppress the evidence seized from his home and then entered a conditional guilty plea. . . .

. . . "At the very core" of the Fourth Amendment "stands the right of a man to retreat into his own home and there be free from unreasonable governmental intrusion." With few exceptions, the question whether a warrantless search of a home is reasonable and hence constitutional must be answered no.

On the other hand, the antecedent question of whether or not a Fourth Amendment "search" has occurred is not so simple under our precedent. The permissibility of ordinary visual surveillance of a home used to be clear because, well into the 20th century, our Fourth Amendment jurisprudence was tied to

---

[48] Lisa Lit et al., *Handler Beliefs Affect Scent Detection Outcomes*, 14 Animal Cognition 387 (2011).

common-law trespass. Visual surveillance was unquestionably lawful because "the eye cannot by the laws of England be guilty of a trespass." We have since decoupled violation of a person's Fourth Amendment rights from trespassory violation of his property, but the lawfulness of warrantless visual surveillance of a home has still been preserved. As we observed in *California v. Ciraolo*, 476 U.S. 207, (1986), "[t]he Fourth Amendment protection of the home has never been extended to require law enforcement officers to shield their eyes when passing by a home on public thoroughfares." . . .

The present case involves officers on a public street engaged in more than naked-eye surveillance of a home. We have previously reserved judgment as to how much technological enhancement of ordinary perception from such a vantage point, if any, is too much. While we upheld enhanced aerial photography of an industrial complex in *Dow Chemical*, we noted that we found "it important that this is not an area immediately adjacent to a private home, where privacy expectations are most heightened."

It would be foolish to contend that the degree of privacy secured to citizens by the Fourth Amendment has been entirely unaffected by the advance of technology. For example, as the cases discussed above make clear, the technology enabling human flight has exposed to public view (and hence, we have said, to official observation) uncovered portions of the house and its curtilage that once were private. The question we confront today is what limits there are upon this power of technology to shrink the realm of guaranteed privacy. . . .

. . . [I]n the case of the search of the interior of homes — the prototypical and hence most commonly litigated area of protected privacy — there is a ready criterion, with roots deep in the common law, of the minimal expectation of privacy that exists, and that is acknowledged to be reasonable. To withdraw protection of this minimum expectation would be to permit police technology to erode the privacy guaranteed by the Fourth Amendment. We think that obtaining by sense-enhancing technology any information regarding the interior of the home that could not otherwise have been obtained without physical "intrusion into a constitutionally protected area," *Silverman*, 365 U.S., at 512, constitutes a search — at least where (as here) the technology in question is not in general public use. This assures preservation of that degree of privacy against government that existed when the Fourth Amendment was adopted. On the basis of this criterion, the information obtained by the thermal imager in this case was the product of a search.[49]

---

[49] The dissent's repeated assertion that the thermal imaging did not obtain information regarding the interior of the home is simply inaccurate. A thermal imager reveals the relative heat of various rooms in the home. The dissent may not find that information particularly private or important, but there is no basis for saying it is not information regarding the interior of the home. The dissent's comparison of the thermal imaging to various circumstances in which outside observers might be able to perceive, without technology, the heat of the home — for example, by observing snowmelt on the roof — is quite irrelevant. The fact that equivalent information could sometimes be obtained by other means does not make lawful the use of means that violate the Fourth Amendment. The police might, for example, learn how many people are in a particular house by setting up year-round surveillance, but that does not make breaking and entering to find out the same information lawful. In any event, on the night of January 16, 1992, no outside observer could have discerned the relative heat of Kyllo's home without thermal imaging.

The Government maintains, however, that the thermal imaging must be upheld because it detected "only heat radiating from the external surface of the house." The dissent makes this its leading point, contending that there is a fundamental difference between what it calls "off-the-wall" observations and "through-the-wall" surveillance." But just as a thermal imager captures only heat emanating from a house, so also a powerful directional microphone picks up only sound emanating from a house — and a satellite capable of scanning from many miles away would pick up only visible light emanating from a house. We rejected such a mechanical interpretation of the Fourth Amendment in *Katz*, where the eavesdropping device picked up only sound waves that reached the exterior of the phone booth. Reversing that approach would leave the homeowner at the mercy of advancing technology — including imaging technology that could discern all human activity in the home. While the technology used in the present case was relatively crude, the rule we adopt must take account of more sophisticated systems that are already in use or in development. The dissent's reliance on the distinction between "off-the-wall" and "through-the-wall" observation is entirely incompatible with the dissent's belief, which we discuss below, that thermal-imaging observations of the intimate details of a home are impermissible. The most sophisticated thermal imaging devices continue to measure heat "off-the-wall" rather than "through-the-wall"; the dissent's disapproval of those more sophisticated thermal-imaging devices, is an acknowledgement that there is no substance to this distinction. As for the dissent's extraordinary assertion that anything learned through "an inference" cannot be a search, that would validate even the "through-the-wall" technologies that the dissent purports to disapprove. Surely the dissent does not believe that the through-the-wall radar or ultrasound technology produces an 8-by-10 Kodak glossy that needs no analysis (i.e., the making of inferences). And, of course, the novel proposition that inference insulates a search is blatantly contrary to *United States v. Karo*, 468 U.S. 705 (1984), where the police "inferred" from the activation of a beeper that a certain can of ether was in the home. The police activity was held to be a search, and the search was held unlawful.

The Government also contends that the thermal imaging was constitutional because it did not "detect private activities occurring in private areas." . . . The Fourth Amendment's protection of the home has never been tied to measurement of the quality or quantity of information obtained. In *Silverman*, for example, we made clear that any physical invasion of the structure of the home, "by even a fraction of an inch," was too much, and there is certainly no exception to the warrant requirement for the officer who barely cracks open the front door and sees nothing but the nonintimate rug on the vestibule floor. . . .

Limiting the prohibition of thermal imaging to "intimate details" would not only be wrong in principle; it would be impractical in application. . . . To begin with, there is no necessary connection between the sophistication of the surveillance equipment and the "intimacy" of the details that it observes—which means that one cannot say (and the police cannot be assured) that use of the relatively crude equipment at issue here will always be lawful. The Agema Thermovision 210 might disclose, for example, at what hour each night the lady of the house takes her daily sauna and bath—a detail that many would consider "intimate"; and a much more sophisticated system might detect nothing more intimate than the fact that someone left a closet light on. We could not, in other words, develop a rule approving only that through-the-wall surveillance which identifies objects no smaller than 36 by 36 inches, but would have to develop a jurisprudence specifying which home activities are "intimate" and which are not. And even when (if ever) that jurisprudence were fully developed, no police office would be able to know *in advance* whether his through-the-wall surveillance picks up "intimate" details—and thus would be unable to know in advance whether it is constitutional. . . .

We have said that the Fourth Amendment draws "a firm line at the entrance to the house." That line, we think, must be not only firm but also bright — which requires clear specification of those methods of surveillance that require a warrant. While it is certainly possible to conclude from the videotape of the thermal imaging that occurred in this case that no "significant" compromise of the homeowner's privacy has occurred, we must take the long view, from the original meaning of the Fourth Amendment forward. . . .

Where, as here, the Government uses a device that is not in general public use, to explore details of the home that would previously have been unknowable without physical intrusion, the surveillance is a "search" and is presumptively unreasonable without a warrant. . . .

STEVENS, J. joined by REHNQUIST, C.J. and O'CONNOR and KENNEDY, JJ. dissenting. . . . [S]earches and seizures of property in plain view are presumptively reasonable. Whether that property is residential or commercial, the basic principle is the same: "What a person knowingly exposes to the public, even in his own home or office, is not a subject of Fourth Amendment protection." That is the principle implicated here.

While the Court "take[s] the long view" and decides this case based largely on the potential of yet-to-be-developed technology that might allow "through-the-wall surveillance," this case involves nothing more than off-the-wall surveillance by law enforcement officers to gather information exposed to the general public from the outside of petitioner's home. All that the infrared camera did in this case was passively measure heat emitted from the exterior surfaces of petitioner's home; all that those measurements showed were relative differences in emission levels, vaguely indicating that some areas of the roof and outside walls were warmer than others. As still images from the infrared scans show, no details regarding the interior of petitioner's home were revealed. . . .

. . . Heat waves, like aromas that are generated in a kitchen, or in a laboratory or opium den, enter the public domain if and when they leave a building. A subjective expectation that they would remain private is not only implausible but also surely not "one that society is prepared to recognize as 'reasonable.'" . . .

Despite the Court's attempt to draw a line that is "not only firm but also bright," the contours of its new rule are uncertain because its protection apparently dissipates as soon as the relevant technology is "in general public use." Yet how much use is general public use is not even hinted at by the Court's opinion, which makes the somewhat doubtful assumption that the thermal imager used in this case does not satisfy that criterion. In any event, putting aside its lack of clarity, this criterion is somewhat perverse because it seems likely that the threat to privacy will grow, rather than recede, as the use of intrusive equipment becomes more readily available. . . .

Because the new rule applies to information regarding the "interior" of the home, it is too narrow as well as too broad. Clearly, a rule that is designed to protect individuals from the overly intrusive use of sense-enhancing equipment should not be limited to a home. If such equipment did provide its user with the functional equivalent of access to a private place — such as, for example, the telephone booth involved in *Katz*, or an office building — then the rule should apply to such an area as well as to a home. . . .

NOTES & QUESTIONS

1. ***Thermal Imagers vs. Cameras.*** How does the Court distinguish the thermal imager in *Kyllo* from the camera in *Dow Chemical*? Does this distinction make sense?

2. ***Technology in General Public Use.*** The majority based its holding on the fact that a thermal sensor was *"a device not in general public use."* However, a search of eBay reveals different kinds of thermal-imaging devices for sale at a variety of prices. Hence, the thermal sensor device is one that is publicly available. Is this "eBay test" relevant? How should a court decide when a technology is "in general public use"?

3. ***The Home.*** A key component to the Court's holding is that the thermal sensor was used to glean information about activities in the home. The home has long enjoyed significant protection as a private place. The maxim that the home is one's "castle" appeared as early as 1499.[50] *Semayne's Case*, 77 Eng. Rep. 194, 195 (K.B. 1604), was the first recorded case in which the sanctity of the home was mentioned: "[T]he house of every one is to him as his castle and fortress." According to William Blackstone, the law has "so particular and tender a regard to the immunity of a man's house that it stiles it his castle, and will never suffer it to be violated with impunity."[51] William Pitt once remarked: "The poorest man may in his cottage bid defiance to the Crown. It may be frail — its roof may shake — the wind may enter — the rain may enter — but the King of England cannot enter — all his force dares not cross the threshold of the ruined tenement!"[52]

In the United States, the importance of privacy in the home has long been recognized. The Supreme Court recognized in 1886 the importance of protecting "the sanctity of a man's home" in *Boyd v. United States*, 116 U.S. 616 (1886). As the Court later observed in *Payton v. New York*, 445 U.S. 573 (1980): "In none is the zone of privacy more clearly defined when bounded by the unambiguous physical dimensions of an individual's home." In a different case, it stated, "At the very core [of the Fourth Amendment] stands the right

---

[50] See Note, *The Right to Privacy in Nineteenth Century America*, 94 Harv. L. Rev. 1892, 1894 (1981).

[51] 4 William Blackstone, *Commentaries on the Laws of England* 223 (1769).

[52] Charles J. Sykes, *The End of Privacy* 83 (1999).

of a man to retreat into his own home and there be free from unreasonable governmental intrusion." *Silverman v. United States,* 365 U.S. 505 (1961).

The Court has afforded the home the strongest protection under the Fourth Amendment. For example, automobiles can generally be searched without warrants, while homes rarely can be searched without warrants (except under exigent circumstances). Compare *Chambers v. Maroney,* 399 U.S. 42 (1970), with *Mincey v. Arizona,* 437 U.S. 385 (1978).

In *Chapman v. United States,* 365 U.S. 610 (1961), the Court held that the Fourth Amendment protection of the home extends to apartment tenants, even though they do not own the apartment. Further, in *Bumper v. North Carolina,* 391 U.S. 543 (1968), the Court held that a person living in the home of another was entitled to the same Fourth Amendment protection as if it were her own home. Later, in *Minnesota v. Olson,* 495 U.S. 91 (1990), the Court extended the Fourth Amendment protection of the home to overnight guests in another's home or apartment: However, in *Minnesota v. Carter,* 525 U.S. 83 (1998), the Court held that a visitor who was in a friend's apartment for a short duration (not overnight) had no reasonable expectation of privacy in that apartment because that apartment was used to package cocaine and was not being used as a home.

How much does *Kyllo*'s holding rest on the fact that the thermal sensor was used to learn about activities in the home? What if a thermal sensor were used outside the home?

4. *The Courts vs. Congress.* Orin Kerr contends that when new technologies are involved, Congress, not the courts, should be the primary rulemaker. In particular, Kerr critiques the generally held view that "the Fourth Amendment should be interpreted broadly in response to technological change." According to Kerr:

> [C]ourts should place a thumb on the scale in favor of judicial caution when technology is in flux, and should consider allowing legislatures to provide the primary rules governing law enforcement investigations involving new technologies. . . . When technology is in flux, Fourth Amendment protections should remain relatively modest until the technology stabilizes.

Kerr justifies his conclusion by making an argument about the attributes of judicial versus legislative rulemaking:

> The first difference is that legislatures typically create generally applicable rules ex ante, while courts tend to create rules ex post in a case-by-case fashion. That is, legislatures enact generalized rules for the future, whereas courts resolve disputes settling the rights of parties arising from a past event. The difference leads to Fourth Amendment rules that tend to lag behind parallel statutory rules and current technologies by at least a decade, resulting in unsettled and then outdated rules that often make little sense given current technological facts. . . .
>
> A second difference between judicial and legislative rulemaking concerns their operative constraints. . . . Legislatures are up to the task [of adapting to technological change]; courts generally are not. Legislatures can experiment with different rules and make frequent amendments; they can place restrictions on both public and private actors; and they can even "sunset" rules

so that they apply only for a particular period of time. The courts cannot. As a result, Fourth Amendment rules will tend to lack the flexibility that a regulatory response to new technologies may require. . . .

The third important difference between judicial rules and legislative rules relates to the information environment in which rules are generated. Legislative rules tend to be the product of a wide range of inputs, ranging from legislative hearings and poll results to interest group advocacy and backroom compromises. Judicial rules tend to follow from a more formal and predictable presentation of written briefs and oral arguments by two parties. Once again, the difference offers significant advantages to legislative rulemaking. The task of generating balanced and nuanced rules requires a comprehensive understanding of technological facts. Legislatures are well-equipped to develop such understandings; courts generally are not.[53]

Peter Swire responds that Congress's privacy legislation was shaped by judicial decisions concerning the Fourth Amendment:

At least four mutually reinforcing reasons underscore the importance of judicial decisions to how these privacy protections were enacted. First, the Supreme Court decision made the issue more salient, focusing attention on a topic that otherwise would not climb to the top of the legislative agenda. Second, the importance of the decision to the political process was greater because of what social scientists have called the "endowment effect" or "status quo bias." . . . [T]he concept is that individuals experience a loss as more important than a gain of equal size. . . . [T]he perceived "loss" of Fourth Amendment protections . . . would be a spur to legislative action. Third, the opinions of the Supreme Court shaped the legislative debates. Vigorous dissents in each case articulated reasons why privacy protections should be considered important. . . . Fourth, once the issue had moved high enough on the agenda to warrant a vote, there were persuasive public-policy arguments that some privacy protections were appropriate.[54]

Daniel Solove also disagrees with Kerr's conclusions: "Where the courts have left open areas for legislative rules to fill in, Congress has created an uneven fabric of protections that is riddled with holes and that has weak protections in numerous places." Further, Solove contends, legislative ex ante rules are not necessarily preferable to judicial ex post rules:

The problem with ex ante laws is that they cannot anticipate all of the new and changing factual situations that technology brings about. Ex post rules, in contrast, are often much better tailored to specific types of technology, because such rules arise as technology changes, rather than beforehand. . . .

Solove argues that the "historical record suggests that Congress is actually far worse than the courts in reacting to new technologies." In response to Kerr's argument that the legislature is better equipped to understand new technologies than the judiciary, Solove responds that "merely shifting to a statutory regime will not eliminate Kerr's concern with judges

---

[53] Orin S. Kerr, *The Fourth Amendment and New Technologies: Constitutional Myths and the Case for Caution*, 102 Mich. L. Rev. 801, 803-05, 868, 871, 875 (2004).

[54] Peter P. Swire, *Katz Is Dead. Long Live Katz,* 102 Mich. L. Rev. 904, 917 (2004).

misunderstanding technology. In fact, many judicial misunderstandings stem from courts trying to fit new technologies into old statutory regimes built around old technologies."[55]

5. **Is the Fourth Amendment Primarily Protective of the Individual or Society?** Consider the following observation by Anthony Amsterdam:

> [Should the Fourth Amendment] be viewed as a collection of protections of atomistic spheres of interest of individual citizens or as a regulation of governmental conduct[?] Does it safeguard *my* person and *your* house and *her* papers and *his* effects against unreasonable searches and seizures; or is it essentially a regulatory canon requiring government to order its law enforcement procedures in a fashion that keeps us collectively secure in our persons, houses, papers, and effects, against unreasonable searches and seizures?[56]

Under what view does the Supreme Court seem to be operating? Which view do you think is the most appropriate?

6. **Is Government Observation Different from Observation by Others?** Amsterdam also argues that one's privacy may be violated by being observed by the police but may not be violated by the very same observation from others:

> [I]f you live in a cheap hotel or in a ghetto flat, your neighbors can hear you breathing quietly even in temperate weather when it is possible to keep the windows and doors closed. For the tenement dweller, the difference between observation by neighbors and visitors who ordinarily use the common hallways and observation by policemen who come into hallways to "check up" or "look around" is the difference between all the privacy that his condition allows and none. Is that small difference too unimportant to claim [F]ourth [A]mendment protection?[57]

Do you agree that our expectations of privacy turn on who is watching rather than simply whether we are being watched? Should the "reasonable expectation of privacy" test be changed to the "reasonable expectation of what the police can observe or search" test?

7. **Beepers and Tracking Devices.** In *United States v. Knotts*, 460 U.S. 276 (1983), the police placed a beeper in a five-gallon drum of chloroform purchased by the defendants and placed in their car. The beeper transmitted signals that enabled the police to track the location of the defendants' vehicle. The Court held that the Fourth Amendment did not apply to the use of this device because a "person traveling in an automobile on public thoroughfares has no reasonable expectation of privacy in his movements from one place to another." Therefore, "[t]he governmental surveillance conducted by means of

---

[55] Daniel J. Solove, *Fourth Amendment Codification and Professor Kerr's Misguided Call for Judicial Deference*, 74 Fordham L. Rev. 747, 761-74 (2005).

[56] Anthony G. Amsterdam, *Perspectives on the Fourth Amendment*, 58 Minn. L. Rev. 349, 367 (1974). For an additional critique of the reasonable expectation of privacy test, see Andrew E. Taslitz, *The Fourth Amendment in the Twenty-First Century: Technology, Privacy, and Human Emotions*, 65 Law & Contemp. Probs. 125 (2002).

[57] Amsterdam, *Fourth Amendment, supra*, at 404.

the beeper in this case amounted principally to the following of an automobile on public streets and highways." In *United States v. Karo*, 468 U.S. 705 (1984), law enforcement officials planted a beeper in a can of ether that the defendant bought from an informant. The officials tracked the movements of the can of ether through a variety of places, including within a residence. While the movements in *Knotts* were in public, the movements within the residence were not, and this amounted to an impermissible search of the residence:

> The monitoring of an electronic device such as a beeper is, of course, less intrusive than a full-scale search, but it does reveal a critical fact about the interior of the premises that the Government is extremely interested in knowing and that it could not have otherwise obtained without a warrant. The case is thus not like *Knotts*, for there the beeper told the authorities nothing about the interior of Knotts' cabin. The information obtained in *Knotts* was "voluntarily conveyed to anyone who wanted to look. . . ."

UNITED STATES V. JONES

132 S. Ct. 945 (2012)

SCALIA J. We decide whether the attachment of a Global-Positioning-System (GPS) tracking device to an individual's vehicle, and subsequent use of that device to monitor the vehicle's movements on public streets, constitutes a search or seizure within the meaning of the Fourth Amendment. . . .

In 2004 respondent Antoine Jones, owner and operator of a nightclub in the District of Columbia, came under suspicion of trafficking in narcotics and was made the target of an investigation by a joint FBI and Metropolitan Police Department task force. Officers employed various investigative techniques, including visual surveillance of the nightclub, installation of a camera focused on the front door of the club, and a pen register and wiretap covering Jones's cellular phone.

Based in part on information gathered from these sources, in 2005 the Government applied to the United States District Court for the District of Columbia for a warrant authorizing the use of an electronic tracking device on the Jeep Grand Cherokee registered to Jones's wife. A warrant issued, authorizing installation of the device in the District of Columbia and within 10 days.

On the 11th day, and not in the District of Columbia but in Maryland,[58] agents installed a GPS tracking device on the undercarriage of the Jeep while it was parked in a public parking lot. Over the next 28 days, the Government used the device to track the vehicle's movements, and once had to replace the device's battery when the vehicle was parked in a different public lot in Maryland. By means of signals from multiple satellites, the device established the vehicle's location within 50 to 100 feet, and communicated that location by cellular phone to a Government computer. It relayed more than 2,000 pages of data over the 4-week period.

---

[58] In this litigation, the Government has conceded noncompliance with the warrant and has argued only that a warrant was not required.

The Government ultimately obtained a multiple-count indictment charging Jones and several alleged co-conspirators with, as relevant here, conspiracy to distribute and possess with intent to distribute five kilograms or more of cocaine and 50 grams or more of cocaine base, in violation of 21 U.S.C. §§ 841 and 846 . . . .

In March 2007, a grand jury returned another indictment, charging Jones and others with the same conspiracy. The Government introduced at trial the same GPS-derived locational data admitted in the first trial, which connected Jones to the alleged conspirators' stash house that contained $850,000 in cash, 97 kilograms of cocaine, and 1 kilogram of cocaine base. The jury returned a guilty verdict, and the District Court sentenced Jones to life imprisonment. . . .

The Fourth Amendment provides in relevant part that "[t]he right of the people to be secure in their persons, houses, papers, and effects, against unreasonable searches and seizures, shall not be violated." It is beyond dispute that a vehicle is an "effect" as that term is used in the Amendment. We hold that the Government's installation of a GPS device on a target's vehicle, and its use of that device to monitor the vehicle's movements, constitutes a "search."

It is important to be clear about what occurred in this case: The Government physically occupied private property for the purpose of obtaining information. We have no doubt that such a physical intrusion would have been considered a "search" within the meaning of the Fourth Amendment when it was adopted. . . .

The text of the Fourth Amendment reflects its close connection to property, since otherwise it would have referred simply to "the right of the people to be secure against unreasonable searches and seizures"; the phrase "in their persons, houses, papers, and effects" would have been superfluous.

Consistent with this understanding, our Fourth Amendment jurisprudence was tied to common-law trespass, at least until the latter half of the 20th century. *Kyllo v. United States,* 533 U.S. 27 (2001); Kerr, *The Fourth Amendment and New Technologies: Constitutional Myths and the Case for Caution,* 102 Mich. L. Rev. 801 (2004). Thus, in *Olmstead v. United States,* 277 U.S. 438 (1928), we held that wiretaps attached to telephone wires on the public streets did not constitute a Fourth Amendment search because "[t]here was no entry of the houses or offices of the defendants."

Our later cases, of course, have deviated from that exclusively property-based approach. In *Katz v. United States,* 389 U.S. 347 (1967), we said that "the Fourth Amendment protects people, not places," and found a violation in attachment of an eavesdropping device to a public telephone booth. Our later cases have applied the analysis of Justice Harlan's concurrence in that case, which said that a violation occurs when government officers violate a person's "reasonable expectation of privacy."

The Government contends that the Harlan standard shows that no search occurred here, since Jones had no "reasonable expectation of privacy" in the area of the Jeep accessed by Government agents (its underbody) and in the locations of the Jeep on the public roads, which were visible to all. But we need not address the Government's contentions, because Jones's Fourth Amendment rights do not rise or fall with the *Katz* formulation. At bottom, we must "assur[e] preservation of that degree of privacy against government that existed when the Fourth Amendment was adopted." *Kyllo.* As explained, for most of our history the Fourth Amendment was understood to embody a particular concern for government trespass upon the areas ("persons, houses, papers, and effects") it enumerates.[59] *Katz* did not repudiate that understanding. . . . *Katz* did not narrow the Fourth Amendment's scope.

The Government contends that several of our post-*Katz* cases foreclose the conclusion that what occurred here constituted a search. It relies principally on two cases in which we rejected Fourth Amendment challenges to "beepers," electronic tracking devices that represent another form of electronic monitoring. The first case, *Knotts,* upheld against Fourth Amendment challenge the use of a "beeper" that had been placed in a container of chloroform, allowing law enforcement to monitor the location of the container. We said that there had been no infringement of Knotts' reasonable expectation of privacy since the information obtained—the location of the automobile carrying the container on public roads, and the location of the off-loaded container in open fields near Knotts' cabin—had been voluntarily conveyed to the public. But as we have discussed, the *Katz* reasonable-expectation-of-privacy test has been *added to,* not *substituted for,* the common-law trespassory test. The holding in *Knotts* addressed only the former, since the latter was not at issue. The beeper had been placed in the container before it came into Knotts' possession, with the consent of the then-owner. *Knotts* would be relevant, perhaps, if the Government were making the argument that what would otherwise be an unconstitutional search is not such where it produces only public information. The Government does not make that argument, and we know of no case that would support it.

The second "beeper" case, *United States v. Karo* does not suggest a different conclusion. There we addressed the question left open by *Knotts,* whether the installation of a beeper in a container amounted to a search or seizure. As in *Knotts,* at the time the beeper was installed the container belonged to a third party, and it did not come into possession of the defendant until later. Thus, the specific question we considered was whether the installation "*with the consent of the original owner* constitute[d] a search or seizure . . . when the container is delivered to a buyer having no knowledge of the presence of the beeper" (emphasis added). We held not. The Government, we said, came into physical contact with the container only before it belonged to the defendant Karo; and the transfer of the container with the unmonitored beeper inside did not convey any information and thus did not invade Karo's privacy. That conclusion is perfectly consistent with the one we reach here. Karo accepted the container as it came to

---

[59] Justice ALITO's concurrence (hereinafter concurrence) doubts the wisdom of our approach because "it is almost impossible to think of late–18th-century situations that are analogous to what took place in this case." But in fact it posits a situation that is not far afield—a constable's concealing himself in the target's coach in order to track its movements. There is no doubt that the information gained by that trespassory activity would be the product of an unlawful search— whether that information consisted of the conversations occurring in the coach, or of the destinations to which the coach traveled.

In any case, it is quite irrelevant whether there was an 18th-century analog. Whatever new methods of investigation may be devised, our task, *at a minimum,* is to decide whether the action in question would have constituted a "search" within the original meaning of the Fourth Amendment. Where, as here, the Government obtains information by physically intruding on a constitutionally protected area, such a search has undoubtedly occurred.

him, beeper and all, and was therefore not entitled to object to the beeper's presence, even though it was used to monitor the container's location. . . .

The concurrence begins by accusing us of applying "18th-century tort law." That is a distortion. What we apply is an 18th-century guarantee against unreasonable searches, which we believe must provide *at a minimum* the degree of protection it afforded when it was adopted. The concurrence does not share that belief. It would apply *exclusively Katz* 's reasonable-expectation-of-privacy test, even when that eliminates rights that previously existed. . . .

In fact, it is the concurrence's insistence on the exclusivity of the *Katz* test that needlessly leads us into "particularly vexing problems" in the present case. This Court has to date not deviated from the understanding that mere visual observation does not constitute a search. . . . Thus, even assuming that the concurrence is correct to say that "[t]raditional surveillance" of Jones for a 4–week period "would have required a large team of agents, multiple vehicles, and perhaps aerial assistance," our cases suggest that such visual observation is constitutionally permissible. It may be that achieving the same result through electronic means, without an accompanying trespass, is an unconstitutional invasion of privacy, but the present case does not require us to answer that question.

Justice SOTOMAYOR, concurring. I join the Court's opinion because I agree that a search within the meaning of the Fourth Amendment occurs, at a minimum, "[w]here, as here, the Government obtains information by physically intruding on a constitutionally protected area." . . . The Government usurped Jones' property for the purpose of conducting surveillance on him, thereby invading privacy interests long afforded, and undoubtedly entitled to, Fourth Amendment protection.

Of course, the Fourth Amendment is not concerned only with trespassory intrusions on property. As the majority's opinion makes clear, however, *Katz* 's reasonable-expectation-of-privacy test augmented, but did not displace or diminish, the common-law trespassory test that preceded it. . . . Justice Alito's approach, which discounts altogether the constitutional relevance of the Government's physical intrusion on Jones' Jeep, erodes that longstanding protection for privacy expectations inherent in items of property that people possess or control. By contrast, the trespassory test applied in the majority's opinion reflects an irreducible constitutional minimum: When the Government physically invades personal property to gather information, a search occurs. The reaffirmation of that principle suffices to decide this case.

Nonetheless, as Justice Alito notes, physical intrusion is now unnecessary to many forms of surveillance. With increasing regularity, the Government will be capable of duplicating the monitoring undertaken in this case by enlisting factory- or owner-installed vehicle tracking devices or GPS-enabled smartphones. As Justice Alito incisively observes, the same technological advances that have made possible nontrespassory surveillance techniques will also affect the *Katz* test by shaping the evolution of societal privacy expectations. Under that rubric, I agree with Justice Alito that, at the very least, "longer term GPS monitoring in investigations of most offenses impinges on expectations of privacy."

In cases involving even short-term monitoring, some unique attributes of GPS surveillance relevant to the *Katz* analysis will require particular attention. GPS monitoring generates a precise, comprehensive record of a person's public movements that reflects a wealth of detail about her familial, political, professional, religious, and sexual associations. The Government can store such records and efficiently mine them for information years into the future. . . .

Awareness that the Government may be watching chills associational and expressive freedoms. And the Government's unrestrained power to assemble data that reveal private aspects of identity is susceptible to abuse. . . .

I would take these attributes of GPS monitoring into account when considering the existence of a reasonable societal expectation of privacy in the sum of one's public movements. I would ask whether people reasonably expect that their movements will be recorded and aggregated in a manner that enables the Government to ascertain, more or less at will, their political and religious beliefs, sexual habits, and so on. I do not regard as dispositive the fact that the Government might obtain the fruits of GPS monitoring through lawful conventional surveillance techniques. I would also consider the appropriateness of entrusting to the Executive, in the absence of any oversight from a coordinate branch, a tool so amenable to misuse, especially in light of the Fourth Amendment's goal to curb arbitrary exercises of police power to and prevent "a too permeating police surveillance," *United States v. Di Re,* 332 U.S. 581 (1948).

More fundamentally, it may be necessary to reconsider the premise that an individual has no reasonable expectation of privacy in information voluntarily disclosed to third parties. This approach is ill suited to the digital age, in which people reveal a great deal of information about themselves to third parties in the course of carrying out mundane tasks. People disclose the phone numbers that they dial or text to their cellular providers; the URLs that they visit and the e-mail addresses with which they correspond to their Internet service providers; and the books, groceries, and medications they purchase to online retailers. . . . I for one doubt that people would accept without complaint the warrantless disclosure to the Government of a list of every Web site they had visited in the last week, or month, or year. But whatever the societal expectations, they can attain constitutionally protected status only if our Fourth Amendment jurisprudence ceases to treat secrecy as a prerequisite for privacy. I would not assume that all information voluntarily disclosed to some member of the public for a limited purpose is, for that reason alone, disentitled to Fourth Amendment protection. Resolution of these difficult questions in this case is unnecessary, however, because the Government's physical intrusion on Jones' Jeep supplies a narrower basis for decision. I therefore join the majority's opinion.

Justice ALITO, with whom Justice GINSBURG, Justice BREYER, and Justice KAGAN join, concurring in the judgment. This case requires us to apply the Fourth Amendment's prohibition of unreasonable searches and seizures to a 21st-century surveillance technique, the use of a Global Positioning System (GPS) device to monitor a vehicle's movements for an extended period of time. Ironically, the Court has chosen to decide this case based on 18th-century tort law. By attaching a small GPS device[60] to the underside of the vehicle that respondent drove, the law enforcement officers in this case engaged in conduct that might have provided grounds in 1791 for a suit for trespass to chattels.[61] And for this reason, the Court concludes, the installation and use of the GPS device constituted a search.

This holding, in my judgment, is unwise. It strains the language of the Fourth Amendment; it has little if any support in current Fourth Amendment case law; and it is highly artificial.

I would analyze the question presented in this case by asking whether respondent's reasonable expectations of privacy were violated by the long-term monitoring of the movements of the vehicle he drove. . . .

The Fourth Amendment prohibits "unreasonable searches and seizures," and the Court makes very little effort to explain how the attachment or use of the GPS device fits within these terms. . . .

The Court does claim that the installation and use of the GPS constituted a search, but this conclusion is dependent on the questionable proposition that these two procedures cannot be separated for purposes of Fourth Amendment analysis. If these two procedures are analyzed separately, it is not at all clear from the Court's opinion why either should be regarded as a search. It is clear that the attachment of the GPS device was not itself a search; if the device had not functioned or if the officers had not used it, no information would have been obtained. And the Court does not contend that the use of the device constituted a search either. On the contrary, the Court accepts the holding in *United States v. Knotts* that the use of a surreptitiously planted electronic device to monitor a vehicle's movements on public roads did not amount to a search.

The Court argues—and I agree—that "we must 'assur[e] preservation of that degree of privacy against government that existed when the Fourth Amendment was adopted.' " But it is almost impossible to think of late–18th-century situations that are analogous to what took place in this case. (Is it possible to imagine a case in which a constable secreted himself somewhere in a coach and remained there for a period of time in order to monitor the movements of the coach's owner?[62]) The Court's theory seems to be that the concept of a search, as originally understood, comprehended any technical trespass that led to the gathering of evidence, but we know that this is incorrect. At common law, any unauthorized intrusion on private property was actionable, see Prosser & Keeton 75, but a trespass on open fields, as opposed to the "curtilage" of a home, does not fall within the scope of the Fourth Amendment because private property outside the curtilage is not part of a "hous[e]" within the meaning of the Fourth Amendment. See *Oliver v. United States*, 466 U.S. 170 (1984).

---

[60] Although the record does not reveal the size or weight of the device used in this case, there is now a device in use that weighs two ounces and is the size of a credit card. Tr. of Oral Arg. 27.

[61] At common law, a suit for trespass to chattels could be maintained if there was a violation of "the dignitary interest in the inviolability of chattels," but today there must be "some actual damage to the chattel before the action can be maintained." W. Keeton, D. Dobbs, R. Keeton, & D. Owen, Prosser & Keeton on Law of Torts 87 (5th ed.1984) (hereinafter Prosser & Keeton). Here, there was no actual damage to the vehicle to which the GPS device was attached.

[62] The Court suggests that something like this might have occurred in 1791, but this would have required either a gigantic coach, a very tiny constable, or both—not to mention a constable with incredible fortitude and patience.

The Court's reasoning in this case is very similar to that in the Court's early decisions involving wiretapping and electronic eavesdropping, namely, that a technical trespass followed by the gathering of evidence constitutes a search. . . .

By contrast, in cases in which there was no trespass, it was held that there was no search. Thus, in *Olmstead v. United States* (1928), the Court found that the Fourth Amendment did not apply because "[t]he taps from house lines were made in the streets near the houses." . . .

Katz v. United States(1967) finally did away with the old approach, holding that a trespass was not required for a Fourth Amendment violation. . . . What mattered, the Court now held, was whether the conduct at issue "violated the privacy upon which [the defendant] justifiably relied while using the telephone booth." . . .

Under this approach, as the Court later put it when addressing the relevance of a technical trespass, "an actual trespass is neither necessary *nor sufficient* to establish a constitutional violation." *United States v. Karo,* 468 U.S. 705 (1984) (emphasis added). . . .

Disharmony with a substantial body of existing case law is only one of the problems with the Court's approach in this case.

I will briefly note four others. First, the Court's reasoning largely disregards what is really important (the *use* of a GPS for the purpose of long-term tracking) and instead attaches great significance to something that most would view as relatively minor (attaching to the bottom of a car a small, light object that does not interfere in any way with the car's operation). . . .

Second, the Court's approach leads to incongruous results. If the police attach a GPS device to a car and use the device to follow the car for even a brief time, under the Court's theory, the Fourth Amendment applies. But if the police follow the same car for a much longer period using unmarked cars and aerial assistance, this tracking is not subject to any Fourth Amendment constraints. . . .

Third, under the Court's theory, the coverage of the Fourth Amendment may vary from State to State. If the events at issue here had occurred in a community property State or a State that has adopted the Uniform Marital Property Act, respondent would likely be an owner of the vehicle, and it would not matter whether the GPS was installed before or after his wife turned over the keys. In non-community-property States, on the other hand, the registration of the vehicle in the name of respondent's wife would generally be regarded as presumptive evidence that she was the sole owner.

Fourth, the Court's reliance on the law of trespass will present particularly vexing problems in cases involving surveillance that is carried out by making electronic, as opposed to physical, contact with the item to be tracked. For example, suppose that the officers in the present case had followed respondent by surreptitiously activating a stolen vehicle detection system that came with the car when it was purchased. Would the sending of a radio signal to activate this system constitute a trespass to chattels? Trespass to chattels has traditionally required a physical touching of the property. . . .

The *Katz* expectation-of-privacy test avoids the problems and complications noted above, but it is not without its own difficulties. It involves a degree of circularity, and judges are apt to confuse their own expectations of privacy with those of the hypothetical reasonable person to which the *Katz* test looks. In addition, the *Katz* test rests on the assumption that this hypothetical reasonable person has a well-developed and stable set of privacy expectations. But technology can change those expectations. Dramatic technological change may lead to periods in which popular expectations are in flux and may ultimately produce significant changes in popular attitudes. . . .

Recent years have seen the emergence of many new devices that permit the monitoring of a person's movements. In some locales, closed-circuit television video monitoring is becoming ubiquitous. On toll roads, automatic toll collection systems create a precise record of the movements of motorists who choose to make use of that convenience. Many motorists purchase cars that are equipped with devices that permit a central station to ascertain the car's location at any time so that roadside assistance may be provided if needed and the car may be found if it is stolen.

Perhaps most significant, cell phones and other wireless devices now permit wireless carriers to track and record the location of users—and as of June 2011, it has been reported, there were more than 322 million wireless devices in use in the United States. For older phones, the accuracy of the location information depends on the density of the tower network, but new "smart phones," which are equipped with a GPS device, permit more precise tracking. For example, when a user activates the GPS on such a phone, a provider is able to monitor the phone's location and speed of movement and can then report back real-time traffic conditions after combining ("crowdsourcing") the speed of all such phones on any particular road. Similarly, phone-location-tracking services are offered as "social" tools, allowing consumers to find (or to avoid) others who enroll in these services. The availability and use of these and other new devices will continue to shape the average person's expectations about the privacy of his or her daily movements. . . .

A legislative body is well situated to gauge changing public attitudes, to draw detailed lines, and to balance privacy and public safety in a comprehensive way.

To date, however, Congress and most States have not enacted statutes regulating the use of GPS tracking technology for law enforcement purposes. The best that we can do in this case is to apply existing Fourth Amendment doctrine and to ask whether the use of GPS tracking in a particular case involved a degree of intrusion that a reasonable person would not have anticipated.

Under this approach, relatively short-term monitoring of a person's movements on public streets accords with expectations of privacy that our society has recognized as reasonable. *See Knotts.* But the use of longer term GPS monitoring in investigations of most offenses impinges on expectations of privacy. For such offenses, society's expectation has been that law enforcement agents and others would not—and indeed, in the main, simply could not—secretly monitor and catalogue every single movement of an individual's car for a very long period. In this case, for four weeks, law enforcement agents tracked every movement that respondent made in the vehicle he was driving. We need not identify with precision the point at which the tracking of this vehicle became a search, for the line was surely crossed before the 4-week mark. Other cases may present more difficult questions. But where uncertainty exists with respect to whether a certain period of GPS surveillance is long enough to constitute a Fourth Amendment search, the police may always seek a warrant. We also need not consider whether prolonged GPS monitoring in the context of investigations involving extraordinary offenses would similarly intrude on a constitutionally protected sphere of privacy. In such cases, long-term tracking might have been mounted using previously available techniques.

NOTES & QUESTIONS

1. *A New Direction?* Both concurring opinions, involving five justices, embraced a new theory of privacy. In previous cases, the Court has focused extensively on whether something or not was exposed to the public. The concurrences recognize that extensive and aggregated surveillance can violate a reasonable expectation of privacy regardless of whether or not such surveillance occurred in public:

> Under this approach, relatively short-term monitoring of a person's movements on public streets accords with expectations of privacy that our society has recognized as reasonable. *See Knotts.* But the use of longer term GPS monitoring in investigations of most offenses impinges on expectations of privacy. For such offenses, society's expectation has been that law enforcement agents and others would not—and indeed, in the main, simply could not—secretly monitor and catalogue every single movement of an individual's car for a very long period. In this case, for four weeks, law enforcement agents tracked every movement that respondent made in the vehicle he was driving.

Is this a new direction for the reasonable expectation of privacy test?

2. *Influence on Other Areas of Privacy Law.* Other areas of law often use Fourth Amendment reasonable expectation of privacy determinations as guidance about whether something is a private matter. Will *Jones* affect the privacy torts? Consider *Nader v. General Motors Corp.,* 255 N.E.2d 765 (N.Y. Ct. App. 1970) (excerpted in Chapter 2). There, a court held that "overzealous" surveillance in public could violate privacy and constitute intrusion upon seclusion. To what extent would Justices Alito and Sotomayor agree? Does their approach extend further?

3. *Where Is the Line?* The theory that extensive and aggregated surveillance in public can impinge upon a reasonable expectation of privacy is sometimes referred to as "mosaic theory." Prior to *Jones,* a number of scholars had argued that extensive public surveillance should be viewed as a privacy violation. According to Daniel Solove, "We do many private things in public, such as buy medications and hygiene products in drug stores and browse books and magazines in bookstores. We expect a kind of practical obscurity— to be just another face in the crowd."[63] Helen Nissenbaum notes that "while isolated bits of information (as generated, for example, by merely walking around in public spaces and not taking active steps to avoid notice) are not

---

[63] Daniel J. Solove, *Nothing to Hide: The False Tradeoff Between Privacy and Security* 178 (2011).

especially revealing, assemblages are capable of exposing people quite profoundly."[64] In his concurrence, Justice Alito distinguished between short-term monitoring and extensive surveillance, but he did not indicate where the line would be drawn:

> We need not identify with precision the point at which the tracking of this vehicle became a search, for the line was surely crossed before the 4–week mark. Other cases may present more difficult questions. But where uncertainty exists with respect to whether a certain period of GPS surveillance is long enough to constitute a Fourth Amendment search, the police may always seek a warrant.

Orin Kerr contends that the mosaic theory raises too many questions and is too vague to serve as useful guidance for law enforcement surveillance activities:

> [I]mplementing the mosaic theory would require courts to answer an extensive list of difficult and novel questions. . . . For example, what is the standard for the mosaic? How should courts aggregate conduct to know when a sufficient mosaic has been created? Which techniques should fall within the mosaic approach? Should mosaic searches require a warrant? If so, how can mosaic warrants satisfy the particularity requirement? Should the exclusionary rule apply to violations of the mosaic search doctrine? Who has standing to challenge mosaic searches? Adopting a mosaic theory will require courts to answer all of these questions and more.

Moreover, Kerr notes:

> [T]he amount of private information collected by the surveillance will vary greatly from suspect to suspect. For example, imagine the police know that one suspect rarely uses his car while a second suspect drives several hours a day. The police install GPS devices on both cars for one week, revealing very little about the first suspect and a great deal about the habits of the second. Does the mosaic amount to a search earlier for the second suspect than the first?[65]

4. *Dogs, the Home, and Property-Based Protection of Privacy.* Continuing the trend of strong protection of the home (as in *Kyllo*), and reliance on a trespass theory (as in *Jones*), the Supreme Court found that the use of a drug-sniffing dog on a homeowner's porch to investigate the contents of the home was a "search" within the meaning of the Fourth Amendment. Writing for the majority in *Florida v. Jardines*, 569 U.S. ___ (2013), Justice Scalia began by stating that the area immediately surrounding the home, such as the front porch of a house, was part of its curtilage. This area was protected by the Fourth Amendment and the use of drug-sniffing dog by the police exceeded

---

[64] Helen Nissenbaum, *Protecting Privacy in the Information Age: The Problem of Privacy in Public,* 17 Law & Phil. 559 (1998).

[65] Orin S. Kerr, *The Mosaic Theory of the Fourth Amendment,* 110 Mich. L. Rev. ___ (2012).

the "implicit license" that homeowner's grant to visitors, including "the Nation's Girl Scouts and trick-or-treaters" as well as law enforcement officers who wish to knock on the front door of the house. According to Justice Scalia, however, "the background social norms that invite a visitor to the front door do not invite him there to conduct a search." Referring to *Jones*, he repeated that the *Katz* reasonable expectation test was added to "the traditional property-based understanding of the Fourth Amendment."

Concurring in the opinion, Justice Kagan, joined by Justices Ginsburg and Sotomayor, found that the use of the drug-sniffing dog implicated *Kyllo*. In her view, the trained drug-detection dog was similar to the thermal imaging device in that earlier case, namely a device not in general public use that was being use to explore details of the home that would not otherwise be discovered without entering inside the premises.

In dissent, Justice Alito, joined by Chief Justice Roberts, and Justices Kennedy and Breyer, scoffed at the notion of a violation of any implied license or property interest. The officer in the case simply walked up to the front door, stayed no longer than a minute or two, and used a dog, an animal whose "keen sense of smell has been used in law enforcement for centuries." Moreover, a dog was not a new form of technology or device unlike the thermal imaging device in *Kyllo*.

Is *Florida v. Jardines* best understood as building on *Jones* to re-invigorate property-based theories of privacy? Or does it stand for the narrower proposition that privacy cases involving trespass can gain a slender majority from the current membership of the Supreme Court?

B. INFORMATION GATHERING ABOUT FIRST AMENDMENT ACTIVITIES

In a number of instances, government searches and surveillance implicate First Amendment activities. For example, as Daniel Solove argues:

> First Amendment activities are implicated by a wide array of law enforcement data-gathering activities. Government information gathering about computer and Internet use, for example, can intrude on a significant amount of First Amendment activity. Searching or seizing a computer can reveal personal and political writings. Obtaining e-mail can provide extensive information about correspondence and associations. Similarly, ISP records often contain information about speech, as they can link people to their anonymous communications. AOL, for example, receives about a thousand requests per month for use of its customer records in criminal cases.[66]

Neil Richards contends that government surveillance is particularly dangerous for two reasons:

---

[66] Daniel J. Solove, *The First Amendment as Criminal Procedure*, 82 N.Y.U. L. Rev. 112, 114-15 (2007).

First, surveillance is harmful because it can chill the exercise of our civil liberties. With respect to civil liberties, consider surveillance of people when they are thinking, reading, and communicating with others in order to make up their minds about political and social issues. Such intellectual surveillance is especially dangerous because it can cause people not to experiment with new, controversial, or deviant ideas. To protect our intellectual freedom to think without state oversight or interference, we need what I have elsewhere called "intellectual privacy." A second special harm that surveillance poses is its effect on the power dynamic between the watcher and the watched. This disparity creates the risk of a variety of harms, such as discrimination, coercion, and the threat of selective enforcement, where critics of the government can be prosecuted or blackmailed for wrongdoing unrelated to the purpose of the surveillance.[67]

Government information gathering involving First Amendment activities not only involves Fourth Amendment protections, but also First Amendment protections and sometimes special statutory protections.

The Fourth Amendment was heavily influenced by government information gathering about First Amendment activities. The Framers of the Constitution forged the Fourth Amendment in part due to their strong dislike of general warrants, especially in seditious libel cases. A general warrant authorized sweeping searches for all personal papers related to a particular offense. In English common law, speech criticizing the government could be deemed "seditious libel" — a criminal offense. The American colonists were subject to general warrants, and the Framers particularly detested them as an overbearing form of government power.

In the years preceding the American Revolution, there were several high-profile seditious libel cases in England that generated significant attention in the colonies. These cases involved interests that are now protected by both the First and Fourth Amendments. In *Wilkes v. Wood,* 19 Howell's State Trials 982, 982 (C.P. 1763), a publication called *The North Briton* printed anonymous criticism of the King, but it was commonly known that the author was John Wilkes, a member of Parliament. Pursuant to a general warrant authorizing searches for anything connected with *The North Briton,* the government began raiding the homes of various authors and publishers (including Wilkes) to search and seize their personal documents. Wilkes was arrested. Wilkes brought a civil trespass lawsuit to challenge the general warrant. Wilkes prevailed in a jury trial. The Wilkes case was widely celebrated in the American colonies.[68]

Two years later, John Entick challenged a general warrant in a seditious libel investigation. In *Entick v.* Carrington, 19 Howell's State Trials 1029 (C.P. 1765). Lord Camden found for Entick, criticizing general warrants: "[A person's] house is rifled; his most valuable secrets are taken out of his possession, before the paper for which he is charged is found to be criminal by any competent jurisdiction, and before he is convicted either of writing publishing or being concerned in the paper." The *Entick* case was also widely praised in the colonies, and even towns were named after Wilkes and Lord Camden.

---

[67] Neil M. Richards, *The Dangers of Surveillance,* 126 Harv. L. Rev. 1934, 1935 (2013).

[68] William J. Cuddihy, *The Fourth Amendment: Origins and Original Meaning 602-1781* (2009).

The *Wilkes* and *Entick* cases strongly shaped the Framers' intent behind the Fourth Amendment, as well as subsequent interpretations of the Fourth Amendment.

STANFORD V. TEXAS

379 U.S. 476 (1965)

STEWART, J. . . . . On December 27, 1963, several Texas law-enforcement officers presented themselves at the petitioner's San Antonio home for the purpose of searching it under authority of a warrant issued by a local magistrate. By the time they had finished, five hours later, they had seized some 2,000 of the petitioner's books, pamphlets, and papers. The question presented by this case is whether the search and seizure were constitutionally valid.

The warrant was issued under s 9 of Art. 6889-3A of the Revised Civil Statutes of Texas. The Article, enacted in 1955 and known as the Suppression Act, is a sweeping and many-faceted law which, among other things, outlaws the Communist Party and creates various individual criminal offenses, each punishable by imprisonment for up to 20 years. Section 9 authorizes the issuance of a warrant "for the purpose of searching for and seizing any books, records, pamphlets, cards, receipts, lists, memoranda, pictures, recordings, or any written instruments showing that a person or organization is violating or has violated any provision of this Act." The section sets forth various procedural requirements, among them that "if the premises to be searched constitute a private residence, such application for a search warrant shall be accompanied by the affidavits of two credible citizens." . . .

The district judge issued a warrant which specifically described the premises to be searched, recited the allegations of the applicant's and affiants' belief that the premises were "a place where books, records, pamphlets, cards, receipts, lists, memoranda, pictures, recordings and other written instruments concerning the Communist Party of Texas, and the operations of the Communist Party in Texas are unlawfully possessed and used in violation of Article 6889-3 and Article 6889-3A, Revised Civil Statutes of the State of Texas," and ordered the executing officers "to enter immediately and search the above described premises for such items listed above unlawfully possessed in violation of Article 6889--3 and Article 6889-3A, Revised Civil Statutes, State of Texas, and to take possession of same."

The warrant was executed by the two Assistant Attorneys General who had signed the affidavit, accompanied by a number of county officers. They went to the place described in the warrant, which was where the petitioner resided and carried on a mail order book business under the trade name "All Points of View." The petitioner was not at home when the officers arrived, but his wife was, and she let the officers in after one of them had read the warrant to her. . . .

Under the general supervision of one of the Assistant Attorneys General the officers spent more than four hours in gathering up about half the books they found in the house. Most of the material they took came from the stock in trade of the petitioner's business, but they took a number of books from his personal library as well. The books and pamphlets taken comprised approximately 300 separate titles, in addition to numerous issues of several different periodicals. Among the books taken were works by such diverse writers as Karl Marx, Jean Paul Sartre, Theodore Draper, Fidel Castro, Earl Browder, Pope John XXIII, and MR. JUSTICE HUGO L. BLACK. The officers also took possession of many of the petitioner's private documents and papers, including his marriage certificate, his insurance policies, his household bills and receipts, and files of his personal correspondence. All this material was packed into 14 cartons and hauled off to an investigator's office in the county courthouse. The officers did not find any "records of the Communist Party" or any "party lists and dues payments." . . .

. . . [W]e think it is clear that this warrant was of a kind which it was the purpose of the Fourth Amendment to forbid—a general warrant. Therefore, even accepting the premise that some or even all of the substantive provisions of Articles 6889-3 and 6889-3A of the Revised Civil Statutes of Texas are constitutional and have not been pre-empted by federal law, even accepting the premise that the warrant sufficiently specified the offense believed to have been committed and was issued upon probable cause, the magistrate's order denying the motion to annul the warrant and return the property must nonetheless be set aside. . . .

The Fourth Amendment provides that "no Warrants shall issue, but upon probable cause, supported by Oath or affirmation, and particularly describing the place to be searched, and the persons or things to be seized."

These words are precise and clear. They reflect the determination of those who wrote the Bill of Rights that the people of this new Nation should forever "be secure in their persons, houses, papers, and effects" from intrusion and seizure by officers acting under the unbridled authority of a general warrant. Vivid in the memory of the newly independent Americans were those general warrants known as writs of assistance under which officers of the Crown had so bedeviled the colonists. The hated writs of assistance had given customs officials blanket authority to search where they pleased for goods imported in violation of the British tax laws. They were denounced by James Otis as "the worst instrument of arbitrary power, the most destructive of English liberty, and the fundamental principles of law, that ever was found in an English law book," because they placed "the liberty of every man in the hands of every petty officer." . . .

But while the Fourth Amendment was most immediately the product of contemporary revulsion against a regime of writs of assistance, its roots go far deeper. Its adoption in the Constitution of this new Nation reflected the culmination in England a few years earlier of a struggle against oppression which had endured for centuries. The story of that struggle has been fully chronicled in the pages of this Court's reports, and it would be a needless exercise in pedantry to review again the detailed history of the use of general warrants as instruments of oppression from the time of the Tudors, through the Star Chamber, the Long Parliament, the Restoration, and beyond.

What is significant to note is that this history is largely a history of conflict between the Crown and the press. It was in enforcing the laws licensing the publication of literature and, later, in prosecutions for seditious libel that general warrants were systematically used in the sixteenth, seventeenth, and eighteenth centuries. In Tudor England officers of the Crown were given roving commissions to search where they pleased in order to suppress and destroy the literature of dissent, both Catholic and Puritan. In later years warrants were sometimes more specific in content, but they typically authorized of all persons connected of the premises of all persons connected with the publication of a particular libel, or the arrest and seizure of all the papers of a named person thought to be connected with a libel.

It was in the context of the latter kinds of general warrants that the battle for individual liberty and privacy was finally won—in the landmark cases of *Wilkes v. Wood* and *Entick v. Carrington*. The *Wilkes* case arose out of the Crown's attempt to stifle a publication called The North Briton, anonymously published by John Wilkes, then a member of Parliament—particularly issue No. 45 of that journal. Lord Halifax, as Secretary of State, issued a warrant ordering four of the King's messengers "to make strict and diligent search for the authors, printers, and publishers of a seditious and treasonable paper, entitled, The North Briton, No. 45, . . . and them, or any of them, having found, to apprehend and seize, together with their papers." "Armed with their roving commission, they set forth in quest of unknown offenders; and unable to take evidence, listened to rumors, idle tales, and curious guesses. They held in their hands the liberty of every man whom they were pleased to suspect." Holding that this was "a ridiculous warrant against the whole English nation," the Court of Common Pleas awarded Wilkes damages against the Secretary of State.

John Entick was the author of a publication called Monitor or British Freeholder. A warrant was issued specifically naming him and that publication, and authorizing his arrest for seditious libel and the seizure of his "books and papers." The King's messengers executing the warrant ransacked Entick's home for four hours and carted away quantities of his books and papers. In an opinion which this Court has characterized as a wellspring of the rights now protected by the Fourth Amendment, Lord Camden declared the warrant to be unlawful. "This power," he said, "so assumed by the secretary of state is an execution upon all the party's papers, in the first instance. His house is rifled; his most valuable secrets are taken out of his possession, before the paper for which he is charged is found to be criminal by any competent jurisdiction, and before he is convicted either of writing, publishing, or being concerned in the paper." Thereafter, the House of Commons passed two resolutions condemning general warrants, the first limiting its condemnation to their use in cases of libel, and the second condemning their use generally. . . .

In short, what this history indispensably teaches is that the constitutional requirement that warrants must particularly describe the 'things to be seized' is to be accorded the most scrupulous exactitude when the "things" are books, and the basis for their seizure is the ideas which they contain. No less a standard could be faithful to First Amendment freedoms. The constitutional impossibility of leaving the protection of those freedoms to the whim of the officers charged with executing the warrant is dramatically underscored by what the officers saw fit to seize under the warrant in this case.

Two centuries have passed since the historic decision in *Entick v. Carrington*, almost to the very day. The world has greatly changed, and the voice of nonconformity now sometimes speaks a tongue which Lord Camden might find hard to understand. But the Fourth and Fourteenth Amendments guarantee to John Stanford that no official of the State shall ransack his home and seize his books and papers under the unbridled authority of a general warrant—no less than the law 200 years ago shielded John Entick from the messengers of the King.

NOTES & QUESTIONS

1. *Are Fourth Amendment Warrants Sufficient to Protect First Amendment Activities?* In *Zurcher v. the Stanford Daily*, 436 U.S. 547 (1978), the police searched the offices of a college newspaper, *The Stanford Daily*, to gather evidence relating to a demonstration that had turned violent. The newspaper was not involved in the demonstration and nobody at the newspaper was suspected of criminal activity. The reason for the search was that the journalists had taken photographs of the demonstration and the police wanted these photos for evidence. The newspaper argued that searches of its offices "will seriously threaten the ability of the press to gather, analyze, and disseminate news." The Court, however, concluded that the Fourth Amendment did not prohibit state authorities from searching the premises if the authorities had a warrant supported by probable cause. The Court recognized that First Amendment activities were implicated by the search but noted that "[w]here the materials sought to be seized may be protected by the First Amendment, the requirements of the Fourth Amendment must be applied with 'scrupulous exactitude." The Court then concluded that "the prior cases do no more than insist that the courts apply the warrant requirements with particular exactitude when First Amendment interests would be endangered by the search." Accordingly, First Amendment interests are sufficiently protected by "the preconditions for a warrant." In later cases, the Court clarified that the First Amendment does not require a "higher standard" than a warrant supported by probable cause for seizures of books or films.

2. *The Privacy Protection Act.* In 1980, Congress responded to *Zurcher* by passing the Privacy Protection Act (PPA), 42 U.S.C. § 2000aa. The PPA prohibits government officials from searching or seizing work product materials or documents "possessed by a person reasonably believed to have a purpose to disseminate to the public a newspaper, book, broadcast, or other similar form of public communication, in or affecting interstate or foreign commerce." However, if "there is probable cause to believe that the person possessing such materials has committed or is committing the criminal offense to which the materials relate," then such materials may be searched or seized. The "criminal offense" cannot consist of the mere receipt, possession, or communication of the materials (except if it involves national defense data, classified information, or child pornography). § 2000aa(a)(1). The materials may be searched or seized if "there is reason to believe that the immediate seizure of such materials is necessary to prevent the death of, or serious bodily injury to, a human being."

The effect of the PPA is to require law enforcement officials to obtain a subpoena in order to obtain such information. Unlike search warrants, subpoenas permit the party subject to them to challenge them in court before having to comply. Further, instead of law enforcement officials searching through offices or records, the persons served with the subpoena must produce the documents themselves.

3. *Government Information Gathering About Group Membership.* In *NAACP v. Alabama*, 357 U.S. 449 (1958), the Supreme Court held that the NAACP could not be compelled to publicly disclose the names and addresses of its members. According to the Court, there is a "vital relationship between freedom to associate and privacy in one's associations." Exposing members would subject them "to economic reprisal, loss of employment, threat of physical coercion, and other manifestations of public hostility."

The Court reached a similar conclusion in *Bates v. City of Little Rock*, 361 U.S. 516 (1960), and *Gibson v. Florida Legislative Investigation Commission*, 372 U.S. 539 (1963), cases also involving the compulsory public disclosure of NAACP membership lists.

In *Barenblatt v. United States*, 360 U.S. 109 (1959), a Subcommittee of the House Un-American Activities Committee summoned Lloyd Barenblatt, a 31-year-old teacher of psychology at Vassar College, to testify. The House Un-American Activities Committee was a long-standing Committee that investigated Communist activities by forcing suspected Communist Party members to disclose that they were Party members and reveal the names of other members. Before Barenblatt appeared, his contract with Vassar expired and was not renewed. The Committee wanted to question Barenblatt because another witness had stated that when Barenblatt was a graduate student, he had been associated with a small group of Communists. When called before the Committee, Barenblatt refused to answer questions pertaining to his current and past membership in the Communist Party. He was found in contempt, tried in federal district court, and sentenced to six months in prison. Barenblatt challenged his being compelled to disclose his political associations as a violation of his First Amendment rights. The Supreme Court, however, concluded that Congress's interests in investigating the Communist Party outweighed Barenblatt's rights. Justices Black, Warren, and Douglas dissented:

> The First Amendment says in no equivocal language that Congress shall pass no law abridging freedom of speech, press, assembly or petition. The activities of this Committee, authorized by Congress, do precisely that, through exposure, obloquy and public scorn. . . .

> [The majority] balances the right of the Government to preserve itself, against Barenblatt's right to refrain from revealing Communist affiliations. Such a balance, however, mistakes the factors to be weighed. In the first place, it completely leaves out the real interest in Barenblatt's silence, the interest of the people as a whole in being able to join organizations, advocate causes and make political "mistakes" without later being subjected to governmental penalties for having dared to think for themselves. . . .

In *Shelton v. Tucker*, 364 U.S. 479 (1960), the Court struck down a law requiring teachers to list the organizations they belonged or contributed to within the past five years. The Court held that "the statute's comprehensive interference with associational freedom goes far beyond what might be justified in the exercise of the State's legitimate inquiry into the fitness and competency of its teachers":

> The scope of the inquiry required by [the statute] is completely unlimited. The statute requires a teacher to reveal the church to which he belongs, or to which he has given financial support. It requires him to disclose his political party, and every political organization to which he may have contributed over a five-year period. It requires him to list, without number, every conceivable kind of associational tie — social, professional, political, vocational, or religious. Many such relationships could have no possible bearing upon the teacher's occupational competence or fitness.

Can you reconcile the Court's decision in *Barenblatt* with *Shelton v. Tucker* and *NAACP v. Alabama*?

A number of Supreme Court cases involved challenges to questions about Communist Party membership asked by state bar committees. In *Konigsberg v. State Bar of California*, 366 U.S. 36 (1961), an applicant for membership in the California Bar refused to answer questions about his membership in the Communist Party. The committee refused to certify him. The Court held that the applicant's First Amendment rights were not violated because "[t]here is here no likelihood that deterrence of association may result from foreseeable private action, for bar committee interrogations such as this are conducted in private."

In *Baird v. State Bar*, 401 U.S. 1 (1971), an applicant before the Arizona Bar Committee refused to answer whether she was a member of the Communist Party or any organization "that advocates overthrow of the United States Government by force or violence." As a result, the applicant was denied admission to the bar. The Court held that the questioning was improper because the government cannot attempt to conduct "[b]road and sweeping state inquiries" into people's political views or group associations. "In effect this young lady was asked by the State to make a guess as to whether any organization to which she ever belonged 'advocates overthrow of the United States Government by force or violence.' " The Court reasoned:

> The First Amendment's protection of association prohibits a State from excluding a person from a profession or punishing him solely because he is a member of a particular political organization or because he holds certain beliefs. Similarly, when a State attempts to make inquiries about a person's beliefs or associations, its power is limited by the First Amendment. Broad and sweeping state inquiries into these protected areas, as Arizona has engaged in here, discourage citizens from exercising rights protected by the Constitution.
>
> When a State seeks to inquire about an individual's beliefs and associations a heavy burden lies upon it to show that the inquiry is necessary to protect a legitimate state interest. Of course Arizona has a legitimate interest in determining whether petitioner has the qualities of character and the professional competence requisite to the practice of law. But here petitioner

has already supplied the Committee with extensive personal and professional information to assist its determination. By her answers to questions other than No. 25, and her listing of former employers, law school professors, and other references, she has made available to the Committee the information relevant to her fitness to practice law. And whatever justification may be offered, a State may not inquire about a man's views or associations solely for the purpose of withholding a right or benefit because of what he believes.

Can you distinguish *Baird* from *Barenblatt, Konigsberg*, and the other Communist Party membership cases?

4. ***Intellectual Privacy.*** Neil Richards argues that surveillance is particularly threatening to what he calls "intellectual privacy," which he defines as "the protection from surveillance or unwanted interference by others when we are engaged in the processes of generating ideas and forming beliefs—when we're thinking, reading, and speaking with confidantes before our ideas are ready for public consumption."[69] Richards argues that intellectual privacy is a necessary protection for intellectual freedom and free speech:

> New ideas—political, scientific, artistic, or otherwise . . . depend on access to the ideas of others and the ability to engage with them. And to do this, we need to be able to read freely and then think privately about what we've read in our own time. . . .
>
> Even access to knowledge isn't by itself enough. We need places and spaces (real and virtual) in which to read, to think, to explore. The process of idea generation is one of trial and error. Very often, what seems like a good idea at the time turns out to be a terrible one after testing or further reflection. But to test or examine ideas, we again turn to other people—our friends and confidantes, our family and colleagues. We rely on these people for their frank and confidential assessments of whether we're on to something, or whether we're crazy. . . .
>
> These activities and expectations allow us to discuss, test, and reevaluate our ideas before they are ready for public exposure. . . .
>
> If we're interested in the creation of new ideas, we should want people to experiment with controversial ideas. . . .

Richards goes on to argue that First Amendment law and theory should focus more on how ideas and beliefs area formed:

> First Amendment cases and scholarship are full of explanations about *why* we allow the expression of large amounts of often offensive and harmful speech—for instance, because lots of speech enhances the search for truth, the processes of democratic self-government, or individual autonomy. By contrast, discussions of free speech have only rarely addressed the question of *how* we ensure new and interesting ideas get generated.
>
> This is a curious omission, because if we care about free speech, we should care about speakers having something interesting to say. Many of today's most cherished ideas were once highly controversial. Consider the notion that governments should be elected by the people, or the separation of church and state, or the idea of the equality of all people under law regardless of race, sex, or religion. At various times, believing or promoting each of these ideas was

---

[69] Neil M. Richards, *Intellectual Privacy*, Chapter 6 (forthcoming 2015).

to be done at your peril. Think of the thousands of people killed in early modern Europe for believing differently in matters of faith, or the violent persecution of American civil rights activists who believed in racial equality. Ideas matter because they can be destabilizing, which explains why those in power have resorted to extreme measures—burnings at the stake, lynchings, Selma Bridge—to keep those destabilizing ideas in check.[70]

Is Richards correct? Should the law be concerned with belief formation? Is this too broad an extension of the First Amendment?

5. *The First Amendment as Criminal Procedure.* Daniel Solove contends that the First Amendment should be employed to protect against many forms of government searches and surveillance: "The First Amendment is usually taught separately from the Fourth and Fifth Amendments, and judicial decisions on criminal procedure only occasionally mention the First Amendment. [However,] the First Amendment must be considered alongside the Fourth and Fifth Amendments as a source of criminal procedure."

Solove contends that there is a doctrinal foundation for First Amendment protection against government information gathering. If the First Amendment were to apply to certain government law enforcement activities, what level of protections would it provide? Solove argues:

> Even if an instance of government information gathering triggers First Amendment protection, collection of the data will not necessarily be prohibited. Rather, the First Amendment will require the government to demonstrate (1) a significant interest in gathering the information and (2) that the manner of collection is narrowly tailored to achieving that interest. . . . [T]he use of a warrant supported by probable cause will, in most cases, suffice to satisfy the narrow tailoring requirement. In other words, in cases where the First Amendment applies, it often will require procedures similar to those required by the Fourth Amendment.[71]

Solove also posits that the First Amendment would be enforced by way of an exclusionary rule. To what extent does the First Amendment apply to government law enforcement activities? Should the First Amendment require similar protections to those of the Fourth Amendment?

GONZALES V. GOOGLE

234 F.R.D. 674 (N.D. Cal. 2006)

[The government sought information for its use in *ACLU v. Gonzales*, No. 98-CV-5591, pending in the Eastern District of Pennsylvania. That case involved a challenge by the ACLU to the Children's Online Privacy Protection Act (COPPA). Google was not a party to that case, but the government subpoenaed from Google: (1) URL samples: "[a]ll URL's that are available to be located to a query on your company's search engine as of July 31, 2005" and (2) search

---

[70] *Id.*

[71] Daniel J. Solove, *The First Amendment as Criminal Procedure*, 82 N.Y.U. L. Rev. 112, 114-15, 159 (2007).

queries: "[a]ll queries that have been entered on your company's search engine between June 1, 2005 and July 31, 2005 inclusive." Subsequently, the government narrowed its URL sample demand to 50,000 URLs and it narrowed its search query demand to all queries during a one-week period rather than the two-month period mentioned above. Google still raised a challenge, and the government again narrowed its search query request for only 5,000 entries from Google's query log. It continued to seek a sample of 50,000 URLs from Google's search index. Under Federal Rule of Civil Procedure 26, a subpoena sought must be "reasonably calculated to lead to admissible evidence." It may be quashed if the "burden or expense of the proposed discovery outweighs its likely benefit."]

WARE, J. . . . As narrowed by negotiations with Google and through the course of this Miscellaneous Action, the Government now seeks a sample of 50,000 URLs from Google's search index. In determining whether the information sought is reasonably calculated to lead to admissible evidence, the party seeking the information must first provide the Court with its plans for the requested information. The Government's disclosure of its plans for the sample of URLs is incomplete. The actual methodology disclosed in the Government's papers as to the search index sample is, in its entirety, as follows: "A human being will browse a random sample of 5,000-10,000 URLs from Google's index and categorize those sites by content" and from this information, the Government intends to "estimate . . . the aggregate properties of the websites that search engines have indexed." The Government's disclosure only describes its methodology for a study to categorize the URLs in Google's search index, and does not disclose a study regarding the effectiveness of filtering software. Absent any explanation of how the "aggregate properties" of material on the Internet is germane to the underlying litigation, the Government's disclosure as to its planned categorization study is not particularly helpful in determining whether the sample of Google's search index sought is reasonably calculated to lead to admissible evidence in the underlying litigation.

Based on the Government's statement that this information is to act as a "test set for the study" and a general statement that the purpose of the study is to "evaluate the effectiveness of content filtering software," the Court is able to envision a study whereby a sample of 50,000 URLs from the Google search index may be reasonably calculated to lead to admissible evidence on measuring the effectiveness of filtering software. In such a study, the Court imagines, the URLs would be categorized, run through the filtering software, and the effectiveness of the filtering software ascertained as to the various categories of URLs. The Government does not even provide this rudimentary level of general detail as to what it intends to do with the sample of URLs to evaluate the effectiveness of filtering software, and at the hearing neither confirmed nor denied the Court's speculations about the study. In fact, the Government seems to indicate that such a study is not what it has in mind: "[t]he government seeks this information *only* to perform a study, in the aggregate, of trends on the Internet" (emphasis added), with no explanation of how an aggregate study of Internet trends would be reasonably calculated to lead to admissible evidence in the underlying suit where the efficacy of filtering software is at issue. . . .

Given the broad definition of relevance in Rule 26, and the current narrow scope of the subpoena, despite the vagueness with which the Government has disclosed its study, the Court gives the Government the benefit of the doubt. The Court finds that 50,000 URLs randomly selected from Google's data base for use in a scientific study of the effectiveness of filters is relevant to the issues in the case of *ACLU v. Gonzales.*[72]

In its original subpoena the Government sought a listing of the text of all search queries entered by Google users over a two month period. As defined in the Government's subpoena, "queries" include only the text of the search string entered by a user, and not "any additional information that may be associated with such a text string that would identify the person who entered the text string into the search engine, or the computer from which the text string was entered." The Government has narrowed its request so that it now seeks only a sample of 5,000 such queries from Google's query log. The Government discloses its plans for the query log information as follows: "A random sample of approximately 1,000 Google queries from a one-week period will be run through the Google search engine. A human being will browse the top URLs returned by each search and categorize the sites by content." . . .

Google also argues that it will be unduly burdened by loss of user trust if forced to produce its users' queries to the Government. Google claims that its success is attributed in large part to the volume of its users and these users may be attracted to its search engine because of the privacy and anonymity of the service. According to Google, even a perception that Google is acquiescing to the Government's demands to release its query log would harm Google's business by deterring some searches by some users.

Google's own privacy statement indicates that Google users could not reasonably expect Google to guard the query log from disclosure to the Government. . . . Google's privacy policy does not represent to users that it keeps confidential any information other than "personal information." Neither Google's URLs nor the text of search strings with "personal information" redacted, are reasonably "personal information" under Google's stated privacy policy. Google's privacy policy indicates that it has not suggested to its users that non-"personal information" such as that sought by the Government is kept confidential.

However, even if an expectation by Google users that Google would prevent disclosure to the Government of its users' search queries is not entirely reasonable, the statistic cited by Dr. Stark that over a quarter of all Internet searches are for pornography indicates that at least some of Google's users expect some sort of privacy in their searches. The expectation of privacy by some Google users may not be reasonable, but may nonetheless have an appreciable impact on the way in which Google is perceived, and consequently the frequency with which users use Google. Such an expectation does not rise to the level of an absolute privilege, but does indicate that there is a potential burden as to

---

[72] To the extent that the Government is gathering this information for some other purpose than to run the sample of Google's search index through various filters to determine the efficacy of those filters, the Court would take a different view of the relevance of the information. For example, the Court would not find the information relevant if it is being sought just to characterize the nature of the URL's in Google's database.

Google's loss of goodwill if Google is forced to disclose search queries to the Government.

Rule 45(c)(3)(B) provides additional protections where a subpoena seeks trade secret or confidential commercial information from a nonparty. . . . Because Google still continues to claim information about its entire search index and entire query log as confidential, the Court will presume that the requested information, as a small sample of proprietary information, may be somewhat commercially sensitive, albeit not independently commercially sensitive. Successive disclosures, whether in this lawsuit or pursuant to subsequent civil subpoenas, in the aggregate could yield confidential commercial information about Google's search index or query log. . . .

What the Government has not demonstrated, however, is a substantial need for *both* the information contained in the sample of URLs and sample of search query text. Furthermore, even if the information requested is not a trade secret, a district court may in its discretion limit discovery on a finding that "the discovery sought is unreasonably cumulative or duplicative, or is obtainable from some other source that is more convenient, less burdensome, or less expensive." Rule 26(b)(2)(i).

Faced with duplicative discovery, and with the Government not expressing a preference as to which source of the test set of URLs it prefers, this Court exercises its discretion pursuant to Rule 26(b)(2) and determines that the marginal burden of loss of trust by Google's users based on Google's disclosure of its users' search queries to the Government outweighs the duplicative disclosure's likely benefit to the Government's study. Accordingly, the Court grants the Government's motion to compel only as to the sample of 50,000 URLs from Google's search index.

The Court raises, sua sponte, its concerns about the privacy of Google's users apart from Google's business goodwill argument. . . .

Although the Government has only requested the text strings entered, basic identifiable information may be found in the text strings when users search for personal information such as their social security numbers or credit card numbers through Google in order to determine whether such information is available on the Internet. The Court is also aware of so-called "vanity searches," where a user queries his or her own name perhaps with other information. . . . This concern, combined with the prevalence of Internet searches for sexually explicit material — generally not information that anyone wishes to reveal publicly — gives this Court pause as to whether the search queries themselves may constitute potentially sensitive information.

The Court also recognizes that there may a difference between a private litigant receiving potentially sensitive information and having this information be produced to the Government pursuant to civil subpoena. . . . Even though counsel for the Government assured the Court that the information received will only be used for the present litigation, it is conceivable that the Government may have an obligation to pursue information received for unrelated litigation purposes under certain circumstances regardless of the restrictiveness of a protective order. The Court expressed this concern at oral argument as to queries such as "bomb placement white house," but queries such as "communist berkeley parade route protest war" may also raise similar concerns. In the end, the Court need not express an opinion on this issue because the Government's motion is granted only as to the sample of URLs and not as to the log of search queries.

The Court also refrains from expressing an opinion on the applicability of the Electronic Communications Privacy Act. . . . The Court only notes that the ECPA does not bar the Government's request for sample of 50,000 URLs from Google's index though civil subpoena.

NOTES & QUESTIONS

1. ***URL Samples vs. Search Queries.*** The sought-after subpoena in *Gonzales v. Google* concerned information about both URL samples and search queries. What decision did the district court reach for each type of data? Are there different privacy implications for governmental access to the two kinds of information?

2. ***Can People Be Identified from Anonymous Search Data?*** An incident involving AOL proved that individuals can be identified based on their search queries. In August 2006, AOL revealed that it had released to researchers about 20 million search queries made by over 650,000 users of its search engine. Although AOL had substituted numerical IDs for the subscribers' actual user names, the personal identity of the user could be found based on the search queries. The *New York Times* demonstrated as much by tracking down AOL user No. 4417749; it linked this person's data trail to a 62-year old widow who lived in Lilburn, Georgia, and admitted to the reporter, "Those are my searches."[73]

C. FEDERAL ELECTRONIC SURVEILLANCE LAW

1. SECTION 605 OF THE FEDERAL COMMUNICATIONS ACT

Recall that in 1928, the Court in *Olmstead* declared that wiretapping did not constitute a Fourth Amendment violation. By the time *Olmstead* was decided, more than 25 states had made wiretapping a crime.

Six years later, responding to significant criticism of the *Olmstead* decision, Congress enacted the Federal Communications Act (FCA) of 1934. Section 605 of the Act provided that "no person not being authorized by the sender shall intercept any communication and divulge or publish the existence, contents, substance, purport, effect, or meaning of such intercepted communications to any person." Although § 605 did not expressly provide for an exclusionary rule, the Court in *Nardone v. United States*, 302 U.S. 379 (1937), held that federal officers could not introduce evidence obtained by illegal wiretapping in federal court.

Section 605 had significant limitations. States could still use evidence in violation of § 605 in state prosecutions. Further, § 605 only applied to wire com-

---

[73] Michael Barbaro & Tom Zeller, Jr., *A Face is Exposed for AOL Searcher No. 4417749*, N.Y. Times, Aug. 9, 2006.

munications and wiretapping, not to eavesdropping on nonwire communications. Thus, bugging was not covered.

In the words of Attorney General Nicholas Katzenback, § 605 was the "worst of all possible solutions." It prevented law enforcement from using information gleaned from wiretaps in court — even if pursuant to a warrant supported by probable cause. And it did little to restrict government wiretapping since it was interpreted not to prohibit such activity so long as the evidence was not used in court.

With the absence of Fourth Amendment protections and the limited protections of § 605, the federal government engaged in extensive wiretapping. During World War II, J. Edgar Hoover, the director of the FBI, successfully urged President Franklin Roosevelt to allow FBI wiretapping to investigate subversive activities and threats to national security. During the Truman Administration, the justification for electronic surveillance expanded to include domestic security as well. In the 1950s, the FBI then expanded its electronic surveillance due to national concern about Communism and communist infiltration of government. During the Cold War Era and beyond, Hoover ordered wiretapping of hundreds of people, including political enemies, dissidents, Supreme Court Justices, professors, celebrities, writers, and others. Among Hoover's files were dossiers on John Steinbeck, Ernest Hemingway, Charlie Chaplin, Marlon Brando, Muhammad Ali, Albert Einstein, John Lennon, and numerous presidents and members of Congress.[74]

The FBI also placed Martin Luther King Jr. under extensive surveillance. Hoover believed King was a Communist (which he was not), and disliked him personally. When the FBI's electronic surveillance of King revealed King's extramarital affairs, the FBI sent copies of the tapes to King along with a letter insinuating that he should commit suicide or else the tapes would be leaked to the public. The FBI also sent the tapes to King's wife and played them to President Lyndon Johnson.[75] In reflecting on the FBI's campaign against King, Frederick Schwarz and Aziz Huq note that an important role was played by Hoover's "personal animus against King, and his profound distaste for the social changes pressed by the civil rights movement." Schwarz and Huq also observe: "But without an institutional underpinning, Hoover's bias would not have taken the form of a massive, multiyear surveillance and harassment campaign. The war against King highlights what happens when checks and balances are abandoned."[76]

During this time, state police also conducted wiretapping. To the extent that this wiretapping was regulated, this regulation was purely that of the individual states. Section 605 only applied at the federal level. In an influential study, Samuel Dash, Richard Schwartz, and Robert Knowlton revealed that regulation of wiretapping by the states was often ineffective. There were numerous unauthorized wiretaps and few checks against abuses.[77]

---

[74] Daniel J. Solove, *Reconstructing Electronic Surveillance Law,* 72 Geo. Wash. L. Rev. 1264, 1273-74 (2004).

[75] David J. Garrow, *The FBI and Martin Luther King, Jr.* (1980).

[76] Frederick A.O. Schwarz, Jr. & Aziz Z. Huq, *Unchecked and Unbalanced: Presidential Power in a Time of Terror* 23 (2007).

[77] *See* Samuel Dash, Richard Schwartz & Robert Knowlton, *The Eavesdroppers* (1959).

2. TITLE III

In 1968, in response to *Katz v. United States* and *Berger v. New York*, Congress enacted Title III of the Omnibus Crime Control and Safe Streets Act of 1968, Pub. L. No. 90-351, codified at 18 U.S.C. §§ 2510–2520. This Act is commonly referred to as "Title III" or, subsequent to its amendment in 1986, as the "Wiretap Act."

Title III extended far beyond § 605; it applied to wiretaps by federal and state officials as well as by private parties. Title III required federal agents to apply for a warrant before wiretapping. The Act criminalized private wiretaps. However, if any party to the conversation consented to the tapping, then there was no violation of Title III.

Title III authorized the Attorney General to apply to a federal judge for an order authorizing the interception of a "wire or oral communication." A judge could not issue a court order unless there was probable cause. Many other procedural safeguards were established.

Title III excluded wiretaps for national security purposes from any restrictions at all. President Nixon frequently used the national security exception to place internal dissidents and radicals under surveillance. However, in *United States v. United States District Court* (the *Keith* case), 407 U.S. 297 (1972), the Court unanimously rejected Nixon's approach, stating that Title III's national security exception does not apply to internal threats but only to foreign threats.

3. THE ELECTRONIC COMMUNICATIONS PRIVACY ACT

In 1986, Congress modernized federal wiretap law by passing the Electronic Communications Privacy Act (ECPA).[78] The ECPA amended Title III (the Wiretap Act), and it also included two new acts in response to developments in computer technology and communication networks. Hence, federal electronic surveillance law on the domestic side contains three parts: (1) the Wiretap Act (the updated version of Title III, which ECPA shifted to its first Title); (2) the Stored Communications Act (SCA); and (3) the Pen Register Act.

Many of the provisions of federal electronic surveillance law apply not only to government officials, but to private individuals and entities as well. In particular, cases involving the violation of federal electronic surveillance law by private parties often occur in the employment context when employers desire to use forms of electronic surveillance on their employees.

Electronic surveillance law operates independently of the Fourth Amendment. Even if a search is reasonable under the Fourth Amendment,

---

[78] For more background on electronic surveillance law, see Patricia L. Bellia, *Surveillance Law Through Cyberlaw's Lens,* 72 Geo. Wash. L. Rev. 1375 (2004); Deirdre K. Mulligan, *Reasonable Expectations in Electronic Communications: A Critical Perspective on the Electronic Communications Privacy Act,* 72 Geo. Wash. L. Rev. 1557 (2004); Paul K. Ohm, *Parallel-Effect Statutes and E-mail "Warrants": Reframing the Internet Surveillance Debate,* 72 Geo. Wash. L. Rev. 1599 (2004); Susan Freiwald, *Online Surveillance: Remembering the Lessons of the Wiretap Act,* 56 Ala. L. Rev. 9 (2004). *See generally* Symposium, *The Future of Internet Surveillance Law,* 72 Geo. Wash. L. Rev. 1139-1617 (2004).

electronic surveillance law may bar the evidence. Even if a search is authorized by a judge under federal electronic surveillance law, the Fourth Amendment could still prohibit the wiretap.

Moreover, procedures for obtaining a court order under the Wiretap Act are more stringent than those for obtaining a search warrant under the Fourth Amendment. As an example of how the Wiretap Act is stricter, under the Fourth Amendment, any law enforcement official can apply for a warrant. Under the Wiretap Act, in contrast, only certain officials (prosecuting attorneys) can apply.

In at least one significant way, federal electronic surveillance law is broader than the Fourth Amendment. Under the Fourth Amendment, search warrants generally authorize a single entry and prompt search. Warrants must be narrowly circumscribed. They are not a license for unlimited and continued investigation. Under the Wiretap Act, however, courts can authorize continuing surveillance — 24 hours a day for a 30-day period. This period can also be extended.

In order to comprehend how each of the three acts comprising ECPA works, it is important to know that ECPA classifies all communications into three types: (1) "wire communications"; (2) "oral communications"; and (3) "electronic communications." Each type of communication is protected differently. As a general matter, wire communications receive the most protection and electronic communications receive the least.

Wire Communications. A "wire communication," defined in § 2510(1), involves all "aural transfers" that travel through a wire or a similar medium:

> (1) "wire communication" means any aural transfer made in whole or in part through the use of facilities for the transmission of communications by the aid of wire, cable, or other like connection between the point of origin and the point of reception (including the use of such connection in a switching station) furnished or operated by any person engaged in providing or operating such facilities for the transmission of interstate or foreign communications or communications affecting interstate or foreign commerce.

An "aural transfer" is a communication containing the human voice at any point. § 2510(18). The human voice need only be a minor part of the communication. Further, the human voice need not always be present throughout the journey of the communication. Therefore, a communication that once consisted of the human voice that has been translated into code or tones still qualifies as an "aural transfer."

The aural transfer must travel through wire (i.e., telephone wires or cable wires) or a similar medium. The entire journey from origin to destination need not take place through wire, as many communications travel through a host of different mediums — wire, radio, satellite, and so on. Only part of the communication's journey must be through a wire.

Oral Communications. The second type of communication under federal wiretap law is "oral communications." Pursuant to § 2510(2), an "oral communication" is a communication "uttered by a person exhibiting an expectation that such communication is not subject to interception under circumstances justifying such expectation." Oral communications are typically intercepted through bugs and other recording or transmitting devices.

Electronic Communications. The final type of communication is an "electronic communication." Under § 2510(12), an electronic communication consists of all non-wire and non-oral communications:

> (12) "electronic communication" means any transfer of signs, signals, writing, images, sounds, data, or intelligence of any nature transmitted in whole or in part by a wire, radio, electromagnetic, photoelectronic or photooptical system that affects interstate or foreign commerce, but does not include —
>
> (A) any wire or oral communication. . . .

In other words, an electronic communication consists of all communications that do not constitute wire or oral communications. An example of an electronic communication is an e-mail — at least as long as it does not contain the human voice.

Although electronic communications are protected under the Stored Communications Act as well as the Wiretap Act, they are treated differently than wire and oral communications. The most notable difference is that the exclusionary rule in the Wiretap Act does not apply to electronic communications. Therefore, wire or oral communications that fall within the Wiretap Act are protected by the exclusionary rule, but not when they fall within the Stored Communications Act (which has no exclusionary rule). Electronic communications are not protected by the exclusionary rule in the Wiretap Act or the Stored Communications Act.

(a) The Wiretap Act

Interceptions. The Wiretap Act, which is codified at Title I of ECPA, 18 U.S.C. §§ 2510–2522, governs the interception of communications. In particular, § 2511 provides that:

> (1) Except as otherwise specifically provided in this chapter any person who —
>
> > (a) intentionally intercepts, endeavors to intercept, or procures any other person to intercept or endeavor to intercept, any wire, oral, or electronic communication;
> >
> > (b) intentionally uses, endeavors to use, or procures any other person to use or endeavor to use any electronic, mechanical, or other device to intercept any oral communication when —
> >
> > > (i) such device is affixed to, or otherwise transmits a signal through, a wire, cable, or other like connection used in wire communication; or
> > >
> > > (ii) such device transmits communications by radio, or interferes with the transmission of such communication; or

(iii) such person knows, or has reason to know, that such device or any component thereof has been sent through the mail or transported in interstate or foreign commerce. . . .

(c) intentionally discloses, or endeavors to disclose, to any other person the contents of any wire, oral, or electronic communication, knowing or having reason to know that the information was obtained through the interception of a wire, oral, or electronic communication in violation of this subsection;

(d) intentionally uses, or endeavors to use, the contents of any wire, oral, or electronic communication, knowing or having reason to know that the information was obtained through the interception of a wire, oral, or electronic communication in violation of this subsection. . . .

As this provision indicates, the Wiretap Act applies to the intentional interception of a communication. To "intercept" a communication means to acquire its contents through the use of any "electronic, mechanical, or other device." § 2510(4). The classic example of an activity covered by the Act is the wiretapping of a phone conversation — a device is being used to listen to a conversation as it is occurring, as the words are moving through the wires. The Wiretap Act applies when communications are intercepted contemporaneously with their transmission. Once the communication is completed and stored, then the Wiretap Act no longer applies.

In *Bartnicki v. Vopper*, 532 U.S. 514 (2001) (Chapter 2), the Court held that § 2511(1)(c) violated the First Amendment by restricting disclosures involving matters of public concern.

Exclusionary Rule. Under the Wiretap Act, "any aggrieved person . . . may move to suppress the contents of any wire or oral communication intercepted pursuant to this chapter, or evidence derived therefrom." § 2518 (10)(a).

Penalties. Violations of the Wiretap Act can result in fines of a minimum of $10,000 per violation as well as up to five years' imprisonment. *See* §§ 2511(4)(a); 2520(c)(2)(B).

Court Orders. Pursuant to § 2518, an application for a court wiretapping or electronic surveillance order must be made under oath and contain a variety of information, including details to justify the agent's belief that a crime has been, is being, or will be committed; specific description of place where communications will be intercepted; description of the type of communication; and period of time of interception. The judge may require the applicant to furnish additional testimony or documentary evidence in support of the application. The judge must find probable cause and that the particular communications concerning that offense will be obtained through the interception. Further, the court must find that alternatives to wiretapping were attempted and failed, or reasonably appear to be unlikely to succeed or to be too dangerous. The order can last for up to 30 days and can be renewed.

Under the Wiretap Act, only certain government officials are able to apply to a court for a wiretapping order — for federal law enforcement agencies, the relevant party is the attorney general, or a deputy or assistant attorney general;

for state officials, the relevant party is the principal prosecuting attorney of a state or a local government, or any government attorney. In other words, the police themselves cannot obtain a wiretap order alone. The Wiretap Act also provides an exclusive list of crimes for which a wiretap order can be issued. The list is broad and includes most felonies. A wiretap order cannot be obtained, however, to investigate a misdemeanor.

Minimization. The Wiretap Act requires that interception must be minimized to avoid sweeping in communications beyond the purpose for which the order was sought. Pursuant to § 2518(6): "Every order and extension thereof shall contain a provision that the authorization to intercept shall be executed as soon as practicable, shall be conducted in such a way as to minimize the interception of communications not otherwise subject to interception under this chapter, and must terminate upon attainment of the authorized objective." For example, if law enforcement officials are wiretapping the home phone line of a person suspected of running an illegal gambling operation and the person's daughter is talking on the line to a friend about going to the movies, the officials should stop listening to the conversation.

Notice. After the surveillance is over, copies of the recorded conversations must be turned over to the court issuing the order. The court must notify the party that surveillance was undertaken within 90 days after the denial of a surveillance order or after the completion of the surveillance authorized by a granted surveillance order. § 2518(8)(d).

Exceptions. There are two notable exceptions under the Wiretap Act. First, the Act does not apply if one of the parties to the communication consents. § 2511(2)(c). For example, a person can secretly tap and record a communication to which that person is a party. Thus, secretly recording one's own phone conversations is not illegal under federal wiretap law. If they participate in the conversation, government agents and informants can record others without their knowledge. An exception to the consent exception is when an interception is carried out for the purpose of committing any criminal or tortious act. In that case, even when a party has consented, interception is illegal. § 2511(2)(d).

Second, a communications service provider is permitted "to intercept, disclose, or use that communication in the normal course of his employment while engaged in any activity which is a necessary incident to the rendition of his service or to the protection of the rights or property of the provider of that service." § 2511(2)(a). Also, a service provider may intentionally disclose intercepted communications to the proper authorities when criminal activity is afoot; with the consent of the originator, addressee, or intended recipient; or to any intermediary provider. § 2511(3).

(b) The Stored Communications Act

Stored Communications. Whereas communications in transmission are covered by the Wiretap Act, communications in storage are protected by the Stored Communications Act (SCA), codified at 18 U.S.C. §§ 2701–2711.[79] With many forms of modern communication, such as Internet service, communications and subscriber records are often maintained in storage by the electronic communications service provider. Section 2701 states:

> (a) Offense. — Except as provided in subsection (c) of this section whoever —
>
>> (1) intentionally accesses without authorization a facility through which an electronic communication service is provided; or
>>
>> (2) intentionally exceeds an authorization to access that facility; and thereby obtains, alters, or prevents authorized access to a wire or electronic communication while it is in electronic storage in such system shall be punished as provided in subsection (b) of this section.

The definition of "electronic storage" in the Wiretap Act also applies to the term as used in the SCA. "Electronic storage" means:

> (A) any temporary, intermediate storage of a wire or electronic communication incidental to the electronic transmission thereof; and
>
> (B) any storage of such communication by an electronic communications service for purposes of backup protection of such communication. § 2510(17).

Section 2701(a) does not apply to "the person or entity providing a wire or electronic communications service" (such as Internet Service Providers) or to "a user of that service with respect to a communication of or intended for that user." § 2701(c).

The SCA also forbids the disclosure of the contents of stored communications by communications service providers. *See* § 2702(a). There are a number of exceptions, including disclosures to the intended recipient of the communication, disclosures with the consent of the creator or recipient of the communication, disclosures that are "necessarily incident to the rendition of the service or to the protection of the rights or property of the provider of that service," and disclosures to a law enforcement agency under certain circumstances. *See* § 2702(b).

Penalties. The SCA has less severe criminal penalties and civil liability than Title I. Under § 2701(b), violations can result in fines of a minimum of $1,000 per violation and up to six months imprisonment. If the wiretap is done for commercial advantage or gain, then a violation can result in up to one year of imprisonment.

Exclusionary Rule. The SCA does not provide for an exclusionary rule.

Judicial Authority for Obtaining Stored Communications. Under the SCA, the judicial process required for obtaining permission to access stored

---

[79] For more background about the SCA, see Orin S. Kerr, *A User's Guide to the Stored Communications Act, and a Legislator's Guide to Amending It,* 72 Geo. Wash. L. Rev. 1208 (2004).

communications held by electronic communications service providers is much less rigorous than under the Wiretap Act. If the government seeks access to the contents of a communication that has been in storage for 180 days or less, then it must first obtain a warrant supported by probable cause. § 2703(a). If the government wants to access a communication that has been in storage for more than 180 days, the government must provide prior notice to the subscriber and obtain an administrative subpoena, a grand jury subpoena, a trial subpoena, or a court order. § 2703(b). The court order does not require probable cause, only "specific and articulable facts showing that there are reasonable grounds" to believe communications are relevant to the criminal investigation. 18 U.S.C. § 2703(d). However, if the government seeks to access a communication that has been in storage for more than 180 days and does not want to provide prior notice to the subscriber, it must obtain a warrant. § 2703(b). Notice to the subscriber that the government obtained her communications can be delayed for up to 90 days. § 2705.

Court Orders to Obtain Subscriber Records. According to § 2703(c)(1)(B), communication service providers must disclose subscriber information (i.e., identifying information, address, phone number, etc.) to the government under certain circumstances:

> (B) A provider of electronic communication service or remote computing service shall disclose a record or other information pertaining to a subscriber to or customer of such service (not including the contents of communications covered by subsection (a) or (b) of this section) to a governmental entity only when the governmental entity —
>
>> (i) obtains a warrant issued under the Federal Rules of Criminal Procedure or equivalent State warrant;
>> (ii) obtains a court order for such disclosure under subsection (d) of this section;
>> (iii) has the consent of the subscriber or customer to such disclosure

Communications service providers who disclose stored communications in accordance with any of the above orders or subpoenas cannot be held liable for that disclosure. *See* § 2703(e).

Exceptions. Similar to the Wiretap Act, the SCA also has a consent exception, see § 2702(b), and a service provider exception, see § 2701(c)(1). Unlike the service provider exception for the Wiretap Act, which allows interceptions on a limited basis (those necessary to provide the communications service), the SCA's exception is broader, entirely exempting "the person or entity providing a wire or electronic communications service." § 2701(c)(1).

(c) The Pen Register Act

The Pen Register Act, codified at 18 U.S.C. §§ 3121–3127, governs pen registers and trap and trace devices — and their modern analogues. Recall *Smith v. Maryland,* earlier in this chapter, where the Court held that the Fourth Amendment did not extend to pen register information. The Pen Register Act

no 4th Amd protection

provides some limited protection for such information. Subject to certain exceptions, "no person may install or use a pen register or a trap and trace device without first obtaining a court order." § 3121(a). Traditionally, a pen register was a device that records the telephone numbers dialled from a particular telephone line (phone numbers of outgoing calls). A trap and trace device is the reverse of a pen register — it records the telephone numbers where incoming calls originate.

Definition of "Pen Register." The Pen Register Act defines pen registers more broadly than phone number information:

> [T]he term "pen register" means a device or process which records or decodes dialing, routing, addressing, or signaling information transmitted by an instrument or facility from which a wire or electronic communication is transmitted, provided, however, that such information shall not include the contents of any communication . . . 18 U.S.C. § 3127(3)

Court Orders. If the government certifies that "the information likely to be obtained by such installation and use is relevant to an ongoing investigation," § 3123(a), then courts "shall authorize the installation and use of a pen register or a trap and trace device for a period not to exceed sixty days." § 3123(c). This standard is a low threshold. As Susan Freiwald contends: "[T]he language of the [pen register] court order requirement raises doubt as to its efficacy as a guard against fishing expeditions. . . . The relevance standard in the transaction records provision allows law enforcement to obtain records of people who may be tangentially involved in a crime, even as innocent victims."[80]

Enforcement. There is no exclusionary rule for violations of the Pen Register Act. Rather than a suppression remedy, the Pen Register Act provides: "Whoever knowingly violates subsection (a) shall be fined under this title or imprisoned not more than one year, or both." § 3121(d).

4. THE COMMUNICATIONS ASSISTANCE FOR LAW ENFORCEMENT ACT

In *United States v. New York Telephone*, 434 U.S. 159 (1977), the Supreme Court held that 18 U.S.C. § 2518(4) required telecommunications providers to furnish "any assistance necessary to accomplish an electronic interception." However, the issue of whether a provider had to create and design its technology to facilitate authorized electronic surveillance remained an open question.

In the 1980s, new communications technology was developed to enable more wireless communications — cellular telephones, microwave, and satellite communications. As a result of fears that these new technologies would be harder to monitor, the law enforcement community successfully convinced Congress to

---

[80] Susan Freiwald, *Uncertain Privacy: Communications Attributes After the Digital Telephony Act*, 69 S. Cal. L. Rev. 949, 1005-06 (1996).

force telecommunications providers to ensure that the government could continue to monitor electronic communications.[81]

The Communications Assistance for Law Enforcement Act (CALEA) of 1994, Pub. L. No. 103-414, (also known as the "Digital Telephony Act") requires telecommunication providers to help facilitate the government in executing legally authorized surveillance. Congress appropriated federal funding of $500 million to telephone companies to make the proposed changes.

Requirements. CALEA requires all telecommunications providers to be able to isolate and intercept electronic communications and be able to deliver them to law enforcement personnel. If carriers provide an encryption service to users, then they must decrypt the communications. CALEA permits the telecommunications industry to develop the technology. Under a "safe harbor" provision, carriers that comply with accepted industry standards are in compliance with CALEA. 47 U.S.C. § 1006(a)(2).

Limits. CALEA contains some important limits. Carriers must "facilitat[e] authorized communications interceptions and access to call-identifying information . . . in a manner that protects . . . the privacy and security of communications and call-identifying information not authorized to be intercepted." § 1002(a)(4)(A). Further, CALEA is designed to provide "law enforcement no more and no less access to information than it had in the past." H.R. Rep. No. 103-827, pt. 1, at 22. Additionally, CALEA does not apply to "information services," such as e-mail and Internet access. §§ 1001(8)(C)(i), 1002(b)(2)(A).

Voice over Internet Protocol (VoIP). A new way to make telephone calls is to use a broadband Internet connection to transmit the call. This technique, VoIP, converts a voice signal into a digital signal that travels over the Internet and connects to a phone number. On August 4, 2004, the FCC unanimously adopted a Notice of Proposed Rulemaking and Declaratory Ruling regarding VoIP and CALEA. *In the Matter of Communications Assistance for Law Enforcement Act and Broadband Access and Services*, FCC 04-187 (Aug. 4, 2004). It tentatively declared that CALEA applies to any facilities-based providers of any type of broadband Internet access service — including wireline, cable modem, satellite, wireless, and powerline — and to managed or mediated VoIP services. This conclusion was based on an FCC judgment that these services fall under CALEA statutory language as "a replacement for a substantial portion of the local telephone service." 47 U.S.C. § 1001(8)B)(ii).

Susan Landau and Whitfield Diffie argue that inserting wiretap requirements into Internet protocols will make the Internet less secure. A system that permits "legally authorized security breaches" (such as a wiretap by law enforcement officers) is also more open to unauthorized security breaches (such as hacking and other kinds of unlawful intrusions). They argue that "[o]n balance we are

---

[81] For a detailed analysis of CALEA, see Susan Freiwald, *Uncertain Privacy: Communication Attributes After the Digital Telephony Act*, 69 S. Cal. L. Rev. 949 (1996).

better off with a secure computer infrastructure than with one that builds surveillance into the network fabric."[82]

5. THE USA PATRIOT ACT

On the morning of September 11, 2001, terrorists hijacked four planes and crashed three of them into the World Trade Center and the Pentagon, killing thousands of people. The nation was awakened into a world filled with new frightening dangers. Shortly after the September 11 attacks, a still unknown person or persons sent letters laced with the deadly bacteria anthrax through the mail to several prominent individuals in the news media and in politics. Acting with great haste, Congress passed a sweeping new law expanding the government's electronic surveillance powers in many significant ways.[83] Called the "Uniting and Strengthening America By Providing Appropriate Tools Required To Intercept and Obstruct Terrorism Act" (USA PATRIOT Act), the Act made a number of substantial changes to several statutes, including the federal electronic surveillance statutes.

Definition of Terrorism. Section 802 of the USA PATRIOT Act added to 18 U.S.C. § 2331 a new definition of "domestic terrorism." According to the Act, domestic terrorism involves "acts dangerous to human life that are a violation of the criminal laws of the United States or of any State" that "appear to be intended: (i) to intimidate or coerce a civilian population; (ii) to influence the policy of a government by intimidation or coercion; or (iii) to affect the conduct of a government by mass destruction, assassination, or kidnapping; and . . . occur primarily within the territorial jurisdiction of the United States." According to many proponents of civil liberties, this definition is very broad and could potentially encompass many forms of civil disobedience, which, although consisting of criminal conduct (minor violence, threats, property damage), includes conduct that has historically been present in many political protests and has never been considered to be terrorism.

Delayed Notice of Search Warrants. Under the Fourth Amendment, the government must obtain a warrant and provide notice to a person before conducting a search or seizure. Case law provided for certain limited exceptions. Section 213 of the USA PATRIOT Act adds a provision to 18 U.S.C. § 3103a, enabling the government to delay notice if the court concludes that there is "reasonable cause" that immediate notice will create an "adverse result" such as physical danger, the destruction of evidence, delayed trial, flight from prosecution, and other circumstances. § 3103a(b). Warrants enabling a covert search with delayed notice are often referred to as "sneak and peek" warrants. Civil libertarians consider "sneak and peek" warrants dangerous because they authorize covert searches, thus preventing individuals from safeguarding their rights during the search. Moreover, there is little supervision of the government's

---

[82] Susan Landau & Whitfield Diffie, *Privacy on the Line* 331, 328 (2d ed. 2007).

[83] For background about the passage of the USA PATRIOT Act, see Beryl A. Howell, *Seven Weeks: The Making of the USA Patriot Act*, 72 Geo. Wash. L. Rev. 1145 (2004).

carrying out of the search. Law enforcement officials argue that covert searches are necessary to avoid tipping off suspects that there is an investigation under way.

New Definition of Pen Registers and Trap and Trace Devices. Under the Pen Register Act of the ECPA, §§ 3121 *et seq.*, the definitions of pen registers and trap and trace devices focused primarily on telephone numbers. A pen register was defined under 18 U.S.C. § 3127(3) as

> a device which records or decodes electronic or other impulses which identify the numbers dialed or otherwise transmitted on the telephone line to which such device is attached. . . .

Section 216 of the USA PATRIOT Act changed the definition to read:

> a device *or process* which records or decodes *dialing, routing, addressing, or signaling information transmitted by an instrument or facility from which a wire or electronic communication is transmitted, provided, however, that such information shall not include the contents of any communication* is attached . . . (changes emphasized).

These changes altered the definition of a pen register from applying not only to telephone numbers but also to Internet addresses, e-mail addressing information (the "to" and "from" lines on e-mail), and the routing information of a wide spectrum of communications. The inclusion of "or process" after "device" enlarges the means by which such routing information can be intercepted beyond the use of a physical device. The definition of a trap and trace device was changed in a similar way. Recall that under the Pen Register Act, a court order to obtain such information does not require probable cause, but merely certification that "the information likely to be obtained by such installation and use is relevant to an ongoing criminal investigation." 18 U.S.C. § 3123. The person whose communications are subject to this order need not even be a criminal suspect; all that the government needs to certify is relevance to an investigation.

Recall *Smith v. Maryland* earlier in this chapter, where the Court held that pen registers were not protected under the Fourth Amendment. Does the new definition of pen register and trap and trace device under the USA PATRIOT Act go beyond *Smith v. Maryland*? Are Internet addresses and e-mail addressing information analogous to pen registers?

Private Right of Action for Government Disclosures. The USA PATRIOT Act adds a provision to the Stored Communications Act that provides for civil actions against the United States for any "willful" violations. 18 U.S.C. § 2712. The court may assess actual damages or $10,000 (whichever is greater) and litigation costs. Such an action must first be presented before the "appropriate department or agency under the procedures of the Federal Tort Claims Act."

6. STATE ELECTRONIC SURVEILLANCE LAW

A number of states have enacted their own versions of electronic surveillance law, some of which are more protective than federal electronic surveillance law. For example, several states require the consent of all parties to a conversation. Unless all parties consent, these states require a warrant for a wiretap. In contrast, federal wiretap law allows law enforcement to listen in to a conversation if any party to it consents to the surveillance.

One prominent example of a more protective state law was the indictment on July 30, 1999, of Linda Tripp on two counts of violating Maryland's wiretapping law. At the request of the Office of the Independent Counsel, Linda Tripp had secretly taped a phone conversation she had with Monica Lewinsky about Lewinsky's affair with President Clinton. Tripp then disclosed the contents of that conversation to a news magazine. Possible penalties under Maryland law included up to ten years' imprisonment and a $20,000 fine. Maryland's wiretapping law, in contrast to federal wiretap law, requires the consent of the other party to a communication. Tripp was indicted by a Maryland grand jury. Although Tripp was protected by a federal grant of immunity from prosecution, Maryland was not part of the immunity agreement and could prosecute Tripp. After a judicial ruling suppressing certain evidence, the case against Tripp was dropped.

Massachusetts also has an all-party-consent electronic surveillance law. Consider *Commonwealth v. Hyde,* 750 N.E.2d 963 (Mass. 2001). The defendant Michael Hyde was stopped by the police for a routine auto stop. The police searched the defendant, his passenger, and his car. No traffic citation was issued. Hyde filed a complaint at the police station about the stop, and he provided a hidden audio recording he had made of the encounter. The police subsequently charged Hyde with illegal electronic surveillance in violation of state law, G.L. c. 272, § 99, which provides that "any person who willfully commits an interception, attempts to commit an interception, or procures any other person to commit an interception or to attempt to commit an interception of any wire or oral communication shall be fined not more than ten thousand dollars, or imprisoned in the state prison for not more than five years, or imprisoned in a jail or house of correction for not more than two and one half years, or both so fined and given one such imprisonment." Hyde was convicted and sentenced to six months probation and a $500 fine.

The *Hyde* court concluded:

> We conclude that the Legislature intended G.L. c. 272, § 99, strictly to prohibit all secret recordings by members of the public, including recordings of police officers or other public officials interacting with members of the public, when made without their permission or knowledge. . . .
>
> We reject the defendant's argument that the statute is not applicable because the police officers were performing their public duties, and, therefore, had no reasonable expectation of privacy in their words. The statute's preamble expresses the Legislature's general concern that "the uncontrolled development and unrestricted use of modern electronic surveillance devices pose[d] grave dangers to the privacy of all citizens of the commonwealth" and this concern

was relied on to justify the ban on the public's clandestine use of such devices. While we recognize that G.L. c. 272, § 99, was designed to prohibit the use of electronic surveillance devices by private individuals because of the serious threat they pose to the "privacy of all citizens," the plain language of the statute, which is the best indication of the Legislature's ultimate intent, contains nothing that would protect, on the basis of privacy rights, the recording that occurred here. In *Commonwealth v. Jackson, supra* at 506, 349 N.E.2d 337, this court rejected the argument that, because a kidnapper has no legitimate privacy interest in telephone calls made for ransom purposes, the secret electronic recording of that conversation by the victim's brother would not be prohibited under G.L. c. 272, § 99: "[W]e would render meaningless the Legislature's careful choice of words if we were to interpret 'secretly' as encompassing only those situations where an individual has a reasonable expectation of privacy." . . .

Further, if the tape recording here is deemed proper on the ground that public officials are involved, then the door is opened even wider to electronic "bugging" or secret audio tape recording (both are prohibited by the statute and both are indistinguishable in the injury they inflict) of virtually every encounter or meeting between a person and a public official, whether the meeting or encounter is one that is stressful (like the one in this case or, perhaps, a session with a tax auditor) or nonstressful (like a routine meeting between a parent and a teacher in a public school to discuss a good student's progress). The door once opened would be hard to close, and the result would contravene the statute's broad purpose and the Legislature's clear prohibition of *all* secret interceptions and recordings by private citizens.

In dissent, Chief Justice Marshall wrote:

The purpose of G.L. c. 272, § 99, is not to shield public officials from exposure of their wrongdoings. I have too great a respect for the Legislature to read any such meaning into a statute whose purpose is plain, and points in another direction entirely. Where the legislative intent is explicit, it violates a fundamental rule of statutory construction to reach a result that is plainly contrary to that objective. To hold that the Legislature intended to allow police officers to conceal possible misconduct behind a cloak of privacy requires a more affirmative showing than this statute allows.

In our Republic the actions of public officials taken in their public capacities are not protected from exposure. Citizens have a particularly important role to play when the official conduct at issue is that of the police. Their role cannot be performed if citizens must fear criminal reprisals when they seek to hold government officials responsible by recording — secretly recording on occasion — an interaction between a citizen and a police officer. . . .

The court's ruling today also threatens the ability of the press — print and electronic — to perform its constitutional role of watchdog. As the court construes the Massachusetts wiretapping statute, there is no principled distinction to explain why members of the media would not be held to the same standard as all other citizens.

A few years later, Hyde was convicted again of secretly recording a police officer who had pulled him over in a traffic stop. Are all-party electronic surveillance laws too broad? What kinds of exceptions, if any, should be made?

Note as well that these all-party-consent statutes will also regulate surveillance by private sector entities. In *Kearney v. Salomon Smith Barney*, 137 P.2d 914 (Cal. 2006), two California clients sued a financial institution because their telephone calls to brokers in the institution's Georgia office were recorded without their consent. A California statute prohibited recording a telephone conversation without consent of all parties to it. In contrast, a Georgia statute permitted recording a telephone conversation if consent of one party had been granted. The California Supreme Court concluded that "comparative impairment analysis supports the application of California law in this context." It reached this conclusion by assessing the relative harm suffered to each state due to this conflict of law:

> [I]n light of the substantial number of businesses operating in California that maintain out-of-state offices or telephone operators, a resolution of this conflict permitting all such businesses to regularly and routinely record telephone conversations made to or from California clients or consumers without the clients' or consumers' knowledge or consent would significantly impair the privacy policy guaranteed by California law, and potentially would place local California businesses (that would continue to be subject to California's protective privacy law) at an unfair competitive disadvantage vis-à-vis their out-of-state counterparts. At the same time, application of California law will not have a significant detrimental effect on Georgia's interests as embodied in the applicable Georgia law, because applying California law (1) will not adversely affect any privacy interest protected by Georgia law, (2) will affect only those business telephone calls in Georgia that are made to or are received from California clients, and (3) with respect to such calls, will not prevent a business located in Georgia from implementing or maintaining a practice of recording *all* such calls, but will require only that the business *inform* its clients or customers, at the outset of the call, of the company's policy of recording such calls. (. . . if a business informs a client or customer at the outset of a telephone call that the call is being recorded, the recording would not violate the applicable California statute.)

When state government officials are engaging in electronic surveillance, they are often subject to much less public scrutiny than their federal counterparts. Charles Kennedy and Peter Swire have concluded that there are likely to be significant differences between federal and state electronic surveillance because of differences in the respective "[i]nstitutions, procedures and training" of law enforcement personnel:

> Because state procedures are watched less systematically by the press and civil liberties organizations, abuses at the state level, whether deliberate or the result of inexperience, may not be detected. The under-reporting of state wiretaps . . . is both a symptom of and a contributing factor to this relative lack of oversight. The simple fact is that half of the states have wiretap powers, yet reported no wiretaps in 2001. The utter failure to file the annual wiretap report would be unthinkable at the federal level. In addition, the under-reporting of state wiretaps keeps the use and possible misuse of state wiretaps less visible.[84]

As noted above, moreover, wiretap orders over the last decade have increasingly become a phenomenon of state rather than federal courts. Yet, as Kennedy and Swire observe, we know far less about how state law enforcement

---

[84] Charles H. Kennedy & Peter P. Swire, *State Wiretaps and Electronic Surveillance After September 11,* 54 Hastings L.J. 971 (2003).

agencies make use of their wiretap powers than federal ones. As for the lack of state wiretap reports from many states, the obligation to file a report with the Administrative Office of the U.S. Courts extends only to instances when the states actually make use of these powers. In other words, the Administrative Office does not require reports to be filed if no interception activity took place in the state during a given year.[85] As a simple, initial step at ending the ambiguity about the possible under-reporting of state wiretap orders, should states be required to file a report even if no surveillance activity takes place in it during a particular year?

D. DIGITAL SEARCHES AND SEIZURES

1. SEARCHING COMPUTERS AND ELECTRONIC DEVICES

The Scope of Warrants to Search Computers. In *United States v. Lacy,* 119 F.3d 742 (9th Cir. 1997), the defendant challenged a search warrant authorizing the seizure of his computer hard drive and disks. The defendant contended that the warrant was too general because it applied to his entire computer system. The court upheld the warrant because "this type of generic classification is acceptable when a more precise description is not possible." Several other courts have followed a similar approach as in *Lacy,* upholding generic warrants. In *United States v. Upham,* 168 F.3d 532 (1st Cir. 1999), the court reasoned: "A sufficient chance of finding some needles in the computer haystack was established by the probable-cause showing in the warrant application; and a search of a computer and co-located disks is not inherently more intrusive than the physical search of an entire house for a weapon or drugs." *See also United States v. Hay,* 231 F.3d 630 (9th Cir. 2000) (following *Lacy* and upholding a "generic" warrant application).[86]

However, there are limits to the scope of a search of a computer. In *United States v. Carey,* 172 F.3d 1268 (10th Cir. 1999), an officer obtained a warrant to search a computer for records about illegal drug distribution. When the officer stumbled upon a pornographic file, he began to search for similar files. The court concluded that these actions amounted to an expansion of the scope of the search and would require the obtaining of a second warrant.

In *United States v. Campos,* 221 F.3d 1143 (10th Cir. 2000), the defendant e-mailed two images of child pornography to a person he talked to in a chat room. The person informed the FBI, and the FBI obtained a warrant to search the defendant's home and computer. The agents seized the defendant's computer, and a search revealed the two images of child pornography as well as six other images of child pornography. The defendant challenged the search as beyond the scope of the warrant because the agents "had grounds to search only for the two

---

[85] Paul Schwartz, *German and U.S. Telecommunications Privacy Law,* 54 Hastings L.J. 751, 760 (2003).

[86] For more about computer searches, see Raphael Winnick, *Searches and Seizures of Computers and Computer Data,* 88 Harv. J.L. & Tech. 75 (1994).

images that had been sent." However, the court rejected the defendant's contention, quoting from the FBI's explanation why it is not feasible to search only for particular computer files in one's home:

> . . . Computer storage devices . . . can store the equivalent of thousands of pages of information. Especially when the user wants to conceal criminal evidence, he often stores it in random order with deceptive file names. This requires searching authorities to examine all the stored data to determine whether it is included in the warrant. This sorting process can take weeks or months, depending on the volume of data stored, and it would be impractical to attempt this kind of data search on site. . . .
>
> Searching computer systems for criminal evidence is a highly technical process requiring expert skill and a properly controlled environment. The wide variety of computer hardware and software available requires even computer experts to specialize in some systems and applications, so it is difficult to know before a search which expert should analyze the system and its data. . . . Since computer evidence is extremely vulnerable to tampering or destruction (both from external sources or from destructive code embedded into the system as "booby trap"), the controlled environment of a laboratory is essential to its complete analysis. . . .

Computer Searches and Seizures. Searches and seizures for digital information in computers present some unique conceptual puzzles for existing Fourth Amendment doctrine. Thomas Clancy contends:

> [C]omputers are containers. . . . They . . . contain electronic evidence, that is, a series of digitally stored 0s and 1s that, when combined with a computer program, yield such items as images, words, and spreadsheets. Accordingly, the traditional standards of the Fourth Amendment regulate obtaining the evidence in containers that happen to be computers.[87]

But is a computer a single container or is each computer file its own container? Orin Kerr argues:

> A single physical storage device can store the private files of thousands of different users. It would be quite odd if looking at one file on a server meant that the entire server had been searched, and that the police could then analyze everything on the server, perhaps belonging to thousands of different people, without any restriction.[88]

Is copying a computer file or other digital information a seizure under the Fourth Amendment? In *United States v. Gorshkov*, 2001 WL 1024026 (W.D. Wash. 2001), the FBI remotely copied the contents of the defendant's computer in Russia. The court held: "The agents' act of copying the data on the Russian computers was not a seizure under the Fourth Amendment because it did not interfere with Defendant's or anyone else's possessory interest in the data." However, as Susan Brenner and Barbara Frederiksen contend:

---

[87] Thomas K. Clancy, *The Fourth Amendment Aspects of Computer Searches and Seizures: A Perspective and a Primer*, 75 Miss. L.J. 193, 196 (2005).

[88] Orin S. Kerr, *Searches and Seizures in a Digital World*, 119 Harv. L. Rev. 531, 556 (2005).

[T]he information contained in computer files clearly belongs to the owner of the files. The ownership of information is similar to the contents of a private conversation in which the information belongs to the parties to the conversation. Copying computer data is analogous to recording a conversation. . . . Therefore, copying computer files should be treated as a seizure.[89]

Password-Protected Files. In *Trulock v. Freeh,* 275 F.3d 391 (4th Cir. 2001), Notra Trulock and Linda Conrad shared a computer but maintained separate files protected by passwords. They did not know each other's password and could not access each other's files. When FBI officials, without a warrant, asked to search and seize the computer, Conrad consented. The court held that the FBI could not search Trulock's files since Trulock had not consented:

> Consent to search in the absence of a warrant may, in some circumstances, be given by a person other than the target of the search. Two criteria must be met in order for third party consent to be effective. First, the third party must have authority to consent to the search. Second, the third party's consent must be voluntary. . . .
>
> We conclude that, based on the facts in the complaint, Conrad lacked authority to consent to the search of Trulock's files. Conrad and Trulock both used a computer located in Conrad's bedroom and each had joint access to the hard drive. Conrad and Trulock, however, protected their personal files with passwords; Conrad did not have access to Trulock's passwords. Although Conrad had authority to consent to a general search of the computer, her authority did not extend to Trulock's password-protected files.

UNITED STATES V. ANDRUS

483 F.3d 711 (10th Cir. 2007)

[Federal authorities believed that Ray Andrus was downloading child pornography to his home computer. Ray Andrus resided at his parents' house. Federal officials obtained the consent of Dr. Andrus (Andrus's father) to search the home. He also consented to their searching any computers in the home. The officials went into Ray Andrus's bedroom and a forensic expert examined the contents of the computer's hard drive with forensic software. The software enabled direct access to the computer, bypassing any password protection the user put on it. The officials discovered child pornography on the computer. Later, the officials learned that Ray Andrus had protected his computer with a password and that his father did not know the password. Is the father's consent to search the computer valid since he did not know the password?]

MURPHY, J. . . . Subject to limited exceptions, the Fourth Amendment prohibits warrantless searches of an individual's home or possessions. Voluntary consent to a police search, given by the individual under investigation or by a third party with authority over the subject property, is a well-established exception to the warrant requirement. Valid third party consent can arise either

---

[89] Susan W. Brenner & Barbara A. Frederiksen, *Computer Searches and Seizures: Some Unresolved Issues,* 8 Mich. Telecomm. & Tech. L. Rev. 39, 111-12 (2002).

through the third party's actual authority or the third party's apparent authority. A third party has actual authority to consent to a search "if that third party has either (1) mutual use of the property by virtue of joint access, or (2) control for most purposes." Even where actual authority is lacking, however, a third party has apparent authority to consent to a search when an officer reasonably, even if erroneously, believes the third party possesses authority to consent. *See Georgia v. Randolph,* 547 U.S. 103 (2006).

Whether apparent authority exists is an objective, totality-of-the-circumstances inquiry into whether the facts available to the officers at the time they commenced the search would lead a reasonable officer to believe the third party had authority to consent to the search. When the property to be searched is an object or container, the relevant inquiry must address the third party's relationship to the object. In *Randolph,* the Court explained, "The constant element in assessing Fourth Amendment reasonableness in consent cases . . . is the great significance given to widely shared social expectations." For example, the Court said, "[W]hen it comes to searching through bureau drawers, there will be instances in which even a person clearly belonging on the premises as an occupant may lack any perceived authority to consent." . . .

It may be unreasonable for law enforcement to believe a third party has authority to consent to the search of an object typically associated with a high expectation of privacy, especially when the officers know or should know the owner has indicated the intent to exclude the third party from using or exerting control over the object.

Courts considering the issue have attempted to analogize computers to other items more commonly seen in Fourth Amendment jurisprudence. Individuals' expectations of privacy in computers have been likened to their expectations of privacy in "a suitcase or briefcase." Password-protected files have been compared to a "locked footlocker inside the bedroom." *Trulock v. Freeh,* 275 F.3d 391, 403 (4th Cir. 2001).

Given the pervasiveness of computers in American homes, this court must reach some, at least tentative, conclusion about the category into which personal computers fall. A personal computer is often a repository for private information the computer's owner does not intend to share with others. . . .

The inquiry into whether the owner of a highly personal object has indicated a subjective expectation of privacy traditionally focuses on whether the subject suitcase, footlocker, or other container is physically locked. Determining whether a computer is "locked," or whether a reasonable officer should know a computer may be locked, presents a challenge distinct from that associated with other types of closed containers. Unlike footlockers or suitcases, where the presence of a locking device is generally apparent by looking at the item, a "lock" on the data within a computer is not apparent from a visual inspection of the outside of the computer, especially when the computer is in the "off" position prior to the search. Data on an entire computer may be protected by a password, with the password functioning as a lock, or there may be multiple users of a computer, each of whom has an individual and personalized password-protected "user profile." . . .

Courts addressing the issue of third party consent in the context of computers, therefore, have examined officers' knowledge about password protection as an indication of whether a computer is "locked" in the way a footlocker would be. For example, in *Trulock,* the Fourth Circuit held a live-in girlfriend lacked actual authority to consent to a search of her boyfriend's computer files where the girlfriend told police she and her boyfriend shared the household computer but had separate password-protected files that were inaccessible to the other. The court in that case explained, "Although Conrad had authority to consent to a general search of the computer, her authority did not extend to Trulock's password-protected files." . . .

In addition to password protection, courts also consider the location of the computer within the house and other indicia of household members' access to the computer in assessing third party authority. Third party apparent authority to consent to a search has generally been upheld when the computer is located in a common area of the home that is accessible to other family members under circumstances indicating the other family members were not excluded from using the computer. In contrast, where the third party has affirmatively disclaimed access to or control over the computer or a portion of the computer's files, even when the computer is located in a common area of the house, courts have been unwilling to find third party authority.

Andrus' case presents facts that differ somewhat from those in other cases. Andrus' computer was located in a bedroom occupied by the homeowner's fifty-one year old son rather than in a true common area. Dr. Andrus, however, had unlimited access to the room. Law enforcement officers did not ask specific questions about Dr. Andrus' use of the computer, but Dr. Andrus said nothing indicating the need for such questions. *Cf. Trulock,* 275 F.3d at 398 (when law enforcement questioned third party girlfriend about computer, she indicated she and boyfriend had separate password-protected files). The resolution of this appeal turns on whether the officers' belief in Dr. Andrus' authority was reasonable, despite the lack of any affirmative assertion by Dr. Andrus that he used the computer and despite the existence of a user profile indicating Ray Andrus' intent to exclude other household members from using the computer. For the reasons articulated below, this court concludes the officers' belief in Dr. Andrus' authority was reasonable. . . .

First, the officers knew Dr. Andrus owned the house and lived there with family members. Second, the officers knew Dr. Andrus' house had internet access and that Dr. Andrus paid the Time Warner internet and cable bill. Third, the officers knew the email address bandrus@kc.rr.com had been activated and used to register on a website that provided access to child pornography. Fourth, although the officers knew Ray Andrus lived in the center bedroom, they also knew that Dr. Andrus had access to the room at will. Fifth, the officers saw the computer in plain view on the desk in Andrus' room and it appeared available for use by other household members. Furthermore, the record indicates Dr. Andrus did not say or do anything to indicate his lack of ownership or control over the computer when Cheatham asked for his consent to conduct a computer search. It is uncontested that Dr. Andrus led the officers to the bedroom in which the computer was located, and, even after he saw Kanatzar begin to work on the computer, Dr. Andrus remained silent about any lack of authority he had over the computer. Even if Ray Andrus' computer was protected with a user name and password, there is no indication in the record that the officers knew or had reason to believe such protections were in place.

Andrus argues his computer's password protection indicated his computer was "locked" to third parties, a fact the officers would have known had they asked questions of Dr. Andrus prior to searching the computer. Under our case law, however, officers are not obligated to ask questions unless the circumstances are ambiguous. In essence, by suggesting the onus was on the officers to ask about password protection prior to searching the computer, despite the absence of any indication that Dr. Andrus' access to the computer was limited by a password, Andrus necessarily submits there is inherent ambiguity whenever police want to search a household computer and a third party has not affirmatively provided information about his own use of the computer or about password protection. Andrus' argument presupposes, however, that password protection of home computers is so common that a reasonable officer ought to know password protection is likely. Andrus has neither made this argument directly nor proffered any evidence to demonstrate a high incidence of password protection among home computer users. . . .

Viewed under the requisite totality-of-the-circumstances analysis, the facts known to the officers at the time the computer search commenced created an objectively reasonable perception that Dr. Andrus was, at least, *one* user of the computer. That objectively reasonable belief would have been enough to give Dr. Andrus apparent authority to consent to a search. Even if Dr. Andrus had no actual ability to use the computer and the computer was password protected, these mistakes of fact do not negate a determination of Dr. Andrus' apparent authority. In this case, the district court found Agent Cheatham properly halted the search when further conversation with Dr. Andrus revealed he did not use the computer and that Andrus' computer was the only computer in the house. These later revelations, however, have no bearing on the reasonableness of the officers' belief in Dr. Andrus' authority at the outset of the computer search.

McKAY, J., dissenting. This case concerns the reasonable expectation of privacy associated with password-protected computers. In examining the contours of a third party's apparent authority to consent to the search of a home computer, the majority correctly indicates that the extent to which law enforcement knows or should reasonably suspect that password protection is enabled is critical. . . . I take issue with the majority's implicit holding that law enforcement may use software deliberately designed to automatically bypass computer password protection based on third-party consent without the need to make a reasonable inquiry regarding the presence of password protection and the third party's access to that password.

The presence of security on Defendant's computer is undisputed. Yet, the majority curiously argues that Defendant's use of password protection is inconsequential because Defendant failed to argue that computer password protection is "commonplace." Of course, the decision provides no guidance on what would constitute sufficient proof of the prevalence of password protection, nor does it explain why the court could not take judicial notice that password protection is a standard feature of operating systems. Despite recognizing the "pervasiveness of computers in American homes," and the fact that the "personal computer is often a repository for private information the computer's owner does not intend to share with others," the majority requires the invocation of magical language in order to give effect to Defendant's subjective intent to exclude others from accessing the computer. . . .

The unconstrained ability of law enforcement to use forensic software such as the EnCase program to bypass password protection without first determining whether such passwords have been enabled does not "exacerbate[]" this difficulty; rather, it avoids it altogether, simultaneously and dangerously sidestepping the Fourth Amendment in the process. Indeed, the majority concedes that if such protection were "shown to be commonplace, law enforcement's use of forensic software like EnCase . . . may well be subject to question." But the fact that a computer password "lock" may not be *immediately* visible does not render it unlocked. I appreciate that unlike the locked file cabinet, computers have no handle to pull. But, like the padlocked footlocker, computers do exhibit outward signs of password protection: they display boot password screens, username/password log-in screens, and/or screen-saver reactivation passwords.

The fact remains that EnCase's ability to bypass security measures is well known to law enforcement. Here, ICE's forensic computer specialist found Defendant's computer turned off. Without turning it on, he hooked his laptop directly to the hard drive of Defendant's computer and ran the EnCase program. The agents made no effort to ascertain whether such security was enabled prior to initiating the search. . . .

The majority points out that law enforcement "did not ask specific questions" about Dr. Andrus' use of the computer or knowledge of Ray Andrus' use of password protection, but twice criticizes Dr. Andrus' failure to affirmatively disclaim ownership of, control over, or knowledge regarding the computer. Of course, the computer was located in Ray Andrus' very tiny bedroom, but the majority makes no effort to explain how this does not create an ambiguous situation as to ownership.

The burden on law enforcement to identify ownership of the computer was minimal. A simple question or two would have sufficed. Prior to the computer search, the agents questioned Dr. Andrus about Ray Andrus' status as a renter and Dr. Andrus' ability to enter his 51-year-old son's bedroom in order to determine Dr. Andrus' ability to consent to a search of the room, but the agents did not inquire whether Dr. Andrus used the computer, and if so, whether he had access to his son's password. At the suppression hearing, the agents testified that they were not immediately aware that Defendant's computer was the only one in the house, and they began to doubt Dr. Andrus' authority to consent when they learned this fact. The record reveals that, upon questioning, Dr. Andrus indicated that there was a computer in the house and led the agents to Defendant's room. The forensic specialist was then summoned. It took him approximately fifteen to twenty minutes to set up his equipment, yet, bizarrely, at no point during this period did the agents inquire about the presence of any other computers. . . .

Accordingly, in my view, given the case law indicating the importance of computer password protection, the common knowledge about the prevalence of password usage, and the design of EnCase or similar password bypass mechanisms, the Fourth Amendment and the reasonable inquiry rule, mandate that in consent-based, warrantless computer searches, law enforcement personnel inquire or otherwise check for the presence of password protection and, if a password is present, inquire about the consenter's knowledge of that password and joint access to the computer. . . .

NOTES & QUESTIONS

1. *A Question of Perspective?* Orin Kerr contends:

> From a virtual user's perspective, the child pornography was hidden to the father; it was behind a password-protected gate. Under these facts, the father couldn't consent to a search because he would lack common authority over it. From a physical perspective, however, the file was present on the hard drive just like all the other information. Under these facts, the father could consent to the search because he had access rights to the machine generally. . . .
>
> Viewed from the physical perspective, the investigators reasonably did not know about the user profile and reasonably believed that the father had rights to consent to that part of the hard drive.[90]

2. *Checking for Password Protection.* Was the investigators' belief about the father's authority over the computer reasonable? Should the investigators have asked the father more questions about his use of the computer first? Should they have turned on the machine to see if it was password-protected before hooking up the forensic software? What kinds of incentives does this decision engender for officers doing an investigation?

3. *The Right to Delete.* Paul Ohm contends that the Fourth Amendment should be read to encompass a right to delete: "The text of the Fourth Amendment seems broad enough to protect this 'right to destroy' or, in the computer context, 'right to delete' by its terms through its prohibition on unreasonable seizure."[91] If the government has engaged in an unreasonable search of a computer under the Fourth Amendment, the typical remedy is that the data is excluded from trial. Does it follow that people should also have the right to demand that the data seized by the government be deleted?

4. *Computer Searches at the Border—and Beyond.* Under the border search doctrine, the government need not obtain a warrant or even demonstrate reasonable suspicion to justify a search of persons or property at the international border. According to the Supreme Court, "It is axiomatic that the United States, as sovereign, has the inherent authority to protect, and a paramount interest in protecting, its territorial integrity." *United States v. Flores-Montano*, 541 U.S. 149 (2004). The Court has recognized only a few limits on the government's power to engage in searches at the border without any particularized suspicion, such as "invasive searches of the person." *Id.*

---

[90] Orin Kerr, *Virtual Analogies, Physical Searches, and the Fourth Amendment*, Volokh Conspiracy, Apr. 26, 2007, http://www.volokh.com/posts/1177562355.shtml.

[91] Paul Ohm, *The Fourth Amendment Right to Delete*, 119 Harv. L. Rev. F. 10 (2005). For an extensive normative argument for the right to delete, see Viktor Mayer-Schönberger, *Delete: The Virtues of Forgetting in the Digital Age* (2009).

In *United States v. Arnold*, 533 F.3d 1003 (9th Cir. 2008), the Ninth Circuit considered whether this doctrine applied to computers and electronic devices at the border. The defendant argued that computers should be treated differently from regular property:

> Arnold argues that "laptop computers are fundamentally different from traditional closed containers," and analogizes them to "homes" and the "human mind." Arnold's analogy of a laptop to a home is based on his conclusion that a laptop's capacity allows for the storage of personal documents in an amount equivalent to that stored in one's home. He argues that a laptop is like the "human mind" because of its ability to record ideas, e-mail, internet chats and web-surfing habits.

The court rejected this argument:

> With respect to these searches, the Supreme Court has refused to draw distinctions between containers of information and contraband with respect to their quality or nature for purposes of determining the appropriate level of Fourth Amendment protection. Arnold's analogy to a search of a home based on a laptop's storage capacity is without merit. The Supreme Court has expressly rejected applying the Fourth Amendment protections afforded to homes to property which is *"capable of functioning as a home"* simply due to its size, or, distinguishing between "'worthy' and 'unworthy' containers."

In *United States v. Cotterman*, 637 F.3d 1068 (9th Cir. 2011), the Ninth Circuit upheld a search of a laptop computer that began at the nation's border and ended two days later in a governmental forensic computer laboratory that was 170 miles away from the border. The court stated, "So long as property has not been officially cleared for entry into the United States and remains in the control of the Government, any further search is simply a continuation of the original border search—the entirety of which is justified by the Government's border search power." According to the court, the defendant never regained his normal expectation of privacy in his computer, the 40-hour detention was reasonably related in scope to the circumstances justifying the initial detention at the border, and requiring forensic computer laboratories at all ports of entry throughout the United States would place an unreasonable burden on the government.

In dissent, Judge Betty Fletcher worried that "the scope of the search will be determined by the Government's desire to be thorough, and the length of seizure by the Government's convenience."

RILEY V. CALIFORNIA

2014 WL 2864483 (2014)

ROBERTS, C.J.: These two cases raise a common question: whether the police may, without a warrant, search digital information on a cell phone seized from an individual who has been arrested.

[In the first case, a police officer searched David Riley incident to arrest and found items associated with a street gang. The officer also seized a smart phone from Riley's pants pocket and accessed some information on it. At the station approximately two hours later, a detective specializing in gangs further went through the phone looking for evidence of other crimes. He found a photo of Riley by a car suspected of being involved in a shooting a few weeks earlier. Eventually Riley was also charged with firing at an occupied vehicle, assault with a semiautomatic firearm, and attempted murder in connection with that earlier shooting. He moved to suppress the evidence derived from the search of his cell phone, arguing that the searches violated the Fourth Amendment because they were performed without a warrant and were not otherwise justified by any exceptions to the warrant requirement. Riley was convicted and sentenced to 15 years to life.

In the second case, police officers observed respondent Brima Wurie make an apparent drug sale from a car and subsequently arrested him. After taking him to the station, they seized two cell phones from him, with the one at issue here being a flip phone, which generally has fewer features than a smart phone. The officers noticed that this phone was repeatedly receiving calls from a source labeled as "my house" on the phone's external screen. They opened the phone, accessed the phone's call log, and found the number associated with the "my house" label. After tracing the number to an apartment building, the officers obtained and executed a search warrant for the location, and found and seized 215 grams of crack cocaine, marijuana, drug paraphernalia, a firearm and ammunition, and cash. After being charged with distributing crack cocaine, possessing crack cocaine with intent to distribute, and being a felon in possession of a firearm and ammunition, Wurie moved to suppress the evidence found at the apartment as being the fruit of a warrantless search of his cell phone in violation of the Fourth Amendment. The district court denied the motion and Wurie was convicted and sentenced to 262 months in prison.]

"[T]he ultimate touchstone of the Fourth Amendment is 'reasonableness.' " *Brigham City v. Stuart,* 547 U.S. 398, 403 (2006). Our cases have determined that "[w]here a search is undertaken by law enforcement officials to discover evidence of criminal wrongdoing, . . . reasonableness generally requires the obtaining of a judicial warrant." *Vernonia School Dist. 47J v. Acton,* 515 U.S. 646, 653 (1995). In the absence of a warrant, a search is reasonable only if it falls within a specific exception to the warrant requirement. See *Kentucky v. King,* 131 S. Ct. 1849 (2011).

The two cases before us concern the reasonableness of a warrantless search incident to a lawful arrest . . . . Three related precedents set forth the rules governing such searches: The first, *Chimel v. California,* 395 U.S. 752 (1969), laid the groundwork for most of the existing search incident to arrest doctrine. Police officers in that case arrested Chimel inside his home and proceeded to search his entire three-bedroom house, including the attic and garage. . . . The Court crafted the following rule for assessing the reasonableness of a search incident to arrest.

"When an arrest is made, it is reasonable for the arresting officer to search the person arrested in order to remove any weapons that the latter might seek to use in order to resist arrest or effect his escape . . . . In addition, it is entirely reasonable for the arresting officer to search for and seize any evidence on the arrestee's person in order to prevent its concealment or destruction. . . ."

Four years later, in *United States v. Robinson,* 414 U.S. 218 (1973), the Court applied the *Chimel* analysis in the context of a search of the arrestee's person. A police officer had arrested Robinson for driving with a revoked license. The officer conducted a patdown search and felt an object that he could not identify in Robinson's coat pocket. He removed the object, which turned out to be a crumpled cigarette package, and opened it. Inside were 14 capsules of heroin. . . .

This Court . . . reject[ed] the notion that "case-by-case adjudication" was required . . . [and] explained, "[t]he authority to search the person incident to a lawful custodial arrest, while based upon the need to disarm and to discover evidence, does not depend on what a court may later decide was the probability in a particular arrest situation that weapons or evidence would in fact be found upon the person of the suspect." *Id.* Instead, a "custodial arrest of a suspect based on probable cause is a reasonable intrusion under the Fourth Amendment; that intrusion being lawful, a search incident to the arrest requires no additional justification." *Id.* A few years later, the Court clarified that this exception was limited to "personal property . . . immediately associated with the person of the arrestee." *United States v. Chadwick,* 433 U.S. 1 (1977).

The search incident to arrest trilogy concludes with [*Arizona v. Gant,* 556 U.S. 332 (2009)], which analyzed searches of an arrestee's vehicle. *Gant,* like *Robinson,* recognized that the *Chimel* concerns for officer safety and evidence preservation underlie the search incident to arrest exception. *Gant* added, however, an independent exception for a warrantless search of a vehicle's passenger compartment "when it is 'reasonable to believe evidence relevant to the crime of arrest might be found in the vehicle.' ". . .

These cases require us to decide how the search incident to arrest doctrine applies to modern cell phones . . . . We first consider each *Chimel* concern in turn. In doing so, [r]ather than requiring the "case-by-case adjudication" that *Robinson* rejected, we ask instead whether application of the search incident to arrest doctrine to this particular category of effects would "untether the rule from the justifications underlying the *Chimel* exception."

Digital data stored on a cell phone cannot itself be used as a weapon to harm an arresting officer or to effectuate the arrestee's escape. Once an officer has secured a phone and eliminated any potential physical threats . . . data on the phone can endanger no one.

The United States and California focus primarily on the second *Chimel* rationale: preventing the destruction of evidence.

Both Riley and Wurie concede that officers could have seized and secured their cell phones to prevent destruction of evidence while seeking a warrant . . . . And once law enforcement officers have secured a cell phone, there is no longer any risk that the arrestee himself will be able to delete incriminating data from the phone.

The United States and California argue that information on a cell phone may nevertheless be vulnerable to two types of evidence destruction unique to digital data—remote wiping and data encryption. Remote wiping occurs when a phone, connected to a wireless network, receives a signal that erases stored data. . . . Encryption is a security feature that some modern cell phones use in addition to password protection. When such phones lock, data becomes protected by sophisticated encryption that renders a phone all but "unbreakable" unless police know the password . . . .

With respect to remote wiping, the Government's primary concern turns on the actions of third parties who are not present at the scene of arrest. And data encryption is even further afield . . . . Moreover, in situations in which an arrest might trigger a remote-wipe attempt or an officer discovers an unlocked phone, it is not clear that the ability to conduct a warrantless search would make much of a difference. The need to effect the arrest, secure the scene, and tend to other pressing matters means that law enforcement officers may well not be able to turn their attention to a cell phone right away. . . . Cell phone data would be vulnerable to remote wiping from the time an individual anticipates arrest to the time any eventual search of the phone is completed . . . .

The search incident to arrest exception rests not only on the heightened government interests at stake in a volatile arrest situation, but also on an arrestee's reduced privacy interests upon being taken into police custody. . . .

The fact that an arrestee has diminished privacy interests does not mean that the Fourth Amendment falls out of the picture entirely. Not every search "is acceptable solely because a person is in custody." To the contrary, when "privacy-related concerns are weighty enough" a "search may require a warrant, notwithstanding the diminished expectations of privacy of the arrestee." One such example, of course, is *Chimel*. . . . Because a search of the arrestee's entire house was a substantial invasion beyond the arrest itself, the Court concluded that a warrant was required. . . .

Cell phones differ in both a quantitative and a qualitative sense from other objects that might be kept on an arrestee's person. The term "cell phone" is itself misleading shorthand; many of these devices are in fact minicomputers that also happen to have the capacity to be used as a telephone. They could just as easily be called cameras, video players, rolodexes, calendars, tape recorders, libraries, diaries, albums, televisions, maps, or newspapers.

One of the most notable distinguishing features of modern cell phones is their immense storage capacity. Before cell phones, a search of a person was limited by physical realities and tended as a general matter to constitute only a narrow intrusion on privacy. See Kerr, *Foreword: Accounting for Technological Change*, 36 Harv. J.L. & Pub. Pol'y 403, 404-405 (2013). Most people cannot lug around every piece of mail they have received for the past several months, every picture they have taken, or every book or article they have read . . . . But the possible intrusion on privacy is not physically limited in the same way when it comes to cell phones. The current top-selling smart phone has a standard capacity of 16 gigabytes (and is available with up to 64 gigabytes). Sixteen gigabytes translates to millions of pages of text, thousands of pictures, or hundreds of videos . . . .

The storage capacity of cell phones has several interrelated consequences for privacy. First, a cell phone collects in one place many distinct types of information—an address, a note, a prescription, a bank statement, a video—that reveal much more in combination than any isolated record. Second, a cell phone's capacity allows even just one type of information to convey far more than previously possible. The sum of an individual's private life can be reconstructed through a thousand photographs labeled with dates, locations, and descriptions; the same cannot be said of a photograph or two of loved ones tucked into a wallet. Third, the data on a phone can date back to the purchase of the phone, or even earlier. A person might carry in his pocket a slip of paper reminding him to call Mr. Jones; he would not carry a record of all his communications with Mr. Jones for the past several months, as would routinely be kept on a phone.

Finally, there is an element of pervasiveness that characterizes cell phones but not physical records. Prior to the digital age, people did not typically carry a cache of sensitive personal information with them as they went about their day. . . . . A decade ago police officers searching an arrestee might have occasionally stumbled across a highly personal item such as a diary. But those discoveries were likely to be few and far between. Today, by contrast, it is no exaggeration to say that many of the more than 90% of American adults who own a cell phone keep on their person a digital record of nearly every aspect of their lives—from the mundane to the intimate. . . .

Although the data stored on a cell phone is distinguished from physical records by quantity alone, certain types of data are also qualitatively different. An Internet search and browsing history, for example, can be found on an Internet-enabled phone and could reveal an individual's private interests or concerns . . . . Historic location information is a standard feature on many smart phones and can reconstruct someone's specific movements down to the minute, not only around town but also within a particular building. See *United States v. Jones*, 132 S. Ct. 945, 955 (2012) (SOTOMAYOR, J., concurring) ("GPS monitoring generates a precise, comprehensive record of a person's public movements that reflects a wealth of detail about her familial, political, professional, religious, and sexual associations.") . . . . Mobile application software on a cell phone, or "apps," offer a range of tools for managing detailed information about all aspects of a person's life. . . . The average smart phone user has installed 33 apps, which together can form a revealing montage of the user's life. . . In 1926, Learned Hand observed (in an opinion later quoted in *Chimel*) that it is "a totally different thing to search a man's pockets and use against him what they contain, from ransacking his house for everything which may incriminate him." *United States v. Kirschenblatt*, 16 F.2d 202, 203 (C.A.2). If his pockets contain a cell phone, however, that is no longer true. Indeed, a cell phone search would typically expose to the government far *more* than the most exhaustive search of a house: A phone not only contains in digital form many sensitive records previously found in the home; it also contains a broad array of private information never found in a home in any form—unless the phone is. . . .

We . . . reject the United States' final suggestion that officers should always be able to search a phone's call log, as they did in Wurie's case. The Government relies on *Smith v. Maryland*, 442 U.S. 735 (1979), which held that no warrant was required to use a pen register at telephone company premises to identify numbers dialed by a particular caller. The Court in that case, however, concluded that the use of a pen register was not a "search" at all under the Fourth Amendment. There is no dispute here that the officers engaged in a search of Wurie's cell phone. Moreover, call logs typically contain more than just phone numbers; they include any identifying information that an individual might add, such as the label "my house" in Wurie's case.

Finally, at oral argument California suggested a different limiting principle, under which officers could search cell phone data if they could have obtained the same information from a pre-digital counterpart. . . . But the fact that a search in the pre-digital era could have turned up a photograph or two in a wallet does not justify a search of thousands of photos in a digital gallery . . . . And to make matters worse, such an analogue test would allow law enforcement to search a range of items contained on a phone, even though people would be unlikely to carry such a variety of information in physical form. In Riley's case, for example, it is implausible that he would have strolled around with video tapes, photo albums, and an address book all crammed into his pockets. But because each of those items has a pre-digital analogue, police under California's proposal would be able to search a phone for all of those items—a significant diminution of privacy . . . .

We cannot deny that our decision today will have an impact on the ability of law enforcement to combat crime. Cell phones have become important tools in facilitating coordination and communication among members of criminal enterprises, and can provide valuable incriminating information about dangerous criminals. Privacy comes at a cost.

Holding

Our holding, of course, is not that the information on a cell phone is immune from search; it is instead that a warrant is generally required before such a search, even when a cell phone is seized incident to arrest. Our cases have historically recognized that the warrant requirement is "an important working part of our machinery of government," not merely "an inconvenience to be somehow 'weighed' against the claims of police efficiency." *Coolidge v. New Hampshire,* 403 U.S. 443 (1971) . . . . Moreover, even though the search incident to arrest exception does not apply to cell phones, other case-specific exceptions may still justify a warrantless search of a particular phone. "One well-recognized exception applies when the exigencies of the situation make the needs of law enforcement so compelling that [a] warrantless search is objectively reasonable under the Fourth Amendment." . . . . Our cases have recognized that the Fourth Amendment was the founding generation's response to the reviled "general warrants" and "writs of assistance" of the colonial era, which allowed British officers to rummage through homes in an unrestrained search for evidence of criminal activity. Opposition to such searches was in fact one of the driving forces behind the Revolution itself. In 1761, the patriot James Otis delivered a speech in Boston denouncing the use of writs of assistance. A young John Adams was there, and he would later write that "[e]very man of a crowded audience appeared to me to go away, as I did, ready to take arms against writs of assistance." 10 Works of John Adams 247–248 (C. Adams ed. 1856). According to Adams, Otis's speech was "the first scene of the first act of opposition to the arbitrary claims of Great Britain. Then and there the child Independence was born." *Id.,* at 248. . . .

Modern cell phones are not just another technological convenience. With all they contain and all they may reveal, they hold for many Americans "the privacies of life." The fact that technology now allows an individual to carry such information in his hand does not make the information any less worthy of the protection for which the Founders fought. Our answer to the question of what police must do before searching a cell phone seized incident to an arrest is accordingly simple—get a warrant.

NOTES & QUESTIONS

1. *A Quantitative Difference?* The Supreme Court focused on the quantity of information that people store in a cell phone and noted that this was different than carrying a few photos or other items. Likewise, in *Jones,* the Court focused on the quantity of information gathered by GPS. What is the operative test that separates a search of a cell phone or via GPS from other searches?

2. *Implications for* **Smith v. Maryland.** Recall the third party doctrine in *Smith v. Maryland,* where the Court held that a person lacks an expectation of privacy in the numbers a person dials on the phone. The government in *Riley* invoked *Smith v. Maryland* to argue that "officers should always be able to search a phone's call log." The Court, however, rejected this argument because "call logs typically contain more than just phone numbers; they include any identifying information that an individual might add, such as the label 'my house' in Wurie's case." Today, it is quite easy to link phone numbers to identifiable people. Should the fact that phone numbers are already identified in the phone's call log matter if the police can readily identify the phone numbers in a pen register by looking them up online? Does the reasoning of *Smith v. Maryland* still hold up today in light of *Riley*?

3. *Implications for the Third Party Doctrine.* The third party doctrine in *Smith v. Maryland* and *United States v. Miller* was crafted in the 1970s when only certain forms of data were maintained by third parties. Now, much of our activity involves information that is stored with third parties. As Daniel Solove notes: "The Court's reasoning in *Riley* suggests that perhaps the Court is finally recognizing that old physical considerations — location, size, etc. — are no longer as relevant in light of modern technology. What matters is the data involved and how much it reveals about a person's private life. If this is the larger principle the Court is recognizing today, then it strongly undermines some of the reasoning behind the third party doctrine."[92] Do you agree with this assessment? Is there a way that the third party doctrine can be made consistent with the reasoning in *Riley*?

2. ENCRYPTION

Encryption includes the ability to keep communications secure by concealing the contents of a message. With encryption, even if a communication is

---

[92] Daniel J. Solove, *Does the U.S. Supreme Court's Decision on the 4th Amendment and Cell Phones Signal Future Changes to the Third Party Doctrine?* LinkedIn, June 25, 2014, https://www.linkedin.com/today/post/article/20140625172659-2259773-does-the-u-s-supreme-court-s-decision-on-the-4th-amendment-and-cell-phones-signal-future-changes-to-the-third-party-doctrine.

intercepted, it still remains secure. Encryption works by translating a message into a code of letters or numbers called "cypher text." The parties to the communication hold a *key*, which consists of the information necessary to translate the code back to the original message, or "plain text." Since ancient times, code-makers have devised cryptographic systems to encode messages. But along with the code-makers arose code-breakers, who were able to figure out the keys to cryptographic systems by, for example, examining the patterns in the encoded messages and comparing them to patterns in a particular language and the frequency of use of certain letters in that language. Today, computers have vastly increased the complexity of encryption.

Encryption presents a difficult trade-off between privacy and surveillance. It is an essential technique to protect the privacy of electronic communications in an age when such communications can so easily be intercepted and monitored. On the other hand, it enables individuals to disguise their communications from detection by law enforcement officials.[93] As Whitfield Diffie and Susan Landau observe:

> The explosion in cryptography and the US government's attempts to control it have given rise to a debate between those who hail the new technology's contribution to privacy, business, and security and those who fear both its interference with the work of police and its adverse effect on the collection of intelligence. Positions have often been extreme. The advocates for unfettered cryptography maintain that a free society depends on privacy to protect freedom of association, artistic creativity, and political discussion. The advocates of control hold that there will be no freedom at all unless we can protect ourselves from criminals, terrorists, and foreign threats. Many have tried to present themselves as seeking to maintain or restore the status quo. For the police, the status quo is the continued ability to wiretap. For civil libertarians, it is the ready availability of conversational privacy that prevailed at the time of the country's founding.[94]

The Clipper Chip. The U.S. government has become increasingly concerned that the growing sophistication of encryption would make it virtually impossible for the government to decrypt. In 1994, the government proposed implementing the "Clipper Chip," a federal encryption standard in which the government would retain a copy of the key in a system called "key escrow." By holding a "spare key," the government could readily decrypt encrypted communications if it desired. The Clipper Chip was strongly criticized, and the government's encryption standard has not been widely used.

---

[93] For more background on encryption, see Simon Singh, *The Code: The Evolution of Secrecy from Mary, Queen of Scots to Quantum Cryptography* (1999); Steven Levy, *Crypto: How the Code Rebels Beat the Government — Saving Privacy in the Digital Age* (2002); A. Michael Froomkin, *The Metaphor Is the Key: Cryptography, the Clipper Chip, and the Constitution*, 143 U. Pa. L. Rev. 709 (1995); Robert C. Post, *Encryption Source Code and the First Amendment*, 15 Berkeley Tech. L.J. 713 (2000); A. Michael Froomkin, *The Constitution and Encryption Regulation: Do We Need a "New Privacy"?*, 3 N.Y.U. J. Legis. & Pub. Pol'y 25 (1999).

[94] Whitfield Diffie & Susan Landau, *Privacy on the Line: The Politics of Wiretapping and Encryption* (1998).

Encryption and the First Amendment. In *Junger v. Daley*, 209 F.3d 481 (6th Cir. 2000), the Sixth Circuit concluded that encryption was protected speech under the First Amendment:

> Much like a mathematical or scientific formula, one can describe the function and design of encryption software by a prose explanation; however, for individuals fluent in a computer programming language, source code is the most efficient and precise means by which to communicate ideas about cryptography.

Junger relied on the reasoning of *Bernstein v. United States Dep't of Justice,* 176 F.3d 1132 (9th Cir. 1999) (opinion withdrawn), where the Ninth Circuit struck down a licensing scheme on encryption source code as a violation of the First Amendment:

> Bernstein has submitted numerous declarations from cryptographers and computer programmers explaining that cryptographic ideas and algorithms are conveniently expressed in source code. . . . [T]he chief task for cryptographers is the development of secure methods of encryption. While the articulation of such a system in layman's English or in general mathematical terms may be useful, the devil is, at least for cryptographers, often in the algorithmic details. By utilizing source code, a cryptographer can express algorithmic ideas with precision and methodological rigor that is otherwise difficult to achieve. . . .
>
> Thus, cryptographers use source code to express their scientific ideas in much the same way that mathematicians use equations or economists use graphs. . . .
>
> In light of these considerations, we conclude that encryption software, in its source code form and as employed by those in the field of cryptography, must be viewed as expressive for First Amendment purposes. . . .

Orin Kerr takes issue with *Junger*'s holding: "the court viewed source code using the close-up paradigm of what the code looked like, rather than the deeper functional perspective of what the code was actually supposed to do. . . . Just as viewing a Seurat painting from inches away reveals only dots, the *Junger* court's myopic view of source code revealed only communications that looked like speech in form, but lacked the deeper significance required to establish constitutional expression."[95]

In the view of Robert Post, the question of First Amendment coverage turns on a "constitutional sociology."[96] The relevant discussion for Post is "between encryption source code that is itself part of public dialogue and encryption source code that is meant merely to be used." He adds, moreover, that "even if encryption source code in not itself a subject of public discussion, its regulation might nevertheless affect public discussion in ways that ought to trigger First Amendment coverage." As an example, a licensing scheme for encryption code that engaged in viewpoint discrimination would be flawed. Even beyond viewpoint discrimination, a viewpoint neutral scheme of regulating encryption software would be flawed if it had a sufficient constitutional impact on "the various First Amendment media that employ" such software.

---

[95] Orin S. Kerr, *Are We Overprotecting Code? Thoughts on First-Generation Internet Law*, 57 Wash. & Lee L. Rev. 1287, 1292-93 (2000).

[96] Robert Post, *Encryption Source Code and the First Amendment*, 15 Berkeley Tech. L.J. 713 (2000).

Consider *Karn v. United States Dep't of State*, 925 F. Supp. 1 (D.D.C. 1996), where the court came to the contrary conclusion from *Junger*:

. . . The government regulation at issue here is clearly content-neutral. . . . The defendants are not regulating the export of the diskette because of the expressive content of the comments and or source code, but instead are regulating because of the belief that the combination of encryption source code on machine readable media will make it easier for foreign intelligence sources to encode their communications. . . .

. . . [A] content-neutral regulation is justified . . . if it is within the constitutional power of the government, it "furthers an important or substantial governmental interest," and "the incidental restriction on alleged First Amendment freedoms is no greater than is essential to the furtherance of that interest." . . .

. . . By placing cryptographic products on the ITAR, the President has determined that the proliferation of cryptographic products will harm the United States. . . .

. . . [T]he plaintiff has not advanced any argument that the regulation is "substantially broader than necessary" to prevent the proliferation of cryptographic products. Nor has the plaintiff articulated any present barrier to the spreading of information on cryptography "by any other means" other than those containing encryption source code on machine-readable media. Therefore, the Court holds that the regulation of the plaintiff's diskette is narrowly tailored to the goal of limiting the proliferation of cryptographic products and that the regulation is justified. . . .

Encryption and the Fourth Amendment. Suppose law enforcement officials legally obtain an encrypted communication. Does the Fourth Amendment require a warrant before the government can decrypt an encrypted communication? Consider the following argument by Orin Kerr:

Encryption is often explained as a lock-and-key system, in which a "key" is used to "lock" plaintext by turning it into ciphertext, and then a "key" is used to "unlock" the ciphertext by turning it into plaintext. We know that locking a container is a common way to create a reasonable expectation of privacy in its contents: the government ordinarily cannot break the lock and search a closed container without a warrant. . . .

When we use a "lock" and "unlock" in the metaphorical sense to denote understanding, however, a lock cannot trigger the rights-based Fourth Amendment. If I tell you a riddle, I do not have a right to stop you from figuring it out. Although figuring out the secret of an inscrutable communication may "unlock" its meaning, the Fourth Amendment cannot regulate such a cognitive discovery. . . .[97]

Encryption and the Fifth Amendment. Can the government compel the production of a private key if it is stored on a personal computer? What if the key is known only to the individual and not stored or recorded?

---

[97] Orin S. Kerr, *The Fourth Amendment in Cyberspace: Can Encryption Create a "Reasonable Expectation of Privacy?,"* 33 Conn. L. Rev. 503, 520-21, 522 (2001).

3. VIDEO SURVEILLANCE

Prior to the enactment of the ECPA, video surveillance was not encompassed within the language of Title III. When it amended federal electronic surveillance law in 1986 by enacting the ECPA, Congress again failed to address video surveillance. Of course, if the government intercepts a *communication* consisting of video images (such as a transmission of a webcam image or an e-mail containing a video clip), then the Wiretap Act applies. If the government accesses an individual's stored video clip, then the SCA applies. However, being watched by video *surveillance* (such as a surveillance camera) does not involve an interception or an accessing of stored images. The video surveillance must be silent video surveillance, or else it could be an "oral" communication subject to the Wiretap Act. In sum, silent video surveillance is not covered under federal electronic surveillance law. *See, e.g., United States v. Biasuci*, 786 F.2d 504 (2d Cir. 1986); *United States v. Koyomejian*, 970 F.2d 536 (9th Cir. 1992); *United States v. Falls*, 34 F.3d 674 (8th Cir. 1994).

In *United States v. Mesa-Rincon*, 911 F.2d 1433 (10th Cir. 1990), the court observed that although federal electronic surveillance law did not apply to video surveillance, the Fourth Amendment did:

> Unfortunately, Congress has not yet specifically defined the constitutional requirements for video surveillance. Nevertheless, the general fourth amendment requirements are still applicable to video surveillance; and suppression is required when the government fails to follow these requirements.
>
> Title III establishes elaborate warrant requirements for wiretapping and bugging. Unfortunately, Title III does not discuss television surveillance in any way. Thus, its requirements are not binding on this court in the context of video surveillance. However, the fact that Title III does not discuss television surveillance is no authority for the proposition that Congress meant to outlaw the practice.

4. E-MAIL AND ONLINE COMMUNICATIONS

STEVE JACKSON GAMES, INC. V. UNITED STATES SECRET SERVICE

36 F.3d 457 (5th Cir. 1994)

BARKSDALE, J. Appellant Steve Jackson Games, Incorporated (SJG), publishes books, magazines, role-playing games, and related products. Starting in the mid-1980s, SJG operated an electronic bulletin board system, called "Illuminati" (BBS), from one of its computers. SJG used the BBS to post public information about its business, games, publications, and the role-playing hobby; to facilitate play-testing of games being developed; and to communicate with its customers and free-lance writers by electronic mail (E-mail).

Central to the issue before us, the BBS also offered customers the ability to send and receive private E-mail. Private E-mail was stored on the BBS computer's hard disk drive temporarily, until the addressees "called" the BBS (using their computers and modems) and read their mail. After reading their E-mail, the recipients could choose to either store it on the BBS computer's hard drive or delete it. In February 1990, there were 365 BBS users. Among other uses, appellants Steve Jackson, Elizabeth McCoy, William Milliken, and Steffan O'Sullivan used the BBS for communication by private E-mail. . . . [In addition, Lloyd Blankenship, an employee of Steve Jackson Games, operated a computer bulletin board system (BBS).] Blankenship had the ability to review, and perhaps delete any data on the BBS.

On February 28, 1990, [Secret Service] Agent Foley applied for a warrant to search SJG's premises and Blankenship's residence for evidence of violations of 18 U.S.C. §§ 1030 (proscribes interstate transportation of computer access information) and 2314 (proscribes interstate transportation of stolen property). A search warrant for SJG was issued that same day, authorizing the seizure of [computer hardware, software, and computer data.]

The next day, March 1, the warrant was executed by the Secret Service, including Agents Foley and Golden. Among the items seized was the computer which operated the BBS. At the time of the seizure, 162 items of unread, private E-mail were stored on the BBS, including items addressed to the individual appellants. . . .

Appellants filed suit in May 1991 against, among others, the Secret Service and the United States, claiming [among other things, a violation of] the Federal Wiretap Act, as amended by Title I of the Electronic Communications Privacy Act (ECPA), 18 U.S.C. §§ 2510-2521; and Title II of the ECPA, 18 U.S.C. §§ 2701-2711. . . .

As stated, the sole issue is a very narrow one: whether the seizure of a computer on which is stored private E-mail that has been sent to an electronic bulletin board, but not yet read (retrieved) by the recipients, constitutes an "intercept" proscribed by 18 U.S.C. § 2511(1)(a).

Section 2511 was enacted in 1968 as part of Title III of the Omnibus Crime Control and Safe Streets Act of 1968, often referred to as the Federal Wiretap Act. Prior to the 1986 amendment by Title I of the ECPA, it covered only wire and oral communications. Title I of the ECPA extended that coverage to electronic communications. In relevant part, § 2511(1)(a) proscribes "intentionally intercept[ing] . . . any wire, oral, or electronic communication," unless the intercept is authorized by court order or by other exceptions not relevant here. Section 2520 authorizes, *inter alia*, persons whose electronic communications are intercepted in violation of § 2511 to bring a civil action against the interceptor for actual damages, or for statutory damages of $10,000 per violation or $100 per day of the violation, whichever is greater. 18 U.S.C. § 2520.

The Act defines "intercept" as "the aural or other acquisition of the contents of any wire, electronic, or oral communication through the use of any electronic, mechanical, or other device." 18 U.S.C. § 2510(4). . . .

Webster's Third New International Dictionary (1986) defines "aural" as "of or relating to the ear" or "of or relating to the sense of hearing." And, the Act defines "aural transfer" as "a transfer containing the human voice at any point between and including the point of origin and the point of reception." 18 U.S.C. § 2510(18). This definition is extremely important for purposes of understanding the definition of a "wire communication," which is defined by the Act as any aural transfer made in whole or in part through the use of facilities for the transmission of communications by the aid of wire, cable, or other like connection between the point of origin and the point of reception (including the use of such connection in a switching station) . . . *and such term includes any electronic storage of such communication.*

18 U.S.C. § 2510(1) (emphasis added). In contrast, as noted, an "electronic communication" is defined as "any *transfer* of signs, signals, writing, images, sounds, data, or intelligence of any nature transmitted in whole or in part by a wire, radio, electromagnetic, photoelectronic or photooptical system . . . but does not include . . . any wire or oral communication. . . ." 18 U.S.C. § 2510(12) (emphasis added).

Critical to the issue before us is the fact that, unlike the definition of "wire communication," *the definition of "electronic communication" does not include electronic storage of such communications. See* 18 U.S.C. § 2510(12). "Electronic storage" is defined as

(A) any *temporary*, intermediate *storage* of a wire or *electronic communication incidental to the electronic transmission thereof;* and
(B) any storage of such communication by an electronic communication service for purposes of backup protection of such communication. . . .

18 U.S.C. § 2510(17) (emphasis added). The E-mail in issue was in "electronic storage." Congress' use of the word "transfer" in the definition of "electronic communication," and its omission in that definition of the phrase "any electronic storage of such communication" (part of the definition of "wire communication") reflects that Congress did not intend for "intercept" to apply to "electronic communications" when those communications are in "electronic storage." . . .

Title II generally proscribes unauthorized access to stored wire or electronic communications. Section 2701(a) provides:

Except as provided in subsection (c) of this section whoever —

> (1) intentionally accesses without authorization a facility through which an electronic communication service is provided; or
> (2) intentionally exceeds an authorization to access that facility; and thereby obtains, alters, or prevents authorized access to a wire or electronic communication *while it is in electronic storage in such system* shall be punished. . . .

18 U.S.C. § 2701(a) (emphasis added).

As stated, the district court found that the Secret Service violated § 2701 when it

intentionally accesse[d] without authorization a facility [the computer] through which an electronic communication service [the BBS] is provided . . . and thereby obtain[ed] [and] prevent[ed] authorized access [by appellants] to a[n] . . . electronic communication while it is in electronic storage in such system.

18 U.S.C. § 2701(a). The Secret Service does not challenge this ruling. We find no indication in either the Act or its legislative history that Congress intended for conduct that is clearly prohibited by Title II to furnish the basis for a civil remedy under Title I as well. . . .

NOTES & QUESTIONS

1. *Interception vs. Electronic Storage.* Is unread e-mail in storage because it is sitting on a hard drive at the ISP? Or is it in transmission because the recipient hasn't read it yet? Is the court applying an overly formalistic and strict reading of "interception"?

2. *The Fourth Amendment and E-mail: A Question of Perspective?* Suppose the police sought to obtain a person's unread e-mail messages that were stored with her ISP waiting to be downloaded. *Steve Jackson Games* demonstrates how ECPA would apply — the weaker provisions of the Stored Communications Act rather than the stronger protections of the Wiretap Act apply to e-mail temporarily stored with a person's ISP. *Steve Jackson Games* is a civil case. In the criminal law context, the Stored Communications Act requires a warrant to obtain e-mails stored at the ISP for 180 days or less. If the e-mails have been stored over 180 days, then the government can obtain them with a mere subpoena.

   Would the Fourth Amendment apply? Orin Kerr argues that the answer depends upon the perspective by which one views the Internet. In the "internal perspective," the Internet is viewed as a virtual world, analogous to real space. From the "external perspective," we view the Internet as a network and do not analogize to real space. Kerr provides the following example:

   > Does the Fourth Amendment require [the police] to obtain a search warrant [to obtain an e-mail]? . . . The answer depends largely upon whether they apply an internal or external perspective of the Internet.
   >
   > Imagine that the first officer applies an internal perspective of the Internet. To him, e-mail is the cyberspace equivalent of old-fashioned postal mail. His computer announces, "You've got mail!" when an e-mail message arrives and shows him a closed envelope. When he clicks on the envelope, it opens, revealing the message. From his internal perspective, the officer is likely to conclude that the Fourth Amendment places the same restriction on government access to e-mail that it places on government access to ordinary postal mail. He will then look in a Fourth Amendment treatise for the black letter rule on accessing postal mail. That treatise will tell him that accessing a suspect's mail ordinarily violates the suspect's "reasonable expectation of privacy," and that therefore the officer must first obtain a warrant. Because e-mail is the equivalent of postal mail, the officer will conclude that the Fourth Amendment requires him to obtain a warrant before he can access the e-mail.
   >
   > Imagine that the second police office approaches the same problem from an external perspective. To him, the facts look quite different. Looking at how the Internet actually works, the second police officer sees that when A sent the e-mail to B, A was instructing his computer to send a message to his Internet Service Provider (ISP) directing the ISP to forward a text message to B's ISP. To simplify matters, let's say that A's ISP is EarthLink, and B's ISP is America Online (AOL). . . .
   >
   > What process does the Fourth Amendment require? The second officer will reason that A sent a copy of the e-mail communication to a third party (the EarthLink computer), disclosing the communication to the third party and instructing it to send the communication to yet another third party (AOL). The officer will ask, what process does the Fourth Amendment require to obtain

information that has been disclosed to a third party and is in the third party's possession? The officer will look in a Fourth Amendment treatise and locate to the black letter rule that the Fourth Amendment permits the government to obtain information disclosed to a third party using a mere subpoena. The officer can simply subpoena the system administrator to compel him to produce the e-mails. No search warrant is required.

Who is right? The first officer or the second? The answer depends on whether you approach the Internet from an internal or external perspective. From an internal perspective, the officers need a search warrant; from the external perspective, they do not.[98]

3. ***Previously Read E-mail Stored at an ISP.*** The e-mail stored on the ISP server in *Steve Jackson Games* had not yet been downloaded and read by the recipients. Many people continue to store their e-mail messages with their ISP even after having read them. Does the Stored Communications Act protect them in the same way? The answer to this question is currently in dispute. Daniel Solove observes:

> Because these messages are now stored indefinitely, according to the DOJ's interpretation . . . the e-mail is no longer in temporary storage and is "simply a remotely stored file." Therefore, under this view, it falls outside of much of the Act's protections. Since many people store their e-mail messages after reading them and the e-mail they send out, this enables the government to access their communications with very minimal limitations.[99]

In *Theofel v. Farey-Jones,* 359 F.3d 1066 (9th Cir. 2004), the court concluded that

> [t]he [Stored Communications] Act defines "electronic storage" as "(A) any temporary, intermediate storage of a wire or electronic communication incidental to the electronic transmission thereof; and (B) any storage of such communication by an electronic communication service for purposes of backup protection of such communication." Id. § 2510(17), incorporated by id. § 2711(1). Several courts have held that subsection (A) covers e-mail messages stored on an ISP's server pending delivery to the recipient. Because subsection (A) applies only to messages in "temporary, intermediate storage," however, these courts have limited that subsection's coverage to messages not yet delivered to their intended recipient.
>
> Defendants point to these cases and argue that messages remaining on an ISP's server after delivery no longer fall within the Act's coverage. But, even if such messages are not within the purview of subsection (A), they do fit comfortably within subsection (B). . . .
>
> An obvious purpose for storing a message on an ISP's server after delivery is to provide a second copy of the message in the event that the user needs to download it again — if, for example, the message is accidentally erased from the user's own computer. The ISP copy of the message functions as a "backup" for the user. Notably, nothing in the Act requires that the backup

---

[98] Orin S. Kerr, *The Problem of Perspective in Internet Law,* 91 Geo. L.J. 357, 361-62, 365-67 (2003).

[99] Daniel J. Solove, *Reconstructing Electronic Surveillance Law,* 72 Geo. Wash. L. Rev. 1264 (2004).

protection be for the benefit of the ISP rather than the user. Storage under these circumstances thus literally falls within the statutory definition.

See also Fraser v. Nationwide Mutual Insurance Co., 352 F.3d 108 (3d Cir. 2003) (suggesting that such e-mail messages were in backup storage under the definition of electronic storage).

4. ***What Constitutes an Interception?*** In *United States v. Councilman,* 373 F.3d 197 (1st Cir. 2004), an Internet bookseller, Interloc, Inc., provided e-mail service for its customers, who were book dealers. Councilman, the vice president of Interloc, directed Interloc employees to draft a computer program to intercept all incoming communications from Amazon.com to the book dealers and make copies of them. Councilman and other Interloc employees then read the e-mails in order to gain a commercial advantage. Councilman was charged with criminal violations of the Wiretap Act. Councilman argued that he did not violate the Wiretap Act because the e-mails were in electronic storage, albeit very briefly, when they were copied. The court followed *Steve Jackson Games* and concluded that the e-mail was in temporary storage and therefore subject to the Stored Communications Act, not the Wiretap Act. However, unlike *Steve Jackson Games,* Interloc accessed the e-mails "as they were being transmitted and in real time."

The *Councilman* case received significant criticism by academic commentators and experts in electronic surveillance law for misunderstanding the fundamental distinction between the interception of a communication and the accessing of a stored communication. An interception occurs contemporaneously — as the communication is being transmitted. Accessing a stored communication occurs later, as the communication sits on a computer. This distinction has practical consequences, since interceptions are protected by the much more protective Wiretap Act rather than the Stored Communications Act. Does such a distinction still make sense? Is the contemporaneous interception of communications more troublesome than the accessing of the communications in *Steve Jackson Games*?

The case was reheard en banc, and the en banc court reversed the panel. *See United States v. Councilman,* 418 F.3d 67 (1st Cir. 2005) (en banc). The court concluded that "the term 'electronic communication' includes transient electronic storage that is intrinsic to the communication process, and hence that interception of an e-mail message in such storage is an offense under the Wiretap Act." The court declined to further elaborate on what constitutes an "interception."

5. ***Carnivore.*** Beginning in 1998, the FBI began using a hardware and software mechanism called "Carnivore" to intercept people's e-mail and instant messaging information from their Internet Service Providers (ISPs). After obtaining judicial authorization, the FBI would install Carnivore by connecting a computer directly to the ISP's server and initiating the program. Carnivore was designed to locate the e-mails of a suspect at the ISP when the ISP did not have the capacity to do so.

Carnivore was capable of analyzing the entire e-mail traffic of an ISP, although the FBI maintained it was only used to search for the e-mails of a suspect. The program filtered out the e-mail messages of ISP subscribers who are not the subject of the investigation; but to do so, it had to scan the e-mail headers that identify the senders and recipients. The FBI likened e-mail headers to the information captured by a pen register, a device that registers the phone numbers a person dials.

However, Carnivore could be programmed to search through the entire text of all e-mails, to capture e-mails with certain key words. In this way, Carnivore resembles a wiretap. Recall that under federal wiretap law, judicial approval for obtaining pen register information only requires a certification that "the information likely to be obtained by such installation and use is relevant to an ongoing investigation." 18 U.S.C. § 3123. In contrast, judicial approval of a wiretap requires a full panoply of requirements under Title I, including a showing of probable cause.

To eliminate the negative associations with the term "Carnivore," the device was renamed "DCS1000." Many members of Congress viewed Carnivore with great suspicion. Congress held hearings over the summer of 2000 pertaining to Carnivore, and several bills were proposed to halt or limit the use of Carnivore.

The anti-Carnivore sentiment abruptly ended after the September 11, 2001, World Trade Center and Pentagon terrorist attacks. Section 216 of the USA PATRIOT Act of 2001, in anticipation of the use of Carnivore, required reports on the use of Carnivore to be filed with a court. These reports, filed under seal, require (1) the names of the officers using the device; (2) when the device was installed, used, and removed; (3) the configuration of the device; and (4) the information collected by the device. 18 U.S.C. § 3133(a)(3).

The FBI discontinued use of Carnivore because ISPs can readily produce the information the FBI desires without the assistance of the Carnivore device and because commercially available software has similar functionality.

UNITED STATES V. WARSHAK

631 F.3d 266 (6th Cir. 2010)

[Steven Warshak ran several small businesses that sold products and advertisements, including a popular herbal supplement called "Enzyte," which was touted as increasing a man's potency. This supplement was made by Warshak's company, Berkeley Premium Nutraceuticals, Inc., which had 1,500 employees and sales of $250 million per year. A key component of Berkeley's business was the ability to process credit card payments. To do so, it had banks provide a line of credit. In 2002, one of the banks — the Bank of Kentucky — terminated its relationship with Berkeley because of too many "chargebacks" — when customers dispute a charge. In future applications to banks for similar lines of credit, Warshak filed false applications, including lying that he never had an account terminated. To prevent future problems with excessive chargebacks, Berkeley found ways to falsify the figures.

Warshak (along with his mother, Harriet Warshak, who was involved in the scheme) was eventually indicted for various crimes, including mail, wire, and bank fraud, making false statements to banks, and money laundering. He sought to exclude from evidence about 27,000 of his private e-mails seized from his ISP (NuVox). The trial court denied his motion, and he was convicted, sentenced to 25 years in prison, and ordered to forfeit nearly $500 million worth of proceeds.]

BOGGS, J. Warshak argues that the government's warrantless, *ex parte* seizure of approximately 27,000 of his private emails constituted a violation of the Fourth Amendment's prohibition on unreasonable searches and seizures. The government counters that, even if government agents violated the Fourth Amendment in obtaining the emails, they relied in good faith on the Stored Communications Act ("SCA"), 18 U.S.C. §§ 2701 *et seq.*, a statute that allows the government to obtain certain electronic communications without procuring a warrant. The government also argues that any hypothetical Fourth Amendment violation was harmless. We find that the government *did violate* Warshak's Fourth Amendment rights by compelling his Internet Service Provider ("ISP") to turn over the contents of his emails. However, we agree that agents relied on the SCA in good faith, and therefore hold that reversal is unwarranted. . . .

The Stored Communications Act ("SCA"), 18 U.S.C. §§ 2701 *et seq.*, "permits a 'governmental entity' to compel a service provider to disclose the contents of [electronic] communications in certain circumstances." *Warshak II,* 532 F.3d at 523. As this court explained in *Warshak II:*

> . . . The compelled-disclosure provisions give different levels of privacy protection based on whether the e-mail is held with an electronic communication service or a remote computing service and based on how long the e-mail has been in electronic storage. The government may obtain the contents of e-mails that are "in electronic storage" with an electronic communication service for 180 days or less "only pursuant to a warrant." 18 U.S.C. § 2703(a). The government has three options for obtaining communications stored with a remote computing service and communications that have been in electronic storage with an electronic service provider for more than 180 days: (1) obtain a warrant; (2) use an administrative subpoena; or (3) obtain a court order under § 2703(d). *Id.* § 2703(a), (b). . . .

The Fourth Amendment provides that "[t]he right of the people to be secure in their persons, houses, papers, and effects, against unreasonable searches and seizures, shall not be violated, and no Warrants shall issue, but upon probable cause. . . ." U.S. Const. amend. IV. . . .

A "search" occurs when the government infringes upon "an expectation of privacy that society is prepared to consider reasonable." This standard breaks down into two discrete inquiries: "first, has the [target of the investigation] manifested a subjective expectation of privacy in the object of the challenged search? Second, is society willing to recognize that expectation as reasonable?"

Turning first to the subjective component of the test, we find that Warshak plainly manifested an expectation that his emails would be shielded from outside scrutiny. As he notes in his brief, his "entire business and personal life was contained within the . . . emails seized." Given the often sensitive and sometimes damning substance of his emails, we think it highly unlikely that Warshak expected them to be made public, for people seldom unfurl their dirty laundry in plain view. Therefore, we conclude that Warshak had a subjective expectation of privacy in the contents of his emails.

The next question is whether society is prepared to recognize that expectation as reasonable. This question is one of grave import and enduring consequence, given the prominent role that email has assumed in modern communication. Since the advent of email, the telephone call and the letter have waned in importance, and an explosion of Internet-based communication has taken place. People are now able to send sensitive and intimate information, instantaneously, to friends, family, and colleagues half a world away. Lovers exchange sweet nothings, and businessmen swap ambitious plans, all with the click of a mouse button. Commerce has also taken hold in email. Online purchases are often documented in email accounts, and email is frequently used to remind patients and clients of imminent appointments. In short, "account" is an apt word for the conglomeration of stored messages that comprises an email account, as it provides an account of its owner's life. By obtaining access to someone's email, government agents gain the ability to peer deeply into his activities. Much hinges, therefore, on whether the government is permitted to request that a commercial ISP turn over the contents of a subscriber's emails without triggering the machinery of the Fourth Amendment.

2 considerations

In confronting this question, we take note of two bedrock principles. First, the very fact that information is being passed through a communications network is a paramount Fourth Amendment consideration. Second, the Fourth Amendment must keep pace with the inexorable march of technological progress, or its guarantees will wither and perish.

With those principles in mind, we begin our analysis by considering the manner in which the Fourth Amendment protects traditional forms of communication. In *Katz,* the Supreme Court was asked to determine how the Fourth Amendment applied in the context of the telephone. There, government agents had affixed an electronic listening device to the exterior of a public phone booth, and had used the device to intercept and record several phone conversations. The Supreme Court held that this constituted a search under the Fourth Amendment, notwithstanding the fact that the telephone company had the capacity to monitor and record the calls. . . .

Letters receive similar protection. While a letter is in the mail, the police may not intercept it and examine its contents unless they first obtain a warrant based on probable cause. This is true despite the fact that sealed letters are handed over to perhaps dozens of mail carriers, any one of whom could tear open the thin paper envelopes that separate the private words from the world outside. Put another way, trusting a letter to an intermediary does not necessarily defeat a reasonable expectation that the letter will remain private.

Given the fundamental similarities between email and traditional forms of communication, it would defy common sense to afford emails lesser Fourth Amendment protection. It follows that email requires strong protection under the Fourth Amendment; otherwise, the Fourth Amendment would prove an ineffective guardian of private communication, an essential purpose it has long been recognized to serve.

If we accept that an email is analogous to a letter or a phone call, it is manifest that agents of the government cannot compel a commercial ISP to turn over the contents of an email without triggering the Fourth Amendment. An ISP is the intermediary that makes email communication possible. Emails must pass through an ISP's servers to reach their intended recipient. Thus, the ISP is the functional equivalent of a post office or a telephone company. As we have discussed above, the police may not storm the post office and intercept a letter, and they are likewise forbidden from using the phone system to make a clandestine recording of a telephone call—unless they get a warrant, that is. It only stands to reason that, if government agents compel an ISP to surrender the contents of a subscriber's emails, those agents have thereby conducted a Fourth Amendment search, which necessitates compliance with the warrant requirement absent some exception. . . .

[Earlier in the litigation of this case,] the government argued that this conclusion was improper, pointing to the fact that NuVox contractually reserved the right to access Warshak's emails for certain purposes. While we acknowledge that a subscriber agreement might, in some cases, be sweeping enough to defeat a reasonable expectation of privacy in the contents of an email account, we doubt that will be the case in most situations, and it is certainly not the case here.

As an initial matter, it must be observed that the mere *ability* of a third-party intermediary to access the contents of a communication cannot be sufficient to extinguish a reasonable expectation of privacy. In *Katz,* the Supreme Court found it reasonable to expect privacy during a telephone call despite the ability of an operator to listen in. Similarly, the ability of a rogue mail handler to rip open a letter does not make it unreasonable to assume that sealed mail will remain private on its journey across the country. Therefore, the threat or possibility of access is not decisive when it comes to the reasonableness of an expectation of privacy. . . .

Our conclusion finds additional support in the application of Fourth Amendment doctrine to rented space. Hotel guests, for example, have a reasonable expectation of privacy in their rooms. *See United States v. Allen,* 106 F.3d 695, 699 (6th Cir. 1997). This is so even though maids routinely enter hotel rooms to replace the towels and tidy the furniture. Similarly, tenants have a legitimate expectation of privacy in their apartments. *See United States v. Washington,* 573 F.3d 279, 284 (6th Cir. 2009). That expectation persists, regardless of the incursions of handymen to fix leaky faucets. Consequently, we are convinced that some degree of routine access is hardly dispositive with respect to the privacy question.

Again, however, we are unwilling to hold that a subscriber agreement will *never* be broad enough to snuff out a reasonable expectation of privacy. As the panel noted in *Warshak I* [an earlier case in this litigation], if the ISP expresses an intention to "audit, inspect, and monitor" its subscriber's emails, that might be enough to render an expectation of privacy unreasonable. But where, as here, there is no such statement, the ISP's "control over the [emails] and ability to access them under certain limited circumstances will not be enough to overcome an expectation of privacy." might be sweeping enough

We recognize that our conclusion may be attacked in light of the Supreme Court's decision in *United States v. Miller,* 425 U.S. 435 (1976). In *Miller,* the Supreme Court held that a bank depositor does not have a reasonable expectation of privacy in the contents of bank records, checks, and deposit slips. The Court's holding in *Miller* was based on the fact that bank documents, "including financial statements and deposit slips, contain only information voluntarily conveyed to the banks and exposed to their employees in the ordinary course of business."

But *Miller* is distinguishable. First, *Miller* involved simple business records, as opposed to the potentially unlimited variety of "confidential communications" at issue here. Second, the bank depositor in *Miller* conveyed information to the bank so that the bank could put the information to use "in the ordinary course of business." By contrast, Warshak received his emails through NuVox. NuVox was an intermediary, not the intended recipient of the emails. Thus, *Miller* is not controlling.

Accordingly, we hold that a subscriber enjoys a reasonable expectation of privacy in the contents of emails "that are stored with, or sent or received through, a commercial ISP." The government may not compel a commercial ISP to turn over the contents of a subscriber's emails without first obtaining a warrant based on probable cause. Therefore, because they did not obtain a warrant, the government agents violated the Fourth Amendment when they obtained the contents of Warshak's emails. Moreover, to the extent that the SCA purports to permit the government to obtain such emails warrantlessly, the SCA is unconstitutional. . . .

Even though the government's search of Warshak's emails violated the Fourth Amendment, the emails are not subject to the exclusionary remedy if the officers relied in good faith on the SCA to obtain them. In [*Illinois v. Krull*, 480 U.S. 340 (1987),] the Supreme Court noted that the exclusionary rule's purpose of deterring law enforcement officers from engaging in unconstitutional conduct would not be furthered by holding officers accountable for mistakes of the legislature. Thus, even if a statute is later found to be unconstitutional, an officer "cannot be expected to question the judgment of the legislature." However, an officer cannot "be said to have acted in good-faith reliance upon a statute if its provisions are such that a reasonable officer should have known that the statute was unconstitutional."

Naturally, Warshak argues that the provisions of the SCA at issue in this case were plainly unconstitutional. He argues that any reasonable law enforcement officer would have understood that a warrant based on probable cause would be required to compel the production of private emails. . . .

However, we disagree that the SCA is so conspicuously unconstitutional as to preclude good-faith reliance. As we noted in *Warshak II,* "[t]he Stored Communications Act has been in existence since 1986 and to our knowledge has not been the subject of any successful Fourth Amendment challenges, in any context, whether to § 2703(d) or to any other provision." Furthermore, given the complicated thicket of issues that we were required to navigate when passing on the constitutionality of the SCA, it was not plain or obvious that the SCA was unconstitutional, and it was therefore reasonable for the government to rely upon the SCA in seeking to obtain the contents of Warshak's emails.

But the good-faith reliance inquiry does not end with the facial validity of the statute at issue. In *Krull,* the Supreme Court hinted that the good-faith exception does not apply if the government acted "outside the scope of the statute" on which it purported to rely. . . . Once the officer steps outside the scope of an unconstitutional statute, the mistake is no longer the legislature's, but the officer's. . . .

Warshak argues that the government violated several provisions of the SCA and should therefore be precluded from arguing good-faith reliance. First, Warshak argues that the government violated the SCA's notice provisions. Under § 2703(b)(1)(B), the government must provide notice to an account holder if it seeks to compel the disclosure of his emails through either a § 2703(b) subpoena or a § 2703(d) order. However, § 2705 permits the government to delay notification in certain situations. The initial period of delay is 90 days, but the government may seek to extend that period in 90-day increments. In this case, the government issued both a § 2703(b) subpoena and a § 2703(d) order to NuVox, seeking disclosure of Warshak's emails. At the time, the government made the requisite showing that notice should be delayed. However, the government did not seek to renew the period of delay. In all, the government failed to inform Warshak of either the subpoena or the order for over a year.

Conceding that it violated the notice provisions, the government argues that such violations are irrelevant to the issue of whether it reasonably relied on the SCA in *obtaining* the contents of Warshak's emails. We agree. As the government notes, the violations occurred *after* the emails had been obtained. Thus, the mistakes at issue had no bearing on the constitutional violations. Because the exclusionary rule was designed to deter constitutional violations, we decline to invoke it in this situation.

But Warshak does not hang his hat exclusively on the government's violations of the SCA's notice provisions. He also argues that the government exceeded its authority under another SCA provision — § 2703(f) — by requesting NuVox to engage in *prospective* preservation of his future emails. Under § 2703(f), "[a] provider of wire or electronic communication services or a remote computing service, upon the request of a governmental entity, shall take all necessary steps to *preserve* records and other evidence *in its possession* pending the issuance of a court order or other process." 18 U.S.C. § 2703(f) (emphasis added). Warshak argues that this statute permits only *retrospective* preservation — in other words, preservation of emails already in existence. . . .

Ultimately, however, this statutory violation, whether it occurred or not, is irrelevant to the issue of good-faith reliance. The question here is whether the government relied in good faith on § 2703(b) and § 2703(d) to *obtain* copies of Warshak's emails. True, the government might not have been able to gain access to the emails without the prospective preservation request, as it was NuVox's practice to delete all emails once they were downloaded to the account holder's computer. Thus, in a sense, the government's use of § 2703(f) was a but-for cause of the constitutional violation. But the actual violation at issue was obtaining the emails, and the government did not rely on § 2703(f) specifically to do that. Instead, the government relied on § 2703(b) and § 2703(d). The proper inquiry, therefore, is whether the government violated either of *those* provisions, and the preservation request is of no consequence to that inquiry. . . .

NOTES & QUESTIONS

1. ***E-mail and the Third Party Doctrine.*** Does the court convincingly distinguish e-mail maintained by an ISP from the third party doctrine cases (*Smith v. Maryland* and *United States v. Miller*)?

2. ***The SCA and E-mail.*** Do the SCA's different levels of protection of e-mail make sense? Consider Patricia Bellia and Susan Freiwald:

> [W]arrant-level protection for stored e-mail should persist whether or not an e-mail has been opened, accessed, or downloaded. It is hard to imagine why the act of reading or preparing to read an e-mail, which is the entire point of communicating by e-mail, should somehow deprive a user of his reasonable expectation of privacy in the electronic communication. As discussed, the government's distinctions on this basis derive from a strained reading of out-of-date statutory provisions, and neither reflect nor should impact the Fourth Amendment status of stored e-mail.[100]

3. ***Keystroke Logging Systems.*** In *United States v. Scarfo*, 180 F. Supp. 2d 572 (D.N.J. 2001), the FBI wanted to search Nicodemo S. Scarfo's computer for evidence of illegal gambling activities. They obtained a warrant to search his office and computer, but they were unable to access an encrypted file called "Factors." FBI officials obtained additional search warrants to install a key logging system (KLS) on Scarfo's computer to record his keystrokes. The KLS was designed to work only when Scarfo was offline and not using his model to connect to his America Online account.

   Scarfo challenged the use of the KLS device under the Wiretap Act, under which a mere search warrant would be insufficient and a special court order would be required. The court, however, concluded:

> Recognizing that Scarfo's computer had a modem and thus was capable of transmitting electronic communications via the modem, the F.B.I. configured the KLS to avoid intercepting electronic communications typed on the keyboard and simultaneously transmitted in real time via the communication ports. . . . Hence, when the modem was operating, the KLS did not record keystrokes. It was designed to prohibit the capture of keyboard keystrokes whenever the modem operated. Since Scarfo's computer possessed no other means of communicating with another computer save for the modem, the KLS did not intercept any wire communications.

   Suppose the court concluded that the FBI violated the Wiretap Act. Would Scarfo be able to suppress the evidence?

   Note that the FBI designed the KLS to avoid triggering the Wiretap Act. Some might argue that this is an unfortunate game of technological cat-and-mouse because the privacy invasion was just as significant regardless of whether Scarfo's modem was on or off. Consider the following argument by Raymond Ku:

---

[100] Patricia L. Bellia & Susan Freiwald, *Fourth Amendment Protection for Stored E-Mail,* 2008 U. Chi. Legal F. 121, 135 (2008).

. . . By monitoring what an individual enters into her computer as she enters it, the government has the ability to monitor thought itself. Keystroke-recording devices allow the government to record formless thoughts and ideas an individual never intended to share with anyone, never intended to save on the hard drive and never intended to preserve for future reference in any form. The devices also allow the government to record thoughts and ideas the individual may have rejected the moment they were typed.[101]

Today, ironically, technology would likely forestall the use of the KLS because dial-up modems are increasingly being replaced by always-connected Internet service. This change might expand the coverage of the Wiretap Act. But it raises a broader question: Should interceptions of communications in transmission be protected more stringently than accessing communications that are not in transmission?

5. ISP ACCOUNT INFORMATION

UNITED STATES V. HAMBRICK

55 F. Supp. 2d 504 (W.D. Va. 1999)

MICHAEL, J. Defendant Scott M. Hambrick seeks the suppression of all evidence obtained from his Internet Service Provider ("ISP"), MindSpring, and seeks the suppression of all evidence seized from his home pursuant to a warrant issued by this court. For the reasons discussed below, the court denies the defendant's motion.

On March 14, 1998, J. L. McLaughlin, a police officer with the Keene, New Hampshire Police Department, connected to the Internet and entered a chat room called "Gay dads 4 sex." McLaughlin's screen name was "Rory14." In this chat room, Detective McLaughlin encountered someone using the screen name "Blowuinva." Based on a series of online conversations between "Rory14" (Det. McLaughlin) and "Blowuinva," McLaughlin concluded that "Blowuinva" sought to entice a fourteen-year-old boy to leave New Hampshire and live with "Blowuinva." Because of the anonymity of the Internet, Detective McLaughlin did not know the true identity of the person with whom he was communicating nor did he know where "Blowuinva" lived. "Blowuinva" had only identified himself as "Brad."

To determine Blowuinva's identity and location, McLaughlin obtained a New Hampshire state subpoena that he served on Blowuinva's Internet Service Provider, MindSpring, located in Atlanta, Georgia. The New Hampshire state subpoena requested that MindSpring produce "any records pertaining to the billing and/or user records documenting the subject using your services on March 14th, 1998 at 1210HRS (EST) using Internet Protocol Number 207.69.169.92." MindSpring complied with the subpoena. On March 20, 1998, MindSpring supplied McLaughlin with defendant's name, address, credit card number, e-mail address, home and work telephone numbers, fax number, and the fact that the

---

[101] Raymond Ku, *Think Twice Before You Type*, 163 N.J. L.J. 747 (Feb. 19, 2001).

Defendant's account was connected to the Internet at the Internet Protocol (IP) address.

A justice of the peace, Richard R. Richards, signed the New Hampshire state subpoena. Mr. Richards is not only a New Hampshire justice of the peace, but he is also a detective in the Keene Police Department, Investigation Division. Mr. Richards did not issue the subpoena pursuant to a matter pending before himself, any other judicial officer, or a grand jury. At the hearing on the defendant's motion, the government conceded the invalidity of the warrant. The question before this court, therefore, is whether the court must suppress the information obtained from MindSpring, and all that flowed from it, because the government failed to obtain a proper subpoena. . . .

. . . [Under *Katz v. United States*,] the Fourth Amendment applies only where: (1) the citizen has manifested a subjective expectation of privacy, and (2) the expectation is one that society accepts as "objectively reasonable." . . . Applying the first part of the *Katz* analysis, Mr. Hambrick asserts that he had a subjective expectation of privacy in the information that MindSpring gave to the government. However, resolution of this matter hinges on whether Mr. Hambrick's expectation is one that society accepts as "objectively reasonable."

The objective reasonableness prong of the privacy test is ultimately a value judgment and a determination of how much privacy we should have as a society. In making this constitutional determination, this court must employ a sort of risk analysis, asking whether the individual affected should have expected the material at issue to remain private. The defendant asserts that the Electronic Communications Privacy Act ("ECPA") "legislatively resolves" this question. . . .

The information obtained through the use of the government's invalid subpoena consisted of the defendant's name, address, social security number, credit card number, and certification that the defendant was connected to the Internet on March 14, 1998. Thus, this information falls within the provisions of Title II of the ECPA.

The government may require that an ISP provide stored communications and transactional records only if (1) it obtains a warrant issued under the Federal Rules of Criminal Procedure or state equivalent, or (2) it gives prior notice to the online subscriber and then issues a subpoena or receives a court order authorizing disclosure of the information in question. *See* 18 U.S.C. § 2703(a)-(c)(1)(B). When an ISP discloses stored communications or transactional records to a government entity without the requisite authority, the aggrieved customer's sole remedy is damages.

Although Congress is willing to recognize that individuals have some degree of privacy in the stored data and transactional records that their ISPs retain, the ECPA is hardly a legislative determination that this expectation of privacy is one that rises to the level of "reasonably objective" for Fourth Amendment purposes. Despite its concern for privacy, Congress did not provide for suppression where a party obtains stored data or transactional records in violation of the Act. Additionally, the ECPA's concern for privacy extends only to government invasions of privacy. ISPs are free to turn stored data and transactional records over to nongovernmental entities. *See* 18 U.S.C. § 2703(c)(1)(A) ("[A] provider of electronic communication service or remote computing service may disclose a record or other information pertaining to a subscriber to or customer of such service . . . to any person other than a governmental entity."). For Fourth Amendment purposes, this court does not find that the ECPA has legislatively determined that an individual has a reasonable expectation of privacy in his name, address, social security number, credit card number, and proof of Internet connection. The fact that the ECPA does not proscribe turning over such information to private entities buttresses the conclusion that the ECPA does not create a reasonable expectation of privacy in that information. This, however, does not end the court's inquiry. This court must determine, within the constitutional framework that the Supreme Court has established, whether Mr. Hambrick's subjective expectation of privacy is one that society is willing to recognize.

To have any interest in privacy, there must be some exclusion of others. To have a reasonable expectation of privacy under the Supreme Court's risk-analysis approach to the Fourth Amendment, two conditions must be met: (1) the data must not be knowingly exposed to others, and (2) the Internet service provider's ability to access the data must not constitute a disclosure. In *Katz*, the Supreme Court expressly held that "what a person knowingly exposes to the public, even in his home or office, is not a subject of Fourth Amendment protection." Further, the Court "consistently has held that a person has no legitimate expectation of privacy in information he voluntarily turns over to third parties." *Smith v. Maryland*, 442 U.S. 735, 743-44 (1979). . . .

When Scott Hambrick surfed the Internet using the screen name "Blowuinva," he was not a completely anonymous actor. It is true that an average member of the public could not easily determine the true identity of "Blowuinva." Nevertheless, when Mr. Hambrick entered into an agreement to obtain Internet access from MindSpring, he knowingly revealed his name, address, credit card number, and telephone number to MindSpring and its employees. Mr. Hambrick also selected the screen name "Blowuinva." When the defendant selected his screen name it became tied to his true identity in all MindSpring records. MindSpring employees had ready access to these records in the normal course of MindSpring's business, for example, in the keeping of its records for billing purposes, and nothing prevented MindSpring from revealing this information to nongovernmental actors.[102] Also, there is nothing in the record to suggest that there was a restrictive agreement between the defendant and MindSpring that would limit the right of MindSpring to reveal the defendant's personal information to nongovernmental entities. Where such dissemination of information to nongovernment entities is not prohibited, there can be no reasonable expectation of privacy in that information.

Although not dispositive to the outcome of this motion, it is important to note that the court's decision does not leave members of cybersociety without privacy protection. Under the ECPA, Internet Service Providers are civilly liable when they reveal subscriber information or the contents of stored communications to the government without first requiring a warrant, court order, or subpoena. Here, nothing suggests that MindSpring had any knowledge that the facially valid

---

[102] It is apparently common for ISPs to provide certain information that Mr. Hambrick alleges to be private to marketing firms and other organizations interested in soliciting business from Internet users.

subpoena submitted to it was in fact an invalid subpoena. Had MindSpring revealed the information at issue in this case to the government without first requiring a subpoena, apparently valid on its face, Mr. Hambrick could have sued MindSpring. This is a powerful deterrent protecting privacy in the online world and should not be taken lightly. . . .

NOTES & QUESTIONS

1. *Is There a Reasonable Expectation of Privacy in ISP Records?* The court in *Hambrick* concludes that there is no reasonable expectation of privacy in ISP records based on the third party doctrine in *Smith v. Maryland.* In *United States v. Kennedy,* 81 F. Supp. 2d 1103 (D. Kan. 2000), the court reached a similar conclusion:

   > Defendant has not demonstrated an objectively reasonable legitimate expectation of privacy in his subscriber information. . . . "[A] person has no legitimate expectation of privacy in information he voluntarily turns over to third parties." *Smith v. Maryland,* 442 U.S. 735 (1979). When defendant entered into an agreement with [his ISP], he knowingly revealed all information connected to [his IP address]. He cannot now claim to have a Fourth Amendment privacy interest in his subscriber information.

   Is *Smith v. Maryland* controlling on this issue? Is there a way to distinguish *Smith*?

2. *Statutes as a Basis for a Reasonable Expectation of Privacy?* Hambrick was not seeking relief directly under the Stored Communications Act of ECPA. Why not? Instead, Hambrick asserted he had Fourth Amendment protection in his subscriber records. He argued that under the *Katz* reasonable expectation of privacy test, the ECPA "legislatively resolves" that there is a reasonable expectation of privacy in information that Mindspring gave to the government. Should statutes that protect privacy serve as an indication of a societal recognition of a reasonable expectation of privacy? What are the consequences of using statutes such as ECPA to conclude that the Fourth Amendment applies?

3. *Is There a Remedy?* Mindspring couldn't release information to the government without a warrant or subpoena or else it would face civil liability. However, in this case, the government presented Mindspring with a subpoena that Mindspring had no knowledge was invalid. Therefore, it is unlikely that Mindspring would be liable. If the court is correct in its conclusion that 18 U.S.C. § 2703(a)-(c)(1)(B) of the ECPA only applies to the conduct of Internet Service Providers, then is there any remedy against Officer Richards's blatantly false subpoena? Could a police officer obtain a person's Internet subscriber information by falsifying a subpoena and escape without any civil liability or exclusionary rule?

   In *McVeigh v. Cohen,* 983 F. Supp. 215 (D.D.C. 1998), Timothy McVeigh (a different person from the Oklahoma City bomber) was an enlisted Navy serviceman who had served in the Navy for 17 years. A Navy volunteer coordinated a toy drive for the crew members of the submarine that McVeigh was serving on, and she received an email reply from an America Online (AOL) account with the screen name "boysrch" but signed by a "tim." The volunteer searched through AOL's profile directory and found that "boysrch" was a subscriber named Tim who lived in Honolulu, Hawaii, worked in the military, and who listed his marital status as "gay." The volunteer forwarded the email to her husband, an officer aboard the submarine. The email eventually was forwarded to the ship's captain, who called in Lieutenant Karin Morean, the ship's legal advisor, to investigate. They suspected that Tim might be Timothy McVeigh. Lieutenant Morean requested that a paralegal on her staff contact AOL to find out if the "boysrch" profile could be connected to Timothy McVeigh. The paralegal called AOL and stated he had received a fax from "boysrch" and wanted to confirm who it belonged to. The AOL representative informed him that it was indeed Timothy McVeigh.

The Navy initiated proceedings under the "Don't Ask, Don't Tell, Don't Pursue" policy of the U.S. Military. Under this policy, adopted in 1993, the military cannot investigate sexual orientation unless there is "credible information" that a gay serviceman or servicewoman has the "propensity or intent to engage in homosexual acts." The Navy sought to discharge McVeigh under this policy for "homosexual conduct."

McVeigh sued in federal court to prevent his discharge. He argued that he did not "tell" under the policy but was instead "pursued." The court agreed with McVeigh:

> All that the Navy had was an email message and user profile that it suspected was authored by Plaintiff. Under the military regulation, that information alone should not have triggered any sort of investigation. When the Navy affirmatively took steps to confirm the identity of the email respondent, it violated the very essence of "Don't Ask, Don't Pursue" by launching a search and destroy mission. Even if the Navy had a factual basis to believe that the email message and profile were written by Plaintiff, it was unreasonable to infer that they were necessarily intended to convey a propensity or intent to engage in homosexual conduct. . . .

The court then examined how the Navy's contacting AOL to identify "boysrch" violated ECPA:

> The subsequent steps taken by the Navy in its "pursuit" of the Plaintiff were not only unauthorized under its policy, but likely illegal under the Electronic Communications Privacy Act of 1986 ("ECPA"). The ECPA, enacted by Congress to address privacy concerns on the Internet, allows the government to obtain information from an online service provider — as the Navy did in this instance from AOL — but only if a) it obtains a warrant issued under the Federal Rules of Criminal Procedure or state equivalent; or b) it gives prior notice to the online subscriber and then issues a subpoena or receives a court order authorizing disclosure of the information in question. See 18 U.S.C. § 2703(b)(1)(A)-(B), (c)(1)(B).
>
> In soliciting and obtaining over the phone personal information about the Plaintiff from AOL, his private on-line service provider, the government in this case invoked neither of these provisions and thus failed to comply with the ECPA. From the record, it is undisputed that the Navy directly solicited by phone information from AOL. Lieutenant Karin S. Morean, the ship's

principal legal counsel and a member of the JAG corps, personally requested Legalman Kaiser to contact AOL and obtain the identity of the subscriber. Without this information, Plaintiff credibly contends that the Navy could not have made the necessary connection between him and the user profile which was the sole basis on which to commence discharge proceedings.

The government, in its defense, contends that the Plaintiff cannot succeed on his ECPA claim. It argues that the substantive provision of the statute that Plaintiff cites, 18 U.S.C. § 2703(c)(1)(B), puts the obligation on the online service provider to withhold information from the government, and not vice versa. In support of its position, Defendants cite to the Fourth Circuit opinion in *Tucker v. Waddell*, 83 F.3d 688 (4th Cir. 1996), which held that § 2703(c)(1)(B) only prohibits the actions of online providers, not the government. Accordingly, Defendants allege that Plaintiff has no cause of action against the government on the basis of the ECPA. . . .

. . . [However,] Section 2703(c)(1)(B) must be read in the context of the statute as a whole. In comparison, § 2703(a) and (b) imposes on the government a reciprocal obligation to obtain a warrant or the like before requiring disclosure. It appears from the face of the statute that all of the subsections of § 2703 were intended to work in tandem to protect consumer privacy. Even if, however, the government ultimately proves to be right in its assessment of § 2703(c)(1)(B), the Plaintiff has plead § 2703(a) and (b) as alternative grounds for relief. In his claim that the government, at the least, solicited a violation of the ECPA by AOL, the Court finds that there is likely success on the merits with regard to this issue. The government knew, or should have known, that by turning over the information without a warrant, AOL was breaking the law. Yet the Navy, in this case, directly solicited the information anyway. What is most telling is that the Naval investigator did not identify himself when he made his request. While the government makes much of the fact that § 2703(c)(1)(B) does not provide a cause of action against the government, it is elementary that information obtained improperly can be suppressed where an individual's rights have been violated. In these days of "big brother," where through technology and otherwise the privacy interests of individuals from all walks of life are being ignored or marginalized, it is imperative that statutes explicitly protecting these rights be strictly observed. . . .

The Stored Communications Act does not have a suppression remedy; the court is creating an exclusionary rule for the Stored Communications Act. Is this appropriate? Without a suppression remedy for the conduct of the government in this case, what would deter the government from violating the Stored Communications Act?

Subsequent to *McVeigh v. Cohen,* Congress amended §§ 2703(a)-(c) to make it clear that these provisions applied not just to ISPs but also to government conduct. However, an exclusionary rule was not added.

4. *Cell Site Location Information.* Recall *United States v. Jones* from earlier in this chapter, where the U.S. Supreme Court held that the Fourth Amendment required a warrant before using a GPS tracking device on a car to track movement and location in public. There is another way to obtain data about a person's movements or location — via records maintained by telecommunications service providers. Providers of cell phone or smart phone service have data about the location of that phone, which most often is the

location of the user too. In *United State v. Quartavious*, 754 F.3d 1205 (11th Cir. 2014), the government obtained the defendant's cell site location information under the Stored Communications Act (SCA). Under the SCA, the government need only establish "specific and articulable facts showing that there are reasonable grounds to believe that the information sought is relevant and material to an ongoing criminal investigation." The court held that in light of *Jones*, the Fourth Amendment required a warrant supported by probable cause:

> In light of the confluence of the three opinions in the Supreme Court's decision in Jones, we accept the proposition that the privacy theory is not only alive and well, but available to govern electronic information of search and seizure in the absence of trespass. . . .
>
> *Jones*, as we noted, involved the movements of the defendant's automobile on the public streets and highways. Indeed, the district court allowed the defendant's motion to suppress information obtained when the automobile was not in public places. The circuit opinion and the separate opinions in the Supreme Court concluded that a reasonable expectation of privacy had been established by the aggregation of the points of data, not by the obtaining of individual points. Such a mosaic theory is not necessary to establish the invasion of privacy in the case of cell site location data.
>
> One's car, when it is not garaged in a private place, is visible to the public, and it is only the aggregation of many instances of the public seeing it that make it particularly invasive of privacy to secure GPS evidence of its location. As the circuit and some justices reasoned, the car owner can reasonably expect that although his individual movements may be observed, there will not be a "tiny constable" hiding in his vehicle to maintain a log of his movements. In contrast, even on a person's first visit to a gynecologist, a psychiatrist, a bookie, or a priest, one may assume that the visit is private if it was not conducted in a public way. One's cell phone, unlike an automobile, can accompany its owner anywhere. Thus, the exposure of the cell site location information can convert what would otherwise be a private event into a public one. When one's whereabouts are not public, then one may have a reasonable expectation of privacy in those whereabouts. Therefore, while it may be the case that even in light of the *Jones* opinion, GPS location information on an automobile would be protected only in the case of aggregated data, even one point of cell site location data can be within a reasonable expectation of privacy. In that sense, cell site data is more like communications data than it is like GPS information. That is, it is private in nature rather than being public data that warrants privacy protection only when its collection creates a sufficient mosaic to expose that which would otherwise be private.

The court rejected the government's argument that the third party doctrine applied to location information because, quoting the court in *In re Application of U.S. for an Order Directing a Provider of Elec. Communication Service to Disclose Records to Gov't*, 620 F.3d 304 (3d Cir.2010): "[W]hen a cell phone user makes a call, the only information that is voluntarily and knowingly conveyed to the phone company is the number that is dialed, and there is no indication to the user that making that call will also locate the caller."

The Fifth Circuit in *In re Application of the United State for Historical Cell Site Data*, 724 F.3d 600 (5th Cir. 2013), reached a contrary conclusion:

The third party can store data disclosed to it at its discretion. And once an individual exposes his information to a third party, it can be used for any purpose. . . .

Cell phone users . . . understand that their service providers record their location information when they use their phones at least to the same extent that the landline users in *Smith* understood that the phone company recorded the numbers they dialed. . . .

Their use of their phones, moreover, is entirely voluntary. The Government does not require a member of the public to own or carry a phone. As the days of monopoly phone companies are past, the Government does not require him to obtain his cell phone service from a particular service provider that keeps historical cell site records for its subscribers, either. And it does not require him to make a call, let alone to make a call at a specific location. . . .

Because a cell phone user makes a choice to get a phone, to select a particular service provider, and to make a call, and because he knows that the call conveys cell site information, the provider retains this information, and the provider will turn it over to the police if they have a court order, he voluntarily conveys his cell site data each time he makes a call.

Susan Freiwald concludes that the Fourth Amendment requires a warrant to obtain cell site location data:

Because government compulsion of disclosure of location data constitutes a search under the Fourth Amendment, the judicial oversight inherent in the probable cause warrant requirement is required. The power and intrusiveness of the method, and its susceptibility to abuse, mean that anything less would violate Fourth Amendment rights. While the probable cause standard will not necessarily be that much more demanding than the showing needed for a ["specific and articulable" facts] order [under the SCA], the need to provide notice to the target, after the fact judicial review, and meaningful remedies should make a significant difference. A warrant must be required for location data acquisition as a matter of law, and no Supreme Court precedents pertaining to bumper-beepers, bank records, or telephone numbers counsel a different result.[103]

5. *Historical vs. Real-Time Location Data.* Is there a difference between historical versus real-time location data? Some courts have concluded that real-time location data requires a warrant whereas historical data does not. One rationale for the distinction is that historical data is stored in records and falls under the third party doctrine. According to Susan Freiwald, the distinction is spurious:

[H]istorical location data may be at least as informative to law enforcement agents as prospective location data. Historical data may indicate with whom, where, and for how long targets have met. It may put a target at the scene of a crime at the time the crime was committed and thereby refute the target's alibi. Magistrate Judge Lenihan appropriately found that "the privacy and associational interests implicated [by acquisition of location data] are not meaningfully diminished by a delay in disclosure." Other courts have also

---

[103] Susan Freiwald, *Cell Phone Location Data and the Fourth Amendment: A Question of Law, Not Fact*, 70 Md. L. Rev. 677, 742-43 (2011).

recognized that law enforcement acquisition of records of historical location data, by virtue of creating a target's complete digital profile, should receive the same Fourth Amendment protection as acquisition of location data in real-time or prospectively.[104]

6. IP ADDRESSES, URLS, AND INTERNET SEARCHES

UNITED STATES V. FORRESTER

512 F.3d 500 (9th Cir. 2008)

FISHER, J. . . . Defendants-appellants Mark Stephen Forrester and Dennis Louis Alba were charged with various offenses relating to the operation of a large Ecstasy-manufacturing laboratory, and were convicted on all counts following a jury trial. They now appeal their convictions and sentences. . . .

During its investigation of Forrester and Alba's Ecstasy-manufacturing operation, the government employed various computer surveillance techniques to monitor Alba's e-mail and Internet activity. The surveillance began in May 2001 after the government applied for and received court permission to install a pen register analogue known as a "mirror port" on Alba's account with PacBell Internet. The mirror port was installed at PacBell's connection facility in San Diego, and enabled the government to learn the to/from addresses of Alba's e-mail messages, the IP addresses of the websites that Alba visited and the total volume of information sent to or from his account. Later, the government obtained a warrant authorizing it to employ imaging and keystroke monitoring techniques, but Alba does not challenge on appeal those techniques' legality or the government's application to use them.

Forrester and Alba were tried by jury. At trial, the government introduced extensive evidence showing that they and their associates built and operated a major Ecstasy laboratory. . . .

Alba contends that the government's surveillance of his e-mail and Internet activity violated the Fourth Amendment and fell outside the scope of the then-applicable federal pen register statute. We hold that the surveillance did not constitute a Fourth Amendment search and thus was not unconstitutional. We also hold that whether or not the computer surveillance was covered by the then-applicable pen register statute — an issue that we do not decide — Alba is not entitled to the suppression of any evidence (let alone the reversal of his convictions) as a consequence.

The Supreme Court held in *Smith v. Maryland* that the use of a pen register (a device that records numbers dialed from a phone line) does not constitute a search for Fourth Amendment purposes. According to the Court, people do not have a subjective expectation of privacy in numbers that they dial because they "realize that they must 'convey' phone numbers to the telephone company, since it is through telephone company switching equipment that their calls are completed." Even if there were such a subjective expectation, it would not be one that society is prepared to recognize as reasonable because "a person has no

---

[104] *Id.* at 734.

legitimate expectation of privacy in information he voluntarily turns over to third parties." Therefore the use of a pen register is not a Fourth Amendment search. Importantly, the Court distinguished pen registers from more intrusive surveillance techniques on the ground that "pen registers do not acquire the *contents* of communications" but rather obtain only the addressing information associated with phone calls.

Neither this nor any other circuit has spoken to the constitutionality of computer surveillance techniques that reveal the to/from addresses of e-mail messages, the IP addresses of websites visited and the total amount of data transmitted to or from an account. We conclude that the surveillance techniques the government employed here are constitutionally indistinguishable from the use of a pen register that the Court approved in *Smith*. First, e-mail and Internet users, like the telephone users in *Smith*, rely on third-party equipment in order to engage in communication. *Smith* based its holding that telephone users have no expectation of privacy in the numbers they dial on the users' imputed knowledge that their calls are completed through telephone company switching equipment. Analogously, e-mail and Internet users have no expectation of privacy in the to/from addresses of their messages or the IP addresses of the websites they visit because they should know that this information is provided to and used by Internet service providers for the specific purpose of directing the routing of information. Like telephone numbers, which provide instructions to the "switching equipment that processed those numbers," e-mail to/from addresses and IP addresses are not merely passively conveyed through third party equipment, but rather are voluntarily turned over in order to direct the third party's servers.

Second, e-mail to/from addresses and IP addresses constitute addressing information and do not necessarily reveal any more about the underlying contents of communication than do phone numbers. When the government obtains the to/from addresses of a person's e-mails or the IP addresses of websites visited, it does not find out the contents of the messages or know the particular pages on the websites the person viewed. At best, the government may make educated guesses about what was said in the messages or viewed on the websites based on its knowledge of the e-mail to/from addresses and IP addresses — but this is no different from speculation about the contents of a phone conversation on the basis of the identity of the person or entity that was dialed. Like IP addresses, certain phone numbers may strongly indicate the underlying contents of the communication; for example, the government would know that a person who dialed the phone number of a chemicals company or a gun shop was likely seeking information about chemicals or firearms. Further, when an individual dials a pre-recorded information or subject-specific line, such as sports scores, lottery results or phone sex lines, the phone number may even show that the caller had access to specific content information. Nonetheless, the Court in *Smith* and *Katz* drew a clear line between unprotected addressing information and protected content information that the government did not cross here.[105]

---

[105] Surveillance techniques that enable the government to determine not only the IP addresses that a person accesses but also the uniform resource locators ("URL") of the pages visited might be more constitutionally problematic. A URL, unlike an IP address, identifies the particular document within a website that a person views and thus reveals much more information about the person's

The government's surveillance of e-mail addresses also may be technologically sophisticated, but it is conceptually indistinguishable from government surveillance of physical mail. In a line of cases dating back to the nineteenth century, the Supreme Court has held that the government cannot engage in a warrantless search of the contents of sealed mail, but can observe whatever information people put on the outside of mail, because that information is voluntarily transmitted to third parties. E-mail, like physical mail, has an outside address "visible" to the third-party carriers that transmit it to its intended location, and also a package of content that the sender presumes will be read only by the intended recipient. The privacy interests in these two forms of communication are identical. The contents may deserve Fourth Amendment protection, but the address and size of the package do not. . . .

We therefore hold that the computer surveillance techniques that Alba challenges are not Fourth Amendment searches. However, our holding extends only to these particular techniques and does not imply that more intrusive techniques or techniques that reveal more content information are also constitutionally identical to the use of a pen register. . . .

Alba claims that the government's computer surveillance was not only unconstitutional but also beyond the scope of the then-applicable pen register statute, 18 U.S.C. § 3121-27 (amended October 2001). Under both the old and new versions of 18 U.S.C. § 3122, the government must apply for and obtain a court order before it can install and use a pen register. When the surveillance at issue here took place in May-July 2001, the applicable statute defined a pen register as a "device which records or decodes electronic or other impulses which identify the numbers dialed or otherwise transmitted on the telephone line to which such device is attached." 18 U.S.C. § 3127(3). Notwithstanding the government's invocation of this provision and application for and receipt of a court order, Alba maintains that the computer surveillance at issue here did not come within the statutory definition of a "pen register."

Even assuming that Alba is correct in this contention, he would not be entitled to the suppression of the evidence obtained through the computer surveillance. As both the Supreme Court and this court have emphasized, suppression is a disfavored remedy, imposed only where its deterrence benefits outweigh its substantial social costs or (outside the constitutional context) where it is clearly contemplated by the relevant statute. . . . Alba does not point to any statutory language requiring suppression when computer surveillance that is similar but not technically equivalent to a pen register is carried out. Indeed, he does not even identify what law or regulation the government may have violated if its surveillance did not come within the scope of the then-applicable pen register statute. The suppression of evidence under these circumstances is plainly inappropriate.

Our conclusion is bolstered by the fact that suppression still would not be appropriate even if the computer surveillance was covered by the pen register statute. Assuming the surveillance violated the statute, there is no mention of

---

Internet activity. For instance, a surveillance technique that captures IP addresses would show only that a person visited the New York Times' website at http://www.nytimes.com, whereas a technique that captures URLs would also divulge the particular articles the person viewed.

suppression of evidence in the statutory text. Instead, the only penalty specified is that "[w]hoever knowingly violates subsection (a)" by installing or using a pen register without first obtaining a court order "shall be fined under this title or imprisoned not more than one year, or both." 18 U.S.C. § 3121(d).

NOTES & QUESTIONS

1. *IP Addresses vs. URLs.* The *Forrester* court concludes that e-mail headers and IP addresses are akin to pen registers and that the controlling case is *Smith v. Maryland*. Does *Smith* control because IP address and e-mail header information are not revealing of the contents of the communications or because this information is conveyed to a third party? Recall that in a footnote, the court observes that URLs "might be more constitutionally problematic" because a "URL, unlike an IP address, identifies the particular document within a website that a person views and thus reveals much more information about the person's Internet activity." However, although IP addresses do not reveal specific parts of a websites that a person visits, they do reveal the various websites that a person visits. Why isn't this revealing enough to trigger constitutional protections?

2. *Content vs. Envelope Information.* A key distinction under ECPA, as well as Fourth Amendment law, is between "content" and "envelope" information. Orin Kerr explains the distinction:

> . . . [E]very communications network features two types of information: the contents of communications, and the addressing and routing information that the networks use to deliver the contents of communications. The former is "content information," and the latter is "envelope information."
>
> The essential distinction between content and envelope information remains constant across different technologies, from postal mail to email. With postal mail, the content information is the letter itself, stored safely inside its envelope. The envelope information is the information derived from the outside of the envelope, including the mailing and return addresses, the stamp and postmark, and the size and weight of the envelope when sealed.
>
> Similar distinctions exist for telephone conversations. The content information for a telephone call is the actual conversation between participants that can be captured by an audio recording of the call. The envelope information includes the number the caller dials, the number from which the caller dials, the time of the call, and its duration.[106]

Under ECPA, content information is generally given strong protection (e.g., the Wiretap Act), whereas envelope information is not (e.g., the Pen Register Act). But is such a distinction viable?

Daniel Solove contends that the distinction breaks down:

> When applied to IP addresses and URLs, the envelope/content distinction becomes even more fuzzy. An IP address is a unique number that is assigned to each computer connected to the Internet. Each website, therefore, has an IP

---

[106] Orin S. Kerr, Internet *Surveillance Law After the USA PATRIOT Act: The Big Brother That Isn't,* 97 Nw. U. L. Rev. 607, 611 (2003).

address. On the surface, a list of IP addresses is simply a list of numbers; but it is actually much more. With a complete listing of IP addresses, the government can learn quite a lot about a person because it can trace how that person surfs the Internet. The government can learn the names of stores at which a person shops, the political organizations a person finds interesting, a person's sexual fetishes and fantasies, her health concerns, and so on.

Perhaps even more revealing are URLs. A URL is a pointer — it points to the location of particular information on the Internet. In other words, it indicates where something is located. When we cite to something on the Web, we are citing to its URL. . . . URLs can reveal the specific information that people are viewing on the Web. URLs can also contain search terms. . . .

[Therefore,] the content/envelope distinction is not always clear. In many circumstances, to adapt Marshall McLuhan, the "envelope" *is* the "content." Envelope information can reveal a lot about a person's private activities, sometimes as much (and even more) than can content information.[107]

Orin Kerr disagrees:

Professor Solove appears to doubt the wisdom of offering lower privacy protection for non-content information. He suggests that the acquisition of non-content information should require a full search warrant based on probable cause. . . .

Despite this, Solove's suggestion that the law should not offer lesser privacy protection for non-content information is unpersuasive. The main reason is that it is quite rare for non-content information to yield the equivalent of content information. It happens in very particular circumstances, but it remains quite rare, and usually in circumstances that are difficult to predict ex ante. In the Internet context, for example, non-content surveillance typically consists of collecting Internet packets; the packets disclose that a packet was sent from one IP address to another IP address at a particular time. This isn't very private information, at least in most cases. Indeed, it is usually impossible to know who asked for the packet, or what the packet was about, or what the person who asked for the packet wanted to do, or even if it was a person (as opposed to the computer) who sent for the packet in the first place. Solove focuses on the compelling example of Internet search terms as an example of non-content information that can be the privacy equivalent of content information. This is a misleading example, however, as Internet search terms very well may be contents. . . . Thus, despite the fact that non-content information can yield private information, in the great majority of cases contents of communications implicate privacy concerns on a higher order of magnitude than non-content information, and it makes sense to give greater privacy protections for the former and lesser to the latter.[108]

Solove replies:

Kerr assumes that a compilation of envelope information is generally less revealing than content information. However, a person may care more about protecting the identities of people with whom she communicates than the content of those communications. Indeed, the identities of the people one

---

[107] Solove, *Surveillance Law, supra*, at 1287-88.

[108] Orin S. Kerr, *A User's Guide to the Stored Communications Act — and a Legislator's Guide to Amending It,* 72 Geo. Wash. L. Rev. 1208, 1229 n.142 (2004).

communicates with implicates freedom of association under the First Amendment. The difficulty is that the distinction between content and envelope information does not correlate well to the distinction between sensitive and innocuous information. Envelope information can be quite sensitive; content information can be quite innocuous. Admittedly, in many cases, people do not care very much about maintaining privacy over the identities of their friends and associates. But it is also true that in many cases, the contents of communications are not very revealing as well. Many e-mails are short messages which do not reveal any deep secrets, and even Kerr would agree that this should not lessen their protection under the law. This is because content information has the potential to be quite sensitive — but this is also the case with envelope information.[109]

3. ***The Scope of the Pen Register Act.*** The version of the Pen Register Act in effect when the search took place in *Forrester* was the pre-USA PATRIOT Act version, which defined pen registers more narrowly as "numbers dialed." The USA PATRIOT Act expanded the definition of pen register to include "dialing, routing, addressing, or signaling information . . . provided, however, that such information shall not include the contents of any communication." Prior to the USA PATRIOT Act changes, it was an open question as to whether the Pen Register Act applied to e-mail headers, IP addresses, and URLs. The USA PATRIOT Act changes aimed to clarify that the Pen Register Act did apply beyond telephone numbers. E-mail headers seem to fit readily into the new Pen Register Act definition. But what about IP addresses and URLs? They involve "routing" and "addressing" information, but they may also include "the contents" of communications. Do they involve "contents" or are they merely "envelope" information?

4. ***ECPA and the Exclusionary Rule.*** The *Forrester* court concludes that even if the acquisition of information violated the Pen Register Act, the exclusionary rule is not a remedy under the Act. As discussed earlier in this chapter, many provisions of electronic surveillance law lack an exclusionary rule. In the Wiretap Act, wire and oral communications are protected with an exclusionary rule, but electronic communications are not. Solove argues that "[s]ince e-mail has become a central mode of communication, this discrepancy is baseless."[110] Is it? Can you think of a reason why e-mail should receive lesser protection than a phone conversation, which would be protected by the exclusionary rule under the Wiretap Act? Additionally, the Stored Communications Act and Pen Register Act have no exclusionary remedies for any type of communication.

Orin Kerr argues the absence of an exclusionary rule in many of ECPA's provisions leads to inadequate judicial attention to ECPA. Without an exclusionary rule, Kerr contends, "criminal defendants have little incentive to raise challenges to the government's Internet surveillance practices."

---

[109] Solove, *Surveillance Law, supra*, at 1288. Susan Freiwald contends that "the current categories of the ECPA do not cover web traffic data. At least one other category of protection is needed. Search terms entered, web-pages visited, and items viewed are neither message contents nor their to/from information." Freiwald, *Online Surveillance, supra*, at 71.

[110] Solove, *Surveillance Law, supra*, at 1282.

Therefore, many challenges to Internet surveillance practices "tend to be in civil cases between private parties that raise issues far removed from those that animated Congress to pass the statutes." Adding an exclusionary remedy, Kerr argues, would "benefit both civil libertarian and law enforcement interests alike." He writes:

> On the civil libertarian side, a suppression remedy would considerably increase judicial scrutiny of the government's Internet surveillance practices in criminal cases. The resulting judicial opinions would clarify the rules that the government must follow, serving the public interest of greater transparency. Less obviously, the change could also benefit law enforcement by altering the type and nature of the disputes over the Internet surveillance laws that courts encounter. Prosecutors would have greater control over the types of cases the courts decided, enjoy more sympathetic facts, and have a better opportunity to explain and defend law enforcement interests before the courts. The statutory law of Internet surveillance would become more like the Fourth Amendment law: a source of vital and enforceable rights that every criminal defendant can invoke, governed by relatively clear standards that by and large respect law enforcement needs and attempt to strike a balance between those needs and privacy interests.[111]

5. *The Internet vs. the Telephone.* Susan Freiwald contends that while the 1968 Wiretap Act (Title III) provided powerful and effective protection for telephone communications, ECPA in 1986 did not do the same for online communications:

> . . . [O]nline surveillance is even more susceptible to law enforcement abuse and even more threatening to privacy. Therefore, one might expect regulation of online surveillance to be more privacy-protective than traditional wiretapping law. That could not be further from the truth. The law provides dramatically less privacy protection for online activities than for traditional telephone calls and videotapings. Additionally, what makes the Wiretap Act complex makes online surveillance law chaotic. Almost all of the techniques designed to rein in law enforcement have been abandoned in the online context. And, while Congress resolved much of its ambivalence towards wiretapping in 1968, current law suggests the outright hostility of all branches of government to online privacy.[112]

In what ways does federal electronic surveillance law protect Internet communication differently from telephone communication? Should the privacy protections differ in these areas?

---

[111] Orin S. Kerr, *Lifting the "Fog" of Internet Surveillance: How a Suppression Remedy Would Change Computer Crime Law*, 54 Hastings L.J. 805, 824, 807-08 (2003).

[112] Susan Freiwald, *Online Surveillance: Remembering the Lessons of the Wiretap Act*, 56 Ala. L. Rev. 9, 14 (2004).

CHAPTER 2

NATIONAL SECURITY AND FOREIGN INTELLIGENCE

CHAPTER OUTLINE

A. THE INTELLIGENCE COMMUNITY

B. THE FOURTH AMENDMENT FRAMEWORK

C. FOREIGN INTELLIGENCE GATHERING

    1. The Foreign Intelligence Surveillance Act

    2. The USA-PATRIOT Act

    3. National Security Letters

    4. Internal Oversight

        (a) The Attorney General's FBI Guidelines

        (b) The Homeland Security Act

        (c) The Intelligence Reform and Terrorism Prevention Act

D. NSA SURVEILLANCE

    1. Standing

    2. The Snowden Revelations

Should the law treat investigations involving national security differently than other criminal investigations? This question has long been one that the law has struggled with. Additionally, there are times when government intelligence agencies want to gather foreign intelligence within the United States. One example is when there might be a foreign spy within the United States. Another example is when intelligence agencies just want to spy on a foreign individual who is in the United States to see what can be learned about the activities of foreign nations. These instances might not involve a criminal investigation or even an immediate national security threat — they merely involve gathering useful foreign intelligence.

The difficulty is in delineating between these activities. For example, suppose intelligence agencies are monitoring the activities of individuals with connections to a foreign terrorist organization. There will certainly be an interest in gathering foreign intelligence. National security will likely be implicated. And the case may very likely result in a criminal prosecution if evidence is obtained that the individuals are plotting a terrorist act.

The previous chapter provided an introduction to the Fourth Amendment and to electronic surveillance law, with a focus on the Electronic Communications Privacy Act (ECPA). Ordinarily, government information gathering activities would fall under the Fourth Amendment rules discussed in the previous chapter on law enforcement, and government electronic surveillance would be regulated by ECPA. However, with national security and foreign intelligence gathering, the Fourth Amendment rules are different, and ECPA often does not apply. Instead, other statutes and regulations apply.

A. THE INTELLIGENCE COMMUNITY

The United States intelligence community consists of a number of agencies that gather information about threats domestic and foreign. The three most prominent intelligence agencies are the FBI, CIA, and NSA.

Federal Bureau of Investigation (FBI). The FBI was originally created in 1908 and called the "Bureau of Investigation." It was not until 1935 when the FBI received its current name. The focus of the FBI is on domestic criminal investigations involving federal crimes. However, the FBI also has intelligence, counterintelligence, and counterterrorism functions.

Central Intelligence Agency (CIA). Before the creation of the CIA, its functions were handled by the Office of Strategic Services (OSS), which was created in 1942 by President Franklin D. Roosevelt. The OSS was eliminated at the end of World War II. President Harry Truman created the CIA with the National Security Act of 1947.

National Security Agency (NSA). Located within the Department of Defense, the NSA was created by President Truman in 1952 to engage in cryptology—deciphering encryption codes used in foreign communications. Subsequently the size and activities of the NSA have increased, and the agency is now engaged in large-scale information gathering activities.

Other Intelligence Agencies. There are many other intelligence agencies beyond the FBI, CIA, and NSA. These agencies are located within the Department of Defense, Department of Homeland Security, Department of State, and Department of the Treasury, among others. Some of these entities include the Defense Intelligence Agency (DIA), the State Department's Bureau of Intelligence and Research (INR), and the Treasury Department's Office of Terrorism and Financial Intelligence.

B. THE FOURTH AMENDMENT FRAMEWORK

Does the Fourth Amendment apply differently to national security and foreign intelligence gathering than it does for domestic criminal investigations? These questions long remained unresolved, and are still not fully resolved to this day.

In a footnote to *Katz v. United States,* 389 U.S. 347 (1967), the Court stated that perhaps a warrant might not be required in situations involving national security:

> Whether safeguards other than prior authorization by a magistrate would satisfy the Fourth Amendment in a situation involving the national security is a question not presented by this case.

Justice White, in a concurring opinion, declared:

> In joining the Court's opinion, I note the Court's acknowledgment that there are circumstance in which it is reasonable to search without a warrant. In this connection . . . the Court points out that today's decision does not reach national security cases. Wiretapping to protect the security of the Nation has been authorized by successive Presidents. The present Administration would apparently save national security cases from restrictions against wiretapping. We should not require the warrant procedure and the magistrate's judgment if the President of the United States or his chief legal officer, the Attorney General, has considered the requirements of national security and authorized electronic surveillance as reasonable.

Justices Douglas and Brennan, in another concurring opinion, took issue with Justice White:

> . . . Neither the President nor the Attorney General is a magistrate. In matters where they believe national security may be involved they are not detached, disinterested, and neutral as a court or magistrate must be. . . .
>
> There is, so far as I understand constitutional history, no distinction under the Fourth Amendment between types of crimes. Article III, § 3, gives "treason" a very narrow definition and puts restrictions on its proof. But the Fourth Amendment draws no lines between various substantive offenses. The arrests on cases of "hot pursuit" and the arrests on visible or other evidence of probable cause cut across the board and are not peculiar to any kind of crime.
>
> I would respect the present lines of distinction and not improvise because a particular crime seems particularly heinous. When the Framers took that step, as they did with treason, the worst crime of all, they made their purpose manifest.

The Supreme Court finally confronted these issues more squarely in a case decided in 1972, *United States v. United States District Court,* which has become known as the *Keith* case, named after District Court Judge Damon Keith.

The *Keith* case began when three founding members of a group called "the White Panthers" bombed a CIA office located in Michigan. The group was not a racist group and in fact was supportive of the Black Panthers. The White Panther agenda was to abolish money. According to the group's manifesto: "We demand total freedom for everybody! And we will not be stopped until we get it. . . .

Rock and Roll music is the spearhead of our attack because it is so effective and so much fun."[1]

When it investigated the bombing, the government wiretapped the phone calls of one of the bombers. This was done without a warrant. Recall from the previous chapter that in 1967 the Supreme Court in *United States v. Katz,* 389 U.S. 347 (1967), held that the Fourth Amendment required a warrant in order for the government to wiretap a phone call. Also recall that in 1968 Congress required special court orders for the government to engage in wiretapping when it passed Title III of the Omnibus Crime Control and Safe Streets Act (which now is the Wiretap Act portion of the Electronic Communications Privacy Act (ECPA)).

The Nixon Administration contended that because this case involved a matter of national security, he was able to conduct surveillance without a Fourth Amendment warrant or Title III court order. The Supreme Court, however, in the *Keith* decision below did not agree.

UNITED STATES V. UNITED STATES DISTRICT COURT
(THE *KEITH* CASE)

407 U.S. 297 (1972)

POWELL, J. . . . The issue before us is an important one for the people of our country and their Government. It involves the delicate question of the President's power, acting through the Attorney General, to authorize electronic surveillance in internal security matters without prior judicial approval. Successive Presidents for more than one-quarter of a century have authorized such surveillance in varying degrees, without guidance from the Congress or a definitive decision of this Court. This case brings the issue here for the first time. Its resolution is a matter of national concern, requiring sensitivity both to the Government's right to protect itself from unlawful subversion and attack and to the citizen's right to be secure in his privacy against unreasonable Government intrusion.

This case arises from a criminal proceeding in the United States District Court for the Eastern District of Michigan, in which the United States charged three defendants with conspiracy to destroy Government property. . . . One of the defendants, Plamondon, was charged with the dynamite bombing of an office of the Central Intelligence Agency in Ann Arbor, Michigan.

Title III of the Omnibus Crime Control and Safe Streets Act, 18 U.S.C. §§ 2510-2520, authorizes the use of electronic surveillance for classes of crimes carefully specified in 18 U.S.C. § 2516. Such surveillance is subject to prior court order. Section 2518 sets forth the detailed and particularized application necessary to obtain such an order as well as carefully circumscribed conditions for its use. The Act represents a comprehensive attempt by Congress to promote more effective control of crime while protecting the privacy of individual thought and expression. Much of Title III was drawn to meet the constitutional

---

[1] Trevor W. Morrison, *The Story of United States v. U.S. District Court (Keith): The Surveillance Power, in Presidential Power Stories* 287 (Christopher Schroeder & Curtis Bradley eds., 2008).

requirements for electronic surveillance enunciated by this Court in *Berger v. New York,* and *Katz v. United States.*

The Government relies on § 2511(3). It argues that "in excepting national security surveillances from the Act's warrant requirement Congress recognized the President's authority to conduct such surveillances without prior judicial approval." The section thus is viewed as a recognition or affirmance of a constitutional authority in the President to conduct warrantless domestic security surveillance such as that involved in this case.

We think the language of § 2511(3), as well as the legislative history of the statute, refutes this interpretation. The relevant language is that: "Nothing contained in this chapter . . . shall limit the constitutional power of the President to take such measures as he deems necessary to protect . . ." against the dangers specified. At most, this is an implicit recognition that the President does have certain powers in the specified areas. Few would doubt this, as the section refers — among other things — to protection "against actual or potential attack or other hostile acts of a foreign power." But so far as the use of the President's electronic surveillance power is concerned, the language is essentially neutral.

Section 2511(3) certainly confers no power, as the language is wholly inappropriate for such a purpose. It merely provides that the Act shall not be interpreted to limit or disturb such power as the President may have under the Constitution. In short, Congress simply left presidential powers where it found them.

Our present inquiry, though important, is . . . a narrow one. It addresses a question left open by *Katz*:

> Whether safeguards other than prior authorization by a magistrate would satisfy the Fourth Amendment in a situation involving the national security. . . .

We begin the inquiry by noting that the President of the United States has the fundamental duty, under Art. II, § 1, of the Constitution, to "preserve, protect and defend the Constitution of the United States." Implicit in that duty is the power to protect our Government against those who would subvert or overthrow it by unlawful means. In the discharge of this duty, the President — through the Attorney General — may find it necessary to employ electronic surveillance to obtain intelligence information on the plans of those who plot unlawful acts against the Government. The use of such surveillance in internal security cases has been sanctioned more or less continuously by various Presidents and Attorneys General since July 1946.

Though the Government and respondents debate their seriousness and magnitude, threats and acts of sabotage against the Government exist in sufficient number to justify investigative powers with respect to them.[2] The covertness and complexity of potential unlawful conduct against the Government and the necessary dependency of many conspirators upon the telephone make electronic surveillance an effective investigatory instrument in certain circumstances. The

---

[2] The Government asserts that there were 1,562 bombing incidents in the United States from January 1, 1971, to July 1, 1971, most of which involved Government related facilities. Respondents dispute these statistics as incorporating many frivolous incidents as well as bombings against nongovernmental facilities. The precise level of this activity, however, is not relevant to the disposition of this case.

marked acceleration in technological developments and sophistication in their use have resulted in new techniques for the planning, commission, and concealment of criminal activities. It would be contrary to the public interest for Government to deny to itself the prudent and lawful employment of those very techniques which are employed against the Government and its lawabiding citizens. . . .

But a recognition of these elementary truths does not make the employment by Government of electronic surveillance a welcome development — even when employed with restraint and under judicial supervision. There is, understandably, a deep-seated uneasiness and apprehension that this capability will be used to intrude upon cherished privacy of law-abiding citizens. We look to the Bill of Rights to safeguard this privacy. Though physical entry of the home is the chief evil against which the wording of the Fourth Amendment is directed, its broader spirit now shields private speech from unreasonable surveillance. Our decision in *Katz* refused to lock the Fourth Amendment into instances of actual physical trespass.

. . . [N]ational security cases, moreover, often reflect a convergence of First and Fourth Amendment values not present in cases of "ordinary" crime. Though the investigative duty of the executive may be stronger in such cases, so also is there greater jeopardy to constitutionally protected speech. . . . The danger to political dissent is acute where the Government attempts to act under so vague a concept as the power to protect "domestic security." Given the difficulty of defining the domestic security interest, the danger of abuse in acting to protect that interest becomes apparent.

The price of lawful public dissent must not be a dread of subjection to an unchecked surveillance power. Nor must the fear of unauthorized official eavesdropping deter vigorous citizen dissent and discussion of Government action in private conversation. For private dissent, no less than open public discourse, is essential to our free society.

As the Fourth Amendment is not absolute in its terms, our task is to examine and balance the basic values at stake in this case: the duty of Government to protect the domestic security, and the potential danger posed by unreasonable surveillance to individual privacy and free expression. If the legitimate need of Government to safeguard domestic security requires the use of electronic surveillance, the question is whether the needs of citizens for privacy and the free expression may not be better protected by requiring a warrant before such surveillance is undertaken. We must also ask whether a warrant requirement would unduly frustrate the efforts of Government to protect itself from acts of subversion and overthrow directed against it. . . .

[C]ontentions in behalf of a complete exemption from the warrant requirement, when urged on behalf of the President and the national security in its domestic implications, merit the most careful consideration. We certainly do not reject them lightly, especially at a time of worldwide ferment and when civil disorders in this country are more prevalent than in the less turbulent periods of our history. There is, no doubt, pragmatic force to the Government's position.

[W]e do not think a case has been made for the requested departure from Fourth Amendment standards. The circumstances described do not justify complete exemption of domestic security surveillance from prior judicial scrutiny. Official surveillance, whether its purpose be criminal investigation or ongoing intelligence gathering, risks infringement of constitutionally protected privacy of speech. Security surveillances are especially sensitive because of the inherent vagueness of the domestic security concept, the necessarily broad and continuing nature of intelligence gathering, and the temptation to utilize such surveillances to oversee political dissent. We recognize, as we have before, the constitutional basis of the President's domestic security role, but we think it must be exercised in a manner compatible with the Fourth Amendment. In this case we hold that this requires an appropriate prior warrant procedure.

We cannot accept the Government's argument that internal security matters are too subtle and complex for judicial evaluation. Courts regularly deal with the most difficult issues of our society. There is no reason to believe that federal judges will be insensitive to or uncomprehending of the issues involved in domestic security cases. . . . If the threat is too subtle or complex for our senior law enforcement officers to convey its significance to a court, one may question whether there is probable cause for surveillance.

Nor do we believe prior judicial approval will fracture the secrecy essential to official intelligence gathering. The investigation of criminal activity has long involved imparting sensitive information to judicial officers who have respected the confidentialities involved. Judges may be counted upon to be especially conscious of security requirements in national security cases. Title III of the Omnibus Crime Control and Safe Streets Act already has imposed this responsibility on the judiciary in connection with such crimes as espionage, sabotage, and treason, §§ 2516(1)(a) and (c), each of which may involve domestic as well as foreign security threats. Moreover, a warrant application involves no public or adversary proceedings: it is an ex parte request before a magistrate or judge. Whatever security dangers clerical and secretarial personnel may pose can be minimized by proper administrative measures, possibly to the point of allowing the Government itself to provide the necessary clerical assistance. . . .

We emphasize, before concluding this opinion, the scope of our decision. As stated at the outset, this case involves only the domestic aspects of national security. We have not addressed and express no opinion as to, the issues which may be involved with respect to activities of foreign powers or their agents. . . .

Moreover, we do not hold that the same type of standards and procedures prescribed by Title III are necessarily applicable to this case. We recognize that domestic security surveillance may involve different policy and practical considerations from the surveillance of "ordinary crime." The gathering of security intelligence is often long range and involves the interrelation of various sources and types of information. The exact targets of such surveillance may be more difficult to identify than in surveillance operations against many types of crime specified in Title III. Often, too, the emphasis of domestic intelligence gathering is on the prevention of unlawful activity or the enhancement of the Government's preparedness for some possible future crisis or emergency. Thus, the focus of domestic surveillance may be less precise than that directed against more conventional types of crime.

Given those potential distinctions between Title III criminal surveillances and those involving the domestic security, Congress may wish to consider protective standards for the latter which differ from those already prescribed for specified crimes in Title III. Different standards may be compatible with the Fourth Amendment if they are reasonable both in relation to the legitimate need of Government for intelligence information and the protected rights of our citizens. For the warrant application may vary according to the governmental interest to be enforced and the nature of citizen rights deserving protection. . . .

DOUGLAS, J. concurring. While I join in the opinion of the Court, I add these words in support of it. . . .

If the Warrant Clause were held inapplicable here, then the federal intelligence machine would literally enjoy unchecked discretion. Here, federal agents wish to rummage for months on end through every conversation, no matter how intimate or personal, carried over selected telephone lines, simply to seize those few utterances which may add to their sense of the pulse of a domestic underground. . . .

That "domestic security" is said to be involved here does not draw this case outside the mainstream of Fourth Amendment law. Rather, the recurring desire of reigning officials to employ dragnet techniques to intimidate their critics lies at the core of that prohibition. For it was such excesses as the use of general warrants and the writs of assistance that led to the ratification of the Fourth Amendment. . . .

[W]e are currently in the throes of another national seizure of paranoia, resembling the hysteria which surrounded the Alien and Sedition Acts, the Palmer Raids, and the McCarthy era. Those who register dissent or who petition their governments for redress are subjected to scrutiny by grand juries, by the FBI, or even by the military. Their associates are interrogated. Their homes are bugged and their telephones are wiretapped. They are befriended by secret government informers. Their patriotism and loyalty are questioned. . . .

We have as much or more to fear from the erosion of our sense of privacy and independence by the omnipresent electronic ear of the Government as we do from the likelihood that fomenters of domestic upheaval will modify our form of governing.

NOTES & QUESTIONS

1. ***The Fourth Amendment Framework in* Keith.** The *Keith* Court draws a distinction between electronic surveillance in (1) criminal investigations, regulated under Title III (now ECPA); (2) domestic national security investigations; and (3) foreign intelligence gathering, including investigations involving "activities of foreign powers and their agents."

   (1) Ordinary Criminal Investigations. Regarding ordinary criminal investigations, the *Keith* Court stated that there was no debate regarding "the necessity of obtaining a warrant in the surveillance of crimes unrelated to the national security interest."

   (2) Domestic National Security Investigations. Regarding domestic national security investigations, the focus of the *Keith* Court's opinion,

its holding was that the Fourth Amendment required the issuing of a warrant in domestic security investigations. It also held that the precise requirements for issuing a requirement to investigate domestic security need not be the same as for Title III criminal surveillance.

(3) Foreign Intelligence Gathering. Finally, the *Keith* Court stated that it did not address issues involving foreign powers and their agents.

Does this tripartite distinction seem useful as a policy matter? How does one distinguish between security surveillance (category two) and surveillance for ordinary crime (category one)?

Daniel Solove argues that such a distinction ought not to be made: "'National security' has often been abused as a justification not only for surveillance but also for maintaining the secrecy of government records as well as violating the civil liberties of citizens." He further contends that "the line between national security and regular criminal activities is very blurry, especially in an age of terrorism."[3] In his book, *Nothing to Hide,* Solove further argues:

> It is difficult to distinguish national-security matters from ordinary crime, especially when U.S. citizens are involved. National security threats *are* a form of crime. They are severe crimes. But the rules for investigating ordinary crime are designed to regulate government information gathering no matter how grave the particular crime might be. These rules aren't rigid, and they make allowances for emergencies and unusual circumstances.[4]

On the other hand, Richard Posner contends that the word "unreasonable" in the Fourth Amendment "invites a wide-ranging comparison between the benefits and costs of a search or seizure." He proposes a "sliding scale" standard where "the level of suspicion require to justify the search or seizure should fall . . . as the magnitude of the crime under investigation rises."[5] Paul Rosenzweig argues: "In this time of terror, some adjustment of the balance between liberty and security is both necessary and appropriate. . . . [T]he very text of the Fourth Amendment — with its prohibition only of 'unreasonable' searches and seizures — explicitly recognizes the need to balance the harm averted against the extent of governmental intrusion."[6]

2. ***The Church Committee Report.*** In 1976, a congressional committee led by Senator Frank Church (called the "Church Committee") engaged in an extensive investigation of government national security surveillance. It found extensive abuses, which it chronicled in its famous report known as the Church Committee Report:

---

[3] Solove, *Surveillance Law,* 72 Geo. Wash. L. Rev. 1264, 1301-02 (2004).

[4] Daniel J. Solove, *Nothing to Hide: The False Tradeoff Between Privacy and Security* 66 (2011).

[5] Richard Posner, *Law, Pragmatism, and Democracy* 303 (2003); *see also* Akhil Reed Amar, *The Constitution and Criminal Procedure* 31 (1997) ("The core of the Fourth Amendment . . . is neither a warrant nor probable cause but reasonableness.").

[6] Paul Rosenzweig, *Civil Liberty and the Response to Terrorism,* 42 Duq. L. Rev. 663 (2004).

Too many people have been spied upon by too many Government agencies and too much information has been collected. The Government has often undertaken the secret surveillance of citizens on the basis of their political beliefs, even when those beliefs posed no threat of violence or illegal acts on behalf of a hostile foreign power. The Government, operating primarily through secret informants, but also using other intrusive techniques such as wiretaps, microphone "bugs," surreptitious mail opening, and break-ins, has swept in vast amounts of information about the personal lives, views, and associations of American citizens. . . . Groups and individuals have been harassed and disrupted because of their political views and their lifestyles. Investigations have been based upon vague standards whose breadth made excessive collection inevitable. . . .

The FBI's COINTELPRO — counterintelligence program — was designed to "disrupt" groups and "neutralize" individuals deemed to be threats to domestic security. The FBI resorted to counterintelligence tactics in part because its chief officials believed that existing law could not control the activities of certain dissident groups, and that court decisions had tied the hands of the intelligence community. Whatever opinion one holds about the policies of the targeted groups, many of the tactics employed by the FBI were indisputably degrading to a free society. . . .

Since the early 1930's, intelligence agencies have frequently wiretapped and bugged American citizens without the benefit of judicial warrant. . . .

There has been, in short, a clear and sustained failure by those responsible to control the intelligence community and to ensure its accountability.[7]

The Church Committee Report was influential in the creation of FISA as well as the Attorney General Guidelines.

3. *National Security vs. Civil Liberties.* Eric Posner and Adrian Vermeule argue that the legislature and judiciary should defer to the executive in times of emergency and that it is justified to curtail civil liberties when national security is threatened:

The essential feature of the emergency is that national security is threatened; because the executive is the only organ of government with the resources, power, and flexibility to respond to threats to national security, it is natural, inevitable, and desirable for power to flow to this branch of government. Congress rationally acquiesces; courts rationally defer. . . .

During emergencies, when new threats appear, the balance shifts; government should and will reduce civil liberties in order to enhance security in those domains where the two must be traded off. . . .

In emergencies . . . judges are at sea, even more so than are executive officials. The novelty of the threats and of the necessary responses makes judicial routines and evolved legal rules seem inapposite, even obstructive. There is a premium on the executive's capacities for swift, vigorous, and secretive action.[8]

---

[7] *Intelligence Activities and the Rights of Americans* (Vol. 2), Final Report of the Select Committee to Study Government Operations with Respect to Intelligence Activities 5, 10, 15 (Apr. 26, 1976).

[8] Eric A. Posner & Adrian Vermeule, *Terror in the Balance: Security, Liberty, and the Courts* 4, 5, 18 (2006). For another defense of the curtailment of civil liberties for national security, see Richard A. Posner, *Not a Suicide Pact: The Constitution in a Time of National Emergency* (2006).

4. *The Fourth Amendment and Foreign Intelligence Surveillance. Keith* did not address how the Fourth Amendment would govern foreign intelligence surveillance (category three). Circuit courts examining the issue have concluded that at a minimum, no warrant is required by the Fourth Amendment for foreign intelligence surveillance. In *United States v. Butenko*, 494 F.2d 593 (3d Cir. 1974) (en banc), the court justified this conclusion by reasoning that "foreign intelligence gathering is a clandestine and highly unstructured activity, and the need for electronic surveillance often cannot be anticipated in advance." Reaching a similar conclusion in *United States v. Truong Dinh Hung*, 629 F.2d 908 (4th Cir. 1980), the court reasoned: "[T]he needs of the executive are so compelling in the area of foreign intelligence, unlike the area of domestic security, that a uniform warrant requirement would, following *Keith,* 'unduly frustrate' the President in carrying out his foreign affairs responsibilities."

C. FOREIGN INTELLIGENCE GATHERING

1. THE FOREIGN INTELLIGENCE SURVEILLANCE ACT

In the *Keith* case, the Court explicitly refused to address whether the Fourth Amendment would require a warrant for surveillance of agents of foreign powers.

The Foreign Intelligence Surveillance Act (FISA) of 1978, Pub. L. No. 95-511, codified at 50 U.S.C. §§ 1801–1811, establishes standards and procedures for use of electronic surveillance to collect "foreign intelligence" within the United States. § 1804(a)(7)(B). FISA creates a different regime than ECPA, the legal regime that governs electronic surveillance for law enforcement purposes. The regime created by FISA is designed primarily for intelligence gathering agencies to regulate how they gain general intelligence about foreign powers and agents of foreign powers within the borders of the United States. In contrast, the regime of ECPA is designed for domestic law enforcement to govern the gathering of information for criminal investigations involving people in United States.

Applicability of FISA. When does FISA govern rather than ECPA? FISA generally applies when foreign intelligence gathering is "a significant purpose" of the investigation. 50 U.S.C. § 1804(a)(7)(B) and § 1823(a)(7)(B). The language of "a significant purpose" comes from the USA PATRIOT Act of 2001. Prior to the USA PATRIOT Act, FISA as interpreted by the courts required that the collection of foreign intelligence be the primary purpose for surveillance. After the USA PATRIOT Act, foreign intelligence gathering need no longer be the primary purpose. A further expansion of the FISA occurred in 2008 with amendments to that law, which we discuss below.

The Foreign Intelligence Surveillance Court (FISC). Requests for FISA orders are reviewed by a special court of federal district court judges. The USA PATRIOT Act increased the number of judges on the FISC from 7 to 11. 50 U.S.C. § 1803(a). The proceedings are ex parte, with the Department of Justice (DOJ) making the applications to the court on behalf of the CIA and other agencies. The Court meets in secret, and its proceedings are generally not revealed to the public or to the targets of the surveillance.

In 2007, the FISC declined an ACLU request to access its documents relating to alleged unauthorized surveillance. *In re Motion for Release of Court Records*, 526 F. Supp. 2d (2007). This case was an exception to the usual procedure of *ex parte* only hearings before the FISC. The court found that it had jurisdiction to entertain motions for release of its documents, and then denied the request. It stated:

> The FISC is a unique court. Its entire docket relates to the collection of foreign intelligence by the federal government. The applications submitted to it by the government are classified, as are the overwhelming majority of the FISC's orders. Court sessions are held behind closed doors in a secure facility, and every proceeding in its history prior to this one has been ex parte, with the government the only party. . . . Other courts operate primarily in public with secrecy the exception; the FISC operates primarily in secret, with public access the exception.

Perhaps most importantly, the court noted that "the proper functioning of the FISA process would be adversely affected if submitting sensitive information to the FISC could subject the Executive Branch's classification to a heightened form of judicial review."

 Court Orders. The legal test for surveillance under FISA is not whether probable cause exists that the party to be monitored is involved in criminal activity. Rather, the court must find probable cause that the party to be monitored is a "foreign power" or "an agent of a foreign power." § 1801. Therefore, unlike ECPA or the Fourth Amendment, FISA surveillance is not tied to any required showing of a connection to criminal activity. However, if the monitored party is a "United States person" (a citizen or permanent resident alien), the government must establish probable cause that the party's activities "may" or "are about to" involve a criminal violation. § 1801(b)(2)(A).

The number of FISA electronic surveillance orders expanded from 199 orders (1979) to 886 (1999).[9] In 2001, the FISA court approved 934 applications for electronic surveillance orders. None were denied.[10] The USA PATRIOT Act of 2001 eased the standard for obtaining a FISA order. There were 1,228 orders in 2002, 1,727 orders in 2003 (4 were denied), and 1,758 applications in 2004. This represents an increase of 88 percent from 2001.

---

[9] Foreign Intelligence Surveillance Act Orders 1979-1999, http://www/epic.org/privacy/wiretap/stats/fisa_stats.html.

[10] Office of Attorney General, *2001 Annual FISA Report to Congress,* available at www.usdoj.gov/o4foia/readingrooms/2001annualfisareporttocongress.htm.

Surveillance Without Court Orders. In certain circumstances, FISA authorizes surveillance without having to first obtain a court order. § 1802. In particular, the surveillance must be "solely directed at" obtaining intelligence exclusively from "foreign powers." § 1802(a). There must be "no substantial likelihood that the surveillance will acquire the contents of any communications to which a United States person is a party." § 1802(a)(1)(B). Electronic surveillance without a court order requires the authorization of the President, through the Attorney General, in writing under oath. § 1802(a)(1).

Video Surveillance. Unlike ECPA, FISA explicitly regulates video surveillance. In order to have court approval for video surveillance, the FISA requires the government to submit, among other things, "a detailed description of the nature of the information sought and the type of communications or activities to be subjected to the surveillance," § 1804(a)(6); "a certification . . . that such information cannot reasonably be obtained by normal investigative techniques," § 1804(a)(7); and "a statement of the period of time for which the electronic surveillance is required to be maintained," § 1804(a)(10). Video surveillance orders can last for 90 days.

The FISA Amendments Act. In 2008, Congress enacted significant amendments to FISA. The FISA Amendments Act (FAA) was passed in response to the revelation in 2005 that since 9/11 the National Security Agency (NSA) was engaging in an extensive program of warrantless wiretapping of international phone calls. Subsequently, several lawsuits were brought against the telecommunications companies that participated in the surveillance for violating FISA and ECPA. One of the most controversial aspects of the FAA was a grant of retroactive immunity to these companies. The NSA surveillance program and the ensuing litigation will be discussed later in this chapter.

In its other aspects, the FAA both expanded the government's surveillance abilities and added new privacy protections. The FAA explicitly permits collection of information from U.S. telecommunications facilities where it is not possible in advance to know whether a communication is purely international (that is, all parties to it are located outside of the United States) or whether the communication involves a foreign power or its agents. David Kris explains, "With the advent of web-based communication and other developments, the government cannot always determine — consistently, reliably, and in real time — the location of parties to an e-mail message."[11] It is also possible to collect information and then examine it (through data mining) to look for links with a foreign power or its agents. The perceived need, Kris states, was for a kind of "vacuum-cleaner" capacity that would enable the government to sift through large amounts of information without meeting FISA's traditional warrant requirements.

---

[11] David Kris, *A Guide to the New FISA Bill, Part I*, Balkanization (June 21, 2008), at http://balkin.blogspot.com/2008/06/guide-to-new-fisa-bill-part-i.html. Kris is co-author of the leading treatise, J. Douglas Wilson & David Kris, *National Security Investigations and Prosecutions* (2007).

FAA amends FISA to permit "targeting of persons reasonably believed to be located outside the United States to acquire foreign intelligence information." § 702(a). The person targeted must be a non-U.S. person, or certain more restrictive measures apply. §§ 703–04. The critical substantive requirements are that the "target" of the surveillance be someone overseas and that a "significant purpose" of the surveillance be to acquire "foreign intelligence information," which is broadly defined.

The collection of this information must be carried out in accordance with certain "targeting procedures" to ensure that the collection is directed at persons located outside the United States. § 702(c)(1)(A). The acquisition must also involve new minimization procedures, which the Attorney General is to adopt. § 702(e). The Justice Department and the Director of National Intelligence must certify in advance of the surveillance activity that targeting and minimization procedures meet the statutory standards and that "a significant purpose" of the surveillance is to acquire foreign intelligence information. § 702(g)(2). The FAA also states that the government may not engage in a kind of "reverse-targeting" — the government cannot target "a person reasonably believed to be outside the United States if the purpose of such acquisition is to target a particular, known person reasonably believed to be in the United States." § 702(b)(2).

The FISC is to review certifications and the targeting and minimization procedures adopted. If a certification does not "contain all the required elements" or the procedures "are not consistent with the requirements" of the FAA or the Fourth Amendment to the U.S. Constitution, the FISC is to issue an order directing the government to correct any deficiencies. § 702(i)(3).

As for its expansion of privacy protections, the FAA requires that the FISC approve surveillance of a U.S. citizen abroad based on a showing that includes a finding that the person is "an agent of a foreign power, or an officer or employee of a foreign power." Previously, FISA did not regulate surveillance of targets, whether U.S. citizens or not, when located outside the United States. The FAA also contains new mechanisms for congressional oversight and crafts new audit functions for the Inspector Generals of the Department Justice.

GLOBAL RELIEF FOUNDATION, INC. V. O'NEIL

207 F. Supp. 779 (N.D. Ill. 2002)

. . . [A]gents of the FBI arrived at the corporate headquarters of Global Relief [a U.S.-based Islamic humanitarian relief organization] and the home of its executive director on December 14, 2001 and seized a considerable amount of material they felt was relevant to their investigation of Global Relief's activities. As the defendants have conceded in their briefs, no warrant had been obtained before the FBI arrived either at Global Relief's headquarters or the executive director's residence. Nevertheless, FISA includes a provision which states that, when the Attorney General declares that "an emergency situation exists with respect to the execution of a search to obtain foreign intelligence information" prior to the Foreign Intelligence Surveillance Court acting on the application, a warrantless search is authorized. 50 U.S.C. § 1824(e)(1)(B)(i). When such an emergency situation arises, the government must submit a warrant application to the Foreign Intelligence Surveillance Court within 72 hours of the warrantless search for approval. *See* 50 U.S.C. § 1824(e). In this case, the failure of the FBI agents to present a FISA warrant on December 14 was caused by the Assistant Attorney General's declaration that an emergency situation existed with respect to the targeted documents and material. The defendants did submit a warrant application to the Foreign Intelligence Surveillance Court on December 15, as required by 50 U.S.C. § 1824(e). We have reviewed the warrant that issued and the submissions to the Foreign Intelligence Surveillance Court in support of that warrant.

We conclude that the FISA application established probable cause to believe that Global Relief and the executive director were agents of a foreign power, as that term is defined for FISA purposes, at the time the search was conducted and the application was granted. . . . Given the sensitive nature of the information upon which we have relied in making this determination and the Attorney General's sworn assertion that disclosure of the underlying information would harm national security, it would be improper for us to elaborate further on this subject.

This Court has concluded that disclosure of the information we have reviewed could substantially undermine ongoing investigations required to apprehend the conspirators behind the September 11 murders and undermine the ability of law enforcement agencies to reduce the possibility of terrorist crimes in the future. Furthermore, this Court is persuaded that the search and seizure made by the FBI on December 14 were authorized by FISA. Accordingly, we decline plaintiff's request that we declare the search invalid and order the immediate return of all items seized.

NOTES & QUESTIONS

1. **Probable Cause.** Searches under the Wiretap Act require a "super warrant," including a showing of probable cause that an individual has committed or is about to commit an enumerated offense. 18 U.S.C. § 2518(3). What is the required showing of probable cause for a FISA search? FISA requires a judicial finding, as the *O'Neill* case indicates, that probable cause exists to believe that the target is an agent of a foreign power. It also states that no U.S. person can be considered an agent of a foreign power based solely on First Amendment activities.

2. **Defendants' Rights?** In *Global Relief Foundation*, the court finds that disclosure of the information that it reviewed in deciding on the validity of the search was not to be revealed to the defendant because it "could substantially undermine ongoing investigations required to apprehend the conspirators behind the September 11 murders and undermine the ability of law enforcement agencies to reduce the possibility of terrorist crimes in the future." However, FISA requires that defendants receive notice about "any information obtained or derived from an electronic surveillance of that

aggrieved person" pursuant to FISA when the government seeks to use information at trial or other official proceedings. 50 U.S.C. § 1806(c).

3. ***The Three* Keith *Categories.*** Recall the *Keith* Court's distinction between electronic surveillance in (1) criminal investigations; (2) domestic security investigations; and (3) investigations involving "activities of foreign powers and their agents." Today, ECPA regulates electronic surveillance in criminal investigations (category one above). The Foreign Intelligence Surveillance Act (FISA), as enacted in 1978, regulates electronic and other kinds of surveillance in cases involving foreign powers and their agents (category three).

What then of the *Keith* category of "domestic security investigations" (category two)? Recall that the defendants in the underlying criminal proceeding were charged with a conspiracy to destroy government property. One of the defendants, for example, was charged with "the dynamite bombing" of a CIA office in Michigan. *Keith* makes it clear that it would be consistent with the Fourth Amendment for Congress to create different statutory requirements for issuing warrants for surveillance in cases involving domestic security. But Congress has not enacted such rules, and, as a consequence, law enforcement is required to carry out surveillance of criminal activities similar to those in *Keith* under the requirements of Title III and other parts of ECPA.

4. ***The Lone Wolf Amendment.*** The *Keith* categories and related rules remain unaltered by the "lone wolf" amendment to FISA in 2004. That year, Congress amended FISA to include any non-U.S. person who "engages in international terrorism or activities in preparation therefor" in the definition of "agent of a foreign power." The change means that the "lone wolf" terrorist need not be tied to a foreign power, but must be a non-U.S. person engaged in or plotting "international terrorism." FISA defines "international terrorism" as involving, among other things, activities that "[o]ccur totally outside the U.S., or transcend national boundaries in terms of the means by which they accomplished, the persons they appear intended to coerce or intimidate, or the locale in which their perpetrators operate or seek asylum." 50 U.S.C. § 1801(c). As an illustration of the coverage of the "Lone Wolf" amendment, it would not cover Timothy McVeigh, the Oklahoma City bomber.

5. ***A New Agency for Domestic Intelligence?*** Francesca Bignami notes that in European countries, one governmental agency typically gathers intelligence on threats abroad posed by foreign governments, and another agency "is charged with gathering intelligence at home, on activities sponsored by foreign powers (counter-intelligence) as well as on home-grown security threats."[12] Both of these agencies are generally overseen not by judiciary, but by legislative and executive branches. Both intelligence agencies generally carry out surveillance under a more permissive set of legal rules than the domestic police. In contrast, in the United States, the FBI is charged with both

---

[12] Francesca Bignami, *European versus American Liberty*, 48 B.C. L. Rev. 609, 621 (2007).

domestic intelligence investigations and criminal investigations of violations of federal law.

Judge Richard Posner has emerged as the leading critic of the assignment of this double function to the FBI. He contends that the combination of criminal investigation and domestic intelligence at the FBI has not been successful: "If the incompatibility between the law enforcement and intelligence cultures is conceded, then it follows that an agency 100 percent dedicated to domestic intelligence would be likely to do a better job than the FBI, which is at most 20 percent intelligence and thus at least 80 percent criminal investigation and in consequence dominated by the criminal investigations."[13] Posner calls for creation of a "pure" domestic intelligence agency, one without any law enforcement responsibilities and located outside of the FBI. For Posner, the new U.S. Security Intelligence Surveillance can be modeled on the United Kingdom's MI5 or the Canadian Security Intelligence Service. What should the rules be for such a domestic intelligence agency concerning telecommunications surveillance? Should the FISA rules be applied to it?

UNITED STATES V. ISA

923 F.2d 1300 (8th Cir. 1991)

[The FBI obtained an order pursuant to FISA to bug the home of Zein Hassan Isa and his wife, Maria Matias. The FBI suspected Isa, a naturalized U.S. citizen, of being an agent of the Palestine Liberation Organization (PLO). One evening, the FBI's recording tapes of the bugged home captured Zein and Maria's murder of their 16-year-old daughter, Tina. Zein and Maria became angry at Tina's general rebelliousness and her defiance of their order not to date a particular young man. On the tape, Zein said to Tina: "Here, listen, my dear daughter, do you know that this is the last day? Tonight, you're going to die!" Tina responded in disbelief: "Huh?" Maria held Tina down while Zein stabbed her six times in the chest. While Tina screamed, Zein said: "Quiet, little one! Die my daughter, die!" The FBI turned the tapes over to the State of Missouri, where the Isas resided, where they were used to convict the Isas of murder. The Isas were sentenced to death.[14] Zein Isa argued that the recording should be suppressed because it captured events that had no relevance to the FBI's foreign intelligence gathering.]

GIBSON, J. . . . [A]ppellant argues that his fourth amendment rights were violated because the government failed to comply with the minimization procedures defined in 50 U.S.C. § 1801(h). Specifically, he contends that the tapes turned over to the State of Missouri record a "private domestic matter," which is not relevant material under the Foreign Intelligence Surveillance Act and must therefore be destroyed. In support of this argument, he cites isolated

---

[13] Richard A. Posner, *Uncertain Shield* 101-02 (2006).

[14] The Eighth Circuit opinion contains a very meager account of the facts on this case. The facts contained in this book are taken from *Terror and Death at Home Are Caught in F.B.I. Tape,* N.Y. Times, Oct. 28, 1991, at A14.

sentences regarding required minimization procedures from the legislative history of the Foreign Intelligence Surveillance Act:

> Minimization procedures might also include restrictions on the use of surveillance to times when foreign intelligence information is likely to be obtained, ... [Furthermore, a target's] communications which are clearly not relevant to his clandestine intelligence activities should be destroyed. S. Rep. No. 95-701, 95th Cong., 2d Sess. 4.

Notwithstanding the minimization procedures required by [FISA], the Act specifically authorizes the retention of information that is "evidence of a crime," 50 U.S.C. § 1801(h)(3), and provides procedures for the retention and dissemination of such information. 50 U.S.C. § 1806(b)-(f). There is no requirement that the "crime" be related to foreign intelligence. . . .

Thus, we conclude that the tapes are "evidence of crime" and that the district court correctly denied appellant's motion to suppress. 50 U.S.C. § 1801(h)(3).

NOTES & QUESTIONS

1. *Use of Information Obtained Through FISA Orders.* As the *Isa* court notes, information obtained via FISA can be used in criminal trials. However, the standard to obtain a FISA order does not require probable cause. Is it appropriate to allow the use of evidence that would ordinarily required a warrant with probable cause to obtain? On the other hand, the FISA order in *Isa* was properly obtained, and the agents unexpectedly obtained evidence of a murder. If the order is obtained properly in good faith, and evidence of a crime is unexpectedly gathered, why should it be excluded from use in a criminal prosecution?

2. *Minimization Procedures and Information Screening "Walls."* As illustrated by *Isa,* FISA allows the use of information properly obtained under FISA to be used in a criminal prosecution. What prevents the government from using the often more lax standards of FISA to gather evidence in a criminal investigation? The standards of FISA are often much less stringent than those of ECPA. Government officials would merely need to say that they are conducting "intelligence gathering" and obtain a FISA order rather than an order under ECPA — and then, if they uncover evidence of a crime, they could use it to prosecute. FISA has some built-in protections against this. For example, it requires that "the purpose" of the surveillance be foreign intelligence gathering. This language was interpreted by courts as the "primary" purpose.

   FISA requires that procedures be implemented to minimize the collection, retention, and dissemination of information about U.S. persons. § 1801(h)(1). Minimization procedures are designed to prevent the broad power of "foreign intelligence gathering" from being used for routine criminal investigations. In a number of instances, however, there are overlaps between foreign intelligence gathering and criminal investigations.

   One common minimization procedure is what is known as an "information screening wall." With the "wall," an official not involved in the criminal investigation must review the raw materials gathered by FISA surveillance and only pass on information that might be relevant evidence. The wall is designed to prevent criminal justice personnel from initiating or directing the FISA surveillance. The wall does not prevent the sharing of information; rather, it prevents criminal prosecutors from becoming involved in the front end of the investigation rather than on the back end.

How should terrorism investigations, which involve both intelligence gathering and the collection of evidence for criminal prosecution, fit into this scheme?

2. THE USA PATRIOT ACT

THE 9/11 COMMISSION REPORT

Excerpt from pp. 254-75 (2004)

"The System Was Blinking Red"

As 2001 began, counterterrorism officials were receiving frequent but fragmentary reports about threats. Indeed, there appeared to be possible threats almost everywhere the United States had interests — including at home. . . .

Threat reports surged in June and July, reaching an even higher peak of urgency. The summer threats seemed to be focused on Saudi Arabia, Israel, Bahrain, Kuwait, Yemen, and possibly Rome, but the danger could be anywhere — including a possible attack on the G-8 summit in Genoa. . . .

A terrorist threat advisory distributed in late June indicated a high probability of near-term "spectacular" terrorist attacks resulting in numerous casualties. Other reports' titles warned, "Bin Ladin Attacks May Be Imminent" and "Bin Ladin and Associates Making Near-Term Threats." . . .

Most of the intelligence community recognized in the summer of 2001 that the number and severity of threat reports were unprecedented. Many officials told us that they knew something terrible was planned, and they were desperate to stop it. Despite their large number, the threats received contained few specifics regarding time, place, method, or target. . . .

["Jane," an FBI analyst assigned to the FBI's investigation of the terrorist attack on the USS *Cole*] began drafting what is known as a lead for the FBI's New York Field Office. A lead relays information from one part of the FBI to another and requests that a particular action be taken. . . . [H]er draft lead was not sent until August 28. Her email told the New York agent that she wanted him to get started as soon as possible, but she labeled the lead as "Routine" — a designation that informs the receiving office that it has 30 days to respond.

The agent who received the lead forwarded it to his squad supervisor. That same day, the supervisor forwarded the lead to an intelligence agent to open an intelligence case — an agent who thus was behind "the wall" keeping FBI intelligence information from being shared with criminal prosecutors. He also sent it to the *Cole* case agents and an agent who had spent significant time in Malaysia searching for another Khalid: Khalid Sheikh Mohammad.

The suggested goal of the investigation was to locate Mihdhar, [a member of al Qaeda and a 9/11 hijacker] determine his contacts and reasons for being in the United States, and possibly conduct an interview. Before sending the lead, "Jane" had discussed it with "John," the CIA official on detail to the FBI. . . . The discussion seems to have been limited to whether the search should be classified as an intelligence investigation or as a criminal one. It appears that no one informed higher levels of management in either the FBI or CIA about the case. . . .

One of the *Cole* case agents read the lead with interest, and contacted "Jane" to obtain more information. "Jane" argued, however, that because the agent was designated a "criminal" FBI agent, not an intelligence FBI agent, the wall kept him from participating in any search for Mihdhar. In fact, she felt he had to destroy his copy of the lead because it contained NSA information from reports that included caveats ordering that the information not be shared without OIPR's permission. The agent asked "Jane" to get an opinion from the FBI's National Security Law Unit (NSLU) on whether he could open a criminal case on Mihdhar.

"Jane" sent an email to the *Cole* case agent explaining that according to the NSLU, the case could be opened only as an intelligence matter, and that if Mihdhar was found, only designated intelligence agents could conduct or even be present at any interview. She appears to have misunderstood the complex rules that could apply to this situation.

The FBI agent angrily responded:

> Whatever has happened to this — someday someone will die — and the wall or not — the public will not understand why we were not more effective at throwing every resource we had at certain "problems." . . .

"Jane" replied that she was not making up the rules; she claimed that they were in the relevant manual and "ordered by the [FISA] Court and every office of the FBI is required to follow them including FBI NY."

It is now clear that everyone involved was confused about the rules governing the sharing and use of information gathered in intelligence channels. Because Mihdhar was being sought for his possible connection to or knowledge of the *Cole* bombing, he could be investigated or tracked under the existing *Cole* criminal case. No new criminal case was need for the criminal agent to begin searching for Mihdhar. And as NSA had approved the passage of its information to the criminal agent, he could have conducted a search using all available information. As a result of this confusion, the criminal agents who were knowledgeable about al Qaeda and experienced with criminal investigative techniques, including finding suspects and possible criminal charges, were thus excluded from the search. . . .

We believe that if more resources had been applied and a significantly different approach taken, Mihdhar and Hazmi might have been found. They had used their true names in the United States. Still, the investigators would have needed luck as well as skill to find them prior to September 11 even if such searches had begun as early as August 23, when the lead was first drafted.

Many FBI witnesses have suggested that even if Mihdhar had been found, there was nothing the agents could have done except follow him onto the planes. We believe this is incorrect. Both Hazmi and Mihdhar could have been held for immigration violations or as material witnesses in the *Cole* bombing case. Investigation or interrogation of them, and investigation of their travel and financial activities, could have yielded evidence of connections to other participants in the 9/11 plot. The simple fact of their detention could have derailed the plan. In any case, the opportunity did not arise. . . .

On August 15, 2001, the Minneapolis FBI Field Office initiated an intelligence investigation on Zacarias Moussaoui. . . . [H]e had entered the United States in February 2001, and had begun flight lessons at Airman Flight School in Norman, Oklahoma. He resumed his training at the Pan Am International Flight Academy in Eagan, Minnesota, starting on August 13. He had none of the usual qualifications for light training on Pan Am's Boeing 747 flight simulators. He said he did not intend to become a commercial pilot but wanted the training as an "ego boosting thing." Moussaoui stood out because with little knowledge of flying, he wanted to learn to "take off and land" a Boeing 747.

The agent in Minneapolis quickly learned that Moussaoui possessed jihadist beliefs. Moreover, Moussaoui had $32,000 in a bank account but did not provide a plausible explanation for this sum of money. He traveled to Pakistan but became agitated when asked if he had traveled to nearby countries while in Pakistan. He planned to receive martial arts training, and intended to purchase a global positioning receiver. The agent also noted that Moussaoui became extremely agitated whenever he was questioned regarding his religious beliefs. The agent concluded that Moussaoui was "an Islamic extremist preparing for some future act in furtherance of radical fundamentalist goals." He also believed Moussaoui's plan was related to his flight training.

Moussaoui can be seen as an al Qaeda mistake and a missed opportunity. An apparently unreliable operative, he had fallen into the hands of the FBI. . . . If Moussaoui had been connected to al Qaeda, questions should instantly have arisen about a possible al Qaeda plot that involved piloting airliners, a possibility that had never been seriously analyzed by the intelligence community. . . .

As a French national who had overstayed his visa, Moussaoui could be detained immediately. The INS arrested Moussaoui on the immigration violation. A deportation order was signed on August 17, 2001.

The agents in Minnesota were concerned that the U.S. Attorney's office in Minneapolis would find insufficient probable cause of a crime to obtain a criminal warrant to search Moussaoui's laptop computer. Agents at FBI headquarters believed there was insufficient probable cause. Minneapolis therefore sought a special warrant under the Foreign Intelligence Surveillance Act. . . .

To do so, however, the FBI needed to demonstrate probable cause that Moussaoui was an agent of a foreign power, a demonstration that was not required to obtain a criminal warrant but was a statutory requirement for a FISA warrant. The agent did not have sufficient information to connect Moussaoui to a "foreign power," so he reached out for help, in the United States and overseas. . .

[Based on information supplied by the French government, Moussaoui was linked to a rebel leader in Chechnya.] This set off a spirited debate between the Minneapolis Field Office, FBI headquarters, and the CIA as to whether Chechen rebels . . . were sufficiently associated with a terrorist organization to constitute a "foreign power" for purposes of the FISA statute. FBI headquarters did not believe this was good enough, and its National Security Law Unit declined to submit a FISA application. . . .

Although the Minneapolis agents wanted to tell the FAA from the beginning about Moussaoui, FBI headquarters instructed Minneapolis that it could not share the more complete report the case agent had prepared for the FAA. . . .

NOTES & QUESTIONS

1. ***Confusion About the Law Before 9/11.*** The 9/11 Commission Report excerpted above indicated that many law enforcement officials were confused about what FISA required and how information could be shared. The 9/11 Commission Report stated that the FBI headquarters concluded that Moussaoui's association with Chechen rebels was not adequate to justify a FISA order because Chechen rebels were not "sufficiently associated with a terrorist organization to constitute a 'foreign power' for purposes of the FISA statute." Does FISA require that a foreign power involve a terrorist organization? Consider the following excerpt from a Senate Report discussing the problems with the Moussaoui investigation:

> *First,* key FBI personnel responsible for protecting our country against terrorism did not understand the law. The SSA at FBI Headquarters responsible for assembling the facts in support of the Moussaoui FISA application testified before the Committee in a closed hearing that he did not know that "probable cause" was the applicable legal standard for obtaining a FISA warrant. In addition, he did not have a clear understanding of what the probable cause standard meant. . . . In addition to not understanding the probable cause standard, the SSA's supervisor (the Unit Chief) responsible for reviewing FISA applications did not have a proper understanding of the legal definition of the "agent of a foreign power" requirement.[15]

A footnote in the report explained that the FBI agent "was under the incorrect impression that the statute required a link to an already identified or 'recognized' terrorist organization, an interpretation that the FBI and the supervisor himself admitted was incorrect."

According to Senator Arlen Specter (R-PA), the consequences of this misunderstanding of law were grave:

> The failure to obtain a warrant under the Foreign Intelligence Surveillance Act for Zacarias Moussaoui was a matter of enormous importance, and it is my view that if we had gotten into Zacarias Moussaoui's computer, a treasure trove of connections to Al-Qeada, in combination with the FBI report from Phoenix where the young man with Osama bin Laden's picture seeking flight training, added to [the fact that] the CIA knew about two men who turned out to be terrorist pilots on 9/11 . . . there was a veritable blueprint and 9/11 might well have been prevented. . . .
>
> [I]n a way which was really incredulous, the FBI agents didn't know the standard. They didn't know it when they were dealing with the Moussaoui

---

[15] Senate Report No. 108-040.

case, and they didn't know it almost a year later when we had the closed-door hearing.[16]

Does this indication regarding law enforcement confusion point to a need for changes in the law, changes in FBI training, or some other action?

2. ***What Did the FISA "Wall" Require?*** Since information validly obtained pursuant to a FISA court order can be used for criminal prosecution, the FISA "wall" prevented criminal enforcement officials from directing the implementation of FISA orders. Consider the following remarks by Jamie Gorelick, who was part of the 9/11 Commission:

> At last week's hearing, Attorney General John Ashcroft, facing criticism, asserted that "the single greatest structural cause for September 11 was the wall that segregated criminal investigations and intelligence agents" and that I built that wall through a March 1995 memo. This simply is not true.
>
> First, I did not invent the "wall," which is not a wall but a set of procedures implementing a 1978 statute (the Foreign Intelligence Surveillance Act, or FISA) and federal court decisions interpreting it. In a nutshell, that law, as the courts read it, said intelligence investigators could conduct electronic surveillance in the United States against foreign targets under a more lenient standard than is required in ordinary criminal cases, but only if the "primary purpose" of the surveillance were foreign intelligence rather than a criminal prosecution.
>
> Second, according to the FISA Court of Review, it was the justice departments under Presidents Ronald Reagan and George H.W. Bush in the 1980s that began to read the statute as limiting the department's ability to obtain FISA orders if it intended to bring a criminal prosecution. . . .
>
> [N]othing in the 1995 guidelines prevented the sharing of information between criminal and intelligence investigators. Indeed, the guidelines require that FBI foreign intelligence agents share information with criminal investigators and prosecutors whenever they uncover facts suggesting that a crime has been or may be committed. . . .[17]

According to Gorelick, why was the "wall" in place? What function did it serve? What precisely did it require?

3. ***FISA and the USA PATRIOT Act.*** Prior to the USA PATRIOT Act, FISA applied when foreign intelligence gathering was "the purpose" of the investigation. Courts interpreted "the purpose" to mean that the primary purpose of the investigation had to be foreign intelligence gathering. Criminal enforcement could be a secondary purpose, but not the primary one. The USA PATRIOT Act, § 204, changed this language to make FISA applicable when foreign intelligence gathering is "a significant purpose" of the investigation. 50 U.S.C. §§ 1804(a)(7)(B) and 1823(a)(7)(B). Why do you think that this change was made in the USA PATRIOT Act?

---

[16] *The USA Patriot Act in Practice: Shedding Light on the FISA Process,* S. Hearing 107-947 (Sept. 10, 2002).

[17] Jamie S. Gorelick, *The Truth About "the Wall,"* Wash. Post, Apr. 18, 2004, at B7.

IN RE SEALED CASE

310 F.3d 717 (FIS Ct. Rev. 2002)

[In 2002, Attorney General John Ashcroft submitted to the FISA court new procedures for minimization, which significantly curtailed the screening walls. The procedures were reviewed by the FISA court in *In re All Matters Submitted to the Foreign Intelligence Surveillance Court* (May 17, 2002). The court expressed concern over the new procedures in light of the fact that in September 2000, the government had confessed error in about 75 FISA applications, including false statements that the targets of FISA surveillance were not under criminal investigations, that intelligence and criminal investigations were separate, and that information was not shared with FBI criminal investigators and assistant U.S. attorneys. The FISA court rejected the proposed procedures because they would allow criminal prosecutors to advise on FISA information gathering activities. The government appealed to the Foreign Intelligence Surveillance (FIS) Court of Review, which is composed of three judges on the D.C. Circuit. In 2002, the FIS Court of Review published its first and, thus far, only opinion.]

PER CURIAM. This is the first appeal from the Foreign Intelligence Surveillance Court to the Court of Review since the passage of the Foreign Intelligence Surveillance Act (FISA) in 1978. The appeal is brought by the United States from a FISA court surveillance order which imposed certain restrictions on the government. . . .

The court's decision from which the government appeals imposed certain requirements and limitations accompanying an order authorizing electronic surveillance of an "agent of a foreign power" as defined in FISA. There is no disagreement between the government and the FISA court as to the propriety of the electronic surveillance; the court found that the government had shown probable cause to believe that the target is an agent of a foreign power and otherwise met the basic requirements of FISA. . . . The FISA court authorized the surveillance, but imposed certain restrictions, which the government contends are neither mandated nor authorized by FISA. Particularly, the court ordered that law enforcement officials shall not make recommendations to intelligence officials concerning the initiation, operation, continuation or expansion of FISA searches or surveillances. Additionally, the FBI and the Criminal Division [of the Department of Justice] shall ensure that law enforcement officials do not direct or control the use of the FISA procedures to enhance criminal prosecution, and that advice intended to preserve the option of a criminal prosecution does not inadvertently result in the Criminal Division's directing or controlling the investigation using FISA searches and surveillances toward law enforcement objectives.

To ensure the Justice Department followed these strictures the court also fashioned what the government refers to as a "chaperone requirement"; that a unit of the Justice Department, the Office of Intelligence Policy and Review (OIPR) (composed of 31 lawyers and 25 support staff), "be invited" to all meetings between the FBI and the Criminal Division involving consultations for the purpose of coordinating efforts "to investigate or protect against foreign attack or other grave hostile acts, sabotage, international terrorism, or clandestine intelligence activities by foreign powers or their agents." . . .

[The FISA court opinion below] appears to proceed from the assumption that FISA constructed a barrier between counterintelligence/intelligence officials and law enforcement officers in the Executive Branch — indeed, it uses the word "wall" popularized by certain commentators (and journalists) to describe that supposed barrier.

The "wall" emerges from the court's implicit interpretation of FISA. The court apparently believes it can approve applications for electronic surveillance only if the government's objective is *not* primarily directed toward criminal prosecution of the foreign agents for their foreign intelligence activity. But the court neither refers to any FISA language supporting that view, nor does it reference the Patriot Act amendments, which the government contends specifically altered FISA to make clear that an application could be obtained even if criminal prosecution is the primary counter mechanism.

Instead the court relied for its imposition of the disputed restrictions on its statutory authority to approve "minimization procedures" designed to prevent the acquisition, retention, and dissemination within the government of material gathered in an electronic surveillance that is unnecessary to the government's need for foreign intelligence information. 50 U.S.C. § 1801(h). . . .

. . . [I]t is quite puzzling that the Justice Department, at some point during the 1980s, began to read the statute as limiting the Department's ability to obtain FISA orders if it intended to prosecute the targeted agents — even for foreign intelligence crimes. To be sure, section 1804, which sets forth the elements of an application for an order, required a national security official in the Executive Branch — typically the Director of the FBI — to certify that "the purpose" of the surveillance is to obtain foreign intelligence information (amended by the Patriot Act to read "a significant purpose"). But as the government now argues, the definition of foreign intelligence information includes evidence of crimes such as espionage, sabotage or terrorism. Indeed, it is virtually impossible to read the 1978 FISA to exclude from its purpose the prosecution of foreign intelligence crimes, most importantly because, as we have noted, the definition of an agent of a foreign power — if he or she is a U.S. person — is grounded on criminal conduct. . . .

. . . In October 2001, Congress amended FISA to change "the purpose" language in § 1804(a)(7)(B) to "a significant purpose." It also added a provision allowing "Federal officers who conduct electronic surveillance to acquire foreign intelligence information" to "consult with Federal law enforcement officers to coordinate efforts to investigate or protect against" attack or other grave hostile acts, sabotage or international terrorism, or clandestine intelligence activities, by foreign powers or their agents. 50 U.S.C. § 1806(k)(1). . . . Although the Patriot Act amendments to FISA expressly sanctioned consultation and coordination between intelligence and law enforcement officials, in response to the first applications filed by OIPR under those amendments, in November 2001, the FISA court for the first time adopted the 1995 Procedures, as augmented by the January 2000 and August 2001 Procedures, as "minimization procedures" to apply in all cases before the court.

The Attorney General interpreted the Patriot Act quite differently. On March 6, 2002, the Attorney General approved new "Intelligence Sharing Procedures" to implement the Act's amendments to FISA. The 2002 Procedures supersede prior procedures and were designed to permit the complete exchange of information and advice between intelligence and law enforcement officials. They eliminated the "direction and control" test and allowed the exchange of advice between the FBI, OIPR, and the Criminal Division regarding "the initiation, operation, continuation, or expansion of FISA searches or surveillance." . . .

Unpersuaded by the Attorney General's interpretation of the Patriot Act, the court ordered that the 2002 Procedures be adopted, *with modifications,* as minimization procedures to apply in all cases. . . .

. . . [W]hen Congress explicitly authorizes consultation and coordination between different offices in the government, without even suggesting a limitation on who is to direct and control, it necessarily implies that either could be taking the lead. . . .

That leaves us with something of an analytic conundrum. On the one hand, Congress did not amend the definition of foreign intelligence information which, we have explained, includes evidence of foreign intelligence crimes. On the other hand, Congress accepted the dichotomy between foreign intelligence and law enforcement by adopting the significant purpose test. Nevertheless, it is our task to do our best to read the statute to honor congressional intent. The better reading, it seems to us, excludes from the purpose of gaining foreign intelligence information a sole objective of criminal prosecution. We therefore reject the government's argument to the contrary. Yet this may not make much practical difference. Because, as the government points out, when it commences an electronic surveillance of a foreign agent, typically it will not have decided whether to prosecute the agent (whatever may be the subjective intent of the investigators or lawyers who initiate an investigation). So long as the government entertains a realistic option of dealing with the agent other than through criminal prosecution, it satisfies the significant purpose test.

The important point is — and here we agree with the government — the Patriot Act amendment, by using the word "significant," eliminated any justification for the FISA court to balance the relative weight the government places on criminal prosecution as compared to other counterintelligence responses. If the certification of the application's purpose articulates a broader objective than criminal prosecution — such as stopping an ongoing conspiracy — and includes other potential non-prosecutorial responses, the government meets the statutory test. Of course, if the court concluded that the government's sole objective was merely to gain evidence of past criminal conduct — even foreign intelligence crimes — to punish the agent rather than halt ongoing espionage or terrorist activity, the application should be denied. . . .

It can be argued, however, that by providing that an application is to be granted if the government has only a "significant purpose" of gaining foreign intelligence information, the Patriot Act allows the government to have a primary objective of prosecuting an agent for a non-foreign intelligence crime. Yet we think that would be an anomalous reading of the amendment. . . . That is not to deny that ordinary crimes might be inextricably intertwined with foreign intelligence crimes. For example, if a group of international terrorists were to engage in bank robberies in order to finance the manufacture of a bomb, evidence of the bank robbery should be treated just as evidence of the terrorist act itself. But the FISA process cannot be used as a device to investigate wholly unrelated ordinary crimes.

Having determined that FISA, as amended, does not oblige the government to demonstrate to the FISA court that its primary purpose in conducting electronic surveillance is *not* criminal prosecution, we are obliged to consider whether the statute as amended is consistent with the Fourth Amendment. . . . [I]n asking whether FISA procedures can be regarded as reasonable under the Fourth Amendment, we think it is instructive to compare those procedures and requirements with their Title III counterparts. Obviously, the closer those FISA procedures are to Title III procedures, the lesser are our constitutional concerns. . . .

With limited exceptions not at issue here, both Title III and FISA require prior judicial scrutiny of an application for an order authorizing electronic surveillance. 50 U.S.C. § 1805; 18 U.S.C. § 2518. And there is no dispute that a FISA judge satisfies the Fourth Amendment's requirement of a "neutral and detached magistrate."

The statutes differ to some extent in their probable cause showings. Title III allows a court to enter an *ex parte* order authorizing electronic surveillance if it determines on the basis of the facts submitted in the government's application that "there is probable cause for belief that an individual is committing, has committed, or is about to commit" a specified predicate offense. 18 U.S.C. § 2518(3)(a). FISA by contrast requires a showing of probable cause that the target is a foreign power or an agent of a foreign power. 50 U.S.C. § 1805(a)(3). We have noted, however, that where a U.S. person is involved, an "agent of a foreign power" is defined in terms of criminal activity. . . . FISA surveillance would not be authorized against a target engaged in purely domestic terrorism because the government would not be able to show that the target is acting for or on behalf of a foreign power. . . .

FISA's general programmatic purpose, to protect the nation against terrorists and espionage threats directed by foreign powers, has from its outset been distinguishable from "ordinary crime control." After the events of September 11, 2001, though, it is hard to imagine greater emergencies facing Americans than those experienced on that date.

We acknowledge, however, that the constitutional question presented by this case — whether Congress' disapproval of the primary purpose test is consistent with the Fourth Amendment — has no definitive jurisprudential answer.

. . . Our case may well involve the most serious threat our country faces. Even without taking into account the President's inherent constitutional authority to conduct warrantless foreign intelligence surveillance, we think the procedures and government showings required under FISA, if they do not meet the minimum Fourth Amendment warrant standards, certainly come close.

NOTES & QUESTIONS

1. *Assessing the Benefits and Problems of the "Wall."* Paul Rosenzweig argues: "Prior to the Patriot Act, a very real wall existed. . . . While information could be 'thrown over the wall' from intelligence officials to prosecutors, the decision to do so always rested with national security personnel — even though law-enforcement agents are in a better position to determine what evidence is pertinent to their case."[18]

   Consider Peter Swire:

   > The principal argument [in favor of the wall] is that criminal prosecutions should be based on the normal rules of criminal procedure, not on evidence gathered in a secret court system. The norm should be the usual constitutional protections rather than the exceptional circumstances that arise in foreign intelligence investigations. . . .
   >
   > "[T]he wall" serves essential purposes. . . . [R]emoval of "the wall" may violate the Constitution for investigations that are primarily not for foreign intelligence purposes. At some point an investigation is so thoroughly domestic and criminal that the usual Fourth Amendment and other protections apply. . . . Second, "the wall" may be important in preventing the spread of the secret FISA system over time. As of 2002, seventy-one percent of the federal electronic surveillance orders were FISA orders rather than Title III orders. The Patriot Act reduction of safeguards in the FISA system means that this figure may climb in the future. . . .
   >
   > . . . [E]arly in an investigation, it may be difficult or impossible for investigators to know whether the evidence will eventually be used for intelligence purposes or in an actual prosecution. For instance, imagine that a FISA wiretap is sought for a group of foreign agents who are planning a bomb attack. On these facts, there would be a strong foreign intelligence purpose, to frustrate the foreign attack. In addition, there would be a strong law enforcement basis for surveillance, to create evidence that would prove conspiracy beyond a reasonable doubt. On these facts, it would be difficult for officials to certify honestly that "the primary purpose" of the surveillance was for foreign intelligence rather than law enforcement. The honest official might say that the surveillance has a dual use — both to create actionable foreign intelligence information and to create evidence for later prosecution.
   >
   > Faced with this possibility of dual use, the Patriot Act amendment was to require only that "a significant purpose" of the surveillance be for foreign intelligence. Under the new standard, an official could honestly affirm both a significant purpose for foreign intelligence and a likely use for law enforcement.

   Swire is troubled by the USA PATRIOT Act's changing FISA's requirement that "the purpose" of the investigation be foreign intelligence gathering to a looser requirement that "a significant purpose" of the investigation constituting foreign intelligence gathering:

   > The problem with the "significant purpose" standard, however, is that it allows too much use of secret FISA surveillance for ordinary crimes. The FISCR interpreted the new statute in a broad way: "So long as the government

---

[18] Paul Rosenzweig, *Civil Liberty and the Response to Terrorism*, 42 Duq. L. Rev. 663 (2004).

entertains a realistic option of dealing with the agent other than through criminal prosecution, it satisfies the significant purpose test." The range of "realistic options" would seem to be so broad, however, that FISA orders could issue for an enormous range of investigations that ordinarily would be handled in the criminal system. . . . The Patriot Act amendment, as interpreted by the FISCR, thus allows the slippery slope to occur. A potentially immense range of law enforcement surveillance could shift into the secret FISA system.[19]

In lieu of the standard that "a significant purpose" of the investigation consists of foreign intelligence gathering, Swire recommends that FISA orders should be granted only if the surveillance is "sufficiently important for foreign intelligence purposes." Will Swire's proposed standard ("sufficiently important for foreign intelligence purposes") make a material difference from that of "a significant purpose"?

2. ***The Constitutionality of FISA and the Protect America Act.*** At the end of *In re Sealed Case,* the court concludes: "[W]e think the procedures and government showings required under FISA, if they do not meet the minimum Fourth Amendment warrant standards, certainly come close." Is coming close to meeting minimum warrant standards adequate enough to be constitutional?

Prior to the USA PATRIOT Act amendments, a few courts considered the constitutionality of FISA, with all concluding that the statute passed constitutional muster. For example, in *United States v. Duggan,* 743 F.2d 59 (2d Cir. 1984), the Second Circuit concluded that FISA did not violate the Fourth Amendment because

> [p]rior to the enactment of FISA, virtually every court that had addressed the issue had concluded that the President had the inherent power to conduct warrantless electronic surveillance to collect foreign intelligence information, and that such surveillances constituted an exception to the warrant requirement of the Fourth Amendment. The Supreme Court specifically declined to address this issue in *United States v. United States District Court,* but it had made clear that the requirements of the Fourth Amendment may change when differing governmental interests are at stake, and it observed . . . that the governmental interests presented in national security investigations differ substantially from those presented in traditional criminal investigations. . . .
>
> Against this background, Congress passed FISA to settle what it believed to be the unresolved question of the applicability of the Fourth Amendment warrant requirement to electronic surveillance for foreign intelligence purposes, and to "remove any doubt as to the lawfulness of such surveillance." . . .
>
> We regard the procedures fashioned in FISA as a constitutionally adequate balancing of the individual's Fourth Amendment rights against the nation's need to obtain foreign intelligence information. . . .

In 2008, the Foreign Intelligence Surveillance Court of Review (FISCR) upheld the constitutionality of the Protect America Act (PAA) of 2007, a

---

[19] Peter Swire, *The System of Foreign Intelligence Surveillance Law,* 72 Geo. Wash. L. Rev. 1306, 1342, 1360-65 (2004).

stopgap law enacted before the FISA Amendment Act of 2008. *In re Directives [redacted text]*, 551 F.3d 1004 (FISCR 2008). The FISCR found that the PAA, applied through the relevant directives, satisfied the Fourth Amendment's reasonableness requirements. It observed, "The more important the government's interest, the greater the intrusion that may be constitutionally tolerated under the Fourth Amendment." Moreover, the PAA and accompanying directives provide safeguards, including "targeting procedures, minimization procedures, [and] a procedure to ensure that a significant purpose of a surveillance is to obtain foreign intelligence information." It concluded that "our decision recognizes that where the government has instituted several layers of serviceable safeguards to protect individuals against unwarranted harms and to minimize incidental intrusions, its effort to protect national security should not be frustrated by the courts."

Why should different Fourth Amendment requirements exist for foreign intelligence purposes as opposed to regular domestic law enforcement? Is the distinction between foreign intelligence and domestic law enforcement tenable in light of international terrorism, where investigations often have both a foreign intelligence and domestic law enforcement purpose? Do the USA PATRIOT Act amendments affect FISA's constitutionality?

3. ***After-the-Fact Reasonableness Review?*** In a critique of the FISA warrant-procedure as amended by the PATRIOT Act, a Note in the *Yale Law Journal* proposes that FISA be repealed and that the United States return to use of warrantless foreign intelligence surveillance in which "targets could challenge the reasonableness of the surveillance in an adversary proceeding in an Article III court after the surveillance was complete."[20]

Do you think that the foreign intelligence context is well suited to the proposed warrantless regime? For the Note, "the possibility of after-the-fact reasonableness review of the merits of their decisions in Article III courts (in camera or note) would help guarantee careful and calm DOJ decisionmaking." Is reasonableness a sufficiently strict standard of review? Furthermore, one of the hallmarks of the Fourth Amendment's warrant procedure is before-the-fact review; law enforcement officials must seek judicial authorization *before* they conduct their search. Would after-the-fact review result in hindsight bias? Another consideration is the extent to which warrantless surveillance would allow the government to "bootstrap" an investigation — the government could undertake broad, unregulated surveillance knowing that it could lead to evidence that may be admissible in court.

4. ***The USA PATRIOT Act § 215.*** Section 215 of the USA PATRIOT Act adds a new § 501 to the Foreign Intelligence Surveillance Act (FISA):

(a)(1) The Director of the Federal Bureau of Investigation or a designee of the Director (whose rank shall be no lower than Assistant Special Agent in Charge) may make an application for an order requiring the production of any tangible things (including books, records, papers, documents, and other items) for an investigation to protect against international terrorism or clandestine

---

[20] Nola K. Breglio, Note, *Leaving FISA Behind: The Need to Return to Warrantless Foreign Intelligence Surveillance*, 113 Yale L.J. 179, 203-04, 209, 212 (2003).

intelligence activities, provided that such investigation of a United States person is not conducted solely upon the basis of activities protected by the first amendment to the Constitution.

> (2) An investigation conducted under this section shall —
> (A) be conducted under guidelines approved by the Attorney General under Executive Order 12333 (or a successor order); and
> (B) not be conducted of a United States person solely upon the basis of activities protected by the first amendment to the Constitution of the United States.

Applications for court orders shall be made to a judge and "shall specify that the records are sought for an authorized investigation" and "to protect against international terrorism or clandestine intelligence activities." § 501(b). This section also has a gag order:

> (d) No person shall disclose to any other person (other than those persons necessary to produce the tangible things under this section) that the Federal Bureau of Investigation has sought or obtained tangible things under this section. § 501(d).

The American Library Association (ALA) led a spirited campaign against § 215. It issued a resolution stating, in part, that

> the American Library Association encourages all librarians, library administrators, library governing bodies, and library advocates to educate their users, staff, and communities about the process for compliance with the USA PATRIOT Act and other related measures and about the dangers to individual privacy and the confidentiality of library records resulting from those measures.

In 2003, Attorney General John Ashcroft stated that § 215 had never been used to access library records. He further stated: "The fact is, with just 11,000 FBI agents and over a billion visitors to America's libraries each year, the Department of Justice has neither the staffing, the time nor the inclination to monitor the reading habits of Americans. . . . No offense to the American Library Association, but we just don't care." In 2005, the ALA revealed the results of a survey of librarians indicating a minimum of 137 formal law enforcement inquiries to library officials since 9/11, 49 of which were by federal officials and the remainder by state and local officials. The study did not indicate whether any of these were pursuant to § 215.

The National Security Council relied on § 215 of the USA PATRIOT Act as authorization for its collection of bulk telephone metadata. The existence of this secret program was first revealed through unauthorized disclosures of classified documents by Edward Snowden, a contractor for the NSA, in June 2013. This chapter addresses the NSA's telephone records program below.

3. NATIONAL SECURITY LETTERS

Provisions in several laws permit the FBI to obtain personal information from third parties merely by making a written request in cases involving national security. No court order is required. These requests are called "National Security Letters" (NSLs).

The Stored Communications Act. ECPA's Stored Communications Act contains an NSL provision, 18 U.S.C. § 2709. This provision allows the FBI to compel communications companies (ISPs, telephone companies) to release customer records when the FBI makes a particular certification. Before the USA PATRIOT Act, the FBI had to certify that the records were "relevant to an authorized foreign counterintelligence investigation" and that "there are specific and articulable facts giving reason to believe that the person or entity to whom the information sought pertains is a foreign power or an agent of a foreign power as defined in section 101 of the Foreign Intelligence Surveillance Act of 1978 (50 U.S.C. 1801)."

Section 505 of the USA PATRIOT Act amended the National Security Letters provision of ECPA by altering what must be certified. The existing requirements regarding counterintelligence and specific and articulable facts that the target was an agent of a foreign power were deleted. The FBI now needs to certify that the records are "relevant to an authorized investigation to protect against terrorism or clandestine intelligence activities, provided that such an investigation of a United States person is not conducted solely on the basis of activities protected by the first amendment to the Constitution of the United States." 18 U.S.C. § 2709.

This provision also has a gag order:

> No wire or electronic communication service provider, or officer, employee, or agent thereof, shall disclose to any person that the Federal Bureau of Investigation has sought or obtained access to information or records under this section. § 2709(c).

Unlike § 215, Ashcroft made no statement about § 505.[21]

The Right to Financial Privacy Act. The Right to Financial Privacy Act (RFPA) also contains an NSL provision. As amended by the Patriot Act, this provision states that the FBI can obtain an individual's financial records if it "certifies in writing to the financial institution that such records are sought for foreign counter intelligence purposes to protect against international terrorism or clandestine intelligence activities, provided that such an investigation of a United States person is not conducted solely upon the basis of activities protected by the first amendment to the Constitution of the United States." 12 U.S.C. § 3414(a)(5)(A). As with the Stored Communications Act NSL provision, the RFPA NSL provision contains a "gag" rule prohibiting the financial institution from disclosing the fact it received the NSL. § 3414(a)(5)(D).

The Fair Credit Reporting Act. Likewise, the Fair Credit Reporting Act provides for NSLs. Pursuant to a written FBI request, consumer reporting agencies "shall furnish to the Federal Bureau of Investigation the names and addresses of all financial institutions . . . at which a customer maintains or has maintained an account." 15 U.S.C. § 1681u(a). Consumer reporting agencies must also furnish "identifying information respecting a consumer, limited to

---

[21] Mark Sidel, *More Secure, Less Free?: Antiterrorism Policy and Civil Liberties After September 11*, at 14 (2004).

name, address, former addresses, places of employment, or former places of employment." 15 U.S.C. § 1681u(b). To obtain a full consumer report, however, the FBI must obtain a court order ex parte. 15 U.S.C. § 1681u(c). Like the other NSL provisions, the FCRA NSL provisions restrict NSLs for investigations based "solely" upon First Amendment activities. The FCRA NSL also has a "gag" rule. 15 U.S.C. § 1681u(d).

The USA PATRIOT Reauthorization Act. In the USA PATRIOT Reauthorization Act of 2005, Congress made several amendments that affected NSLs. It explicitly provided for judicial review of NSLs. It also required a detailed examination by the DOJ's Inspector General "of the effectiveness and use, including any improper or illegal use" of NSLs. This kind of audit proved its value in March 2006 when the Inspector General issued its review of the FBI's use of NSLs. First, the Inspector General found a dramatic underreporting of NSLs. Indeed, the total number of NSL requests between 2003 and 2005 totaled at least 143,074. Of these NSLs requests, as the Inspector General found, "[t]he overwhelming majority . . . sought telephone toll billing records information, subscriber information (telephone or e-mail) or electronic communication transaction records under the ECPA NSL statute." [22]

The Inspector General also carried out a limited audit of investigative case files, and found that 22 percent of them contained at least one violation of investigative guidelines or procedures that was not reported to any of the relevant internal authorities at the FBI. Finally, the Inspector General also found over 700 instances in which the FBI obtained telephone records and subscriber information from telephone companies based on the use of a so-called "exigent letter" authority. This authority, absent from the statute, was invented by the FBI's Counterterrorism Division. Having devised this new power, the FBI did not set limits on its use, or track how it was employed. Witnesses told the Inspector General that many of these letters "were not issued in exigent circumstances, and the FBI was unable to determine which letters were sent in emergency circumstances due to inadequate recordkeeping." Indeed, "in most instances, there was no documentation associating the requests with pending national security investigations."[23]

NSL Litigation. In *Doe v. Ashcroft*, 334 F. Supp. 2d 471 (S.D.N.Y. 2004), a federal district court invalidated 18 U.S.C. § 2709 (*Doe I*). It found that § 2709 violated the Fourth Amendment because, at least as applied, it barred or at least substantially deterred a judicial challenge to an NSL request. It did so by prohibiting an NSL recipient from revealing the existence of an NSL inquiry. The court also found that the "all inclusive sweep" of § 2709 violated the First Amendment as a prior-restraint and content-based restriction on sweep that was subject to strict scrutiny review. Additionally, the court found that in some instances the use of an NSL might infringe upon people's First Amendment rights. For example, suppose that the FBI uses an NSL to find out the identity of

---

[22] Office of the Inspector General, *A Review of the Federal Bureau of Investigations Use of National Security Letters* x-xiv (Mar. 2007).

[23] *Id.* at xxxviii, xxxiv.

an anonymous speaker on the Internet. Does the First Amendment limit using an NSL in this manner? Does the First Amendment restriction on the NSL provisions, which prohibits NSLs for investigations based "solely" upon First Amendment activities, adequately address these potential First Amendment problems?

Shortly after *Doe I,* another district court invalidated 18 U.S.C. § 2709(c), which prevented a recipient of an NSL to disclose information about the government's action. *Doe v. Gonzales,* 386 F. Supp. 2d 66, 82 (D. Conn. 2005) (*Doe II*).

While appeals in *Doe I* and *Doe II* were pending, Congress enacted the USA PATRIOT Reauthorization Act of 2005, which made several changes to § 2709 and added several provisions concerning judicial review of NSLs, which were codified at 18 U.S.C. § 3511. Following enactment of these provisions, plaintiffs challenged the amended nondisclosure provisions of §§ 2709(c) and 3511. The same district court that issued the *Doe I* opinion then found §§ 2709(c) and 3511(b) to be facially unconstitutional. *Doe v. Gonzales,* 500 F. Supp. 2d 379 (S.D.N.Y. 2007) (*Doe III*).

The newly enacted § 3511 provided for judicial review of NSLs. As a result, the *Doe III* plaintiffs did not challenge it on Fourth Amendment grounds as in *Doe I.* Instead, they argued, and the court agreed, that the nondisclosure provisions of § 2709(c) remained an unconstitutional prior restraint and content-based restriction on speech. The court also concluded that § 3511(b) was unconstitutional under the First Amendment and the doctrine of separation of powers. Among its conclusions, the court noted that Congress in amending § 2709(c) allowed the FBI to certify on a case-by-case basis whether nondisclosure was necessary. Yet, this narrowing of the statute to reduce the possibility of unnecessary limitation of speech also means that the FBI could conceivably engage in viewpoint discrimination. As a consequence, the amended statute was a content-based restriction as well as a prior restraint on speech and, therefore, subject to strict scrutiny.

The Second Circuit modified the district court's opinion. In *Doe v. Mukasey,* 549 F.3d 861 (2008), the court found that the challenged statutes did not comply with the First Amendment, although not to the extent that the district court found. It also concluded that the lower court's ordered relief was too broad. The Second Circuit began by construing § 2709(c) to permit a nondisclosure requirement only when senior FBI officials certify that disclosure may result in an enumerated harm that is related to "an authorized investigation to protect against international terrorism or clandestine intelligence activities." It also interpreted § 3511(b)(2) and (b)(3) as placing the burden on the Government "to show that a good reason exists to expect that disclosure of receipt of an NSL will risk an enumerated harm." Additionally, it held the relevant subsections unconstitutional to the extent that they would impose a nondisclosure requirement without placing the burden on the government to initiate judicial review of that obligation, and to the extent that judicial review would treat "a government official's certification that disclosure may endanger the national security of the United States or interfere with diplomatic relations . . . as conclusive."

More recently, the Northern District of California declared NSLs to be unconstitutional due to the statute's nondisclosure and judicial review provisions.

In re: National Security Letter, 930 F.Supp.2d 1064 (N.D. Cali 2013) found that the nondisclosure provisions represented a significant infringement on speech regarding controversial government powers that violated the First Amendment. The restrictions on judicial review violated the First Amendment as well as separation of powers principles. Given the significant constitutional and national security issues at stake, the district court judge stayed enforcement of the court's order. This decision is now on appeal to the Ninth Circuit as *In re: National Security Letter, Under Seal v. Holder*. Although the litigation is proceeding as a sealed matter, the Ninth Circuit has ordered various litigation documents to be made public and created a website devoted to the case due to the high level of interest in it.[24]

4. INTERNAL OVERSIGHT

Judicial oversight is not the only mechanism that regulates intelligence agencies. There are also several guidelines, internal governance structures and processes, privacy officials, and oversight boards that regulate the activities of various intelligence agencies.

(a) The Attorney General's FBI Guidelines

Unlike many government agencies, the FBI was not created by Congress through a statute. In 1907, Attorney General Charles Bonaparte requested that Congress authorize him to create a national detective force in the Department of Justice (DOJ). The DOJ had been using investigators from the Secret Service, but Bonaparte wanted a permanent force. Congress rejected his request due to concerns over this small group developing into a secret police system. Nevertheless, Bonaparte went ahead with his plans and formed a new subdivision of the DOJ, called the "Bureau of Investigation." President Theodore Roosevelt later authorized the subdivision through an executive order in 1908. J. Edgar Hoover began running the Bureau, which was renamed the Federal Bureau of Investigation in 1935.[25]

The FBI grew at a great pace. In 1933, the FBI had 353 agents and 422 support staff; in 1945, it had 4,380 agents and 7,422 support staff.[26] Today, the FBI has 11,000 agents and 16,000 support staff, as well as 56 field offices, 400 satellite offices, and 40 foreign liaison posts.[27]

FBI surveillance activities are regulated through the U.S. Constitution and electronic surveillance laws, as well as by guidelines promulgated by the Attorney General. In 1976, responding to Hoover's abuses of power, Attorney General Edward Levi established guidelines to control FBI surveillance activities.[28] As William Banks and M.E. Bowman observe:

---

[24] *In re: National Security Letter, Under Seal v. Holder (Sealed)*, at http://www.ca9.uscourts.gov/content/view.php?pk_id=0000000715.

[25] Curt Gentry, *J. Edgar Hoover: The Man and the* Secrets 111-13 (1991).

[26] Ronald Kessler, *The Bureau: The Secret History of the FBI* 57 (2002).

[27] Federal Bureau of Investigation, Frequently Asked Questions, http://www.fbi.gov/aboutus/faqs/faqsone.html (Dec. 4, 2003).

[28] *See* United States Attorney General Guidelines on Domestic Security Investigation (1976).

The most pertinent Levi Guidelines focused on freedom of speech and freedom of the press. First, investigations based solely on unpopular speech, where there is no threat of violence, were prohibited. Second, techniques designed to disrupt organizations engaged in protected First Amendment activity, or to discredit individuals would not be used in any circumstance.

At the same time, Attorney General Levi emphasized that the Guidelines were intended to permit domestic security investigations where the activities under investigation "involve or will involve the use of force or violence and the violation of criminal law." . . .

On March 7, 1983, Attorney General William French Smith revised the Guidelines regarding domestic security investigations. . . .

The Smith Guidelines were intended to increase the investigative avenues available to the FBI in domestic terrorism cases. Where the Levi/Civiletti Guidelines had established a predicate investigative standard of "specific and articulable facts," the Smith version lowered the threshold to require only a "reasonable indication" as the legal standard for opening a "full" investigation. . . . The "reasonable indication" standard is significantly lower than the Fourth Amendment standard of probable cause required in law enforcement. To balance the lowered threshold for opening an investigation, Attorney General Smith emphasized that investigations would be regulated and would "not be based solely on activities protected by the First Amendment or the lawful exercise of other rights secured by the Constitution."

Nonetheless, the Smith Guidelines authorized FBI Headquarters to approve the use of informants to infiltrate a group "in a manner that may influence the exercise of rights protected by the First Amendment." The Smith Guidelines also stated: "In the absence of any information indicating planned violence by a group or enterprise, mere speculation that force or violence might occur during the course of an otherwise peaceable demonstration is not sufficient grounds for initiation of an investigation." . . .

According to the criminal guidelines, a full investigation may be opened where there is "reasonable indication" that two or more persons are engaged in an enterprise for the purpose of furthering political or social goals wholly or in part through activities that involve force or violence and are a violation of the criminal laws of the United States. . . .

In order to determine whether an investigation should be opened, the FBI must also take into consideration the magnitude of the threat, the likelihood that the threat will come to fruition, and the immediacy of the jeopardy. In addition to physical danger, the FBI must consider the danger to privacy and free expression posed by an investigation. For example, unless there is a reasonable indication that force or violence might occur during the course of a demonstration, initiation of an investigation is not appropriate. . . .[29]

In 2002, Attorney General John Ashcroft issued revised FBI guidelines. Whereas under the preexisting guidelines, the FBI could engage in surveillance of public political activity and search the Internet when "facts or circumstances reasonably indicate that a federal crime has been, is being, or will be committed,"[30] Ashcroft's guidelines eliminate this requirement. The FBI is

---

[29] William C. Banks & M.E. Bowman, *Executive Authority for National Security Surveillance,* 50 Am. U. L. Rev. 1, 69-74 (2000).

[30] The Attorney General's Guidelines on General Crimes, Racketeering Enterprise and Domestic Security/Terrorism Investigations § II.C.1 (Mar. 21, 1989).

permitted to gather "publicly available information, whether obtained directly or through services or resources (whether nonprofit or commercial) that compile or analyze such information; and information voluntarily provided by private entities." The FBI can also "carry out general topical research, including conducting online searches and accessing online sites and forums."[31]

Daniel Solove argues that Congress should pass a legislative charter to regulate the FBI:

> . . . [E]xecutive orders and guidelines can all be changed by executive fiat, as demonstrated by Ashcroft's substantial revision to the guidelines in 2002. Moreover, the Attorney General Guidelines are not judicially enforceable. The problem with the current system is that it relies extensively on self-regulation by the executive branch. Much of this regulation has been effective, but it can too readily be changed in times of crisis without debate or discussion. Codifying the internal executive regulations of the FBI would also allow for public input into the process. The FBI is a very powerful arm of the executive branch, and if we believe in separation of powers, then it is imperative that the legislative branch, not the executive alone, become involved in the regulation of the FBI. The guidelines should be judicially enforceable to ensure that they are strictly followed.[32]

Should other government security agencies have more oversight? Does Solove overlook the FBI's internal administrative processes that serve to limit its power?

(b) The Homeland Security Act

In 2002, Congress passed the Homeland Security Act, 6 U.S.C. § 222, which consolidated 22 federal agencies into the Department of Homeland Security (DHS). Agencies and other major components at the DHS include the Transportation Security Administration, Customs and Border Protection, Federal Emergency Management Agency, U.S. Citizenship and Immigration Services, U.S. Coast Guard, and U.S. Secret Service. The Office of the Secretary of DHS includes the Office of the Chief Privacy Officer, the Office of Civil Rights and Civil Liberties, the Office of Counter Narcotics, and the Office of State and Local Government Coordination.

Among other things, the Act creates a Privacy Office. 6 U.S.C. § 222. The Secretary must "appoint a senior official to assume primary responsibility for privacy policy." The privacy official's responsibilities include ensuring compliance with the Privacy Act of 1974; evaluating "legislative and regulatory proposals involving the collection, use, and disclosure of personal information by the Federal Government"; and preparing an annual report to Congress.

(c) The Intelligence Reform and Terrorism Prevention Act

Information Sharing and Institutional Culture. The 9/11 Commission found that in addition to the legal restrictions on sharing of foreign intelligence

---

[31] The Attorney General's Guidelines on General Crimes, Racketeering Enterprise and Terrorism Enterprise Investigations § VI (May 30, 2002).

[32] Daniel J. Solove, *Reconstructing Electronic Surveillance Law,* 72 Geo. Wash. L. Rev. 1264, 1304 (2004).

information, limitations in the FBI's institutional culture as well as technology had also prevented the circulation of data. In its final report, the 9/11 Commission stated: "The importance of integrated, all-source analysis cannot be overstated. Without it, it is not possible to 'connect the dots.' "[33] The 9/11 Commission called for a restructuring of the United States Intelligence Community (USIC) through creation of a National Intelligence Director to oversee this process.

In an Executive Order of August 27, 2004, President Bush required executive branch agencies to establish an environment to facilitate sharing of terrorism information.[34] Responding to the 9/11 Commission Report, Congress passed the Intelligence Reform and Terrorism Prevention Act of 2004 (IRPTA), codifying the requirements in Bush's Executive Order. The Act mandates that intelligence be "provided in its most shareable form" that the heads of intelligence agencies and federal departments "promote a culture of information sharing."

The Long and Winding Road: The Creation of the Privacy and Civil Liberties Oversight Board. The IRTPA seeks to establish protection of privacy and civil liberties by setting up a five-member Privacy and Civil Liberties Oversight Board (PCLOB). The Board gives advice to the President and agencies of the executive branch and provides an annual report of activities to Congress. Among its oversight activities, the Board is to review whether "the information sharing practices of the departments, agencies, and elements of the executive branch . . . appropriately protect privacy and civil liberties." The Board is also to "ensure that privacy and civil liberties are appropriately considered in the development and implementation of . . . regulations and executive branch policies." Regarding FISA surveillance, IRTPA mandates that the Attorney General provide more detailed reporting to Congress on governmental surveillance practices and the government's legal interpretations of FISA.

The Privacy and Civil Liberties Board has been the subject of controversy. A year after its creation, in February 2006, the Board still had not met a single time. When the Board issued its first annual report in May 2007, it led to the resignation of Lanny Davis, the Board's only Democratic member. The Bush Administration made more than 200 revisions to the report. The White House defending the actions as "standard operating procedure," and stated that it was appropriate because the board was legally under the President's supervision. In his resignation letter, Davis contested "the extensive redlining of the board's report to Congress by administration officials and the majority of the Board's willingness to accept most [of the edits.]"

Later that year, Congress enacted legislation to strengthen the independence and authority of the Board. It is now an "independent agency" located within the executive branch. No more than three members of the same political party can be appointed to the Board, and the Senate is to confirm all appointments to it. As before, however, the Board cannot issue subpoenas itself. Rather, a majority of

---

[33] The 9/11 Commission Report 408 (2004).

[34] Exec. Order No. 13356, 69 Fed. Reg. 53,599, 53,600-01 (Sept. 1, 2004).

Board members have the power to ask the Attorney General to issue a subpoena.[35]

Finally, in August 2012, the Senate confirmed the Board's four part-time members. The Senate confirmed David Medine, the Board's chairman and its only full-time member, in late May 2013. The timing was auspicious as it was five days before news stories began to appear based on Edward Snowden's leaked NSA documents. PCLOB has now issued semi-annual reports to Congress summarizing its initial activities as well as detailed studies of the NSA's telephone records program conduction under Section 214 of the PATRIOT Act and the NSA's surveillance program under Section 702 of the Foreign Intelligence Surveillance Act.[36] We discuss both NSA programs and the PCLOB reports below.

D. NSA SURVEILLANCE

In December 2005, a front page article in the *New York Times* first revealed that the National Security Agency (NSA) was intercepting communications where one party was located outside the United States and another party inside the United States.[37] The Bush Administration named this surveillance program the "Terrorist Surveillance Program" (TSP).

Created in 1952, the NSA collects and analyzes foreign communications. As Frederick Schwarz and Aziz Huq explain, "The NSA collects signals intelligence from telegrams, telephones, faxes, e-mails, and other electronic communications, and then disseminates this information among other agencies of the executive branch."[38] Schwarz and Huq also point out that the Church Committee investigation in 1975-76 found that "the NSA had not exercised its vast power with restraint or due regard for the Constitution." In the past, the NSA had engaged in activities such as collecting every international telegram sent from the United States and maintaining watch lists of U.S. citizens involved in political protests.

After 9/11, the NSA again began secret surveillance activities within the United States. Although the Bush Administration has discussed aspects of the NSA surveillance of telecommunications, the complete dimensions of the NSA activities remain unknown. And while the Department of Justice has issued a

---

[35] Ronald D. Lee & Paul M. Schwartz, *Beyond the "War on Terrorism": Towards the New Intelligence Network*, 103 Mich. L. Rev. 1446 (2005).

[36] PCLOB, *Report on the Surveillance Program Operated Pursuant to Section 702 of the Foreign Intelligence Surveillance Act* (July 2, 2014); PCLOB, *Report on the Telephone Records Program Conducted under Section 215 of the USA PATRIOT Act and on the Operations of the Foreign Intelligence Surveillance Court* (Jan. 23, 2014).

[37] James Risen & Eric Lichtblau, *Bush Lets U.S. Spy on Callers Without Courts*, N.Y. Times, Dec. 16. 2005, at A1.

[38] Frederick A.O. Schwarz Jr. & Aziz Z. Huq, *Unchecked and Unbalanced: Presidential Power in a Time of Terror* 127 (2007).

white paper justifying these activities,[39] the legal opinions said to declare the program lawful are secret.

Several lawsuits ensued, challenging the legality of the NSA surveillance. Some of these cases were brought against telecommunications companies that cooperated with the NSA in conducting the surveillance. Plaintiffs alleged that these companies violated FISA and ECPA.

Early in 2007, a secret FISC decision denied permission for certain NSA surveillance activities. The FISC judgment was said to concern a NSA request for a so-called "basket warrant," under which warrants are issued not on a case-by-case basis for specific suspects, but more generally for surveillance activity involving multiple targets. One anonymous official was quoted as saying that the FISC ruling concerned cases "where one end is foreign and you don't know where the other is."[40] The Administration leaked information about this ruling and argued that it impeded the government's ability to investigate threats of imminent terrorist attacks.

In the summer of 2007, Congress enacted the Protect America Act to authorize the NSA surveillance program.[41] This statute was subject to sunset in 120 days, and it expired without Congress enacting a new law or renewing it.[42] At that point, without the Protect America Act's amendments, the original FISA once again took effect, until Congress enacted FAA in July 2008.

A major roadblock to amending FISA had been the subject of immunity for the telecommunications companies that participated or participate in TSP or similar programs. President Bush stated that telecommunications immunity was needed to provide "meaningful liability protection to those who are alleged to have assisted our nation following the attacks of September 11, 2001." FISA already did contain immunity provisions, and this language was in effect at the time that the TSP began. *See* 18 U.S.C. § 2511(2)(a)(ii). The cooperation of the telecommunication companies with the NSA must have been outside the existing safe harbor language.

The FAA of 2008, discussed earlier in this chapter, establishes new rules for at least some of this NSA behavior. Title II of the FAA raises a new challenge to the litigation against the NSA behavior prior to its enactments — it provides statutory defenses for the telecommunications companies that assisted the NSA. Specifically, the FAA prohibits "a civil action" against anyone "for providing assistance to an element of the intelligence community" in connection "with an intelligence activity involving communications" following a specific kind of certification by the Attorney General. § 802. The certification in question requires a determination that the assistance was (1) authorized by the President

---

[39] United States Department of Justice, *Legal Authorities Supporting the Activities of the National Security Agency Described by the President* (Jan. 19, 2006).

[40] Greg Miller, *Court Puts Limits on Surveillance Abroad*, L.A. Times, Aug. 2, 2007.

[41] The Protect America Act created an exception to FISA's requirements. The exception was found in the statute's § 105A. This part of the law exempted all communications "directed at" people outside of the United States from FISA's definition of "electronic surveillance." Once a communication fell within § 105A, the government could carry it out subject to § 105B and its requirements — rather than FISA and its obligation to seek a warrant from the FISC.

[42] As discussed above, the Foreign Intelligence Surveillance Court of Review upheld the constitutionality of the PAA. *In re Directives [redacted text]*, 551 F.3d 1004 (FISCR 2008).

during the period beginning on September 11, 2001 and ending on January 17, 2007; (2) designed to detect or prevent a terrorist attack; and (3) the subject of a written request from the Attorney General or the head of the intelligence community. A court presented with such a certificate is to review it for the support of "substantial evidence."

As noted above, the FAA of 2008 added a new provision, Section 702, to FISA, which permits the Attorney General and the Director of National Intelligence to jointly authorize surveillance conducted within the U.S. but targeting only non-U.S. persons reasonably believed to be located outside of the U.S. In *Clapper v. Amnesty International USA*, the Supreme Court deciding a standing issue that determined whether a challenge against Section 702 could be brought by "attorneys and human rights, labor, legal, and media organizations whose work allegedly requires them to engage in sensitive and sometimes privileged telephone and e-mail communications with colleagues, clients, sources, and other individuals located abroad."

1. STANDING

CLAPPER V. AMNESTY INTERNATIONAL USA
133 S. Ct. (2013)

ALITO, J. . . . Section 702 of the Foreign Intelligence Surveillance Act of 1978, 50 U.S.C. § 1881a, allows the Attorney General and the Director of National Intelligence to acquire foreign intelligence information by jointly authorizing the surveillance of individuals who are not "United States persons"[43] and are reasonably believed to be located outside the United States. Before doing so, the Attorney General and the Director of National Intelligence normally must obtain the Foreign Intelligence Surveillance Court's approval. Respondents are United States persons whose work, they allege, requires them to engage in sensitive international communications with individuals who they believe are likely targets of surveillance under § 1881a. Respondents seek a declaration that § 1881a is unconstitutional, as well as an injunction against §1881a-authorized surveillance. The question before us is whether respondents have Article III standing to seek this prospective relief.

Respondents assert that they can establish injury in fact because there is an objectively reasonable likelihood that their communications will be acquired under § 1881a at some point in the future. But respondents' theory of *future* injury is too speculative to satisfy the well-established requirement that threatened injury must be "certainly impending." And even if respondents could demonstrate that the threatened injury is certainly impending, they still would not be able to establish that this injury is fairly traceable to § 1881a. As an alternative argument, respondents contend that they are suffering *present* injury because the risk of § 1881a-authorized surveillance already has forced them to take costly and burdensome measures to protect the confidentiality of their international

---

43 The term "United States person" includes citizens of the United States, aliens admitted for permanent residence, and certain associations and corporations. 50 U.S.C. § 1801(i); see § 1881(a).

communications. But respondents cannot manufacture standing by choosing to make expenditures based on hypothetical future harm that is not certainly impending. We therefore hold that respondents lack Article III standing.. . .

In 1978, after years of debate, Congress enacted the Foreign Intelligence Surveillance Act (FISA) to authorize and regulate certain governmental electronic surveillance of communications for foreign intelligence purposes. In enacting FISA, Congress legislated against the backdrop of our decision in *United States v. United States Dist. Court for Eastern Dist. of Mich.*, 407 U.S. 297 (1972) (*Keith*), in which we explained that the standards and procedures that law enforcement officials must follow when conducting "surveillance of 'ordinary crime' " might not be required in the context of surveillance conducted for domestic national-security purposes.

When Congress enacted the FISA Amendments Act of 2008 (FISA Amendments Act), it left much of FISA intact, but it "established a new and independent source of intelligence collection authority, beyond that granted in traditional FISA." As relevant here, § 702 of FISA, 50 U.S.C. § 1881a, which was enacted as part of the FISA Amendments Act, supplements pre-existing FISA authority by creating a new framework under which the Government may seek the FISC's authorization of certain foreign intelligence surveillance targeting the communications of non-U.S. persons located abroad. Unlike traditional FISA surveillance, § 1881a does not require the Government to demonstrate probable cause that the target of the electronic surveillance is a foreign power or agent of a foreign power. And, unlike traditional FISA, § 1881a does not require the Government to specify the nature and location of each of the particular facilities or places at which the electronic surveillance will occur.

The present case involves a constitutional challenge to § 1881a. . . .

Respondents are attorneys and human rights, labor, legal, and media organizations whose work allegedly requires them to engage in sensitive and sometimes privileged telephone and e-mail communications with colleagues, clients, sources, and other individuals located abroad. Respondents believe that some of the people with whom they exchange foreign intelligence information are likely targets of surveillance under § 1881a. Specifically, respondents claim that they communicate by telephone and e-mail with people the Government "believes or believed to be associated with terrorist organizations," "people located in geographic areas that are a special focus" of the Government's counterterrorism or diplomatic efforts, and activists who oppose governments that are supported by the United States Government.

Respondents claim that § 1881a compromises their ability to locate witnesses, cultivate sources, obtain information, and communicate confidential information to their clients. Respondents also assert that they "have ceased engaging" in certain telephone and e-mail conversations. According to respondents, the threat of surveillance will compel them to travel abroad in order to have in-person conversations. In addition, respondents declare that they have undertaken "costly and burdensome measures" to protect the confidentiality of sensitive communications. . . .

Article III of the Constitution limits federal courts' jurisdiction to certain "Cases" and "Controversies." As we have explained, "[n]o principle is more fundamental to the judiciary's proper role in our system of government than the constitutional limitation of federal-court jurisdiction to actual cases or controversies." *DaimlerChrysler Corp. v. Cuno,* 547 U.S. 332 (2006) (internal quotation marks omitted). "One element of the case-or-controversy requirement" is that plaintiffs "must establish that they have standing to sue."

The law of Article III standing, which is built on separation-of-powers principles, serves to prevent the judicial process from being used to usurp the powers of the political branches. . . .

To establish Article III standing, an injury must be "concrete, particularized, and actual or imminent; fairly traceable to the challenged action; and redressable by a favorable ruling." *Monsanto Co. v. Geertson Seed Farms,* 561 U.S. 139 (2010). . . . Thus, we have repeatedly reiterated that "threatened injury must be *certainly impending* to constitute injury in fact," and that "[a]llegations of *possible* future injury" are not sufficient. . . .

Respondents assert that they can establish injury in fact that is fairly traceable to § 1881a because there is an objectively reasonable likelihood that their communications with their foreign contacts will be intercepted under § 1881a at some point in the future. This argument fails. [R]espondents' argument rests on their highly speculative fear that: (1) the Government will decide to target the communications of non-U.S. persons with whom they communicate; (2) in doing so, the Government will choose to invoke its authority under § 1881a rather than utilizing another method of surveillance; (3) the Article III judges who serve on the Foreign Intelligence Surveillance Court will conclude that the Government's proposed surveillance procedures satisfy § 1881a's many safeguards and are consistent with the Fourth Amendment; (4) the Government will succeed in intercepting the communications of respondents' contacts; and (5) respondents will be parties to the particular communications that the Government intercepts.

First, it is speculative whether the Government will imminently target communications to which respondents are parties. Section 1881a expressly provides that respondents, who are U.S. persons, cannot be targeted for surveillance under § 1881a. See § 1881a(b)(1)–(3). Accordingly, it is no surprise that respondents fail to offer any evidence that their communications have been monitored under § 1881a, a failure that substantially undermines their standing theory. Indeed, respondents do not even allege that the Government has sought the FISC's approval for surveillance of their communications. Accordingly, respondents' theory necessarily rests on their assertion that the Government will target *other individuals*—namely, their foreign contacts.

Yet respondents have no actual knowledge of the Government's §1881a targeting practices. Instead, respondents merely speculate and make assumptions about whether their communications with their foreign contacts will be acquired under §1881a. . . . Moreover, because §1881a at most *authorizes*—but does not *mandate* or *direct*—the surveillance that respondents fear, respondents' allegations are necessarily conjectural. Simply put, respondents can only speculate as to how the Attorney General and the Director of National Intelligence will exercise their discretion in determining which communications to target.

Second, even if respondents could demonstrate that the targeting of their foreign contacts is imminent, respondents can only speculate as to whether the

Government will seek to use §1881a-authorized surveillance (rather than other methods) to do so. The Government has numerous other methods of conducting surveillance, none of which is challenged here. . . .

Third, even if respondents could show that the Government will seek the Foreign Intelligence Surveillance Court's authorization to acquire the communications of respondents' foreign contacts under § 1881a, respondents can only speculate as to whether that court will authorize such surveillance. . . .

Fourth, even if the Government were to obtain the Foreign Intelligence Surveillance Court's approval to target respondents' foreign contacts under § 1881a, it is unclear whether the Government would succeed in acquiring the communications of respondents' foreign contacts. And fifth, even if the Government were to conduct surveillance of respondents' foreign contacts, respondents can only speculate as to whether *their own communications* with their foreign contacts would be incidentally acquired.

In sum, respondents' speculative chain of possibilities does not establish that injury based on potential future surveillance is certainly impending or is fairly traceable to §1881a. . . .

Respondents' alternative argument—namely, that they can establish standing based on the measures that they have undertaken to avoid § 1881a-authorized surveillance—fares no better. Respondents assert that they are suffering ongoing injuries that are fairly traceable to § 1881a because the risk of surveillance under § 1881a requires them to take costly and burdensome measures to protect the confidentiality of their communications. Respondents claim, for instance, that the threat of surveillance sometimes compels them to avoid certain e-mail and phone conversations, to "tal[k] in generalities rather than specifics," or to travel so that they can have in-person conversations. . . .

Respondents' contention that they have standing because they incurred certain costs as a reasonable reaction to a risk of harm is unavailing—because the harm respondents seek to avoid is not certainly impending. In other words, respondents cannot manufacture standing merely by inflicting harm on themselves based on their fears of hypothetical future harm that is not certainly impending. . . .

Respondents also suggest that they should be held to have standing because otherwise the constitutionality of § 1881a could not be challenged.

. . .[O]ur holding today by no means insulates § 1881a from judicial review. As described above, Congress created a comprehensive scheme in which the Foreign Intelligence Surveillance Court evaluates the Government's certifications, targeting procedures, and minimization procedures—including assessing whether the targeting and minimization procedures comport with the Fourth Amendment. § 1881a(a), (c)(1), (i)(2), (i)(3). Any dissatisfaction that respondents may have about the Foreign Intelligence Surveillance Court's rulings—or the congressional delineation of that court's role—is irrelevant to our standing analysis.

Additionally, if the Government intends to use or disclose information obtained or derived from a § 1881a acquisition in judicial or administrative proceedings, it must provide advance notice of its intent, and the affected person may challenge the lawfulness of the acquisition. §§ 1806(c), 1806(e), 1881e(a). . . .

Finally, any electronic communications service provider that the Government directs to assist in § 1881a surveillance may challenge the lawfulness of that directive before the FISC. § 1881a(h)(4), (6).

We hold that respondents lack Article III standing because they cannot demonstrate that the future injury they purportedly fear is certainly impending and because they cannot manufacture standing by incurring costs in anticipation of non-imminent harm. We therefore reverse the judgment of the Second Circuit and remand the case for further proceedings consistent with this opinion.

BREYER, J. joined by GINSBURG, SOTOMAYOR, and KAGAN, JJ. dissenting. The plaintiffs' standing depends upon the likelihood that the Government, acting under the authority of 50 U.S.C. § 1881a will harm them by intercepting at least some of their private, foreign, telephone, or e-mail conversations. In my view, this harm is not "speculative." Indeed it is as likely to take place as are most future events that commonsense inference and ordinary knowledge of human nature tell us will happen. This Court has often found the occurrence of similar future events sufficiently certain to support standing. I dissent from the Court's contrary conclusion. . . .

. . . No one here denies that the Government's interception of a private telephone or e-mail conversation amounts to an injury that is "concrete and particularized." Moreover, the plaintiffs, respondents here, seek as relief a judgment declaring unconstitutional (and enjoining enforcement of) a statutory provision authorizing those interceptions; and, such a judgment would redress the injury by preventing it. Thus, the basic question is whether the injury, *i.e.,* the interception, is "actual or imminent."

Since the plaintiffs fear interceptions of a kind authorized by § 1881a, it is important to understand just what kind of surveillance that section authorizes. Congress enacted § 1881a in 2008, as an amendment to the pre-existing Foreign Intelligence Surveillance Act of 1978, 50 U.S.C. § 1801 *et seq.* Before the amendment, the Act authorized the Government (acting within the United States) to monitor private electronic communications between the United States and a foreign country if (1) the Government's purpose was, in significant part, to obtain foreign intelligence information (which includes information concerning a "foreign power" or "territory" related to our "national defense" or "security" or the "conduct of ... foreign affairs"), (2) the Government's surveillance target was "a foreign power or an agent of a foreign power," and (3) the Government used surveillance procedures designed to "minimize the acquisition and retention, and prohibit the dissemination, of" any private information acquired about Americans. §§ 1801(e), (h), 1804(a).

In addition the Government had to obtain the approval of the Foreign Intelligence Surveillance Court. To do so, it had to submit an application describing (1) each "specific target," (2) the "nature of the information sought," and (3) the "type of communications or activities to be subjected to the surveillance." § 1804(a). It had to certify that, in significant part, it sought to obtain foreign intelligence information. *Ibid.* It had to demonstrate probable cause to believe that each specific target was "a foreign power or an agent of a foreign power." §§ 1804(a), 1805(a). It also had to describe instance-specific procedures to be used to minimize intrusions upon Americans' privacy (compliance with which the court subsequently could assess). §§ 1804(a), 1805(d)(3).

The addition of § 1881a in 2008 changed this prior law in three important ways. First, it eliminated the requirement that the Government describe to the court each specific target and identify each facility at which its surveillance would be directed, thus permitting surveillance on a programmatic, not necessarily individualized, basis. § 1881a(g). Second, it eliminated the requirement that a target be a "foreign power or an agent of a foreign power." *Ibid.* Third, it diminished the court's authority to insist upon, and eliminated its authority to supervise, instance-specific privacy-intrusion minimization procedures (though the Government still must use court-approved general minimization procedures). § 1881a(e). Thus, using the authority of § 1881a, the Government can obtain court approval for its surveillance of electronic communications between places within the United States and targets in foreign territories by showing the court (1) that "a significant purpose of the acquisition is to obtain foreign intelligence information," and (2) that it will use general targeting and privacy-intrusion minimization procedures of a kind that the court had previously approved. § 1881a(g).

Several considerations, based upon the record along with commonsense inferences, convince me that there is a very high likelihood that Government, *acting under the authority of § 1881a,* will intercept at least some of the communications just described. First, the plaintiffs have engaged, and continue to engage, in electronic communications of a kind that the 2008 amendment, but not the prior Act, authorizes the Government to intercept. These communications include discussions with family members of those detained at Guantanamo, friends and acquaintances of those persons, and investigators, experts and others with knowledge of circumstances related to terrorist activities. These persons are foreigners located outside the United States. They are not "foreign power[s]" or "agent[s] of ... foreign power [s]." And the plaintiffs state that they exchange with these persons "foreign intelligence information," defined to include information that "relates to" "international terrorism" and "the national defense or the security of the United States." See 50 U.S.C. § 1801.

Second, the plaintiffs have a strong *motive* to engage in, and the Government has a strong *motive* to listen to, conversations of the kind described. A lawyer representing a client normally seeks to learn the circumstances surrounding the crime (or the civil wrong) of which the client is accused. . . . .Journalists and human rights workers have strong similar motives to conduct conversations of this kind.

At the same time, the Government has a strong motive to conduct surveillance of conversations that contain material of this kind. The Government, after all, seeks to learn as much as it can reasonably learn about suspected terrorists (such as those detained at Guantanamo), as well as about their contacts and activities, along with those of friends and family members. And the Government is motivated to do so, not simply by the desire to help convict those whom the Government believes guilty, but also by the critical, overriding need to protect America from terrorism.

Third, the Government's *past behavior* shows that it has sought, and hence will in all likelihood continue to seek, information about alleged terrorists and detainees through means that include surveillance of electronic communications. As just pointed out, plaintiff Scott McKay states that the Government (under the authority of the pre-2008 law) "intercepted some 10,000 telephone calls and 20,000 email communications involving [his client] Mr. Al-Hussayen."

Fourth, the Government has the *capacity* to conduct electronic surveillance of the kind at issue. To some degree this capacity rests upon technology available to the Government. See 1 D. Kris & J. Wilson, National Security Investigations & Prosecutions § 16:6, p. 562 (2d ed. 2012) ("NSA's technological abilities are legendary"); *id.,* § 16:12, at 572-577 (describing the National Security Agency's capacity to monitor "*very* broad facilities" such as international switches). . . .

Of course, to exercise this capacity the Government must have intelligence court authorization. But the Government rarely files requests that fail to meet the statutory criteria. As the intelligence court itself has stated, its review under § 1881a is "narrowly circumscribed." In re Proceedings Required by § 702(i) of the FISA Amendments Act of 2008, No. Misc. 08-01 (Aug. 17, 2008). There is no reason to believe that the communications described would all fail to meet the conditions necessary for approval. Moreover, compared with prior law, § 1881a simplifies and thus expedites the approval process, making it more likely that the Government will use § 1881a to obtain the necessary approval.

The upshot is that (1) similarity of content, (2) strong motives, (3) prior behavior, and (4) capacity all point to a very strong likelihood that the Government will intercept at least some of the plaintiffs' communications, including some that the 2008 amendment, § 1881a, but not the pre–2008 Act, authorizes the Government to intercept.

At the same time, nothing suggests the presence of some special factor here that might support a contrary conclusion. . . . One can, of course, always imagine some special circumstance that negates a virtual likelihood, no matter how strong. But the same is true about most, if not all, ordinary inferences about future events. Perhaps, despite pouring rain, the streets will remain dry (due to the presence of a special chemical). But ordinarily a party that seeks to defeat a strong natural inference must bear the burden of showing that some such special circumstance exists. And no one has suggested any such special circumstance here. . . .

The majority more plausibly says that the plaintiffs have failed to show that the threatened harm is "*certainly impending*." But . . . *certainty* is not, and never has been, the touchstone of standing. The future is inherently uncertain. Yet federal courts frequently entertain actions for injunctions and for declaratory relief aimed at preventing future activities that are reasonably likely or highly likely, but not absolutely certain, to take place. And that degree of certainty is all that is needed to support standing here.

The Court's use of the term "certainly impending" is not to the contrary. Sometimes the Court has used the phrase "certainly impending" as if the phrase described a *sufficient,* rather than a *necessary,* condition for jurisdiction. See *Pennsylvania v. West Virginia,* 262 U.S. 553 (1923) ("If the injury is certainly impending that is enough"). . . . Taken together the case law uses the word "certainly" as if it emphasizes, rather than literally defines, the immediately following term "impending." . . .

In some standing cases, the Court has found that a reasonable probability of *future* injury comes accompanied with *present* injury that takes the form of reasonable efforts to mitigate the threatened effects of the future injury or to prevent it from occurring. Thus, in *Monsanto Co.*, plaintiffs, a group of conventional alfalfa growers, challenged an agency decision to deregulate genetically engineered alfalfa. Without expressing views about that probability, we found standing because the plaintiffs would suffer present harm by trying to combat the threat. *Ibid.* The plaintiffs, for example, "would have to conduct testing to find out whether and to what extent their crops have been contaminated." And they would have to take "measures to minimize the likelihood of potential contamination and to ensure an adequate supply of non-genetically-engineered alfalfa." *Ibid.* We held that these "harms, which [the plaintiffs] will suffer even if their crops are not actually infected with" the genetically modified gene, "are sufficiently concrete to satisfy the injury-in-fact prong of the constitutional standing analysis."

Virtually identical circumstances are present here. Plaintiff McKay, for example, points out that, when he communicates abroad about, or in the interests of, a client (*e.g.*, a client accused of terrorism), he must "make an assessment" whether his "client's interests would be compromised" should the Government "acquire the communications." If so, he must either forgo the communication or travel abroad. ("I have had to take measures to protect the confidentiality of information that I believe is particularly sensitive," including "travel that is both time-consuming and expensive").

Since travel is expensive, since forgoing communication can compromise the client's interests, since McKay's assessment itself takes time and effort, this case does not differ significantly from *Monsanto*. And that is so whether we consider the plaintiffs' present necessary expenditure of time and effort as a separate concrete, particularized, imminent harm, or consider it as additional evidence that the future harm (an interception) is likely to occur. . . .

While I express no view on the merits of the plaintiffs' constitutional claims, I do believe that at least some of the plaintiffs have standing to make those claims. I dissent, with respect, from the majority's contrary conclusion.

NOTES & QUESTIONS

1. *The Holding in* **Clapper.** By a 5-4 vote, the Clapper Court found a lack of standing. For the majority, the claimants were unable to demonstrate a future injury in fact that was "certainly impending" by allegations regarding likely government surveillance pursuant to Section 702. Writing in dissent, Justice Breyer argued that it was constitutionally justifiable to rely on "ordinary inferences about future events." He notes: "Perhaps, despite pouring rain, the streets will remain dry (due to the presence of a special chemical)." Indeed, at some point, a party that seeks to defeat a strong natural inference bears the burden of defeating it. In the national security context, how would you assess the merit of requiring certainly impending future harm, as the *Clapper* majority does, versus relying on certain "ordinary inferences," as Breyer would do?

2. **The FISA Amendment Act and TSP.** In *Hepting v. AT&T Corp.*, 439 F. Supp. 974 (N.D. Cal 2006), the plaintiffs alleged that AT&T was collaborating with the NSA in a massive warrantless surveillance program, namely, the TSP. As customers of AT&T, the plaintiffs alleged that they suffered injury from this surveillance.

The *Hepting* court found that the existence of the TSP was itself not subject to the state secret privilege. This common law evidentiary privilege protects information from discovery when disclosure of it would harm national security. The *Hepting* court found that (1) the Bush Administration had disclosed "the general contours" of the TSP, which (2) "requires the assistance of a telecommunications provider," and (3) AT&T helps the government in classified matters when asked.

This litigation ended, however, due to *In re NSA Telecommunications Records Litigation,* 633 F. Supp. 2d 949 (N.D. Cal. 2008). In that case, the district court found that the FISA Amendment Act had provided retroactive immunity for the defendants and dismissed the action. The court found that Congress in enacting the statute "manifested an unequivocal intention to create an immunity that will shield the telecommunications company defendants from liability in these actions."

At the time of the debates around this law, Congress also considered laws that would have capped the possible liability exposure of the telecommunications companies at fairly modest amounts, but allow the litigation against them to proceed. Do you think that this approach would have been superior to the FISA Amendment Act's outright grant of immunity?

3. **The End of FISA?** William Banks argues: "At a minimum, the unraveling of FISA and emergence of the TSP call into question the virtual disappearance of effective oversight of our national security surveillance. The Congress and federal courts have become observers of the system, not even participants, much less overseers."[44] He proposes: "If FISA is to have any meaningful role for the next thirty years, its central terms will have to be restored, one way or another."

In contrast, John Yoo argues that such surveillance should be permitted where there is a reasonable chance that terrorists will appear, or communicate, even if we do not know their specific identities. A law professor, Yoo was in government service at the time of the TSP and wrote the government memorandums at the Department of Justice's Office of Legal Counsel that approved the program.[45] Subsequently, he has proposed that in cases where there is a likelihood, perhaps "a 50 percent chance" that terrorists would use a certain kind of avenue for reaching each other, "[a] FISA-based approach would prevent computers from searching through that channel for keywords or names that might suggest terrorist communications."[46]

---

[44] William C. Banks, *The Death of FISA*, 91 Minn. L. Rev. 1209, 1297 (2007).

[45] For a discussion of Yoo's role, see *In re: National Security Telecommunications Records Litigation*, 2010 U.S. Dist. LEXIS 136156, *38-*40 (N.D. Cal. 2010)

[46] John Yoo, *War By Other Means: An Insider's Accounts of the War on Terror* 112 (2006).

A third approach is proposed by Orin Kerr, who would update FISA beyond its current approach, which depends "on the identity and location of who is being monitored."[47] In contrast to this "person-focused" approach, Kerr would add "a complementary set of data-focused authorities" to the statute. Under this second approach, "Surveillance practices should be authorized when the government establishes a likelihood that surveillance would yield what I call 'terrorist intelligence information' — information relevant to terrorism investigations. . . ." Kerr is unwilling to state, however, whether the data-focused approach ("used when identities and/or location are unknown") should or should not require any kind of warrant.

2. THE SNOWDEN REVELATIONS

In June 2013, government contractor Edward Snowden began to leak classified National Security Agency (NSA) materials. This material appeared in the *Guardian* in the United Kingdom, the *Washington Post*, and other periodicals. Snowden revealed widespread NSA wiretapping and data collection previously unknown to the public. Senator Diane Feinstein called Snowden's action an "act of treason." A warrant was to be issued for his arrest. In contrast, Daniel Ellsberg, who leaked the Pentagon Papers, said, "there has not been in American history a more important leak" than Snowden's and praised his "civil courage." John Cassidy in the *New Yorker* called Snowden "a hero."[48] In that same periodical, Jeffrey Toobin called him "a grandiose narcissist who deserves to be in prison."[49]

The leaks have affected international relations through the disclosures of NSA spying in foreign nations. Snowden's actions have affected the ongoing development of the Proposed Data Protection Regulation at the European Union, led European Union officials to demand reforms to the Safe Harbor Agreement with the United States, and harmed U.S. technology companies seeking international business. Brazil's president called off a state dinner with President Obama, and Germany cancelled a Cold War surveillance cooperation agreement in reaction to revelations of NSA spying in their country. Germany's Chancellor, Angela Merkel, had a "strongly worded" conversation with President Obama about NSA surveillance of her cell phone.[50] At a European Summit in Brussels, Merkel said, "Spying between friends, that's just not done." She added: "Now trust has to be rebuilt."

What are the chief Snowden revelations in a nutshell? We can break the flood of information about the NSA into categories concerning (1) targeting of non-U.S. persons outside the United States through surveillance occurring in the United States (pursuant to Section 702 of FISA); (2) collecting telephone metadata (pursuant to Section 215 of the Patriot Act); (3) spying on foreign countries and their leadership; and (4) acting to weaken encryption standards.

---

[47] Orin Kerr, *Updating the Foreign Intelligence Surveillance Act*, 75 U. Chi. L. Rev. 238 (2008).

[48] John Cassidy, *Why Edward Snowden is a Hero*, New Yorker (June 10, 2013).

[49] Jeffrey Toobin, *Edward Snowden is No Hero*, New Yorker (June 10, 2013).

[50] *Embassy Espionage: The NSA's Secret Hub in Berlin*, Der Spiegel (Oct. 13, 2013).

Surveillance of Non-U.S. Persons Outside the United States Conducted Within the United States (Section 702). As the President's Civil Liberties Oversight Board (PCLOB) notes, "Section 702 has its roots in the President's Surveillance Program developed in the immediate aftermath of the September 11th attacks."[51] Following the press disclosures about the Terrorist Surveillance Program in December 2005, the FISA Amendment Acts of 2008 added Section 702 to create a statutory framework for this collection program. Drawing on this section, the NSA then carried out a wide range of surveillance. In particular, and as PCLOB has explained, the NSA has drawn on Section 702 to carry out surveillance under its PRISM program and collection of so-called "upstream communications."

PRISM targets Internet communications and stored data of "non-US persons" outside the United States.[52] In PRISM collection, the government sends a "selector," such as an e-mail address, to a U.S.-based electronic service provider, such as an ISP, and the provider shares communications delivered to that "selector" with the government. PRISM collection does not include telephone calls. Susan Landau notes: "The PRISM documents mention 'direct access' to Microsoft, Yahoo, Google, Facebook, and other U.S. technology companies, but that might be a casual claim rather than a precise statement. Several of the companies involved clarified that this occurs only under legal process—and not through direct access at company servers."[53]

Under "upstream collection," acquisition occurs through the compelled assistance of providers that control the telecommunications backbone. "Upstream collection" also includes telephone calls as well as Internet communications.[54]

Telephone Metadata Collection (Section 215). Leaks by Snowden detailed the bulk collection of domestic telephony metadata. Section 215 of the PATRIOT Act allowed for the collection of individual suspects' "business records." The NSA broadened the scope of Section 215 to include all call detail records generated by certain telephone companies in the United States.[55] Although technically requiring FISC warrants, telephone companies generally complied voluntarily until news media reported on the practice in 2006.[56] Snowden's disclosures also revealed the existence of FISC orders authorizing this practice. Unlike a wiretap, metadata does not describe the content of a phone call, but rather the caller's location, call times and lengths, and which phone numbers the phone contacted. The NSA used metadata to understand webs of relations by

---

[51] PCLOB, *Report on the Surveillance Program Operated Pursuant to Section 702 of the Foreign Intelligence Surveillance Act* 5 (July 2, 2014).

[52] Susan Landau, *Making Sense from Snowden: What's Significant in the NSA Surveillance Revelations*, 11:4 IEEE Security & Privacy 54, 54 (July/Aug. 2013).

[53] *Id.* at 58.

[54] PCLOB, *Report on the 702 Surveillance Program*, 7.

[55] For a clear description of the program and its history, see PCLOB, *Report on the Telephone Records Program Conducted Under Section 215* (Jan. 23, 2014).

[56] Landau, *Making Sense from Snowden, Part II*, IEE Security & Privacy Web Extra v (Jan./Feb. 2014). For a discussion of the Section 215 program, see Joseph D. Mornin, *NSA Metadata Collection and the Fourth Amendment*, 29 BTLJ 985 (2014).

"contact chaining" that compares groups of three "hops" from any "seed." In other words, government analysts would retrieve numbers not only directly in contact with the seed number (the "first hop'), but also numbers in contact with all first hop numbers (the "second hop") and all numbers in contact with all second hop numbers (the "third hop").[57]

Spying on China, G20 leaders, Brazil, Germany, and Other Countries. Snowden claimed that the NSA compromised Chinese telecommunications networks. With the help of the British GCHQ, the UK's NSA-equivalent, the NSA spied on G20 leaders during a 2009 summit in London. The NSA is also said to have spied on Petrobas, Brazil's largest oil and gas company. In Germany, the NSA targeted Chancellor's Merkel's cell phone and ran major listening operations from within the U.S. embassy in Berlin and U.S. military bases throughout the company. In France, initial reports of widespread NSA-spying in that country were followed by reports in *Le Monde* that the activity had been carried out with the cooperation of French intelligence agencies.

Weakening of Encryption Standards. Leaked documents from Snowden showed that the NSA worked to insert vulnerabilities into commercial encryption standards. It did so to make these systems "exploitable" by it. As part of this effort, the NSA covertly influenced the standard-setting process at the National Institute of Standards and Technology. As Susan Landau states, "It appears that NSA [...] viewed corrupting cryptography standards as a goal."[58]

In the two cases that follow, *Klayman v. Obama* and *In re FBI*, a district court and the FISC respectively evaluated the legal sufficiency of Section 215.

KLAYMAN V. OBAMA
957 F. Supp. 2d 1 (D.D.C. 2013)

LEON, J. On June 6, 2013, plaintiffs brought the first of two related lawsuits challenging the constitutionality and statutory authorization of certain intelligence-gathering practices by the United States government relating to the wholesale collection of the phone record metadata of all U.S. citizens. These related cases are two of several lawsuits arising from public revelations over the past six months that the federal government, through the National Security Agency ("NSA"), and with the participation of certain telecommunications and internet companies, has conducted surveillance and intelligence-gathering programs that collect certain data about the telephone and internet activity of American citizens within the United States.

On June 5, 2013, the British newspaper *The Guardian* reported the first of several "leaks" of classified material from Edward Snowden, a former NSA contract employee, which have revealed — and continue to reveal — multiple U.S. government intelligence collection and surveillance programs. *See* Glenn

---

[57] PCLOB, *Telephone Records Program, supra,* 9.
[58] *Id.* at vii.

Greenwald, *NSA collecting phone records of millions of Verizon customers daily,* GUARDIAN (London), June 5, 2013. That initial media report disclosed a FISC order dated April 25, 2013, compelling Verizon Business Network Services to produce to the NSA on "an ongoing daily basis ... all call detail records or 'telephony metadata' created by Verizon for communications (i) between the United States and abroad; or (ii) wholly within the United States, including local telephone calls." Secondary Order, *In re Application of the [FBI] for an Order Requiring the Production of Tangible Things from Verizon Business Network Services, Inc. on Behalf of MCI Communication Services, Inc. d/b/a Verizon Business Services, No. BR 13–80* at 2 (FISC Apr. 25, 2013). According to the news article, this order "show[ed] . . . that under the Obama administration the communication records of millions of US citizens are being collected indiscriminately and in bulk—regardless of whether they are suspected of any wrongdoing." Greenwald, *supra.* In response to this disclosure, the Government confirmed the authenticity of the April 25, 2013 FISC Order, and, in this litigation and in certain public statements, acknowledged the existence of a "program" under which "the FBI obtains orders from the FISC pursuant to Section 215 [of the USA PATRIOT Act] directing certain telecommunications service providers to produce to the NSA on a daily basis electronic copies of 'call detail records.'" Follow-on media reports revealed other Government surveillance programs, including the Government's collection of internet data pursuant to a program called "PRISM." *See* Glenn Greenwald & Ewen MacAskill, *NSA Prism program taps in to user data of Apple, Google and others,* GUARDIAN (London), June 6, 2013. . . .

FISA created a procedure for the Government to obtain ex parte judicial orders authorizing domestic electronic surveillance upon a showing that, *inter alia,* the target of the surveillance was a foreign power or an agent of a foreign power. 50 U.S.C. §§ 1804(a)(3), 1805(a)(2). In enacting FISA, Congress also created two new Article III courts—the Foreign Intelligence Surveillance Court ("FISC"), composed of eleven U.S. district judges, "which shall have jurisdiction to hear applications for and grant orders approving" such surveillance, § 1803(a)(1), and the FISC Court of Review, composed of three U.S. district or court of appeals judges, "which shall have jurisdiction to review the denial of any application made under [FISA]," § 1803(b).

Following the September 11, 2001 terrorist attacks, Congress passed the USA PATRIOT Act, which made changes to FISA and several other laws. Pub. L. No. 107–56, 115 Stat. 272 (2001). Section 215 of the PATRIOT Act replaced FISA's business-records provision with a more expansive "tangible things" provision. Codified at 50 U.S.C. § 1861, it authorizes the FBI to apply "for an order requiring the production of any tangible things (including books, records, papers, documents, and other items) for an investigation to obtain foreign intelligence information not concerning a United States person or to protect against international terrorism or clandestine intelligence activities." § 1861(a)(1). While this provision originally required that the FBI's application "shall specify that the records concerned are sought for" such an investigation, § 1861(b)(2), Congress amended the statute in 2006 to provide that the FBI's application must include "a statement of facts showing that there are reasonable grounds to believe that the tangible things sought are relevant to an authorized investigation ... to obtain foreign intelligence information not concerning a United States person or to protect against international terrorism or clandestine intelligence activities." § 1861(b)(2)(A); *see* USA PATRIOT Improvement and Reauthorization Act of 2005, Pub. L. No. 109–177, § 106(b), 120 Stat. 192 ("USA PATRIOT Improvement and Reauthorization Act").

Section 1861 also imposes other requirements on the FBI when seeking to use this authority. For example, the investigation pursuant to which the request is made must be authorized and conducted under guidelines approved by the Attorney General under Executive Order No. 12,333 (or a successor thereto). 50 U.S.C. § 1861(a)(2)(A), (b)(2)(A). And the FBI's application must "enumerat[e] . . . minimization procedures adopted by the Attorney General . . . that are applicable to the retention and dissemination by the [FBI] of any tangible things to be made available to the [FBI] based on the order requested." § 1861(b)(2)(B). . . .

While the recipient of a production order must keep it secret, Section 1861 does provide the recipient — but only the recipient — a right of judicial review of the order before the FISC pursuant to specific procedures. Prior to 2006, recipients of Section 1861 production orders had no express right to judicial review of those orders, but Congress added such a provision when it reauthorized the PATRIOT Act that year.

To say the least, plaintiffs and the Government have portrayed the scope of the Government's surveillance activities very differently. For purposes of resolving these preliminary injunction motions, however, as will be made clear in the discussion below, it will suffice to accept the Government's description of the phone metadata collection and querying program.

In broad overview, the Government has developed a "counterterrorism program" under Section 1861 in which it collect, compiles, retains, and analyzes certain telephone records, which it characterizes as "business records" created by certain telecommunications companies (the "Bulk Telephony Metadata Program"). The records collected under this program consist of "metadata," such as information about what phone numbers were used to make and receive calls, when the calls took place, and how long the calls lasted. According to the representations made by the Government, the metadata records collected under the program do *not* include *any* information about the content of those calls, or the names, addresses, or financial information of any party to the calls. Through targeted computerized searches of those metadata records, the NSA tries to discern connections between terrorist organizations and previously unknown terrorist operatives located in the United States.

The Government has conducted the Bulk Telephony Metadata Program for more than seven years. Beginning in May 2006 and continuing through the present,[59] the FBI has obtained production orders from the FISC under Section 1861 directing certain telecommunications companies to produce, on an ongoing daily basis, these telephony metadata records, which the companies create and maintain as part of their business of providing telecommunications services to customers. The NSA then consolidates the metadata records provided by

---

[59] The most recent FISC order authorizing the Bulk Telephony Metadata Program that the Government has disclosed (in redacted form, directed to an unknown recipient) expires on January 3, 2014. *See* Oct. 11, 2013 Primary Order at 17.

different telecommunications companies into one database, and under the FISC's orders, the NSA may retain the records for up to five years. According to Government officials, this aggregation of records into a single database creates "an historical repository that permits retrospective analysis," enabling NSA analysts to draw connections, across telecommunications service providers, between numbers reasonably suspected to be associated with terrorist activity and with other, unknown numbers.

The FISC orders governing the Bulk Telephony Metadata Program specifically provide that the metadata records may be accessed only for counterterrorism purposes (and technical database maintenance). Specifically, NSA intelligence analysts, *without seeking the approval of a judicial officer,* may access the records to obtain foreign intelligence information only through "queries" of the records performed using "identifiers," such as telephone numbers, associated with terrorist activity. An "identifier" (i.e., selection term, or search term) used to start a query of the database is called a "seed," and "seeds" must be approved by one of twenty-two designated officials in the NSA's Homeland Security Analysis Center or other parts of the NSA's Signals Intelligence Directorate. Such approval may be given only upon a determination by one of those designated officials that there exist facts giving rise to a "reasonable, articulable suspicion" ("RAS") that the selection term to be queried is associated with one or more of the specified foreign terrorist organizations approved for targeting by the FISC. In 2012, for example, fewer than 300 unique identifiers met this RAS standard and were used as "seeds" to query the metadata, but "the number of unique identifiers has varied over the years."

When an NSA intelligence analyst runs a query using a "seed," the minimization procedures provide that query results are limited to records of communications within three "hops" from the seed. The query results thus will include only identifiers and their associated metadata having a direct contact with the seed (the first "hop"), identifiers and associated metadata having a direct contact with first "hop" identifiers (the second "hop"), and identifiers and associated metadata having a direct contact with second "hop" identifiers (the third "hop"). In plain English, this means that if a search starts with telephone number (123) 456–7890 as the "seed," the first hop will include all the phone numbers that (123) 456–7890 has called or received calls from in the last five years (say, 100 numbers), the second hop will include all the phone numbers that each of *those* 100 numbers has called or received calls from in the last five years (say, 100 numbers for each one of the 100 "first hop" numbers, or 10,000 total), and the third hop will include all the phone numbers that each of *those* 10,000 numbers has called or received calls from in the last five years (say, 100 numbers for each one of the 10,000 "second hop" numbers, or 1,000,000 total). The actual number of telephone numbers and their associated metadata captured in any given query varies, of course, but in the absence of any specific representations from the Government about typical query results, it is likely that the quantity of phone numbers captured in any given query would be very large.

Once a query is conducted and it returns a universe of responsive records (i.e., a universe limited to records of communications within three hops from the seed), trained NSA analysts may then perform new searches and otherwise perform intelligence analysis *within* that universe of data without using RAS-approved search terms. According to the Government, following the "chains of communication" — which, for chains that cross different communications networks, is only possible if the metadata is aggregated—allows the analyst to discover information that may not be readily ascertainable through other, targeted intelligence-gathering techniques. For example, the query might reveal that a seed telephone number has been in contact with a previously unknown U.S. telephone number — i.e., on the first hop. And from there, "contact-chaining" out to the second and third hops to examine the contacts made by that telephone number may reveal a contact with other telephone numbers already known to the Government to be associated with a foreign terrorist organization. In short, the Bulk Telephony Metadata Program is meant to detect: (1) domestic U.S. phone numbers calling *outside* of the U.S. to foreign phone numbers associated with terrorist groups; (2) foreign phone numbers associated with terrorist groups calling *into* the U.S. to U.S. phone numbers; and (3) "possible terrorist-related communications" between U.S. phone numbers *inside* the U.S. . . . .

When ruling on a motion for preliminary injunction, a court must consider "whether (1) the plaintiff has a substantial likelihood of success on the merits; (2) the plaintiff would suffer irreparable injury were an injunction not granted; (3) an injunction would substantially injure other interested parties; and (4) the grant of an injunction would further the public interest." *Sottera, Inc. v. Food & Drug Admin.*, 627 F.3d 891, 893 (D.C. Cir. 2010) (internal quotation marks omitted). I will address each of these factors in turn.

In addressing plaintiffs' likelihood of success on the merits of their constitutional claims, I will focus on their Fourth Amendment arguments, which I find to be the most likely to succeed. First, however, I must address plaintiffs' standing to challenge the various aspects of the Bulk Telephony Metadata Program.

"To establish Article III standing, an injury must be concrete, particularized, and actual or imminent; fairly traceable to the challenged action; and redressable by a favorable ruling." *Clapper v. Amnesty Int'l USA*, 133 S. Ct. 1138 (2013) (internal quotation marks omitted). In *Clapper,* the Supreme Court held that plaintiffs lacked standing to challenge NSA surveillance under FISA because their "highly speculative fear" that they would be targeted by surveillance relied on a "speculative chain of possibilities" insufficient to demonstrate a "certainly impending" injury. Moreover, the *Clapper* plaintiffs' "self-inflicted injuries" (i.e., the costs and burdens of avoiding the feared surveillance) could not be traced to any provable government activity.[60] That is not the case here.

The NSA's Bulk Telephony Metadata Program involves two potential searches: (1) the bulk collection of metadata and (2) the analysis of that data

---

[60] I note in passing one significant difference between the metadata collection at issue in this case and the electronic surveillance at issue in *Clapper*. As the Court noted in *Clapper*, "if the Government intends to use or disclose information obtained or derived from a [50 U.S.C.] § 1881a acquisition in judicial or administrative proceedings, it must provide advance notice of its intent, and the affected person may challenge the lawfulness of the acquisition." 133 S. Ct. at 1154 (citing 50 U.S.C. §§ 1806(c), 1806(e), 1881e(a)). Sections 1806(c) and (e) and 1881e(a), however, apply only to "information obtained or derived from an electronic surveillance" authorized by specific statutes; they do *not* apply to business records collected under Section 1861. Nor does it appear that any other statute requires the Government to notify a criminal defendant if it intends to use evidence derived from an analysis of the bulk telephony metadata collection.

through the NSA's querying process. For the following reasons, I have concluded that the plaintiffs have standing to challenge both. First, as to the collection, the Supreme Court decided *Clapper* just months *before* the June 2013 news reports revealed the existence and scope of certain NSA surveillance activities. Thus, whereas the plaintiffs in *Clapper* could only speculate as to whether they would be surveilled at all, plaintiffs in this case can point to strong evidence that, as Verizon customers, their telephony metadata has been collected for the last seven years (and stored for the last five) and will continue to be collected barring judicial or legislative intervention. In addition, the Government has declassified and authenticated an April 25, 2013 FISC Order signed by Judge Vinson, which confirms that the NSA has indeed collected telephony metadata from Verizon.

. . . [I]n one footnote, the Government asks me to find that plaintiffs lack standing based on the theoretical possibility that the NSA has collected a universe of metadata so incomplete that the program could not possibly serve its putative function.[61] Candor of this type defies common sense and does not exactly inspire confidence!

Likewise, I find that plaintiffs also have standing to challenge the NSA's querying procedures. . . . When the NSA runs such a query, its system must necessarily analyze metadata for *every* phone number in the database by comparing the foreign target number against *all* of the stored call records to determine which U.S. phones, if any, have interacted with the target number. Moreover, unlike a DNA or fingerprint database — which contains only a single "snapshot" record of each person therein — the NSA's database is updated every single day with new information about each phone number. And the NSA can access its database whenever it wants, repeatedly querying any seed approved in the last 180 days (for terms believed to be used by U.S. persons) or year (for all other terms).

The threshold issue that I must address . . . is whether plaintiffs have a reasonable expectation of privacy that is violated when the Government indiscriminately collects their telephony metadata along with the metadata of hundreds of millions of other citizens without any particularized suspicion of wrongdoing, retains all of that metadata for five years, and then queries, analyzes, and investigates that data without prior judicial approval of the investigative targets. If they do — and a Fourth Amendment search has thus occurred — then the next step of the analysis will be to determine whether such a search is "reasonable."

The analysis of this threshold issue of the expectation of privacy must start with the Supreme Court's landmark opinion in *Smith v. Maryland,* 442 U.S. 735 (1979), which the FISC has said "squarely control[s]" when it comes to "[t]he production of telephone service provider metadata." Am. Mem. Op., *In re Application of the [FBI] for an Order Requiring the Production of Tangible Things from [REDACTED],* No. BR 13–109 at 6–9 (FISC Aug. 29, 2013).

---

[61] To draw an analogy, if the NSA's program operates the way the Government suggests it does, then omitting Verizon Wireless, AT & T, and Sprint from the collection would be like omitting John, Paul, and George from a historical analysis of the Beatles. A Ringo-only database doesn't make any sense, and I cannot believe the Government would create, maintain, and so ardently defend such a system.

The question before me is *not* the same question that the Supreme Court confronted in *Smith*. To say the least, "whether the installation and use of a pen register constitutes a 'search' within the meaning of the Fourth Amendment," *id.* at 736, under the circumstances addressed and contemplated in that case — is a far cry from the issue in this case.

Indeed, the question in this case can more properly be styled as follows: When do present-day circumstances — the evolutions in the Government's surveillance capabilities, citizens' phone habits, and the relationship between the NSA and telecom companies — become so thoroughly unlike those considered by the Supreme Court thirty-four years ago that a precedent like *Smith* simply does not apply? The answer, unfortunately for the Government, is now.

In *United States v. Jones* (2012), five justices found that law enforcement's use of a GPS device to track a vehicle's movements for nearly a month violated Jones's reasonable expectation of privacy. Significantly, the justices did so *without* questioning the validity of the Court's earlier decision in *United States v. Knotts,* 460 U.S. 276 (1983), that use of a tracking beeper does not constitute a search because "[a] person travelling in an automobile on public thoroughfares has no reasonable expectation of privacy in his movements from one place to another." Instead, they emphasized the many significant ways in which the short-range, short-term tracking device used in *Knotts* differed from the constant month-long surveillance achieved with the GPS device attached to Jones's car.

Just as the Court in *Knotts* did not address the kind of surveillance used to track Jones, the Court in *Smith* was not confronted with the NSA's Bulk Telephony Metadata Program.[62] Nor could the Court in 1979 have ever imagined how the citizens of 2013 would interact with their phones. For the many reasons discussed below, I am convinced that the surveillance program now before me is so different from a simple pen register that *Smith* is of little value in assessing whether the Bulk Telephony Metadata Program constitutes a Fourth Amendment search. To the contrary, for the following reasons, I believe that bulk telephony metadata collection and analysis almost certainly does violate a reasonable expectation of privacy.

First, the pen register in *Smith* was operational for only a matter of days between March 6, 1976 and March 19, 1976, and there is no indication from the Court's opinion that it expected the Government to retain those limited phone records once the case was over. . . . The NSA telephony metadata program, on the other hand, involves the creation and maintenance of a historical database containing *five years'* worth of data. And I might add, there is the very real prospect that the program will go on for as long as America is combatting terrorism, which realistically could be forever!

Second, the relationship between the police and the phone company in *Smith* is *nothing* compared to the relationship that has apparently evolved over the last seven years between the Government and telecom companies. . . . It's one thing to say that people expect phone companies to occasionally provide information to

---

[62] . . . The Supreme Court itself has recognized that prior Fourth Amendment precedents and doctrines do not always control in cases involving unique factual circumstances created by evolving technology. *See, e.g., Kyllo,* 533 U.S. at 34 ("To withdraw protection of this minimum expectation [of privacy in the home] would be to permit police technology to erode the privacy guaranteed by the Fourth Amendment."). If this isn't such a case, then what is?

law enforcement; it is quite another to suggest that our citizens expect all phone companies to operate what is effectively a joint intelligence-gathering operation with the Government. *Cf. U.S. Dep't of Justice v. Reporters Comm. for Freedom of the Press,* 489 U.S. 749 (1989) ("Plainly there is a vast difference between the public records that might be found after a diligent search of [various third parties' records] and a computerized summary located in a single clearinghouse of information.").

Third, the almost-Orwellian technology that enables the Government to store and analyze the phone metadata of every telephone user in the United States is unlike anything that could have been conceived in 1979. In *Smith,* the Supreme Court was actually considering whether local police could collect one person's phone records for calls made after the pen register was installed and for the limited purpose of a small-scale investigation of harassing phone calls. *See Smith,* 442 U.S. at 737. The notion that the Government could collect similar data on hundreds of millions of people and retain that data for a five-year period, updating it with new data every day in perpetuity, was at best, in 1979, the stuff of science fiction.

Finally, *and most importantly,* not only is the Government's ability to collect, store, and analyze phone data greater now than it was in 1979, but the nature and quantity of the information contained in people's telephony metadata is much greater, as well. . . . In fact, some undoubtedly will be reading this opinion *on their cellphones.* Cell phones have also morphed into multi-purpose devices. They are now maps and music players. They are cameras. They are even lighters that people hold up at rock concerts. They are ubiquitous as well. Count the phones at the bus stop, in a restaurant, or around the table at a work meeting or any given occasion. Thirty-four years ago, *none* of those phones would have been there. Thirty-four years ago, city streets were lined with pay phones. Thirty-four years ago, when people wanted to send "text messages," they wrote letters and attached postage stamps.

Admittedly, what metadata *is* has not changed over time. As in *Smith,* the *types* of information at issue in this case are relatively limited: phone numbers dialed, date, time, and the like.[63] But the ubiquity of phones has dramatically altered the *quantity* of information that is now available and, *more importantly,* what that information can tell the Government about people's lives. Put simply, people in 2013 have an entirely different relationship with phones than they did thirty-four years ago. As a result, people make calls and send text messages now that they would not (really, *could not*) have made or sent back when *Smith* was decided — for example, every phone call today between two people trying to

---

[63] There are, however, a few noteworthy distinctions between the data at issue in *Smith* and the metadata that exists nowadays. For instance, the pen register in *Smith* did not tell the government whether calls were completed or the duration of any calls, *see Smith,* 442 U.S. at 741, whereas that information is captured in the NSA's metadata collection. A much more significant difference is that telephony metadata can reveal the user's location, which in 1979 would have been entirely unnecessary given that landline phones are tethered to buildings. . . . That said, not all FISC orders have been made public, and I have no idea how location data has been handled in the past. . . Recent news reports, though not confirmed by the Government, cause me to wonder whether the Government's briefs are entirely forthcoming about the full scope of the Bulk Telephony Metadata Program. *See, e.g.,* Barton Gellman & Ashkan Soltani, *NSA maps targets by their phones,* WASH. POST, Dec. 5, 2013, at A01.

locate one another in a public place. This rapid and monumental shift towards a cell phone-centric culture means that the metadata from each person's phone "reflects a wealth of detail about her familial, political, professional, religious, and sexual associations," *Jones,* 132 S.Ct. at 955 (Sotomayor, J., concurring), that could not have been gleaned from a data collection in 1979. Records that once would have revealed a few scattered tiles of information about a person now reveal an entire mosaic — a vibrant and constantly updating picture of the person's life.

In sum, the *Smith* pen register and the ongoing NSA Bulk Telephony Metadata Program have so many significant distinctions between them that I cannot possibly navigate these uncharted Fourth Amendment waters using as my North Star a case that predates the rise of cell phones. . . .

[The *Klayman* court next examined the totality of the circumstances to determine whether the search is reasonable within the meaning of the Fourth Amendment. In the absence of individualized suspicion of wrongdoing, the search could only be upheld through the "special needs" caselaw of the Supreme Court.]

The factors I must consider include: (1) "the nature of the privacy interest allegedly compromised" by the search, (2) "the character of the intrusion imposed" by the government, and (3) "the nature and immediacy of the government's concerns and the efficacy of the [search] in meeting them." *Bd. of Educ. v. Earls,* 536 U.S. 822 (2002).

"Special needs" cases, not surprisingly, form something of a patchwork quilt. . . . To my knowledge, however, no court has ever recognized a special need sufficient to justify continuous, daily searches of virtually every American citizen without any particularized suspicion. In effect, the Government urges me to be the first non-FISC judge to sanction such a dragnet.

For reasons I have already discussed at length, I find that plaintiffs have a very significant expectation of privacy in an aggregated collection of their telephony metadata covering the last five years, and the NSA's Bulk Telephony Metadata Program significantly intrudes on that expectation. Whether the program violates the Fourth Amendment will therefore turn on "the nature and immediacy of the government's concerns and the efficacy of the [search] in meeting them." *Earls,* 536 U.S. at 834.

The Government asserts that the Bulk Telephony Metadata Program serves the "programmatic purpose" of "identifying unknown terrorist operatives and preventing terrorist attacks." . . . Yet, turning to the efficacy prong, the Government does *not* cite a single instance in which analysis of the NSA's bulk metadata collection actually stopped an imminent attack, or otherwise aided the Government in achieving any objective that was time-sensitive in nature. In fact, none of the three "recent episodes" cited by the Government that supposedly "illustrate the role that telephony metadata analysis can play in preventing and protecting against terrorist attack" involved any apparent urgency. . . . Given the limited record before me at this point in the litigation—most notably, the utter lack of evidence that a terrorist attack has ever been prevented because searching the NSA database was faster than other investigative tactics—I have serious doubts about the efficacy of the metadata collection program as a means of conducting time-sensitive investigations in cases involving imminent threats of terrorism.

I realize, of course, that such a holding might appear to conflict with other trial courts. . . . Nevertheless, in reaching this decision, I find comfort in the statement in the Supreme Court's recent majority opinion in *Jones* that "[a]t bottom, we must 'assur[e] preservation of that degree of privacy against government that existed when the Fourth Amendment was adopted.'" (quoting *Kyllo*). . . . Indeed, I have little doubt that the author of our Constitution, James Madison, who cautioned us to beware "the abridgement of freedom of the people by gradual and silent encroachments by those in power," would be aghast. . . .

Plaintiffs in this case have also shown a strong likelihood of success on the merits of a Fourth Amendment claim. As such, they too have adequately demonstrated irreparable injury.

. . . [The public interest] looms large in this case, given the significant privacy interests at stake and the unprecedented scope of the NSA's collection and querying efforts, which likely violate the Fourth Amendment. Thus, the public interest weighs heavily in favor of granting an injunction.

. . . [I]n light of the significant national security interests at stake in this case and the novelty of the constitutional issues, I will stay my order pending appeal. In doing so, I hereby give the Government fair notice that should my ruling be upheld, this order will go into effect forthwith.

IN RE FBI

2013 WL 5307991 (FISC 2013)

EAGAN, J. On July 18, 2013, a verified Final "Application for Certain Tangible Things for Investigations to Protect Against International Terrorism" (Application) was submitted to the Court by the Federal Bureau of Investigation (FBI) for an order pursuant to the Foreign Intelligence Surveillance Act of 1978 (FISA or the Act), Title 50, United States Code (U.S.C.), § 1861, as amended (also known as Section 215 of the USA PATRIOT Act), requiring the ongoing daily production to the National Security Agency (NSA) of certain call detail records or "telephony metadata" in bulk. . . .

In conducting its review of the government's application, the Court considered whether the Fourth Amendment to the U.S. Constitution imposed any impediment to the government's proposed collection. Having found none in accord with U.S. Supreme Court precedent, the Court turned to Section 215 to determine if the proposed collection was lawful and that Orders requested from this Court should issue. The Court found that under the terms of Section 215 and under operation of the canons of statutory construction such Orders were lawful and required, and the requested Orders were therefore issued.

Specifically, the government requested Orders from this Court to obtain certain business records of specified telephone service providers. Those telephone company business records consist of a very large volume of each company's call detail records or telephony metadata, but expressly exclude the contents of any communication; the name, address, or financial information of any subscriber or customer; or any cell site location information (CSLI). The government requested production of this data on a daily basis for a period of 90 days. The sole purpose of this production is to obtain foreign intelligence information in support of [TEXT REDACTED] individual authorized investigations to protect against international terrorism and concerning various international terrorist organizations. In granting the government's request, the Court has prohibited the government from accessing the data for any other intelligence or investigative purpose.

By the terms of this Court's Primary Order, access to the data is restricted through technical means, through limits on trained personnel with authorized access, and through a query process that requires a reasonable, articulable suspicion (RAS), as determined by a limited set of personnel, that the selection term (e.g., a telephone number) that will be used to search the data is associated with one of the identified international terrorist organizations. Moreover, the government may not make the RAS determination for selection terms reasonably believed to be used by U.S. persons solely based on activities protected by the First Amendment. To ensure adherence to its Orders, this Court has the authority to oversee compliance, see 50 U.S.C. § 1803(h), and requires the government to notify the Court in writing immediately concerning any instance of non-compliance, see FISC Rule 13(b). According to the government, in the prior authorization period there have been no compliance incidents.[64]

Finally, although not required by statute, the government has demonstrated through its written submissions and oral testimony that this production has been and remains valuable for obtaining foreign intelligence information regarding international terrorist organizations. . . .

The production of telephone service provider metadata is squarely controlled by the U.S. Supreme Court decision in *Smith v. Maryland*, 442 U.S. 735 (1979). The *Smith* decision and its progeny have governed Fourth Amendment jurisprudence with regard to telephony and communications metadata for more than 30 years. Specifically, the *Smith* case involved a Fourth Amendment challenge to the use of a pen register on telephone company equipment to capture information concerning telephone calls, but not the content or the identities of the parties to a conversation. The same type of information is at issue here.[65]

The Supreme Court in Smith recognized that telephone companies maintain call detail records in the normal course of business for a variety of purposes. Furthermore, the Supreme Court found that once a person has transmitted this information to a third party (in this case, a telephone company), the person "has no legitimate expectation of privacy in [the] information...." The telephone user, having conveyed this information to a telephone company that retains the

---

[64] The Court is aware that in prior years there have been incidents of non-compliance with respect to NSA's handling of produced information. Through oversight by this Court over a period of months, those issues were resolved.

[65] The Court is aware that additional call detail data is obtained via this production than was acquired through the pen register acquisition at issue in Smith. Other courts have had the opportunity to review whether there is a *Fourth Amendment* expectation of privacy in call detail records similar to the data sought in this matter and have found that there is none. *See United States v. Reed*, 575 F.3d 900, 914 (9th Cir. 2009) (finding that because "data about the 'call origination, length, and time of call' . . . is nothing more than pen register and trap and trace data, there is no *Fourth Amendment* 'expectation of privacy.' "

information in the ordinary course of business, assumes the risk that the company will provide that information to the government. Thus, the Supreme Court concluded that a person does not have a legitimate expectation of privacy in telephone numbers dialed and, therefore, when the government obtained that dialing information, it "was not a 'search,' and no warrant was required" under the Fourth Amendment.

In *Smith*, the government was obtaining the telephone company's metadata of one person suspected of a crime. Here, the government is requesting daily production of certain telephony metadata in bulk belonging to companies without specifying the particular number of an individual. This Court had reason to analyze this distinction in a similar context in [TEXT REDACTED]. In that case, this Court found that "regarding the breadth of the proposed surveillance, it is noteworthy that the application of the Fourth Amendment depends on the government's intruding into some individual's reasonable expectation of privacy." The Court noted that Fourth Amendment rights are personal and individual, and that "[s]o long as no individual has a reasonable expectation of privacy in meta data, the large number of persons whose communications will be subjected to the . . . surveillance is irrelevant to the issue of whether a Fourth Amendment search or seizure will occur." Put another way, where one individual does not have a Fourth Amendment interest, grouping together a large number of similarly-situated individuals cannot result in a Fourth Amendment interest springing into existence ex nihilo.

In sum, because the Application at issue here concerns only the production of call detail records or "telephony metadata" belonging to a telephone company, and not the contents of communications, *Smith v. Maryland* compels the conclusion that there is no Fourth Amendment impediment to the collection. Furthermore, for the reasons stated in [TEXT REDACTED] and discussed above, this Court finds that the volume of records being acquired does not alter this conclusion. Indeed, there is no legal basis for this Court to find otherwise. . . .

Section 215 of the USA PATRIOT Act created a statutory framework, the various parts of which are designed to ensure not only that the government has access to the information it needs for authorized investigations, but also that there are protections and prohibitions in place to safeguard U.S. person information. . .

.

This Court must verify that each statutory provision is satisfied before issuing the requested Orders.

Because known and unknown international terrorist operatives are using telephone communications, and because it is necessary to obtain the bulk collection of a telephone company's metadata to determine those connections between known and unknown international terrorist operatives as part of authorized investigations, the production of the information sought meets the standard for relevance under Section 215.

As an initial matter and as a point of clarification, the government's burden under Section 215 is not to prove that the records sought are, in fact, relevant to an authorized investigation. The explicit terms of the statute require "a statement of facts showing that there are *reasonable grounds to believe* that the tangible things sought are relevant. . . ." 50 U.S.C. § 1861(b)(2)(A) (emphasis added). In establishing this standard, Congress chose to leave the term "relevant" undefined.

This Court recognizes that the concept of relevance here is in fact broad and amounts to a relatively low standard. Where there is no requirement for specific and articulable facts or materiality, the government may meet the standard under Section 215 if it can demonstrate reasonable grounds to believe that the information sought to be produced has some bearing on its investigations of the identified international terrorist organizations.

This Court has previously examined the issue of relevance for bulk collections. *See* [TEXT REDACTED]. While those matters involved different collections from the one at issue here, the relevance standard was similar. See 50 U.S.C. § 1842(c)(2) ("[R]elevant to an ongoing investigation to protect against international terrorism. . . ."). In both cases, there were facts demonstrating that information concerning known and unknown affiliates of international terrorist organizations was contained within the non-content metadata the government sought to obtain. As this Court noted in 2010, the "finding of relevance most crucially depended on the conclusion that bulk collection is *necessary* for NSA to employ tools that are likely to generate useful investigative leads to help identify and track terrorist operatives." [TEXT REDACTED] Indeed, in [TEXT REDACTED] this Court noted that bulk collections such as these are "necessary to identify the much smaller number of [international terrorist] communications." [TEXT REDACTED] As a result, it is this showing of necessity that led the Court to find that "the entire mass of collected metadata is relevant to investigating [international terrorist groups] and affiliated persons." [TEXT REDACTED]

This case is no different. The government stated, and this Court is well aware, that individuals associated with international terrorist organizations use telephonic systems to communicate with one another around the world, including within the United States. The government argues that the broad collection of telephone company metadata "is necessary to create a historical repository of metadata that enables NSA to find or identify known *and unknown* operatives . . . , some of whom may be in the United States or in communication with U.S. persons." The government would use such information, in part, "to detect and prevent terrorist acts against the United States and U.S. interests." The government posits that bulk telephonic metadata is necessary to its investigations because it is impossible to know where in the data the connections to international terrorist organizations will be found. The government notes also that "[a]nalysts know that the terrorists' communications are located somewhere" in the metadata produced under this authority, but cannot know where until the data is aggregated and then accessed by their analytic tools under limited and controlled queries. As the government stated in its 2006 Memorandum of Law, "[a]ll of the metadata collected is thus relevant, because the success of this investigative tool depends on bulk collection."

The government depends on this bulk collection because if production of the information were to wait until the specific identifier connected to an international terrorist group were determined, most of the historical connections (the entire purpose of this authorization) would be lost. The analysis of past connections is only possible "if the Government has collected and archived a broad set of metadata that contains within it the subset of communications that can later be identified as terrorist-related." Because the subset of terrorist communications is ultimately contained within the whole of the metadata produced, but can only be found after the production is aggregated and then queried using identifiers determined to be associated with identified international terrorist organizations, the whole production is relevant to the ongoing investigation out of necessity.

As the U.S. Supreme Court has stated, "Congress is presumed to be aware of an administrative or judicial interpretation of a statute and to adopt that interpretation when it re-enacts a statute without change." *Lorillard v. Pons*, 434 U.S. 575 (1978). This doctrine of legislative re-enactment, also known as the doctrine of ratification, is applicable here because Congress re-authorized Section 215 of the PATRIOT Act without change in 2011. The record before this Court . . . demonstrates that the factual basis for applying the re-enactment doctrine and presuming that in 2011 Congress intended to ratify Section 215 as applied by this Court is well supported. Members were informed that this Court's "orders generally require production of the business records (as described above) relating to substantially all of the telephone calls handled by the companies, including both calls made between the United States and a foreign country and calls made entirely within the United States." When Congress subsequently re-authorized Section 215 without change, except as to expiration date, that re-authorization carried with it this Court's interpretation of the statute, which permits the bulk collection of telephony metadata under the restrictions that are in place. Therefore, the passage of the PATRIOT Sunsets Extension Act provides a persuasive reason for this Court to adhere to its prior interpretations of Section 215. . . .

This Court is mindful that this matter comes before it at a time when unprecedented disclosures have been made about this and other highly-sensitive programs designed to obtain foreign intelligence information and carry out counter-terrorism investigations. According to NSA Director Gen. Keith Alexander, the disclosures have caused "significant and irreversible damage to our nation." In the wake of these disclosures, whether and to what extent the government seeks to continue the program discussed in this Memorandum Opinion is a matter for the political branches of government to decide.

As discussed above, because there is no cognizable Fourth Amendment interest in a telephone company's metadata that it holds in the course of its business, the Court finds that there is no Constitutional impediment to the requested production. Finding no Constitutional issue, the Court directs its attention to the statute. The Court concludes that there are facts showing reasonable grounds to believe that the records sought are relevant to authorized investigations. This conclusion is supported not only by the plain text and structure of Section 215, but also by the statutory modifications and framework instituted by Congress. Furthermore, the Court finds that this result is strongly supported, if not required, by the doctrine of legislative re-enactment or ratification.

For these reasons, for the reasons stated in the Primary Order appended hereto, and pursuant to 50 U.S.C. § 1861(c)(1), the Court has GRANTED the Orders requested by the government.

Because of the public interest in this matter, pursuant to FISC Rule 62(a), the undersigned FISC Judge requests that this Memorandum Opinion and the Primary Order of July 19, 2013, appended herein, be published.

NOTES & QUESTIONS

1. *Two Different Results:* **Klayman** *and* **In re FBI.** The *Klayman* court found that the time had come to reject *Smith v. Maryland* as valid precedent. In contrast, the FISC in *In re FBI* declared it to be still valid. How do these courts approach the issue of the precedential value of this Supreme Court decision? Which arguments do you find most and least convincing?

2. *PCLOB on Section 215.* In its in-depth study of bulk collection of telephone metadata, the President's Civil Liberties and Oversight Board (PCLOB) reached highly negative conclusions. In its view, Section 215 "has shown minimal value in safeguarding the nation from terrorism."[66] Moreover, the program's "implications for privacy and civil liberties" were serious. The Section 215 surveillance involved the government's ongoing collection of "virtually all telephone records of every American."

   The time had come to end this program. PCLOB concluded: "Any government program that entails such costs requires a strong showing of efficacy. We do not believe that the NSA"s telephone records program conducted under Section 215 meets that standard." Short of its ultimate recommendation to end this surveillance, the PCLOB also called for immediate changes to the program, including reducing the retention period for bulk telephone records from five years to three and restricting the number of "hops" used in contact chaining from three to two. It also called for Congress to enact legislation permitting the FISC to hear from a panel of outside lawyers who would service as Special Advocates before the FISC.

   In separate statements, Board Members Rachel Brand and Elisebeth Collins Cook disagreed with some of the Report. While joining in the Board's recommendation for certain immediate modifications to the program, including removing the "third hop," Brand argued that the program should continue. Brand felt that "the Report gives insufficient weight to the need for a proactive approach to combating terrorism."

   Like Brand, Board Member Cook noted that she had "a different view from the Board as to the efficacy and utility of the Section 215 program." She thought that "a tool that allows investigators to more fully understand our adversaries in a relatively nimble way, allows investigators to verify and reinforce intelligence gathered from other programs or tools, and provides 'peace of mind,' has value."

3. *PCLOB on Section 702.* In contrast to its call for shutting down the Section 215 program, PCLOB had a largely positive reaction to the NSA's surveillance carried out pursuant to Section 702. It stated: "The program has proven valuable in the government's efforts to combat terrorism as well in other areas of foreign intelligence."[67] Perhaps most crucially, "the program has led the government to identify previously unknown individuals who are involved in international terrorism, and it has played a key role in discovering

---

[66] PCLOB, *Telephone Records Program, supra*, 11.

[67] PCLOB, *Section 702 Surveillance Program, supra*, 10.

and disrupting specific terrorist plots aimed at the United States and other countries."

PCLOB also offered specific recommendations regarding this program. It found that the government was unable to assess the precise scope of the incidental collection under the program of information about U.S. persons. As a result, the Board recommended several measures to help provide information about the extent to which the NSA was acquiring and using communications involving U.S. persons or people located in the United States. It also recommended measures to improve accountability and transparency, including the release of declassified versions of the minimization procedures used by the NSA and other government agencies under Section 702.

4. President's Civil Liberties Review Board. Following the Snowden leaks, President Obama created a Review Group on Intelligence and Communications Technologies. The members of the ad hoc committee were Richard A. Clarke, Michael J. Morell, Geoffrey R. Stone, Cass R. Sunstein, and Peter Swire. The announcement of the Review Group took place on August 27, 2013, and on December 12 of that year, the Group released its report, *Liberty and Security in a Changing World*. There were 46 recommendations in this report; of these, several concerned Section 215 and Section 720 oversight.

The Group offered numerous recommendations based on the central principles of protecting both national security and personal privacy as well as fulfilling the central task of risk management. With regard to Section 215 of FISA, it called for an end to the government's storage of bulk telephone metadata and the transition to a system in which such metadata is held privately by telephone companies. The government would then query this information when necessary for national security purposes. As a broad principle for the future, the Group noted: "without senior policy review, the government should not be permitted to collect and store mass, undigested, non-public personal information about US persons for the purpose of enabling future queries and data mining for foreign intelligence purposes."[68]

Regarding Section 702, the President's Review Group recommended that if the government legally intercepts a communication under this authority that "either includes a United States person as a participant or reveals information about a United States person[,]" it should purge any information about that United States person "unless it either has foreign intelligence value or is necessary to prevent serious harm to others." It also recommended that in implementing Section 702, the U.S. government should reaffirm that such surveillance "must be directed *exclusively* at the national security of the United States or our allies" and "must *not* be directed at illicit or illegitimate ends, such as the theft of trade secrets or obtaining commercial gain for domestic industries."[69]

---

[68] President's Review Group on Intelligence and Communication Technologies, *Liberty and Security in a Changing World* 17 (2013).

[69] *Id.* at 29-30 (emphasis in original).

5. ***Bulk Metadata: Private Sector or Governmental Control?*** Regarding the issue of leaving the bulk metadata of the Section 215 program with the private sector, the PCLOB's Rachel Brand took a different view from the President's Review Group's recommendation that it remain with telephone companies. It is worthwhile to contrast the two differing approaches. In her separate statement to the PCLOB's Report on the Telephone Records Program, Brand stated, "I doubt I could support a solution that transfers responsibility for the data to telephone service providers."[70] Legislation would be needed to create a data retention mandate, but this law might also "increase privacy concerns by making the data available for a wide range of purposes other than national security." Indeed, such legislation "would raise a host of questions about the legal status and handling of the data and the role and liabilities of the providers holding it." Brand concludes: "In my view, it would be wiser to leave the program as it is with the NSA than to transfer it to a third party."

6. ***Caselaw on Section 702.*** The FISC has heard multiple cases involving the Section 702 program. In particular, it was troubled by the upstream collection program. In *Redacted*, 2012 WL 9189263 (FISC Sept. 25, 2012), the FISC helpfully summarized its 2011 ruling that "the NSA was annually acquiring tens of thousands of Internet transactions containing at least one wholly domestic communication; that many of these wholly domestic communications were not to, from, or about a targeted facility; and that NSA was also likely acquiring tens of thousands of additional Internet transactions containing one or more targeted communications to and from U.S. persons in the United States."

In its *Redacted* opinion, the FISC decided that the remedial steps taken by the government since October 2011 reduced the risks of past upstream acquisitions under Section 702. For example, the NSA had purged data collected before October 31, 2011 and the utilization of new minimization procedures, which the FISC approved on November 30, 2011. The FISC declared "the outstanding issues raised by NSA's upstream collection of Internet transactions" to be "resolved, subject to the discussion of changes to the minimization procedures that appears below." The subsequent part of the opinion was, however, entirely redacted. Susan Landau argues, "Ultimately, the rules of data minimization should be subject to a public discussion, especially when they directly affect the public." What kind of information do you feel is needed about the Section 702 program to evaluate its policy implications?

In *United States v. Mohamud*, 2014 WL 2866749 (D. Or. 2014), the district court upheld Section 702 against constitutional and other legal challenges. It found that this provision in FISA did not violate the separation of powers doctrine as safeguarded by the Fourth Amendment. FISC review of Section 702 surveillance submissions "provides prior review by a neutral and detached magistrate." The result? This review "strengthens, not undermines, Fourth Amendment rights." The section was also found more generally to

---

[70] PCLOB, *Telephone Records Program, supra*, 6 (Separate Statement by Board Member Rachel Brand).

comport with the Fourth Amendment. The district court found that Section 702 fell within the exception in the *Keith* case for foreign intelligence. Following a FISC opinion, [Caption Redacted], 2011 WL 10945618 (FISC 2011), the *Mohamud* court decided that the collection under Section 702 was still as a whole directed at national security even if the NSA also acquired communications concerning U.S. persons inside the United States. The court also decided that the governmental action was also reasonable under the Fourth Amendment due to the numerous safeguards, such as targeting and minimization procedures, built into Section 702.

7. ***Lack of Investigative Capacity.*** Judge Reggie Walton, the chief judge of the FISC, has told the *Washington Post* that the court lacks tools to provide oversight of the government's surveillance programs. He stated, "The FISC is forced to rely upon the accuracy of the information that is provided to the Court. The FISC does not have the capacity to investigate issues of noncompliance, and in that respect the FISC is in the same position as any other court when it comes to enforcing [government] compliance with its orders."[71] Judge Walton's comments came after the *Post* obtained an NSA classified internal NSA report on its failures to follow certain of the agency's privacy rules and other legal restrictions. Should the FISC's oversight be strengthened, or is such a role best played by the Executive Branch, Congress, or through an internal NSA audit function?

8. ***Reform Proposal: the USA FREEDOM Act.*** Before Congress are numerous reform proposals for FISA. The USA FREEDOM Act, H.R. 3361, is notable for having passed the House of Representatives with 152 Sponsors and for having the support of Senator Patrick Leahy, the Chairman of the Senate Committee on the Judiciary. The USA Freedom Act was introduced in the House by Representative James Sensenbrenner, Jr., one of the sponsors of the USA PATRIOT Act. It reflects his view that the uses made of Section 215 of the PATRIOT Act by the NSA go beyond the intentions of Congress. The USA Freedom Act would end bulk collection of telephone records under Section 215. Call records could still be sought if a judge issued an order finding facts giving rise to a "reasonable articulable suspicions" of wrongdoing. Some have worried, however, that the Bill will not end bulk collection, and that much will turn on the FISC's interpretation of it.

This Bill also alters how the FISA court reaches its decisions. It creates a special advocate position before the FISC. The amicus curiae, a person with "expertise in privacy and civil liberties," would assist the court by reviewing applications, certification, petition, motions, or other submissions as determined by the FISC. As a final matter, the USA FREEDOM Act would encourage transparency by increasing FISA reporting requirements and encouraging declassification of FISC opinions.

---

[71] Carol D. Leonnig, *Court: Ability to Police U.S. Spying Program Limited* (Aug. 15, 2013).

INDEX

Associations, privacy of
  Communist Party members, 43, 82–83,
    86–88, 92, 94
  McCarthy era, 162
  NAACP members, 86–87
Assumption of risk, 36, 37, 54

Bank Secrecy Act, 37–38
Brandeis, Louis, J.
  Fourth Amendment jurisprudence, 17
  Right to Privacy, The, 17, 21, 60

Communications Assistance for Law
  Enforcement Act, 39, 329-30

Databases
  DNA databases, 46–47, 211, 212
  national security. *See* National Security
    Agency

Electronic Communications Privacy Act
  aural transfer, 96, 128–29
  court orders, 39, 96, 98, 101, 102, 105,
    128, 134, 138, 139, 141, 142, 144, 147,
    150, 151, 158
  e-mail, 97, 127–140
  envelope-content distinction, 130, 151–53
  exclusionary rule, 97, 98, 100, 102, 137,
    138, 143, 145, 153–54
  First Amendment, and, 98
  interception, 97–99, 101
  minimization, 99
  oral communications, 96–98
  origins of, 95–96
  Pen Register Act, 35, 95, 101–02, 105,
    151, 153,
  records, ISP, 80, 143,
  Stored Communications Act, 95, 97, 100,
    105, 130, 31, 132, 134, 137, 143, 145,
    146, 152, 53, 186
  Video surveillance, 127, 167
  wire communications, 96, 97, 128, 129,
    139
  Wiretap Act, 37, 95–101, 127, 128, 130,
    132, 139, 140, 151, 153, 154, 158, 169

Electronic surveillance. *See also* Electronic
  Communications Privacy Act; Sense
  enhancement technology
  bugging, 11, 30, 31, 94, 107, 127
  Carnivore, 132–33,
  CCTV, 55–56
  Communications Assistance for Law
    Enforcement Act, and, 39, 329–30
  face recognition technology, 56
  GPS, 70–79, 121, 23, 145–46, 212,
  key logging devices, 139
  pen registers, 32–37, 39, 42, 43, 70, 95,
    101–02, 105, 121, 123, 133, 148–51,
    153, 212, 213, 214, 216
  thermal sensors, 62–67, 80
  trap and trace devices, 37, 101, 102, 105,
    216
  video surveillance, 127, 167
  wiretapping, 11, 12, 16, 17, 18, 25, 31,
    57, 76, 93, 94, 95, 98, 99, 106, 107,
    124, 127, 154, 157, 158, 167, 204
E-mail. *See* Electronic Communications
  Privacy Act
Encryption
  Clipper Chip, 124
  deciphering, 156, 204
  Fifth Amendment, and, 126
  First Amendment, and, 125–126
  Fourth Amendment, and, 126
  security, 119–20, 123–24,

Federal Communications Act
  § 605, 17, 93–94
Fifth Amendment
  self-incrimination, privilege against, 3,
    10–11, 14–16, 20, 126
  origins of, 3
First Amendment
  intellectual privacy, and, 43, 81, 88
  limitations on privacy claims, 57, 188
  surveillance, and, 32, 57–58
Foreign Intelligence Surveillance Act
  § 215 of the USA PATRIOT Act, 184–86,
    204–07, 215, 217–23
  foreign agent, 179, 180, 182

minimization, 168, 171–72, 178–80, 184, 198, 200, 208–09, 221–23
September 11th, and, 104, 133, 169,
USA PATRIOT Act, and, 104–05, 133, 153, 165, 166, 173–87, 207–08, 215, 217, 223
Fourth Amendment. *See* Search and seizure

Genetic information *See* databases
Group association
   freedom of association, value of, 124, 153
   interrogation, 41, 87, 162,
   membership lists, 43, 86
   surveillance, 80–93

Home, 6. 8, 14, 15, 6, 18, 24, 26, 28, 32, 34, 37, 39, 42, 45, 46, 50–52, 58–59, 62–67, 75, 79, 80, 81, 82, 84, 85

National Security Agency, 155, 156, 167, 174, 185, 193–223
National Security Letters, 185–89

Pen Register. *See* Electronic surveillance
Privacy Protection Act. *See* First Amendment
Probable cause. *See* Search and seizure

Reasonable expectation of privacy
   beepers, 48, 69, 70, 72, 73, 147
   doctrine, 4, 25, 32–80
   e-mail, 130–32
   financial records, 35
   garbage, 43–45
   pen registers, 32–39
   plain view. *See* Search and seizure
   third-party records, 32–43
   wiretapping. *See* Electronic surveillance
Right to Financial Privacy Act, 39, 186

Search and seizure
   checkpoints, 7
   exclusionary rule, 7–8
   Fourth Amendment and, 13, 22, 23, 43, 49, 81, 82
   open fields doctrine, 50, 58, 59, 72, 75
   particularized suspicion, 7, 116, 211, 214
   plain view doctrine, 5, 24, 50, 65, 113, 135,
   probable cause, 4–9, 23, 24, 27, 28, 32, 36, 39, 44, 61, 83, 85, 89, 94
   special needs doctrine, 6, 214
   Terry stops, 6, 7
   Third-party doctrine, 32–43, 123, 139, 143, 146,

trespass and, 12, 16, 17,23, 30, 43, 50, 60, 63, 71–73, 75–76, 79, 80, 81, 146, 160
   warrant. *See* Warrant
Sense enhancement technology
   aerial surveillance, 53, 58–60, 63, 73 76
   bugging, 11, 30, 31, 94, 107, 127
   dog sniffs, 48, 61, 62,
   parabolic microphones, 84, 255
   spike mikes, 16, 17
   surveillance cameras, 55–56
   thermal imaging, 62–70, 80
Subpoenas
   administrative subpoenas, 9, 101, 134
   grand jury subpoenas, 9, 11, 101
   records of third parties, 8–11. *See also* Search and seizure, third-party doctrine

Terry Stops. *See* Search and seizure

USA PATRIOT Act. *See* Electronic Communications Privacy Act, Foreign Intelligence Surveillance Act

Warrant
   exceptions, 6–7
   exigent circumstances, 6, 28, 67, 187
   individualized suspicion, 7, 214
   particularity requirement, 27, 79,
   scope of, 4–7
   "special needs," 6, 214
Wiretapping. *See* Electronic surveillance